The [illegible]

Terry Goble

The Literary Way

First paperback edition printed in 2014 in the United Kingdom
The author asserts the moral right to
be identified as the author of this work

A catalogue record for this book is
available from the British Library

ISBN 978-1-910236-05-5

Published by The Creative Peak
www. thecreativepeak.com

For more copies of this book, please email: info@thecreativepeak.com

Book Design: Terry Goble
Photographs: Terry Goble

For further information about this book please visit:
www.theliteraryway.com

Printed and Bound in Great Britain by
CMP (uk) Limited

Acknowledgements follow the last chapter

The Literary Way

The Literary Way is a long distance footpath, which joins places in the Peak District that touched novelists and poets in many different ways. It stretches from the village of Ellastone on the Staffordshire border to the High Peak village of Hayfield.

The Literary Way combines literary masterpieces, inspirational people and wonderful scenery. We will follow rivers, stop at country houses, and stride up on to the open moors. Some of the places we will visit are well-known, while others are not so easy to come across. There is an abundance of old, quaint villages along our route, where we will stop and enjoy the ambience that stimulated creative thoughts. The journey does not rush, but has a level of strolling and drifting through the countryside with frequent stops to admire the scenery and to take in the literary presence. Most of the route is within the confines of the Peak District National Park and has some of the finest scenery in the British Isles.

We will introduce authors and poets who have been influenced in some way by the local area. Some of them lived in the region, while others visited. Some chose to set their books or poems in a specific location, while others used fictional names for places. It is a long and winding route of about 140 miles, and there are certainly much quicker routes between Ellastone and Hayfield, but that would miss the point of savouring the atmosphere and deliberately dawdling to enjoy the countryside and perhaps even reading a snippet from the local works.

Dedication

To my wonderful wife, Cherry

The Literary Way (South)

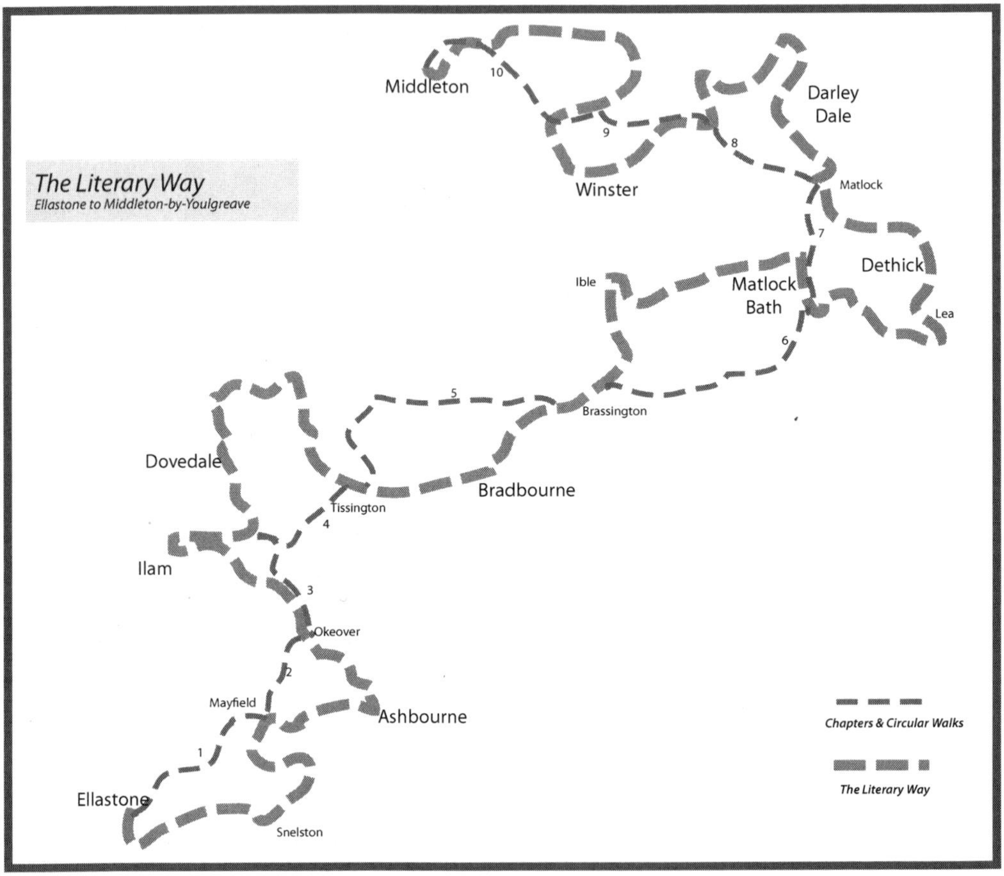

The Literary Way – Walks One to Ten – Ellastone to Middleton-by-Youlgreave

The Literary Way (North)

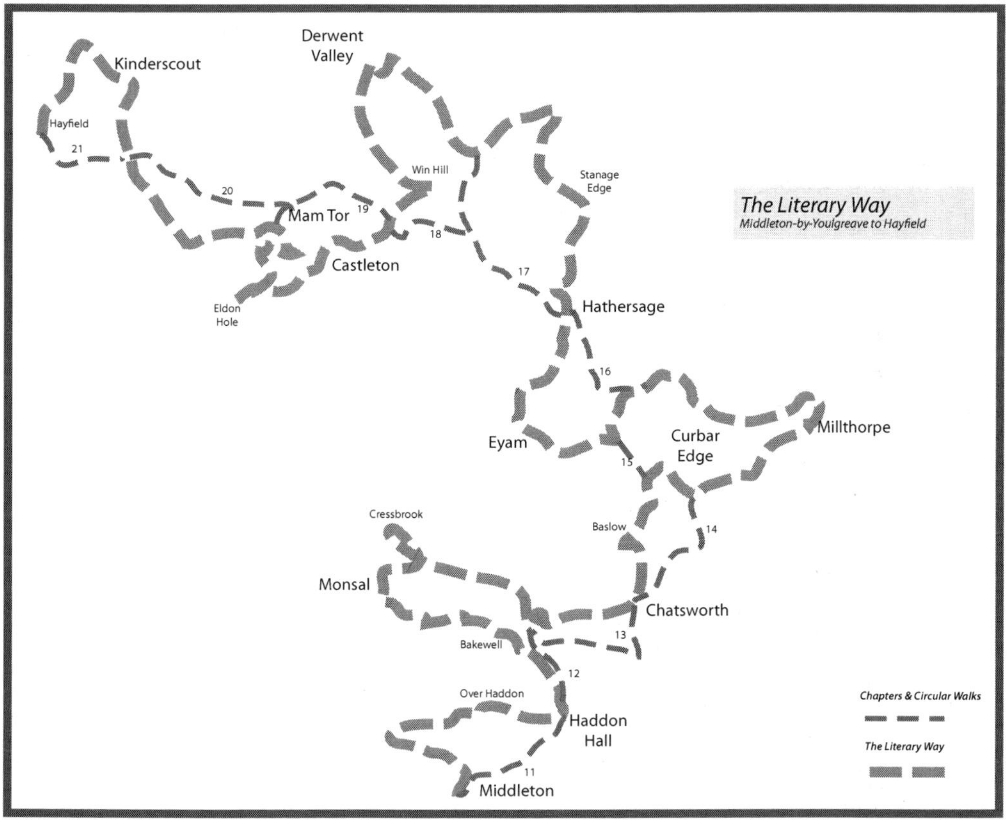

The Literary Way – Walks Eleven to Twenty-One – Middleton-by-Youlgreave to Hayfield

The Literary Way (South)

Detailed Contents – Chapters & Writers

The Literary Way (North)

Detailed Contents – Chapters & Writers

Introduction

The Literary Way brings together authors and poets who range from the sixteenth century to the mid-twentieth century. Amongst the famous, such as Samuel Johnson, George Eliot, Jean-Jacques Rousseau, Sir Walter Scott and Charlotte Bronte, there are some lesser known names, and there are several, such as Thomas Moore, Nat Gould and Mrs Humphrey Ward, who were very popular in their day, but find little favour in the twenty-first century.

Our reflection on literature stretches back to Henry VIII's time. The time-scale for this book finishes in the 1950s, although we do refer to some key films that were inspired by the local literature, and made more recently in the area. On *The Literary Way* we will meet over 130 writers, most of whom are novelists or poets.

We enjoy walking in the British countryside and have also read many fictional books set in the areas in which we have visited. As we explored the Peak District, so it became clear to us that there were many famous literary works set close to each other. When we plotted many of them on a map, a route connecting them began to emerge. *The Literary Way* is the conclusion of that investigation and the development of a route that is so aptly labelled. It is wholly appropriate that the route is a walk, because it gives the real chance of being able to understand what inspired the author or poet to organise their thoughts into the creative richness that evolved from each of them.

One of the most difficult tasks has been selecting the short quotes from the authors' works that best typify the location and its context in the book or poem. We have been relatively brief with the quotes so that the flow of the narrative text does not become fragmented. Some of the quotations have had minor adaptations in punctuation and spelling to make them more readable.

We are well aware that many readers of this book will want to get out into the countryside and enjoy *The Literary Way*. But a 130 mile linear walk is not practical for many reasons. So we have built each chapter around a circular walk which ranges from six to fifteen miles. There is one map for each chapter and our website (www.theliteraryway.com) provides easily printed copies to take with you on the walks. While much of the walk is on regularly used footpaths, there are some less obvious ways, and an Ordnance Survey Explorer map will often help. The circular walks will allow those day visitors to complete the whole of *The Literary Way*, but in a manner suitable to their trips into the country.

It only remains for us to wish you well on the walk, which is through some marvellous countryside. However, you decide to attempt it, either from a long distance walk or a selection of places that give you particular interests, we hope that the information we have provided, will add to your enjoyment. Happy walking and, you never know, we may meet you along the route.

Terry & Cherry Goble

A Cautionary Note

We have for many years walked in this wonderful countryside and this does bring with it duties to respect the land, its owners and the farm animals that we come across. The whole walk follows rights-of-way, concessionary paths or open access land. Can we appeal to any who tackles this route to respect the farm animals, even the most placid of which can be roused when they have young creatures or by the presence of dogs. There are an increasing number of accidents involving the countryside's animals so can we ask you to take every sensible precaution.

There is one other area where we would like to ask for your greatest respect. Churches are often at the heart of the history of a village and in several cases they have links with literature. Our experience is that many churches welcome visitors and, gratefully for us, the incumbents are willing to talk about the church and its locality. So if you are going to find the graves or crosses mentioned in this book please show empathy to the places of religion and the consecrated ground.

With the exception of some of the grander houses where we have sought permission to photograph, all of the pictures that we have taken have been from the public highway or rights-of-way. We have tried, at all times, to respect people's privacy when taking photos. We are very conscious that people live in many of the houses that have been made famous by authors. Some of the most well-known ones will be used to the attention, but we are sure, in many cases, people may well not know that they live in a house that features in a story.

Rural Bliss

Ellastone to Upper Mayfield through Calwich and Snelston

St Peter's Church, Ellastone has connections with George Eliot

Can you imagine today being offered £165,000 pounds for an advance fee on a poem you have yet to write. Well, the equivalent happened to one of the poets in this chapter who, in 1815, was given £3000. This poet moved in the highest social circles and his closest friend was one of England's most evocative Romantic poets, who we will meet at several places on our journey. The beneficiary of the advance lived in a country cottage on the edge of a small village, and many years later, a mysterious novelist also lived in the same house, and wrote three books within as many years.

A seventeenth century poem introduces a football match where the goals are three miles apart. The man, who helped to build one of the goals, was remembered in a poem by a polymath, who will journey with us across his favourite countryside. A future Archbishop of Canterbury resided quietly in one village for many years, before moving on to the national stage and securing his place in history. At one time he was lucky to escape with his life, but returned, for a role in the church close to the King, and an important task at the University of Oxford. Improving the working conditions of children in the nineteenth century was the driving force for one man, who came from the same village. His endeavours for children were celebrated by the young girls from one of the most celebrated literary families. Unfortunately his health failed and others had to take up the reforms he inspired.

We will also turn our attention to a man from Germany who settled in this country and became the King's musician. His friend, the owner of a large country house, placed an organ as the central feature of his main hall as a tribute to him. Another person in that household was a personal friend of the King and Queen and a copious letter writer. Her artistic endeavours are still displayed in the British Museum.

One man who wandered the fields and lanes around Ellastone was a famous Swiss writer, whose works are still read today. He produced some iconic milestones in the history of writing, but never learned to speak English, however, he soon found a French-speaking Englishman who he visited regularly.

A true agricultural village, in the heart of England, is where reality and fiction are blended together by one of the granddaughters of the village. She had an unconventional lifestyle, but it did not stop her many novels becoming some of the most celebrated in the 1800s. In recent times, most of them have

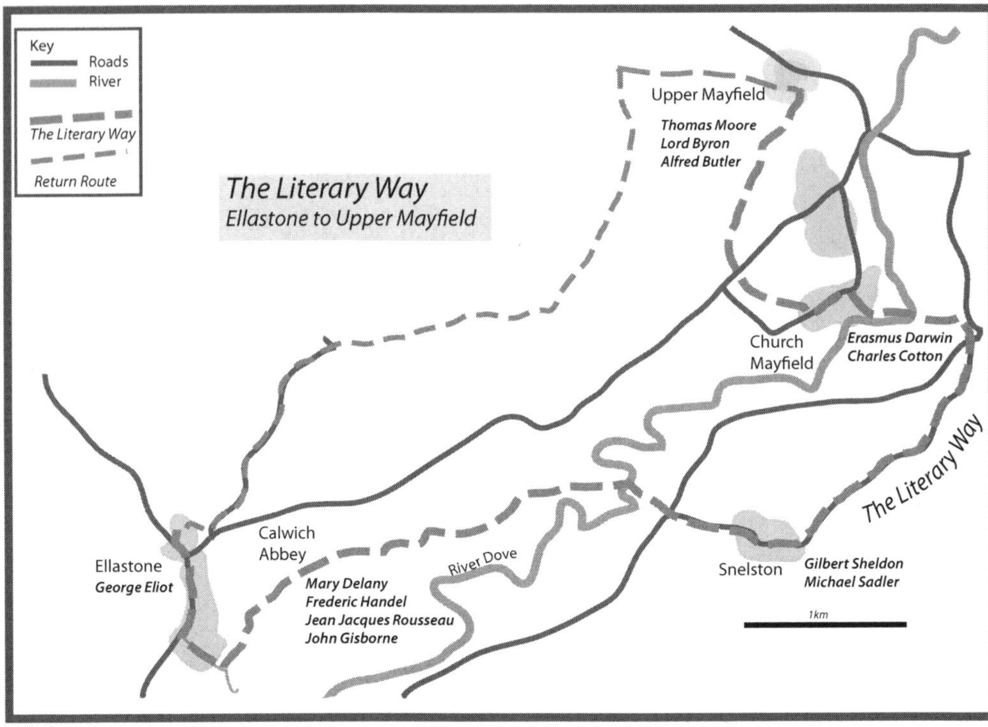

The Literary Way – Walk One – Ellastone to Upper Mayfield

The fictional Donnithorne Arms in George Eliot's Adam Bede

Walk Directions

Ellastone Church to Calwich Abbey (1.45 miles)

The starting point is the car park opposite to the church
Turn right out of the car park, go left at the end of the lane
At the main road junction turn right down the hill
Pass the fictional Donnithorne Arms
Take the first turning left
Before the bridge turn left past the gate house
Follow the track to the remains of Calwich Abbey

Calwich Abbey to Snelston (1.52 miles)

Continue to follow the same track
The summerhouse can be seen near the river
Follow the track until it bends left at 90 degrees
Take the track on the right
Go through gate and join the track at the bottom of the hill
Cross the stile which is immediately in front of you
Follow the path across the field, and cross Toadhole bridge,
Go straight ahead, cross the road and take the lane opposite
Walk up hill for a few hundred yards to enter Snelston

Snelston to Church Mayfield (2.19 miles)

Turn left at the first junction in Snelston
When in sight of the church take the left turn
Follow Parkfield lane for about 1 mile
Turn right at the end and then take the next left turn
Arrive at the 'football goal post'
Take the path opposite to the goal
This leads down to cross the River Dove
Go past the factory and mill cottages
Turn left when reaching the lane
Mayfield Church is then a short walk along the lane

Church Mayfield to Upper Mayfield (1.13 miles)

Take the left path which goes through the church yard
Follow the path into the field
When it branches, follow the right path to the lane
At the junction cross over the road and take the lane opposite
After a short distance turn right along Slack Lane. It becomes a path
Pass Moore's cottage and arrive in Upper Mayfield

Upper Mayfield to Ellastone (3.59 miles)

Turn left at the end of Slack Lane
Walk up the hill and then turn left at the cross roads
At the end of the road go on to the footpath which is ahead
(Ignore the path to the right and the one to left)
Pass through the gate. The path follows the hedge on the right
It then diagonally crosses three fields
You then reach a cross where four paths meet
Take the path to the left which is almost back on oneself
Cross several fields
Continue along path which is The Limestone Way
The path eventually goes down and along the side of the woods
At the end of the woods the path branches
Take right branch which goes downhill across the field
Turn left on to the lane and follow it back to Ellastone
Return across the field to Ellastone Church

Distance: 9.87 miles Ascent: 929ft

been made into films and television series.

The richly grassed valley of the meandering River Dove will be our guide for the first part of our wayfaring. It provides a picturesque backdrop to the three villages on our journey. We start in a linear settlement, built on the acclivity of the river valley. Then the wide valley of the Dove gathers our attention as we stroll along the rich grassy paths. A small footbridge takes us up to a nineteenth century Flemish style model village, which was built in conjunction with the new Gothic-inspired country house, for the lord of the manor. Our final village consists of several distinct nuclei, with the one focused on the church being the most appealing.

Hayslope

The Literary Way starts in the village of Ellastone, which is also the fictional Hayslope. In St Peter's churchyard there is the grave of George Evans. He lived in the scattered hamlet of Roston Common, which is just outside of Ellastone. One of George's sons was born at the family home. He followed the family craft and became a carpenter. However, Ellastone would not be his home for life. He moved to Warwickshire, where he married for a second time, following the death of his first wife. In 1819, a daughter was born and she was named Mary Anne Evans, although she, in later life, often used the name Marian.

She would go on to become one of the foremost authors of her time. In the nineteenth century, many aspiring women writers either used pen-names or published their work anonymously. Marian Evans used the pseudonym of George Eliot. Although she had become famous, and her real name was widely known, she still published under her pen name. Marian was born in the same year as Queen Victoria and when the long-serving British Prime Minister, the Earl of Liverpool, was in office. Her childhood was spent on a farm in Warwickshire and she would take this background to aid her writing with many of her novels being described as 'provincial realism.'

From her origins in the country she gained a different view on society and this led to her understanding some of the new thinking about roles and attitudes. Her thoughts were stimulated when she met literary figures in Coventry, which was near her home farm. These included the philosopher, Herbert Spencer, with whom she fell in love. She pursued her man, but the affection wasn't returned and she had to accept defeat in the end.

Eventually, she moved to London and it wasn't long before she was the leading light in the publishing

All that remains of Calwich Abbey where Handel visited

industry. She was the main editor of the *Westminster Review,* which was a quarterly journal for new thinking in philosophy. However, because she was female her name wasn't used as the official editor. *The Review* had been founded by the Utilitarians, Jeremy Bentham and John Stuart Mill, and was a key journal for many intellectuals at the time. In 1851, through her literary work, Marian met the philosopher, George H Lewes. They decided to live together, which was against the scruples of society at the time, and they were frequently ostracised. However, they were content with their lifestyle and the views of the broader society about them never affected their behaviour. In 1859, Marian published her first book, *Adam Bede,* under her male pseudonym. It was an instant success and it wasn't long before she became renowned in literary circles. She then went on to write novels for the next twenty years. She is best known for *Mill on the Floss, Silas Marner, Middlemarch* and *Daniel Deronda,* which was her last book.

The realism she introduced into her writings showed a close link between people she knew and the characters in her stories. She chose her grandfather's village as the setting for her first novel *Adam Bede.* It is no coincidence that the central character in the book, Adam, is a carpenter. Here is how Marian introduces him:

Such a voice could only come from a broad chest, and the broad chest belonged to a large-boned, muscular man nearly six feet high, with a back so flat and a head so well poised that when he drew himself up to take a more distant survey of his work, he had the air of a soldier standing at ease. The sleeve rolled up above the elbow showed an arm that was likely to win the prize for feats of strength; yet the long supple hand, with its broad finger-tips, looked ready for works of skill. In his tall stalwartness Adam Bede was a Saxon, and justified his name; but the jet-black hair, made the more noticeable by its contrast with the light paper cap, and the keen glance of the dark eyes that shone from under strongly marked, prominent and mobile eyebrows, indicated a mixture of Celtic blood. The face was large and roughly hewn, and when in repose had no other beauty than such as belongs to an expression of good-humoured honest intelligence.
Adam Bede – George Eliot

We leave the church and take the fictional route of Adam Bede though the village. Ellastone is a linear village and stretches from the church down to the river. The imposition of modern main roads has confused its shape a little, but we will take the road steadily downhill towards the bridge. On our left is the imposing grey structure of Ellastone Old Hall, which was formerly the Bromley Arms. It is represented in *Adam Bede* as the Donnithorne Arms, which was named after the local squire's family.

Dove Street takes us towards the river and we enter the wide gateway past the old gate house, and join the track that is straight ahead. The expanse of the flood plain of the Dove stretches out towards the river. George Eliot called this area, the county of Loamshire. The rich red soils of the Triassic sandstone of the area, coupled with the river silts, make for rich grass. The contrast, in George's terms, will be with Stoneyshire when we move on to the grey protruding limestones of Derbyshire with its thin and meagre soils.

Messiah

There are only a few remains, including the stable block and a small summer-house near the river, but along the track, and near the side of the River Dove, once stood a magnificent house. The land had formerly been a priory, but was closed during the reign of Henry VIII.

In 1734 Bernard Granville bought the site, demolished the old priory, and built his new house Calwich Abbey. It is the scant remains of this which can now be seen. Bernard's father was a supporter of King James II. Under pressure from the protestant aristocracy, the King had left the country, to be replaced by William, and the House of Orange, in the 'Glorious Revolution' of 1688. Bernard came into the title of the Duke of Albemarle at about the same time he built Calwich Abbey. However, it wasn't recognised in this country, but it would have been if James III had ever returned to the throne. Both James II and James III had resided in France during their exile.

Before we introduce our musician we need to say a little about Bernard's sister Mary. She was married, when still in her teens to a much older man, and, after he died, she took another husband for many years, and his name was Patrick Delany. She came to fame with her married name and is generally referred to as Mary Delany. In the later part of her life, no doubt inspired by her friend, the Duchess of Portland's love of plants, she took up an interesting hobby. It is probably best described as a delicate collage. She dyed paper and then built pictures of plants. In all she produced 10 volumes of 100 collages each. They are now in the British Museum and represent a unique talent. Mary also became friends with the King and Queen and, after the death of her brother Bernard, she was given a cottage on the Royal Windsor estate. We will let Mary Delany introduce one of King George III's favourite musicians. The encounter took place when Mary was about ten years of age.

I first saw Mr Handel, who was introduced to my Uncle Stanley by Mr Heidegger, the famous manager of the opera. We had no better instrument in the house than a little spinnet of mine, on which that great musician performed wonders.
Autobiography and Correspondence – Mary Delany

George Frideric Handel was to become lifelong friends with both Mary and Bernard and frequently stayed at Calwich Abbey. It is claimed that he wrote both *Messiah* and *Water Music* whilst staying there, and possibly he used the summerhouse, near the River Dove, for inspiration. Handel wrote very little prose himself, and only a few letters, so direct evidence is somewhat hard to find. However, in 1912, information came to light to show the relationship between Bernard, Mary and George. The descendants of Bernard decided to sell the Handel manuscripts in their possession. There was a large variety of them, including fifteen operas all autographed by Handel. The *Messiah* manuscript was of the greatest interest as there were changes from what is thought to be the definitive version. It is believed that the first performance, in Dublin, was from the Granville version. Another twist in the story comes in a letter from King George III to Mrs Delany.

The King has just received the copies of the three operas Mrs Delany so obligingly borrowed for him. He therefore returns the three scores, the two other books that accompanied them, as also the terzetto in the unrivalled author's own hand, and the beautiful song in eight parts. ... The King hopes when the spring is far enough advanced that he may have the pleasure of having that song performed at the Queen's House, to the satisfaction of Mrs Delany.
To Mary Delany – Letter from George III, 11 Feb 1785

The song in eight parts never reached Mary and no copy has ever been found. One significant contribution that George Handel made to Calwich Abbey was the selection of an organ for the house which he would play whenever he visited.

As we go past the former site of the main house, where more recent buildings have been constructed, we can glance down to the river and we can still see the original summer house.

Bernard never married and so his successor at Calwich was his nephew, the Reverend John Granville, who had a friend called John Gisborne, who lived in the next village. We will come to him later on *The Literary Way*, but for now we can look at one of his poems, which was entitled *The Vales of Wever*. In it he described the topography of this local area and the events and places within it. John Gisborne dedicated *The Vales of Wever* to John Granville.

Let's take a few lines from the section that describes Calwich Abbey. When Bernard had the house built, he also arranged for the River Dove, at the bottom of his garden, to be partially re-directed so that the garden had a small lake. The poem was written in 1797.

Come Granville! Thou, whose fostering hand-to-hand
Guards the flows of Albion's land;
For thee, O friend, the placid Spring
Wafts her balm on sweetest wing;
The Vales of Wever – John Gisbourne

Calwich was a very large four-square house with high ceilings and an extensive range of dormers windows.

A Fearful Man

Before we leave Calwich we will introduce a man, who lived locally for a short period, and became a friend of Bernard Granville. Because of Bernard's connection with the exiled King, and as many of his family lived in France, he became a fluent French speaker. About a mile from Calwich is Wootton Hall, it can be seen from the higher ground near

Ellastone church. In that large house stayed a Swiss who could not speak English. He was used to large houses and the upper echelons of society and therefore Bernard's friendship, a few years after the death of George Handel, was very welcome.

Imagine you were walking across these fields and nearby lanes about 250 years ago. The landscape would look very similar to today and you would come across a man who is walking his dog and collecting flowers and plants. He would be carefully studying the flowers and making notes. This was a man who was at home with nature. He would have probably treated you with suspicion as he suspected plots against himself, however, this was more of a persecution complex rather than reality.

His name was Jean-Jacques Rousseau. He was a leading social and political analyst of his day and was, by then, famous throughout Europe. Perhaps his most famous quote comes from the opening of one of his major works, *The Social Contract*.

Man is born free and he is everywhere in chains.
The Social Contract – Jean-Jacques Rousseau

Jean-Jacques was in Derbyshire following the help of the leading British philosopher, David Hume, who managed to obtain a King's pension for Jean-Jacques. Let us consider what he was doing here. Rousseau had fled from France and Switzerland because his writings were heavily criticised and, as a result, he suspected that a number of groups were plotting against him. In 1766, when he came to England, Jean-Jacques was 54 years old and he had completed such major writings as *The Social Contract,* and his views on education in *Emile*.

So why was this famous philosopher collecting plants? Rousseau believed his philosophical works were complete and had moved his attention to botany. He was to produce a volume on botany, that was published posthumously, as well as many full and lengthy letters on the subject. Despite such connections as David Hume, who secured him the King's pension, Jean-Jacques still thought he was being plotted against. After just over a year at Wootton Hall, when he is believed to have written *The Confessions,* his autobiography, he fled back to France, spurning all the help that he had been given.

David Hume in the end believed that he was a mad man who was beyond further support. For another view of Jean-Jacques we can turn, some fifty years later, to Lord Byron. One of his most famous works is the long narrative poem *Childe Harold's Pilgrimage.* Within it, here is what he wrote about Jean-Jacques.

Here the self-torturing sophist, wild Rousseau,
The apostle of affliction, he who threw
Enchantment over passion, and from woe
Wrung overwhelming eloquence, first drew
The breath which made him wretched; yet he knew
How to make madness beautiful, and cast

A House in the Model Village of Snelston

O'er erring deeds and thoughts a heavenly hue
Of words, like sunbeams, dazzling as they past
The eyes, which o'er them shed tears feelingly and fast.

His love was passion's essence - as a tree
On fire by lightning; with ethereal flame
Kindled he was, and blasted; for to be
Thus, and enamoured, were in him the same.
But his was not the love of living dame,
Nor of the dead who rise upon our dreams,
But of Ideal beauty, which became
In him existence, and o'erflowing teems
Along his burning page, distempered though it seems.
Childe Harold's Pilgrimage – Lord Byron

This is our first encounter with Lord Byron. We will leave some of the more enthralling aspects of his life until later. In Mayfield, later in this chapter, we meet his closest friend and eventually his biographer, but it will be at Chatsworth where his tempestuous affairs placed him at the heart of a controversial novel.

Our way now lies across the Dove, which we cross by the small Toadhole footbridge in order to reach the nineteenth century model village of Snelston. We can see that Snelston is uncharacteristic of many local villages. It was re-modelled, in the Flemish style, when the main Snelston Hall was built in the early 1800s. The neo-Gothic Hall was demolished in 1951. However the cottages and buildings in the village have survived and their intricate nature and setting means that it is a pleasure to walk around.

Welcome to the King

On the opposite side of the river from where we are now, amongst the rolling hills, there is a small village, in the parish of Ellastone, called Stanton. In 1598 a baby, Gilbert Sheldon, was born to a father who worked for the Earl of Shrewsbury who owned Alton Towers, a few miles away.

Gilbert would rise to the highest ecclesiastical post in the land at a time of great turmoil, just after the English Civil War. So how is Gilbert Sheldon linked with Snelston? He gradually rose through both the church and the University of Oxford. He became chaplain to King Charles I in the early 1640s and was imminently expected to rise even further. This could not take place because of the outbreak of the civil war, but Gilbert forever remained loyal to the King and, after his death, he transferred that same loyalty to his son.

In 1648 Gilbert was removed from his role of Warden of All Souls College at Oxford University, and was put in jail. However, he was released later and spent a large part of the next ten years living quietly in Snelston. On the restoration of the King, he was made Bishop of London, and also the Dean of the Royal Chapel. He preached a sermon in the presence of the King as part of a solemn thanksgiving for the restoration of the monarchy. He chose Psalm 18, v48, 49. Judging by the length of the sermon it would have taken several hours to deliver. While he was Bishop of London, the Archbishop of Canterbury was in poor health and so Gilbert played a much higher role in the affairs of state by deputising for him. Within three years he took on the role of the head of the English Church. It would then be in another four years, in 1667, that he added the role of Chancellor of Oxford University to his name. He died in 1677, as the incumbent Archbishop of Canterbury, at the age of 79.

Protecting the Children

As we have already learned George Eliot set *Adam Bede* in the nearby village of Ellastone. The story is set in 1799, which is very close to the date when a son of Snelston, Michael Sadler, wrote his first work. He was born on a farm on the edges of the parish, not far from the family home of George Eliot. Before Michael was twenty, he had taken to Methodism and preached locally in the open air in the same theme as is present in *Adam Bede.*

He followed up his religious interest by a publication, *An Apology for Methodists,* which he published in 1797. Soon after, he moved to Leeds and went, with his brother, into industry by starting a textile business. From these early days Michael became aware of the difficulties of the poor. He wanted to alleviate some of their difficulties and his campaigning on their behalf never left him for the rest of his life.

He became an MP and tried to introduce a bill to restrict the use of children in factories. He wanted to ban work for children below 9 years of age and restrict older children to 10-hour days. His bill was rejected, but he did become chairman of a commission into the factory working of children, which produced the *Sadler Report.* It was controversial for its time and was readily criticised in Parliament.

In order to try to emphasise the problems during the period that he developed his report, Michael Sadler wrote the touching *Factory Girl's Last Day.* These are the first two verses.

Twas on a winter's morning,
The weather wet and wild,
Three hours before the dawning
The father roused his child;
Her daily morsel bringing,
The darksome room he paced,
And cried, 'The bell is ringing,
My hapless darling, haste!'

Father, I'm up, but weary,
I scarce can reach the door,
And long the way and dreary,
O carry me once more!
To help us we've no mother;
And you have no employ;
They killed my little brother,

Like him I'll work and die!'
The Factory Girl's Last Day – Michael Sadler

Michael's health began to fail which meant that he would not see his proposals, that he so earnestly desired, come into the laws of this country. He tried to buck the industrialist trend and make lives better for the many children in the factories, but there was a high mortality rate at the time and many orphans died and were buried anonymously. Michael Sadler wasn't a lone voice and we shall encounter a woman, on *The Literary Way* who held Michael's views, but expressed them through a novel.

Michael Sadler and The Brontes

There is an interesting reference to Michael Sadler in 1827, which was several years before his famous report. He was working in Leeds and beginning his campaign for better conditions for children in factories so he would appear in the local politics of the region.

It would be in the vicarage of the small town of Haworth, in the hills of the West Riding, that his name came to be known by a group of four children, who were between the ages of 8 and 12. The three Bronte sisters, Charlotte, Ann and Emily, together with their brother Bramwell, were bored and wanted something to do and so they invented the *The Tales of the Islanders,* which would go on for several years.

The Islanders tales were written in very small books in small writing, the conjecture was that it prevented adults, with poorer eyesight, from reading them. Many of them have survived to this day, and are in the Bronte Museum. Each of them had to pick leading people of the day to run their own island. The extract from the journals is extraordinary as Ann Bronte, who was only eight years old, picked Michael Sadler to be one of her leaders.

We leave Snelston by taking the Clifton road near the church. There are a few remains of Snelston Hall visible and the gate house gives us a good indication of the status of the hall. We pass, on our right, Margery Bower which is a hill with a round barrow tumulus at its summit. It is estimated to be from the Bronze Age. This dates it between 2500 BC and 800 BC. This hill is also thought to be where Cromwell's Roundheads assembled to fire cannons at the retreating Royalist forces in Ashbourne during the English Civil War. It would have been a time when, no doubt, Gilbert Sheldon would have been very well hidden in Snelston.

We reach the valley road from Norbury, and follow it for a hundred yards or so, and turn left down to the river. Just after passing through a cutting in the rocks we emerge onto the flood plain of the river. The old station building is on our left and it is easy to pick out the route of the old railway from Ashbourne to Ellastone. However, on our right there is the site of an old corn mill of which nothing remains. It holds two interests for us on *The Literary Way*. First, the man who was involved in its building, James Brindley, and second how the mill became a set of goalposts for football! We will also introduce one of our friends who will accompany us on our journey. It is Erasmus Darwin.

The Botanic Garden

James Brindley came from a Derbyshire farming family. In his middle teens he went to the nearby town of Leek to become an apprentice millwright. His talents soon came through although he could barely read and write. He set up his own business and this is when he came to Clifton to help in the building of the mill. It is difficult to ascertain his exact involvement because of his illegible notebooks. But it wouldn't be his mills for which he became known.

He became one of the most foremost canal engineers of his day. He worked with Josiah Wedgwood who wanted to join his works at Etruria to the Trent and Mersey navigation systems. Throughout James' life he constructed 365 miles of canals, many of which had complex lock structures and tunnels. Unfortunately James didn't leave us any literary works as he was purely a practical engineer, but those that knew him, left their own tributes to him.

One such person was Erasmus Darwin who was the doctor who treated him in his last year of life. This is the rather flamboyant obituary that Erasmus wrote following James' death at the age of 56.

Nymphs, who erewhile on Brindley's early bier,
On snow-white bosoms shower'd th' incessant tear,
Adorn his tomb! Oh, raise the marble bust,
Proclaim his honours, and protect his dust!
With urns inverted, round the sacred shrine
Their ozier wreaths let weeping Naiads twine,
While on the top mechanic Genius stands,
Counts the fleet waves, and balances the sands!
Botanic Garden – Erasmus Darwin

As we walk the length of *The Literary Way* we will introduce you to some friends of the route who will turn up from place to place and add a little extra literary perspective on the different scenes. Erasmus Darwin is important to us because of the wide-ranging influence he had, and he regularly visited the Peak District.

Erasmus lived most of his life in either nearby Lichfield or Derby. We shall meet him shortly in Ashbourne, concerning his illegitimate daughters, at Arkwright's mills, and also in the upper valley of the Derwent. He was a true polymath and, both inspired, and took inspiration from, a group that he drew together in Lichfield, which was named the Lunar Society. It included such industrial pio-

The site of Brindley's Mill and the Shrovetide football goal

neers as James Watt, Josiah Wedgwood and Joseph Priestly. Erasmus would have known James Brindley quite well as the Darwin and Wedgwood families were united by marriage and Josiah and Erasmus were good friends. Erasmus was fascinated by fossils and he asked many people to collect them for him. James Brindley, in his excavation work for the canals, found many fossils and passed them on to Erasmus. One find occurred when James was constructing the lengthy Harecastle tunnel and Erasmus was delighted with them and spent a long time trying to identify them.

Erasmus was a highly skilled physician in his day and turned down the role of becoming the King's Physician. He had a great thirst for knowledge, both written and practical, and was always conducting experiments. For example, he built a method for steering coaches to help stop them from turning over when cornering. He was an avid letter writer and built a mechanical device that allowed him to keep copies of his letters. The tribute to James Brindley comes from a long poem called *Botanic Garden* which was written in two parts, *The Economy of Vegetation* and *The Love of Plants.* Most of Darwin's poems stray away from the main subject and include information about events and people as well as technology. As an example of this, the obituary for James Brindley appears in *The Economy of Vegetation.*

Anyone for Football!

We mentioned that Brindley's mill was used as goalposts. So if Brindley's mill is one goal, where is the other? For the explanation of this we have to understand where we are. Clifton is a small village on the edge of Ashbourne and is located on Henmore Brook that flows through the centre of the town. At about the same distance on the other side of the centre of Ashbourne is Sturston and a former mill there originally served as the other goal. Both mills have now gone and replica millstones now act as the goals. You might have already guessed, but with 3 miles between the goals it is not the Premier League!

Ashbourne plays host each year, on Shrove Tuesday and Ash Wednesday, to a traditional football match, which probably started in medieval times but its origins are lost in the mists of time. It is known as the Royal Shrovetide Football. It has had its Royal title since 1928 when the Prince of Wales, the future King Edward VIII, started the game. Prince Charles started the game in 2003. The game is between the Up'Ards and Down'Ards, the teams for which are traditionally drawn from either side of the river. But there is no limit and often hundreds of people play, including many visitors.

Interestingly this is not just some local event. Medieval football, or as it is often referred to as, Mob football, has taken place in many parts of the country on Shrovetide. In most towns it has stopped over the years because of the difficulties associated with 'mobs' playing a game with virtually no rules

St John the Baptist Church, Church Mayfield. The resting place of Olivia Byron Moore

throughout a town. Ashbourne has kept with the tradition which now involves shops being boarded up and roads cleared of cars. The origins of this game are quite intriguing but difficult to form a completely coherent picture. As we have just come past Margery Bower, from where the Roundheads fired their cannons, perhaps it is appropriate to consider their leader Oliver Cromwell as a footballer. Unlikely do you think?

During his short residence there (Cambridge University)... he was more famous for his exercises in the fields than in the schools...being one of the chief matchmakers and players of football, cudgels, or any other boysterous sport or game.
Flagellum, or the Life and Death, Birth and Burial of Oliver Cromwell – James Heath

James was Oliver Cromwell's first biographer in 1663 and while there are many doubts about his accuracy, it does show that football was something known and referred to.

Let's conclude our discussion of football with part of a poem from a local man. We will tell you more about him later, for he is another friend of *The Literary Way,* who will turn up from time to time. But for now let's just give a little information. His name was Charles Cotton and he owned a hall further up the River Dove and, by the end of his life, he had written about many subjects. He was born in 1630 so he would have been familiar with the rise of Gilbert Sheldon, who we talked about in Snelston. Charles was also very knowledgeable about games as we shall find out later, but we take a piece from a poem that he sent to his friend John Bradshaw in 1684, a few years before his death in 1687.

In Ashbourne, as in many other places, distinctive settlements within a parish are often called towns or townships. The Aganippe is a fountain in mythology and the Rollerich stones probably refers to the megalithic monuments, the Rollright Stones in Oxfordshire. As the context for the poem the winter had been one of the coldest for years.

Two towns, that long that war had raged
Being at football now engaged
For honour, as both sides pretend,
Left the brave trial to be ended
Till the next thaw for they were frozen
On either part at least a dozen,
With a good handsome space between 'em
Like Rollerich stones, if you've seen 'em
And could no more run, kick, or trip ye
Than I can quaff off Aganippe.
Burlesque on the Great Frost – Charles Cotton

We are standing just near to the old station in Clifton. The sign would have read *Clifton for Mayfield.* So let's go to Mayfield, which is just over the river. Our route takes us over the water and through the mill complex with its delightful row of mill cottages. We are heading for the church a little down the road in Church Mayfield. The St John the Baptist church, and its graveyard, are so typical of how we picture a village church. It has been there since Norman times, and has had alterations, but still retains a quiet and peaceful ambience as it rises above the surrounding fields and the old houses of Mayfield.

Olivia Byron Moore

In 1817 a poet,who lived in Mayfield, received the very large sum of £3000 as an advance for a commissioned poem. During that period, this Irishman was ranked alongside Lord Byron and Sir Walter Scott in literary merit. But such are the vagaries of literary esteem that currently he is far less known that his nineteenth century comparators. His name is Thomas Moore. The poem for which the huge advance was paid was the Oriental Romance, *Lalla Rookh*. The main character, with the title name, is a Princess on her way to be married. She is entertained by a poet who tells traditional romantic stories. She falls in love with the poet, during the journey, but it has a happy ending as it turns out to be the King, who she was travelling to marry, in disguise.

Thomas wrote in a number of different forms stretching from satire to ballads. He felt strongly about the links between the written word and music. His lasting legacy is two songs that still have resonance in the modern era. He was an Irish nationalist and wrote *The Minstrel Boy* which has been widely accepted in both Ireland and the Irish Community abroad. *The Last Rose of Summer* has been popular ever since it was penned, with 21st century interpretations of the song by Sarah Brightman and Charlotte Church.

Thomas Moore's daughter, who sadly died young, had been given the middle name of Byron, because Tom Moore and Lord Byron had a sincere friendship between them, which would last until the untimely death of Byron in Greece.

Olivia is buried in the churchyard at Mayfield. Thomas was much travelled, and only lived in Mayfield for a few years, although he did return on a number of occasions, presumably to visit his young daughter's grave. The death of a young daughter was not the only tragedy he had to bear, as all of his five children pre-deceased him. Also, due to mistakes made by people for whom he was responsible, he built a large debt for which he had to leave the country until means were found to repay it.

There was another lasting legacy from Thomas Moore and this is thought to be directly related to his period in Ashbourne. While he was resident in Mayfield he published a collection of *National Airs* which included words and the music by John Stevenson.

The 'Evening Bells' was under the title, *The Bells of St Petersburg.* Moore said that he originally got the idea from a Russian writer, but it was later translated and amended into Russian and became a very popular song. It is now referred to as a traditional Russian song. It is believed that the bells of St Oswald's in Ashbourne, which can be heard across the fields, gave him the inspiration for the tune and words.

Lord Byron is recognised as one of the leading poets of his time and much of his work is still greatly admired. He is seen as a leading figure in Romanticism. His most famous works are the narrative poems *Childe Harold's Pilgrimage* and *Don Juan.* Byron was much travelled, but spent a period of his life at his ancestral home in Nottinghamshire, and so would have been familiar with the Peak District, before his friend Tom Moore moved to Ashbourne. It was this same friend that in 1835 would publish *The Works of Lord Byron, with his Letters and Journals and his Life,* in seventeen volumes.

My boat is on the shore,
And my bark is on the sea;
But, before I go, Tom Moore,
Here's a double health to thee!
To Thomas Moore – Lord Byron

If we leave the churchyard by the west footpath we cross the fields to take Slack Lane to Upper Mayfield. Tom Moore's house is near the top of the lane and now bears Moore's name. Byron died aged 36 while fighting for Greek Independence against the Ottoman Empire. There has been much use of the so called *'Byronic Hero'* in literature since his time, not least the defining figure of Heathcliff, in *Wuthering Heights* by Emily Bronte. Byron lived a life of excesses typified by an aristocratic background.

Thomas Moore's Cottage

He had little regard for money, but he did have a revolutionary intent that he turned into reality in Greece. One of the friends of both Moore and Byron was the romantic poet Percy Bysshe Shelley. The period when Moore lived at Mayfield, Shelley lived with his wife Mary in Marlow in Buckinghamshire. Tom Moore would, years later, ask for Mary Shelley's help in writing the biography of Lord Byron. Mary is, of course, famous in her own right as an author and we shall return to her in the caves about Matlock.

Thomas Moore was for a long time a leading socialite and, in his early days in London, would frequently sing and recite at the dinner parties of the rich and famous. He produced a very large number of works, mainly poetry, with the collected version running to over 800 pages. To show the circles that he moved in, a memoir of him, and the editing of his letters, was completed by Lord John Russell, who twice served as the British Prime Minster, during Victoria's reign.

Mysterious Writer

Before we leave Tom Moore's cottage we want to introduce another writer who, to say the least, is a little mysterious. A couple of old books, that normally have reliable information, refer to an author called Alfred Butler living in the same cottage as Thomas Moore, but at some time later. Now it is quite easy to find the books that Alfred wrote, but finding anything about him has been much more tricky. He wrote three books, each of three volumes, with each volume being close on 300 pages. The books were produced at the rate of one a year, between 1841 to 1843. The first of the books, entitled *Elphinstone,* is the only one that bears his name. *The Herberts* has no author name, and so in the space on the title page it says, 'by the author of *Elphinstone.* The final book, *Midsummer Eve,* replaces the author with the words 'A Tale'. However, the latter is always ascribed to Alfred Butler.

Let us rest awhile at Upper Mayfield

The gentle meandering of the River Dove has brought us to Upper Mayfield and the end of the first walk in *The Literary Way.* In some of the older references, since we left Ellastone, we had Gilbert Sheldon and Charles Cotton as contemporaries at the Civil War period. It is perhaps speculation to say whether they ever met, but there is clear link between them as we shall find out when we visit Dovedale. Bernard Granville from Calwich Abbey is not a name that history put to the fore, but his household must have been fascinating with such visitors as George Handel and Jean-Jacques Rousseau. Thomas Moore and Lord Byron were good friends, and in the literary maelstrom of the day, they were treated equally, but in modern times it is Lord Byron who is by far the best known.

It is appropriate to finish where we started with Mary Ann Evans, or George Eliot. Although *Adam Bede* was her first novel it is not the one for which she is best known, which must either be *Mill on the Floss* or *Middlemarch.* However, Adam Bede has been in print ever since it was first published in 1859 and was made into a silent film in 1918 and a BBC television production in 1991.

Great Poor Writers
Upper Mayfield to Okeover through Ashbourne

The Old Grammar School, Ashbourne with its coat of arms of the Cockayne Family

We arrive in Ashbourne near to St Oswald's Church with its dominating spire and, in spring, the daffodilled graveyard. Two of the greatest names in literature, a Frenchman and an Englishman, grace this walk. One is linked with the parish church, and the other was a frequent visitor to a house just across the road. They also share the characteristics of the title of this walk. They came from humble stock and, in their early years, wondered how they would earn any money. Pecuniary hardships, however, were not just restricted to those two writers. One woman, born in a poor terrace house in the town, went on to jointly found a major institution that is still with us today.

In the late 1700s Santo Domingo was an island in the Caribbean. Today, that same island is divided into two countries, Haiti and the Dominican Republic. The island's literary link with this Derbyshire market town comes through a prisoner who led a very risky life. His autobiography, written in Ashbourne, gives an insight into the man and his adventures.

We sadly learned of the death of Thomas Moore's young daughter on the last walk and unfortunately there is another young death that has been immortalised in an amazing lifelike sculpture. St Oswald's church is quite magnificent inside and has the famous sculpture of Penelope Boothby. The poor little girl died when she was five years old. We will find a little more about her, and her father, when we pass Ashbourne Hall, at the other end of town. We also said on the previous walk we would look at what brought Erasmus Darwin and his two illegitimate daughters to Ashbourne.

The main part of *The Literary Way* on this walk is set in the historic market town of Ashbourne, which has been relatively untouched by the great expansion of industry in the nineteenth and twentieth centuries, and so we are left with the gentle feel of many of its Georgian features.

Ashbourne is an old town and pre-dates the Domesday Book of 1086. By 1257, it had received its market charter, and over the centuries it gradually grew on either side of the brook, called the Henmore. Our route for this walk concludes at one of the small villages just outside the main town. We took our leave of Upper Mayfield by crossing the River Dove at the Hanging Bridge. Then we had a pleasant walk across the fields which brought us out by the primary school, and near the church.

Opposite the church, is also another school which has an extremely impressive building, it is the

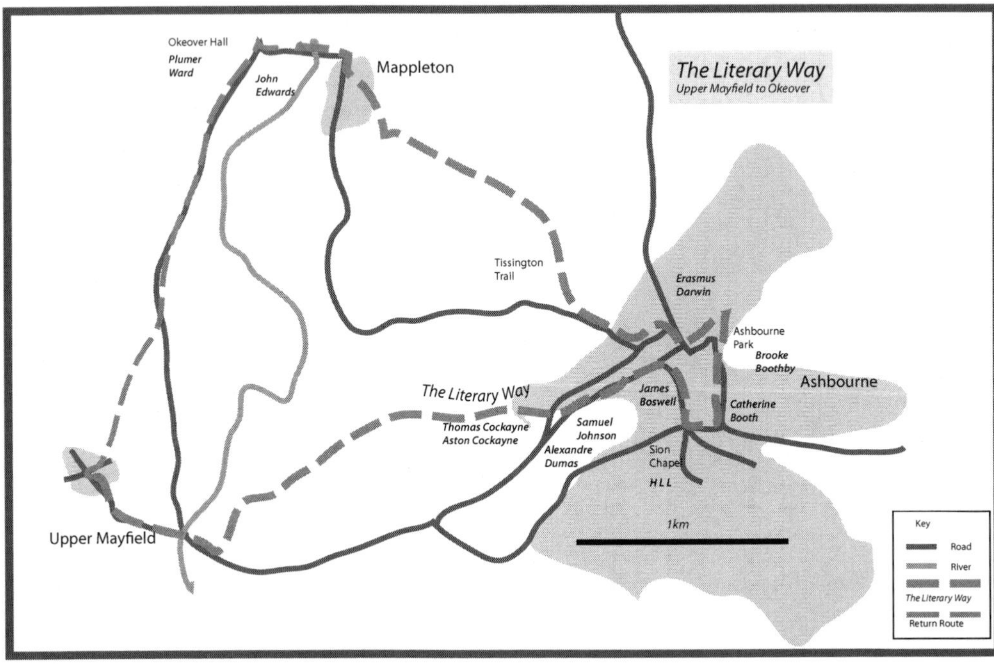

The Literary Way – Walk Two – Upper Mayfield to Okeover

Grade 1 listed Elizabethan Grammar School.

Hunting and Fishing

Sir Thomas Cockayne, who was born in 1520 during the reign of Henry VIII, would create a legacy in Ashbourne that has lasted to this day. The building of the Queen Elizabeth Grammar School was started in 1585 and was completed, just after the turn of the century into the 1600s. The family coat of arms forms the school badge. Whilst the school has now moved to new premises in the town, the magnificent old building still stands opposite St Oswald's church. The family had obtained their honoured status, when Sir Thomas's grandfather had been knighted for services to Henry VIII, during the taking of the Belgian town of Tournai.

However, it was not the fact that Thomas was High Sheriff of Derbyshire on four occasions, or the building of the Grammar School, that we have included him in this book. He wrote one of the first books on hunting. The small volume entitled, *A Treatise of Hunting* was published in 1591. The subtitle adds, *Compiled for the delight of noblemen and gentlemen by Sir Thomas Cockaine, Knight.* This is how he finishes his introduction:

I hope this labour of mine only taken in hand for your delight, shall pass with your most favourable censure thereof. And so with a prayer that both you and I may live and die in the Lord, I bid you all heartily farewell; with this caution, that this disport of hunting be used by you only as recreation to enable both your bodies and minds thereby better exercise, and not as an occupation to spend therein days, months and years, to the hindrance of the service of God, her Majesty or your country. From my house near Ashbourne this last of December, 1590. Your loving friend, T.C.

A Treatise on Hunting – Sir Thomas Cockayne

The Cockayne family, spelled variously as Cockaine and Cokain, lived at Ashbourne Hall, which is on the other side of Ashbourne from St Oswald's. Thomas is buried at St Oswald's, and thanks to George Shaw, a diligent interpreter of the parish records, we know that he was buried at night. The supposition being that as he was Catholic, and in order to perform such a ceremony, it had to take place at night, in the strongly Protestant England. Mary, Queen of Scots, had been executed only a few years earlier.

One other family member, Sir Aston Cockaine, was born in Ashbourne in 1608. He received his baronetcy from Charles I in 1641. Aston was a cavalier and always supported the King. He began to write just before the English Civil War and continued his works after the Restoration.

Aston's first major work was a masque, which is a play with songs and dancing, performed in front of the aristocracy, and in which, they were often invited to take parts. Aston's masque was called *A Masque at Bretbie.* It was performed at the home of the Earl of Chesterfield on Twelfth Night in 1639. Most of his other works came in the later 1650s and early 1660s. He mainly wrote poetry and plays.

Walk Directions

Upper Mayfield to St Oswald's, Ashbourne (1.67 miles)

We start in the hamlet of Upper Mayfield
After passing Tom Moore's cottage we turn right down the hill
At the bottom is Hanging Bridge over the River Dove
We cross the river and take the first footpath on our left
Follow the path until you reach the raised embankment
The path turns right along this embankment
After the gate bear left across the field
The path follows a brook
It then goes diagonally across the meadow
Go through the hedge and follow the path across the grass
It goes into a small wood and then emerges on a drive
Turn right, down the drive, and cross the road
The path goes across the field
We arrive in Ashbourne near the entrance to St Oswald's

St Oswald's to Ashbourne Market (1.19 miles)

Leave St Oswald's and pass the old Grammar School
We also pass the house where Samuel Johnson stayed
We turn right at the traffic lights, just before the wooden arch
Cross the Henmore Brook
At the traffic lights junction turn left
The junction is in sight of HLL's chapel which is on the right
Pass the birth place of Catherine Booth
Turn left at the lights and follow the road to the park
Go into the park and cross to the far corner, where there is a bust of Catherine Booth
Leave the park and on the opposite side of the road is Ashbourne Hall
Turn left towards the town centre
Go straight ahead at the junction
The junction has Erasmus Darwin's daughters' school on the left and then right into the market square.

Ashbourne Market to Okeover (1.64 miles)

Take the local road behind the George and Dragon
Go up the hill and cross the open junction towards Mappleton
Go downhill and turn right to join the Tissington Trail
Follow the trail northwards, and after a dip in the trail take the left footpath
The path goes to Callow Top caravan park
Follow the path through the park
The path then goes downhill
Take the right path diagonally across the fields
Arrive in Mappleton near the Okeover Arms
Turn right on the road and then turn left
Cross the bridge and the old mill is on the right
Okeover Hall can be seen across the estate

Okeover to Upper Mayfield (1.41 miles)

Take the path across Okeover Hall estate
Join the lane and follow it across the cattle grid
Take the second path on the right
It crosses a field in the direction of a farm
Pass close to the farm and follow the path
The path is now parallel to the lane that we have just left
The path goes through a small wooded area
It then emerges onto the main road
Cross the road and take the side road opposite
Turn left at the crossroads in Upper Mayfield

Distance: 5.91 miles Ascent: 667ft

It was Aston's cousin, Charles Cotton, who gave us the description of the football match on the last walk. Aston enjoyed his life of high living and associating with the writers and actors of the day. He was a gambler and during his life managed to spend his inheritance and was forced to sell Ashbourne Hall. He died in poverty.

If we are standing outside the old Grammar School we have a magnificent view of St Oswald's Church and that is where we want to introduce the first of our two world-famous authors.

Le Pasteur D'Ashbourne

Le Pasteur D'Ashbourne was published in France in 1853, and as far was we know, has never been translated into English. However, many works by the same author have become standard texts in English. Perhaps the two of the well known are *The Three Musketeers* and the *Count of Monte Cristo*. We are, of course, talking about Alexandre Dumas. He was certainly an interesting character. Before we look at when he visited Ashbourne, and the novel that he wrote about the town, let's look at the man himself.

His grandparents were a French noble, Marquis de la Pailleterie, and an Afro-Caribbean Haitian slave, Marie-Cesette Dumas. Alexandre's father was a Napoleonic General, but fell out of favour and died when the future writer, Dumas Davy de la Pailleterie, was young. This left his mother in poverty. It would be from that poor beginning that he rose to be one of the foremost literary figures, not only in France, but his works have been translated into languages across the globe. Despite his success, he always had problems with money and was, at one time, made bankrupt and forced to flee from France and live in Belgium. He became a successful playwright, but it wasn't until 1844, at the age of 42, that he turned to writing novels. By 1847 he had enough money to build his own Gothic style mansion, at Le Port-Marly, west of Paris, and to open his own theatre, which went bankrupt within three years.

Alexandre produced about 200 works. He mainly wrote plays and novels but he also produced travel and cookery books. He had a number of 'associates', often his mistresses, who helped him with translations, plots and writing. With such a profusion of works, and coupled with his flamboyant lifestyle, it means that some of the works that he produced with collaborators are not considered his finest writing.

We associate Alexandre with the swashbuckling

St Oswald's Church, which has links with Alexandre Dumas

French novels of *The Three Musketeers, The Count of Monte Cristo* and *The Man in the Iron Mask* but, perhaps surprisingly, he did turn to England for some of his stories. The sequel to *The Three Musketeers, Twenty Years On,* is set to the background of the English Civil War with the four musketeers, two on each side of the fighting. They even pass through Derby on their travels!

There were two English writers that Alexandre greatly admired, they were Sir Walter Scott and Lord Byron. From his admiration of the former, Alexandre wrote two books, one about Robin Hood and the other about Ivanhoe. Alexandre put Lord Byron, along with Victor Hugo, as the two writers he most admired. He said that he learned many of the poems of Lord Byron and was especially fond of *Don Juan* and *Childe Harold.* He included Lord Byron in one of his novels which is called *The Adventures of John Davy.* The hero, and namesake of the story, goes to Turkey and Greece where he meets Lord Byron.

So how did Alexandre come to Ashbourne? In 1850 he went to London for a visit. While he was there he wanted to go on a pilgrimage to the residence of his hero, Lord Byron, who had died some 25 years before. So Alexandre left London and travelled north to Newstead Abbey in Nottingham. He then mixes real life with fiction, when he explains how he came to write the novel *Le Pasteur D'Ashbourn.* He says that while wandering the grounds of Newstead Abbey, he met with the vicar of Ashbourne who invited him back to his home town.

Alexandre says that they travelled by train and arrived at Cheadle, which is about 14 miles from Ashbourne. It is worth noting that, at the time, neither Ashbourne nor Cheadle had a station. However, very near to Cheadle is Alton which did have a station near the country house, Alton Towers. This is Alexandre's description on arriving at the railway station. The word tower could easy refer to Alton Towers close to the railway station

There my fellow stretched out his hand and showing me a tower around which were grouped a hundred houses drowned in a sea of greenery.

Epilogue – Le Pasteur d'Ashbourn – Alexandre Dumas

Alexandre chose the steward of the Earl of Alton as one of the characters in his book. The story is about the cure of the parish in Ashbourne becoming vacant and the rector decides to have a competition between his nephew and the lead in the story, William Bemrose, as to who can produce the best sermon. Aside from this main plot it is a rambling tale which many think is not quite finished.

The Dictionary

Just near the Church there are several seventeenth century buildings. One of them stands out, as it is red brick with a large pillared porch. This house was, at one time, owned by Dr John Taylor, who was a friend of the famous lexicographer Dr

Samuel Johnson. The compiler of the first English dictionary stayed in this Mansion House on several occasions. It was a friendship with John Taylor that started at school and would last for a lifetime. We will be linked in many ways to this doyen of English literature throughout our journey, but let us start by understanding the type of man he was, and why he frequently visited Ashbourne.

Although he is such a well-known name now, he struggled in his early adult life to make a living. He tried unsuccessfully to become a schoolteacher, but then decided to open his own Academy in Lichfield. But it only attracted three attendees. However, one of them was David Garrick, who became the most famous actor of his era and remained a friend of Johnson for the rest of his life.

By 1737 Samuel was penniless and he decided to go to London. He gathered some income by writing about moral and religious issues, but it was some time before he received a commission to compile a dictionary of the English Language. The work was scheduled to take three years but, in the end, it was 1755, and ten years after he started, before it was published.

Fame did not immediately come to Samuel. Although he was a well known figure in London, he did not solve his financial problems until 1761, when the young King George III gave him a modest pension. This was the same year as he met James Boswell, who produced his very well known biography of Samuel.

The favours of fortune did turn for Johnson, when in 1765, he met Henry Thrale, who was a wealthy brewer. They immediately built up a good relationship, which was augmented by Henry Thrale's wife Hester, who also had a lot of time for Samuel. He was very closely associated with the Thrales for the next fifteen years and was often their guest. Samuel eventually died at the age of 75, but his dictionary would never be forgotten. This is the opening of the preface to Samuel's Dictionary:

It is the fate of those who toil at the lower employments of life, to be rather driven by the fear of evil, than attracted by the prospect of good; to be exposed to censure, without hope of praise; to be disgraced by miscarriage, or punished for neglect, where success would have been without applause, and diligence without reward. Among these unhappy mortals is the writer of dictionaries; whom mankind have considered, not as the pupil, but the slave of science, the pioneer of literature, doomed only to remove rubbish and clear obstructions from the paths through which Learning and Genius press forward to conquest and glory, without bestowing a smile on the humble drudge that facilitates their progress. Every other author may aspire to praise; the lexicographer can only hope to escape reproach, and even this negative recompense has been yet granted to very few.

I have, notwithstanding this discouragement, attempted a dictionary of the English language, which, while it was employed in the cultivation of every species of literature, has itself been hitherto neglected; suffered to spread, under the direction of chance, into wild exuberance; resigned to the tyranny of time and fashion; and exposed to the corruptions of ignorance, and caprices of innovation.

English Dictionary – Samuel Johnson

Mansion House where Samuel Johnson stayed with his lifelong friend

Let us pass the wonderful old almshouses and go to the heart of the town. The centre of Ashbourne has narrow streets, and a cobbled market place, which are testimony to the town's age and much of its current charm. Of course, it is not ideally suited to modern traffic, but as the cars and lorries pass through the centre of the town, they go under a wooden arch that straddles the road. It is the pub sign for the Green Man and Black's Head Royal Hotel.

The Making of a Biography

The Green Man was frequented by Samuel Johnson and his biographer James Boswell, and it is to the latter, that we will now pay our attention. James Boswell's biography of Johnson is often cited as a leading example of the form. Even after 200 years it still makes a good read with a fine balance of description, anecdotes and insight into the famous man. This is part of Boswell's description of Ashbourne.

After breakfast I departed, and pursued my journey northwards. I took my post-chaise from the Green Man, a very good inn at Ashbourne, the mistress of which, a mighty civil gentlewoman, curtseying very low, presented me with an engraving of the sign of her house; to which she had subjoined, in her own handwriting, an address in such singular simplicity of style, that I have preserved it, pasted upon one of the boards of my original Journal at this time, and shall here insert it for the amusement of my readers:-

M. KILLINGLEY's duty waits upon Mr. Boswell, is exceedingly obliged to him for this favour; whenever he comes this way, hopes for a continuance of the same. Would Mr. Boswell name the house to his extensive acquaintance, it would be a singular favour conferr'd on one who has it not in her power to make any other return but her most grateful thanks, and sincerest prayers for his happiness in time, and in a blessed eternity.
The Life of Samuel Johnson – James Boswell

What perhaps isn't clear from the writers who we have discussed so far is any relationship between them. Samuel Johnson and James Boswell were contemporaries of both George Frideric Handel and Jean-Jacques Rousseau. Samuel was known for his forthright opinions and never had a good word to say about Jean-Jacques. In fact, he said that he had been hounded out of four countries and the same should apply to England. He also added that he thought Jean-Jacques a much more creditable choice for transportation than many that were sentenced in the English courts.

James Boswell did have a much higher regard for Jean-Jacques than Samuel and had visited him in Paris when James was journeying around Europe. But there is nothing like a bit of scandal. When Jean-Jacques arrived in this country he was initially on his own because his mistress had stayed in France, and delayed joining him. However, as she began her journey, so she was joined by James Boswell and it is believed that they had a brief affair. It would have been a tantalising meeting if Jean-Jacques had come the few miles into Ashbourne when Samuel and James were there! But as far as we know the meeting never took place.

Certainly George and Samuel would have known of each other, as both were famous in the literary and theatrical scenes of London. There is one inn in London that still exists today, it is in Clerkenwell and it is called the Jerusalem Inn. It is claimed that George as a young man visited there, and that Samuel also frequented the ale-house, but given the twenty plus years difference in their age it is unlikely they ever met there.

The main street in Ashbourne just before the Green Man leads us over the Henmore Brook. The old chapel just past the junction is our interest.

Prisoner of War

The title page of a small book gives us the introduction to this section:

A Short Account of the Extraordinary Life and Travels of H. L. L. Native of St Domingo, now a Prisoner of War at Ashbourn in Derbyshire. Showing the remarkable steps of Divine Providence towards him, and the means of his Conversion to God Written by His Own Hand
Life and Travels – H. L. L.

The reader will notice that it does pose a number of interesting questions. Who was H.L.L.? And why was he a prisoner of war in Derbyshire? To which we would have to suppose that being a native of Santo Domingo also intrigues.

Let's start with the prisoner of war. Following the collapse of the Treaty of Amiens, in 1803, between England and France it meant that they were at war again. One particular difficulty that France had at the time was the island in the Caribbean called Santo Domingo. This is the modern-day Haiti and Dominican Republic. Attempts by local people to take the island back from France showed various fortunes. In the overall chaos prevalent in the area at the time, the British captured a French ship and all were treated as prisoners whether they were from France or from Santo Domingo.

Whilst many of these prisoners were kept in the naval bases of Portsmouth and Plymouth, another way of dealing with them was to place them on parole, but a fair distance away from the sea. And so in 1803, 130 prisoners arrived in Ashbourne. There was a jail at Walton Bank, just opposite the chapel, but many were billeted out to the homes in the area. The officers were treated respectfully and they often dined with the senior people of the town. The Green Man was one such location for dinner. After their prisoner of war status was relaxed, some settled in the area. The church records that a few of them married local people.

Our writer Honore Lazarus Lecompte became a convert to Methodism at the chapel at the foot of the hill on the Derby Road. Honore then goes on to give a detailed account of his life, which involved treachery, piracy and many other similar matters. Sometimes he was forced into these circumstances, and at other times, he volunteered in the hope of making his fortune. The political instability, and varying fortunes of different groups in the Caribbean, often found him on the wrong side of trouble. On this walk, two of our writers have background links with Santo Domingo. Honore was a generation older than Alexandre Dumas, but the latter's parents would have been on the same small island when Honore was born.

The Mother of the Salvation Army

This book and the idea of *The Literary Way* were inspired by walking along the different parts of the route on many occasions. It was on one of these times, a pleasant and warm summer's day and we were drifting around Ashbourne. In the park we came across a bust that was dedicated to Catherine Booth, who was born in Ashbourne. Both literature and great writers inspire people. But there is another group of people who create a strong and positive lasting impression on future generations. It seemed appropriate to us, to include any that we came across, as much would be written about them. As we looked at the bust of Catherine in the park it was clear to us that she would fit into this category. At the time we knew little about Catherine Booth except she was married to the founder of the Salvation Army, so it came as a pleasant surprise to us to find that she did write regularly.

At the traffics light we take the road to Belper. A short distance from the junction, there is a row of terraced houses, one of which bears a sign to show that Catherine was born in that house. Before we consider more about Catherine, let's move from the busy road and turn up into the park and find her bust in the eastern top corner.

She was deeply religious as a young girl and frequently suffered from periods of poor health. It was during the period when she was confined to her bed that she began to write articles for magazines about the dangers of alcohol. At the age of 23, she met a Methodist minister called William Booth, who had strong views that the church should extend out into the community and help with food, shelter and clothing. The couple married three years later. By then they were in London, but because of his work, they travelled widely. Catherine shared her husband's view that the Church should reach out to the material needs of the less fortunate in society. It is easy to think of a contented married couple devoting their lives to their church. But there was one area where there was disagreement between the two and that was on the subject of women preachers. William was opposed to the idea, but Catherine became increasingly more adamant that she should be able to preach the same as men. It wasn't just William who held such views and she would attract resistance from a number of different groups in their community. But Catherine would not be deterred and, on one occasion, she took the initiative and stood to speak in public. She rapidly became known as a powerful orator and gradually won round William's support.

It was after nine years of marriage that they jointly opened the Christian Mission in the east end of London. In 1878, the name was changed to Salvation Army and consisted of men and women as officers of equal rank. This was anathema to many parts of society at the time, but the Army went on from strength to strength. Katherine died in 1890, aged 61. She had eight children and after her death, William would carry on the work she had started in making the working conditions of the sweat shops in the east end of London, less injurious to health. Catherine was clearly a woman who would articulately pursue what she believed to be the work of God and which would be a benefit to society. Let's consider the introduction to her work on women preachers.

Making allowance for the novelty of the thing, we cannot discover anything either unnatural or immodest in a Christian woman, becomingly attired, appearing on a platform or in a pulpit. By nature she seems fitted to grace either. God has given to woman a graceful form and attitude, winning manners, persuasive speech, and, above all, a finely-toned emotional nature, all of which appear to us eminent natural qualifications for public speaking. We admit that want of mental culture, the trammels of custom, the force of prejudice, and one-sided interpretations of Scripture, have hitherto almost excluded her from this sphere; but, before such a sphere is pronounced to be unnatural, it must be proved either that woman has not the ability to teach or to preach, or that the possession and exercise of this ability unnaturalizes her in other respects; that so soon as she presumes to step on the platform or into the pulpit, she loses the delicacy and grace of the female character.

Female Ministry: Or Woman's Right to Preach the Gospel – Catherine Booth

The Death of a Daughter

As one would expect in a town that has over a thousand years of history there are several lines of aristocracy either in Ashbourne or in nearby villages. Ashbourne Hall, which is within the confines of the modern town, had a significant occupant in the eighteenth century. Sir Brooke Boothby, who was born in 1744, and was the sixth Baronet in his lineage, lived at Ashbourne Hall, which is just opposite where the bust of Catherine Booth stands in the park. The building, which now fulfills a variety of modern uses, overlooks the park. What is now the graceful park, which we have been walking through, with its gurgling brook, was at one time the grounds and gardens of Ashbourne Hall. The

Penelope Boothby

road between the hall and the park was not opened until the twentieth century, by which time, the hall had left aristocratic hands. Brooke Boothby was an intelligent man and specialised in linguistics and translation. In addition, he wrote a small amount of poetry.

At the height of his engagement with the literary and philosophical communities, Brooke Boothby had his portrait painted by a well known local artist, Joseph Wright. In the picture, he is seen lazing back in a forest glade clutching a book. That forest setting is in the woods of Wootton Hall. The book is the autobiography of the French philosopher, Jean-Jacques Rousseau. Brooke, although he was only in his twenties, when Jean-Jacques took up his residence at Wootton Hall, they became friends for what is likely to be two reasons. First, he was aristocratic, which always suited Jean-Jacques' temperament and second he could speak fluent French. Despite his knowledge of many subjects, Jean-Jacques had never learned to speak English.

Long after Jean-Jacques had left England, Brooke was travelling in France and met up again with Jean-Jacques, who trusted Brooke with a copy of the first part of *The Confessions*, his autobiography. He asked Brooke to ensure that it was published. Brooke duly carried out his task by translating it into English. It was then published in Lichfield. It has since gone on to be published in many languages all over the world.

We referred to the sculpture by Thomas Banks, in St Oswald's church, of Penelope Boothby. This was Brooke's daughter who died aged five. In her short life, she had been painted by Sir Joshua Reynolds, and in death adorned by Banks in the sculpture, and by Henry Fuseli in *The Apotheosis of Peneolope Boothby*.

The death of Penelope caused the start of a decline which would affect Brooke for the rest of his life. He was 47 when his five-year-old daughter died unexpectedly. It was an event from which he would never recover. He lost a sense of purpose about money and finished his life in poor and meagre circumstances. He died in Boulogne aged 80. In tribute to Penelope he wrote *A Book of Sorrows*, including *A Locket of Hair*.

Bright crispéd threads of pure translucent gold!
Ye who were wont with zephyr's breath to play,
Over the warm cheek and ivory forehead stray,
Or clasp her neck in many an amorous fold,
Now, motionless, in this little shrine must hold:
No more to wanton in the eye of day;
Or to the breeze your changeful hues display:
For ever still inanimate, and cold.
A Locket of Hair – Brooke Boothby

Eighteenth Century Female Education

Let's leave the park by the north west corner to the red brick building on the opposite side of the road. On that building, within sight of the park, is a plaque about a school, but before we explain its significance let's look at the intellectual life at the end of the 1700's in the local region. Ashbourne is in mid-Derbyshire and is about 13 miles from the county town of Derby and 26 miles from the large provincial town of Lichfield in Staffordshire.

In the eighteenth century, Lichfield and Derby were intellectual centres for philosophy and literature. Ashbourne became involved in both centres through both residents and visitors. One of leading intelligentsia of the time, we have already introduced, and it was Erasmus Darwin, who earned a substantial amount of money as a physician but his creative mind spanned many topics. His first worries as a doctor were about attracting patients so that he had enough to live on. This concern about money was soon alleviated and he became the doctor of choice for many of the rich and famous, including the Duke and Duchess of Devonshire and the mill-owning Arkwright family.

He drew together in the area, mainly around Lichfield and Derby, a number of leading minds from diverse fields. These included Josiah Wedgwood and James Watt from the fledgling Industrial Revolution, as well as Herbert Spencer, the philosopher, who coined the phrase, 'survival of the fittest'. We see one of our many links in the literary world as we mentioned that Herbert Spencer received the unrequited love of Marian Evans, also known as George Eliot.

Erasmus wrote on an extensive number of topics with perhaps his most important writings being in botany and zoology. His work *Zoonomia, The Laws of Organic Life* was centred on the development of generations in animals. It would be Erasmus's grandson, Charles Darwin, who would develop the ideas of the theory of evolution, in his work *The Origin of Species.* Erasmus lived in the Cathedral Close in Lichfield and caused consternation amongst the clergy when he added to his crest the Latin version of 'Everything from Shells', which was his first rather tentative steps towards the idea of evolution. Regardless of what his inner thoughts were, he never went as far as to alienate his rich and famous clients.

Erasmus Darwin's direct association with Ashbourne took an entirely different line of thought and work. He had five children through his first marriage but his wife died in 1770. He then started a relationship with their governess, Mary Parker. They had two illegitimate daughters Mary Jr. and Susannah. The children stayed in Erasmus's family home and were raised in the same manner as the other children.

Erasmus believed that the education of girls was lacking and proposed his own ideas, when he published, *A Plan for the Conduct of Female Education in Boarding Schools* in 1797, when Mary Jr and Susannah were 23 and 25 years old. They had started their careers as governesses, but Erasmus then helped them set up their school in Ashbourne. The Parker's school was in a red brick building on the corner opposite the park. This building was originally on the Ashbourne Hall estate and was given to Erasmus by Brooke Boothby for use as a school. Brooke frequently attended Erasmus' philosophical and literary meetings.

We can enjoy the traditional old market place as we cross it to go up Union Street. If we go straight on, we pick up the road to Mappleton and once over the brow of the hill we turn onto the footpath and cycle track, the Tissington Trail. After following this north for a short distance there is a footpath on the left to Callow Top Caravan park. We follow this right of way over the hill and down into Mappleton and come out near the Okeover Arms. Further up the road is the bridge of the River Dove which we cross. On our left is the wide estate land of Okeover Hall which we can see with its nearby church and the entrance gates to the drive.

Okeover Hall boasts a writer called Robert Plumer Ward. He was both a novelist and a politician. He was called to the bar, but hankered after politics and served as a member of parliament for 21 years spread over the two constituencies of Cockermouth and Haslemere. During that time he held minor posts in government. He was born in 1765 and would live until he was nearly 80. He published two politically-based books and three novels which he wrote after leaving parliament. *De Vere: A Man*

Erasmus Darwin's daughters' school

Okeover Hall, the home of Robert Plumer Ward

of Independence was published in 1827. It is a long novel that came in four volumes.

De Vere is the central character and as a young man he is groomed by those around him to go into politics. Robert Plumer Ward had a detailed knowledge of politics and its machinations, which come across in the book. De Vere seeks out a quiet moment in the middle of the book and takes himself off to the Dove Valley. In the course of his wandering and looking for somewhere to stay he is welcomed to Okeover Hall. Robert came to live in the Hall in 1832 after he married into the Okeover family, however, he had written *De Vere* some years earlier. It is intriguing to know why it appeared in a book a long time before he married into the Okeover family. He was at the time married and had a family. It was only after his wife's death that he married again and came to live at Okeover, which was well-known for its painting of the Holy Family by Raphael.

Let us leave Okeover with the words of John Edwards in *The Tour of the Dove.* John Edward was a wine merchant from Derby, who wrote his topographical poem as much as a travel guide as a poem. It begins at the confluence of the Dove and Trent and he then makes his way up stream and describes the scenery as he goes.

Oakover's lofty pines in distance seen,
Allured me onward when the morning smiled:
Within the mansion sheltered by that screen
Is Raphael's sweetest work the Virgin mild,
Pictured with Jesus her most holy child.
All things are tranquil here; the River flows
In utter stillness, 'scaped from regions wild;
And those twin streams twice-born join her repose;
Upon her gentle breast their silver pinions close.
The Tour of the Dove – John Edwards

Let us rest awhile at Okeover

No one can doubt, regardless of religious conviction, the sterling work still done by the inspired army of Catherine Booth. Religion, as we will find on *The Literary Way*, plays a major part in many writers' thoughts and works, and it does bring us the remarkable writings of H.L.L. as a social commentary of the time.

We found it quite stunning to discover such a little known work, focused on Ashbourne, as Alexandre Dumas's *Le Pasteur d'Ashbourn.* You will have also noticed that Lord Byron appeared again in the tribute from Alexandre and the reason he came to this part of England. Samuel Johnson once famously said, "a man that is tired of London is tired of life". And while he was always quite keen to return to the capital, he valued his visits and friendship with Dr Taylor.

The aristocratic parts of this chapter, Brooke Boothby and the Cockaynes brought us some writing ranging from deep sorrow to light and humorous verse, but as their lines died out so did their money and privilege, whilst those from humble beginnings became rich. We are back at the River Dove and this will lead our wanderings for most of the next two walks.

A Limestone Desk in Happy Valley

Okeover to Thorpe Cloud through Ilam

Ilam Hall and the River Manifold which has risen from the boil holes

Ilam Hall, and the model village that lays outside of its gates, is the focus for this walk on *The Literary Way.* It gives us the opportunity to bring to you a restoration playwright whose plays were very popular before the bawdy nature of them fell out of favour with the critics, and then the public. His family took the side of the King in the English Civil War and they eventually went to Ireland where our playwright received his early education. He became life long friends with Jonathan Swift, the writer of *Gulliver's Travels,* and the friendship particularly came to the fore when they both moved to London.

In addition, we return to Samuel Johnson, not only for his views of Ilam, especially the river that passes through the ground, but also he used this setting as the basis for one of his novels. We entitled the previous chapter *Great Poor Writers* and we said that Samuel was no exception. His story, inspired by Ilam, was due to a shortage of money, before he became well-known in the haunts of London.

Our route has taken us from Okeover up the Dove Valley on the Staffordshire side of river. When we reached the large Coldwall Bridge, with the village of Thorpe on the hill overlooking it, we entered the Peak District National Park, which was one of the first National Parks created in England and remains one of the busiest.

In this region holidaymakers mix with day-trippers from major towns such as Manchester, Sheffield and Nottingham. Ilam Hall is located in the south of the Peak District and is tucked into the valley of the River Manifold which has steep limestone slopes and a famous disappearing river. The path along the valley takes us past the confluence of the Rivers Dove and Manifold and across the fields to the bridge, behind which we can see the roofs and chimneys of the hall. The village of Ilam, with its 'chalet' style houses and school, seems uncharacteristic of the area, where we tend to expect square limestone buildings, rather than high gables and tiled fronts. These buildings were part of the overall design of the model village that is now Ilam. The development was linked to the Gothic redesign of the main Hall that took place in about the 1830s.

We enter the grounds of Ilam Hall which is now in the custodianship of the National Trust and as we approach the Hall we can see that it is not a large building. There is a reason for this. Currently it does not match its once magnificent opulence, but it still is a truly wonderful setting with many aspects to grip our interest. Ilam Hall has had three main stages to its development.

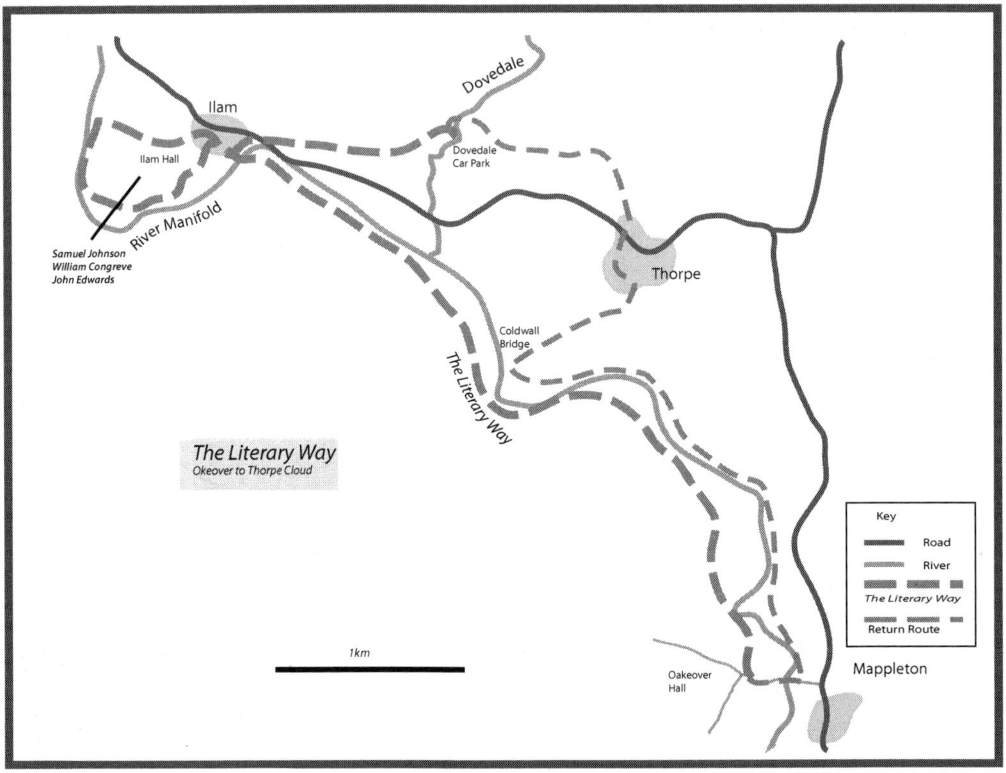

The Literary Way – Walk Three – Okeover to Thorpe Cloud

Walk Directions

Okeover to Ilam (2.98 miles)

Take the path past the old mill
It skirts the fields and then approaches a farm
The path bears left before the farm
Cross the field and enter the wooded area
On emergence from the wood we are at the riverside
This is the west bank of the Dove
After a stile we join a track
This takes us past Coldwall Bridge
We pass through the bushes and trees
The river bank leads us to Ilam Bridge

The Grounds of Ilam Hall

Cross Ilam Bridge and pass the Eleanor Cross
Turn into the hall grounds past the gatehouse
Follow the drive to the house
Pass through the arch to the stable block
Turn left through the gardens and head for the church
From the church go past St Bertram's well to the river
Walk along the river bank and ascend the steps
Enjoy the desk and, over the railings, the boil holes
Carry on down the steps and along Paradise Walk
Turn right near the footbridge
Cross the estate land that has ridge and furrow
Return to the village

Ilam to Dovedale Car Park (1.77 miles)

Turn left at the Eleanor Cross
After a short distance take the footpath on the left
Cross the field and pass the farm
Continue on the path
Enjoy the approach of Bunster Hill and Thorpe Cloud
The path leads to Dovedale Car Park

Dovedale Car Park to Okeover (3.33 miles)

Leave the car park and follow the river northwards
Cross the bridge
Take the path straight ahead
The path goes around Thorpe Cloud
Go through the gate on the right at the rear of Thorpe Cloud
Diagonally cross the field towards the buildings
Cross the road and take the lane opposite
Follow it round, and turn right near Thorpe Church
The lane becomes a track down to Coldwall Bridge
Take the riverside path south on the Thorpe side of the river
Follow the riverside path back to Okeover

Distance: 8.08 miles Ascent: 829ft

Let us explain how things have changed. The hall you see in front of you is the remnants of a much larger one that was built in the 1820s by Jesse Watts-Russell. As we learned in Snelston, the early 1800s saw a revival of Gothic architecture, and this was the style that Jesse wanted. At the beginning of that decade he bought the old Tudor hall and knocked it down to build a new one. The Watts-Russell hall then passed from his family and in the 1930s it was bought with the intention of demolition. This was partly completed before Sir Robert McDougall, the flour magnate, bought it and passed it to the nation.

Sir Robert was a major benefactor to the nation in this area and he donated, not only Ilam Hall, but also parts of Dovedale and other Peak District areas, to the country. He was a descendant of a Victorian teacher who created the first self-raising flour and thereby set up the McDougall flour company. The part of the main hall that survives is a Youth Hostel, the designation of which was part of the bequest from Sir Robert.

If we a pass through the arch towards the old stable block we can turn through the gardens from which the view is excellent and, across the fields, we can see the flat-topped hill, Thorpe Cloud, which dominates over the entrance to Dovedale. In the foreground, is a small quaint church set in the grounds of the old hall and having the wonderful backdrop of the limestone hills. The Holy Cross Church, which is now a mainly seventeenth and nineteenth century building, did have its origins in Saxon times.

The Old Bachelor

Let us now look back in time to the first Ilam Hall. This was a Tudor house built in about 1520 and was owned by the Port family from the 1600s. The family name survives in Derbyshire and has most connections with the village of Etwall, which was the main seat of the family. The family was particularly noted for their work in promoting education. Their name and work lives on in Etwall's comprehensive school which is called the John Port School.

Just a little further along the riverside path is a set of steps that lead us up into the woods. At the top of them is something of a surprise. There is a limestone desk. It is set in a rock grotto in the heavy shadow of the trees. The desk has an angled top

Ilam Hall Gardens with St Bertram's Church and the flat-topped Thorpe Cloud

and a limestone stool. Any one sitting at the desk would have a view down through the woods and over the river. One person who is believed to have sat there, during a period when he was convalescing, was William Congreve. It is supposed that he wrote his first play, a comedy, called *The Old Bachelor* whilst gazing over the valley. The play was first performed in 1693 and was a success. It would be the first step in making him a famous Restoration playwright.

William Congreve was born in Yorkshire, but his father was a cavalier who took up a role in Ireland and so William completed his education at Trinity College Dublin, where he became friends with the writer Jonathan Swift. The main Congreve family home was at Stretton Hall in Staffordshire which is about 65 km from Ilam. It is not entirely clear why he chose to recover from his illness at Ilam.

He was only 23 years old, when the play was first performed and it is likely that he wrote it some years earlier. The Restoration began in 1660 when the monarchy returned to the thrones of the countries of the British Isles. This followed a period of instability in the country caused by the English Civil War.

William spent a lot of time in London and enjoyed the Restoration's relaxation on plays and writing, which had been imposed during the puritanical regime of the middle of the 17th century. While he was in London, as well as Swift, he fell under the wing of one of the foremost poets of the day, John Dryden.

Congreve's Desk where he wrote "The Old Bachelor"

The Old Bachelor was well received on its first performance thanks to Dryden's support, and the play had a long run in Drury Lane, with many of the leading actors of the day. The play is a comedy about the pursuit of love, and as would be expected, one of the principal characters is the old bachelor. It is a humorous, bawdy romp, with many mentions of whores, and sees the final capitulation of the cynical old bachelor. William would have sat at the desk in the grotto and thought about the life in London and around Covent garden for that is where the play is set.

Before the success of the play, Congreve had joined the Middle Temple, in London, to train as a barrister. However, he was never called to the bar. But he needed to work and he made a little money by completing some translation work and publishing an anonymous novel. *The Old Bachelor* changed William's life and he became a celebrated name. Whilst some of his later plays were not that successful, he was well known and did a Royal Command Performance for Queen Anne. Congreve never married, but there was much speculation as to his relationship with Anne Bracegirdle, who appeared in many of his plays.

Despite his relationship with the actress, it is thought that he did have a daughter with the second Duchess of Marlborough. This must have caused a certain amount of problems as she was already married. Although by that time he had moved to Bath and died there following injuries received in a coaching accident.

Let's leave Congreve's desk with one quotation, which is from one of his later plays. It has now become a familiar part of the English language, albeit in a modified form.

Heaven has no rage, like love to hatred turned,
Nor hell a fury, like a woman scorned
The Mourning Bride – William Congreve

Boil Holes

On the riverside just below William's desk there are railings that guard a curve in the river. By carefully studying the surface of the water, it can be seen to be 'boiling' up in two places. This is where water from the Rivers Manifold and Hamps resurfaces after quite substantial journeys underground. Upstream from this point the river will often become a trickle, and it disappears in a dry summer. Downstream from the 'boil holes' there is always a good flow of water. The main waters of the River Manifold disappear into the limestone river bed,

The waters of the Manifold flow from the Boil Holes which are under the footpath

at Wetton, about six kilometres up stream and reappear in these 'boil holes'. This is a significant example of underground flow which is associated with the principal rock of the area, Carboniferous Limestone. The rock covers the entire southern part of the Peak District and is famous for its caves and the sport of caving.

You might wonder what this has to do with our writers. I shall let James Boswell, who was, as we already know, Samuel Johnson's friend and biographer, explain. You will notice that he refers to Ilam as Islam, and Ilam as the residence of the Congreves, in which he is probably mistaken.

Dr. Johnson obligingly proposed to carry me to see Islam, a romantick scene, now belonging to a family of the name of Port, but formerly the seat of the Congreves. I suppose it is well described in some of the Tours. Johnson described it distinctly and vividly, at which I could not but express to him my wonder; because, though my eyes, as he observed, were better than his, I could not by any means equal him in representing visible objects. I said, the difference between us in this respect was as that between a man who has a bad instrument, but plays well on it, and a man who has a good instrument, on which he can play very imperfectly.

I recollect a very fine amphitheatre, surrounded with hills covered with woods, and walks neatly formed along the side of a rocky steep, on the quarter next the house with recesses under projections of rock, overshadowed with trees; in one of which recesses, we were told, Congreve wrote his Old Bachelor. We viewed a remarkable natural curiosity at Islam; two rivers bursting near each other from the rock, not from immediate springs, but after having run for many miles under ground. Plott, in his History of Staffordshire, gives an account of this curiosity; but Johnson would not believe it, though we had the attestation of the gardener, who said, he had put in corks, where the river Manyfold sinks into the ground, and had catched them in a net, placed before one of the openings where the water bursts out. Indeed, such subterraneous courses of water are found in various parts of our globe.

The Life of Samuel Johnson – James Boswell

Samuel Johnson was born in 1709 and would have been familiar with Congreve's work. Samuel would have been twenty years old when Congreve died. The bend in the path leads us to the full aspect of the curved valley. The far side of the river is wooded and rises steeply to tower over the open flat grassed area on our side of the water. We are at the edge of this flat area. On our right is a walkway with a low balustrade over which we can see the full sweep of the valley. This part of the grounds of Ilam Hall is called Paradise Walk.

It is claimed that this valley inspired Samuel Johnson in the writing of *Rasselas*. He wrote it quickly in 1759 to raise money for his mother who was seriously ill. It is a story about an Abyssinian Prince who lived in Happy Valley. We have given you the opening lines so that you may see the links between Johnson's writing and Ilam Hall's Paradise Walk.

Ye who listen with credulity to the whispers of fancy, and pursue with eagerness the phantoms of hope; who expect that age will perform the promises of youth, and that the deficiencies of the present day will be supplied by the morrow, attend to the history of Rasselas, Prince of Abyssinia.
Rasselas was the fourth son of the mighty Emperor in whose dominions the father of waters begins his course - whose bounty

pours down the streams of plenty, and scatters over the world the harvests of Egypt.

According to the custom which has descended from age to age among the monarchs of the torrid zone, Rasselas was confined in a private palace, with the other sons and daughters of Abyssinian royalty, till the order of succession should call him to the throne. The place which the wisdom or policy of antiquity had destined for the residence of the Abyssinian princes was a spacious valley in the kingdom of Amhara, surrounded on every side by mountains, of which the summits overhang the middle part.

The only passage by which it could be entered was a cavern that passed under a rock, of which it had long been disputed whether it was the work of nature or of human industry. The outlet of the cavern was concealed by a thick wood, and the mouth which opened into the valley was closed with gates of iron, forged by the artificers of ancient days, so massive that no man, without the help of engines, could open or shut them.
Rasselas – Samuel Johnson

The story develops as Rasselas decides that he wants to see the real world and so he escapes from his 'paradise' and the story follows him through his travels. There are many interesting links between authors on *The Literary Way*. In this case, *Rasselas* is being read by a character in another famous book. The character is Helen Burns, but you will need to wait until later on *The Literary Way* before we reveal the name of the book and the author.

At the end of Paradise Walk we take the river path that leads us to a small bridge over the Manifold. We don't take the bridge but turn right up the small grassy bank and find ourselves looking over the estate land behind Ilam Hall. This part of the estate is now a Country Park. The familiar estate layout is evident. That is, open grass with trees randomly dotted in the landscape. By looking closely at the ground we see it is not even. There are parallel ridges in the direction we are walking. These grass ridges are about a foot high. The distance between successive ridges is about ten feet. We are looking at a ridge and furrow field system that probably originated in the Middle Ages. The land was allocated in the wide strips, often one to each local family, which were then ploughed down their length. It was the type of plough that created the ridges and furrows. As we would expect it was an arable system of farming. The shape of this ploughed land was preserved when it was grassed over. It is a feature of the countryside that we shall come across many times as we walk across the landscape. It has been preserved for so long because farming moved away from arable to animal farming and therefore the thin soils have never been ploughed with modern equipment.

Let us take our leave of Ilam, and its hall, with the words from a lengthy poem called *The Tour of the Dove.* It was written by John Edwards, in 1821, and was dedicated to the owner of Ilam Hall. This is the section of the poem that describes Ilam Hall. It was written as the new Gothic Hall was being built. The lines refer to William Congreve's grotto as well as the flower gathering of Jean-Jacques Rousseau, who would have passed through the grounds of Ilam on his walks between Ellastone and Dovedale.

Ilam, thy ancient Hall is swept away!
A fairer soon shall lift its domes and towers;
While still thy fountain-deeps ebullient play,
And newborn rivers grace thy laurel bowers
And fossil grots. Strike on, and bring the hours,
Thou clock embosomed deep in ivy bloom!
Time holds the garland yet of Rousseau's flowers;
Still broods antiquity o'er Bertram's tomb,
And Congreve's hermit cell, shrouded in sylvan gloom.
The Tour of the Dove – John Edward

The bridge in the village of Ilam

Let us rest awhile at Ilam Bridge

Our primary focus in this chapter has been the writings of Samuel Johnson and William Congreve, our Restoration playwright. Perhaps a fitting way to end this part of *the Literary Way* is by referring to the description of William by Samuel.

In his retirement he may be supposed to have applied himself to books, for he discovers more literature than the poets have commonly attained. But his studies were in his later days obstructed by cataracts in his eyes, which at last terminated in blindness. This melancholy state was aggravated by the gout, for which he sought relief by a journey to Bath: but, being overturned in his chariot, complained from that time of a pain in his side, and died at his house in Surrey Street in the Strând, January 29, 1728.

Having lain in state in the Jerusalem Chamber, he was buried in Westminster Abbey, where a monument is erected to his memory by Henrietta Duchess of Marlborough, to whom, for reasons either not known or not mentioned, he bequeathed a legacy of about ten thousand pounds, the accumulation of attentive parsimony, which, though to her superfluous and useless, might have given great assistance to the ancient family from which he descended, at that time, by the imprudence of his relation, reduced to difficulties and distress.
The Lives of Poets – Samuel Johnson

A Contemplative Man's Recreation

Thorpe Cloud to Tissington through Milldale

The River Dove flowing past Thorpe Cloud which is on the left

Dovedale has the reputation of being one of the most delightful walks in the United Kingdom and it has been one of our favourites for many years. Because of its popularity it can become very busy so there is a need to carefully choose the time of your walk. We prefer an early morning during the summer, when the freshness of the grass and trees pervades the air with their delicate aromas. One other benefit of walking at this time is the solitude, which allows us to listen to the gentle flowing of the weirs. The range of these sounds is exquisite as the different shapes and falls of the weirs give their individual patterns.

We have a variety of works for our thoughts as we meander alongside the Dove and the exquisite limestone dale that guides the river. There have been many visitors to Dovedale who have extolled its virtues as sublime English scenery, but it is some what surprising that Byron, Coleridge, Moore, Tennyson and Wordsworth did not compose verses about it. Many mention it in their letters, and Wordsworth does refer to the banks of the Dove in a poem, but there are no epic verses that have flowed from the pens of the masters.

In the previous chapters we referred to *A Tour of the Dove* by John Edwards and he comments, in the preface to his work, that he was surprised at the lack of local verse and his lengthy poem was a contribution to resolving the deficit. Two writers, who we have mentioned before, sought out Dovedale. George Eliot refers to it as Eagledale in *Adam Bede,* while it was a favourite destination of Jean-Jacques Rousseau who would have walked the four miles across country from Wootton.

We left Ilam and our route took us across the fields near to the Izaac Walton Hotel, the name of which will become one of our focal points on this walk, and towards the entrance to Dovedale. A fascinating character on this walk is a woman writer from the nineteenth century, who challenged the norms of society, and became one of the first poets extensively recognised by the working class people. An-

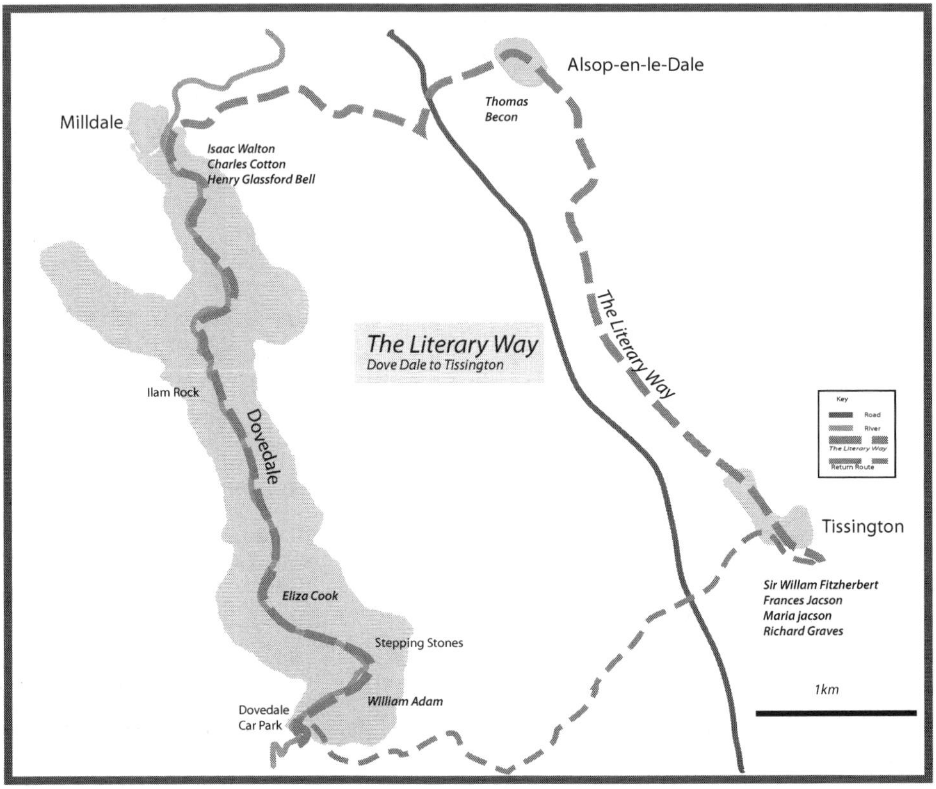

The Literary Way – Walk Four – Thorpe Cloud to Tissington

Stepping Stones in Dovedale

Walk Directions

Dovedale Car Park to Ilam Rock

Take the path from the car park upstream along the river
Cross the footbridge
Go to the top of Thorpe Cloud and then return to the riverside
Take the path past the stepping-stones
The path follows the riverside and then rises to Lovers Leap
Continue past Tissington Spires
Go past Reynard's Arch, which is on the right
You will then reach Ilam Rock which is on the left

Ilam Rock to Milldale (1.17 miles)

Continue on the riverside path
Follow the path past the caves which are called Dove Holes
Continue to follow the path to Viator's Bridge, Milldale
Take path uphill to the right just before Viator's Bridge

Milldale to Alsop-en-le-Dale (1.52 miles)

As the path rises take the left fork of the two paths
The path follows a wall on the left and leads to a stile
Having crossed the stile the wall is now on the right of the footpath
At the path junction, which is at the stile, take the left path to Alsop
The path joins the lane and then turns right
After about 100 metres take the path across the field on the left
Cross the main road, and go down the track to old Alsop station
Take the path straight in front, which goes down across the fields
When you reach the lane, turn right into Alsop
You will go past the Hall and Church

Alsop-en-le-Dale to Tissington (2.26 miles)

Leave the village by continuing along the same lane. Go past the farm.
Take the right footpath at 45 degrees that follows a track.
After the brow of the hill aim to the right of the gate ahead
Cross the stile (which is difficult to find) and head towards the trees
Continue straight ahead
The path then leads under the Tissington Trail
The footpath leaves the track to pass to the left of the farm buildings
Follow the path across the fields
At the path junction take the left path to Tissington
Follow Rakes Lane into Tissington
Go past the Hall and Church

Tissington to Dovedale Car Park (2.46 miles)

To return to start, turn right at the end of the main road
Follow the road along the estate drive
Cross the main road and follow the lane opposite.
The lane bends left and after there is a footpath on the right.
Follow the path across several fields
On the quiet lane turn left and then the footpath is on the right
Follow the path past the back of the hotel
Aim for Thorpe Cloud
Go through the gate and turn left along the slope of Thorpe Cloud
Go down to the bridge and retrace your steps to the car park

Distance: 9.25 miles Ascent: 1427ft

other visitor, a Scottish solicitor, who was on holiday from north of the border, returns us to Isaac.

Churchmen provide some stimulating ideas towards the end of this walk. We shall meet three very different characters and with very different outlooks. The first published under a pseudonym and we shall find out why he took that approach. The second led a two-sided life, one in the church, but the other with some very unchurch-like behaviour. Finally, we have a devout man who lived for a period at one of the Peak District's most magnificent halls.

Thorpe Cloud is situated to the east of the River Dove. Its matching partner, Bunster Hill, is to the west. These two hills form the entrance to the Dove's limestone gorge from the south. They are made of reef limestone, that was formed 300 million years ago in shallow warm seas. These reefs were surrounded, and overlain, by massive piles of calcareous materials which, for us today, have produced this wonderful limestone scenery. On the fringe of this ancient warm sea were the swampy conditions that eventually led to the coal deposits which have been extensively mined to the east and west of the Peak District in Yorkshire, Nottinghamshire and Lancashire.

Let's go up Thorpe Cloud! It is a steep climb, but the view over the countryside, and the perspective of the gorge, make it worthwhile. There are footpaths that approach it from all directions, but the easiest is from the opposite side to the Dove. The exposed limestone is clearly visible on the summit and specks of it can be seen poking through the rough grass on its sides. When you have struggled to the top it is time to take stock and to look over the outstretched hills and the winding gorge of Dovedale. The hotel we passed is visible, as is Ilam Hall.

The route down from Thorpe Cloud on the north side allows us to come into Dovedale from the east. The hill to our right is a flat swathe of rough grass with a single tree on its skyline. Unusually for this part of the country, the hill, according to the Ordnance Survey map, does not have a specific name. The entrance to Dovedale, which is then only a short way down Lin Dale, is quite surprising. All of a sudden we seem to be in the middle of the dale. We join the outside bend of the river with Thorpe Cloud to the left of us, and Bunster Hill in front of us on the other side of the river. The dale curves away from us upstream. At the point of where we join Dovedale there are stepping stones across the river. They provide a great deal of fun for the children, and even adults, in the summer months. There is no public path on the other side of the river beyond the stepping stones, which is the Staffordshire side. On this side of the river we are in Derbyshire.

Gem of the Peak was an early Victorian Guide to the Peak District and had reached its fifth edition by 1851. In it, William Adam, the author, describes the entry into Dovedale with flowing Victorian eloquence:

As we descended over the irregular road-way, if it may be so called, full of ruts, and chiefly over green sward or healthy mountain side, the east end of Dovedale began to open up before us, Thorpe Cloud, rising proudly to our left, Bunster immediately before us, and the lofty point bounding the east entrance to the right. There is an indescribable and overpowering majesty in nature, especially in mountain scenery, that it is difficult to account for; it seems not so much to arise from a minute examination of the parts of which it is composed, as from the combined effect of the whole as it is rapidly traversed with the eye, until the mind is completely filled with its vast dimensions, and inspired with a deep sense of its own insignificance and nothingness, as compared to such monuments of creative wisdom and omnipotent power; and that power reigning in supreme through silent majesty around us.

We experienced the full effect of this as we made out way from the smiling fields and busy haunts of man to plunge into and examine the deeps and narrow recesses of Dovedale, which still retains all its ancient simplicity and beauty, uninjured by the art of man, and its magic charm still unbroken by the intrusions of his dwellings.
Gem of the Peak – William Adam

Dovedale is a limestone gorge that has been eroded and weathered into some fascinating formations. There is a footpath all the way along the east bank to Milldale, which is the first hamlet that is reached.

Ilam Rock

The National Trust, that owns the dale, manages it successfully so that is can cope with the very many visitors that come to this popular part of the River Dove. There are a number of weirs on this section of the Dove. The water flowing over these small rock structures makes this one of the most attractive parts of the river. They not only give differing flows of water, but also provide a relaxing countryside sound to accompany this very peaceful setting. Soon after we begin the walk up Dovedale, the first of the named rock formations is on the far side of the river. It is Dovedale Castle. These noticeable features are resistant rocks that protrude into the air above the remaining rocks and woodlands. There are four principal limestone pinnacles and in the order of meeting them they are, Dovedale Castle, Pickering Tor, Tissington Spires and Ilam Rock. It is only a short walk until we take a steady climb up onto a spur, which is a headland on the inside of the river bend. At the top we find Lover's Leap overlooking the river.

Self Improvement

On Christmas Eve, in 1818, Eliza Cook was born into a large poor family in London. Education was costly and most of her learning would come through a Sunday School. She was diligent in her self studies and was encouraged in her attempts to write poetry at the Sunday meetings. She began to publish poems, and by the time she was 31, she had launched her own Journal. This was published weekly, it was about fifteen to twenty pages in length, and contained a mixture of articles, short stories and poems. Many of the pieces she had written herself, but her widening groups of associates also contributed.

As she had come from such a poor background she wanted to do all she could to support those in similar situations and so looked to giving her support to political causes. One of the first working class political movements, Chartism, was at its zenith at the times and she readily engaged with it. A poem, called *The Old Armchair,* made her name well known throughout the literary and working class world. She was prolific in poetry writing and when she published her collected works it ran to nearly 600 pages. This was in addition to the many other magazines and journals to which she contributed articles. By 1863 her reputation was established and she was awarded a Civil List Pension. We have selected one poem entitled *Derbyshire Dales,* as it contains a verse about Dovedale.

Sweet pass of the Dove mid rock, river, and dingle,
How great is thy charm for the wanderer's breast!
With thy moss-girdled towers and foam-jewelled shingle,
Thy mountains of might, and thy valleys of rest.
Derbyshire Dales – Eliza Cook

She succeeded as a poet in difficult times and, when

she issued her collected works, she ensured that they were cheap enough for ordinary working people to buy, or acquire through the newly formed local libraries.

But we haven't finished with Eliza Cook and Dovedale because there is a fascinating development in the story of her life and poetry. And for what was an intrigue and scandal at the time, we need to cross to the United States of America to put it into context.

Near the time of Eliza's birth, another baby girl was born into the Cushman family in Boston. Her circumstances were similar to Eliza's, the family was poor and little Charlotte had work duties from an early age. But in early adulthood, her occupation and her monetary situation changed. She had desired to become an opera singer but, when this failed, she took to the stage. She became one of the most successful actresses of her age. This brought instant fame and wealth. It enabled her to own houses and to travel to Europe, where she was also hailed as a great actress. However, her lifestyle was far from normal. She created her household solely of women, many of whom would dress as men, but her flamboyance and acting capabilities held the day.

One time, when in England, she read and admired Eliza's poetry. The women met, and then began a close relationship that lasted for a long time. Charlotte Cushman visited Dovedale and stayed at the Izaac Walton Hotel. Eliza Cook wrote a short poem simply entitled *Charlotte Cushman.* It was prompted by Charlotte's first performance in England, in the role of Bianca, in Milman's tragedy *Fazio.* This is the first verse from Eliza's poem.

I thought thee wondrous when thy soul portray'd
The youth Verona bragg'd of; and the love
Of glowing southern blood by thee was made
Entrancing as the breath of orange-grove.
Charlotte Cushman – Eliza Cook

But a far more personal poem was entitled *Our Rambles by the Dove.* It was simply addressed *To CC in America,* and as we rest at the top of the limestone spur called Lover's Leap, let's look at Eliza's words.

Tis well to proudly tell me of the glories of the West,
Of the stream with rapid torrent and the lake with heaving breast;
Of the mountain and the prairie, of the forest and the bluff,
Savannah spot so fragrant, and the jungle dell so rough.
I know that there are wonders in your own gigantic land;
The gorgeous and the beautiful, the startling and the grand;
I know the cataracts are bold, the fields of maize are wide;
I know the pines are thick enough to let the lightnings hide;
But glad I am to hear thee say with warm and clinging love,
Thou thinkest of Old England and our Rambles by the Dove.
Our Rambles by the Dove – Eliza Cook

Let's us leave Eliza and Charlotte. But we have not entirely finished with Charlotte, because she will make another appearance in Matlock, but this time as a character in a novel.

If we stand on Lover's Leap, then directly opposite is the rock formation, which is called the Twelve Apostles. In winter, it is easier to pick out the dozen rock features that make up the formation. In spring and summer the bushes and grass obscure some of them. It's not long after following the path down the north side of the spur that we come to a natural limestone arch that hides a cave. Reynard's Arch is visible from the path only at certain times of the year, when some of the bushes and trees in front of it have lost their leaves. As we reach Pickering Tor, which is on our right, so Ilam Rock can be seen on the far side of the river. Underneath Ilam Rock is a footbridge that is the first public access to the far side of the river since we left the stepping-stones. The path, that crosses the bridge, climbs up and out of Dovedale on its way back to Ilam. We continue the walk along the valley and pass the two large and shallow caves of Dove Holes. The high craggy Nabs is in front of us. We continue on the delightful path along the banks of the Dove. We pass through the last gate in the tree-lined section and the path opens out to a wider expanse of grass.

Soon we can see a small bridge and the hamlet of Milldale. It is a small and narrow bridge, but has been made famous by a writer who lived nearby. Let's set the scene by drawing your attention to the steep hill to the right of the bridge. There is a footpath that comes down that hill.

'Tis Not Two Fingers Broad

This section is about a conversation between two men, one of whom is a member of the local gentry and the other is a visitor to the region. The local gent, in our narrative, is called Piscator and the visitor who is passing through the area, on his way to Lancashire, is called Viator. They have been conversing since joining each other south of Ashbourne. They had stopped at the The Talbot Inn in Ashbourne, where the Piscator offers his country residence, situated by the River Dove, as a place to stay on the journey. This is accepted and after they had finished their ale they travel onwards. They are both on horseback. Their route does not go along the river valley, but follows the limestone hills above the Dove. We'll leave it to the book to explain what happens next.

Piscator: But, sir, we are now come to the descent of the formidable hill I told you of, at the foot of which runs the river Dove, which I cannot but love above all the rest; and therefore prepare yourself to be a little frightened.
Viator: Sir, I see you would fortify me, that I should not shame myself: but I dare follow where you please to lead me; and I see no danger yet; for the descent methinks, is thus far green, even and easy.
Piscator: You will like it worse presently, when you come to the brow of the hill, and now we are there, what think you?

Viator's Bridge at Milldale

Viator: What do I think? Why I think it is the strangest place that ever men and horses went down; and that (if there be any safety at all) the safest way is to alight.
Piscator: I think so too, for you, who are mounted on a beast not acquainted with these slippery stones; although I frequently ride down them, I will alight too, to bear you company, and to lead you the way and if you please, my man shall lead your horse.
Viator: Marry, sir, and thank you too, for I am afraid I shall have enough to do to look to myself; and with my horse in my hand should be in double fear, both of breaking my neck, and my horse falling on me; for it is as steep as a penthouse.
Piscator: To look down from hence it appears so, I confess; but the path winds and turns, and will not be found so troublesome.
Viator: Would I were well down though! Hoist thee! There's one fair 'scape! These stones are so slippery I cannot stand! yet again! I think I were best lay my heels in my neck, and tumble down.
Piscator: If you think your heels will defend your neck, that is the way to be soon at the bottom; but give me your hand at this broad stone, and then the worst is past.
Viator: I thank you, sir, I am now past it, I can go myself. What here the sign of the bridge. Do you use to travel with wheelbarrows in this country?
Piscator: Not that I ever saw sir. Why do you ask that question?
Viator: Because this bridge certainly was made for nothing else; why, a mouse can hardly go over it: 'tis not two fingers broad.
Piscator: You are pleasant, and I am glad to see you so: but I have rid over the bridge many a dark night.
Viator: Why, according to the French proverb, and 'tis a good one, among a great many of worse sense and sounds that language abounds in, 'They whom God takes care of are in safe protection' but, let me tell you, I would not ride over it for a thousand pounds, nor fall off it for two; and yet I think I dare venture on foot, although if you were not by to laugh at me, I should do it on all fours.
Piscator: Well, sir, your mirth becomes you, and I am glad to see you safe over; and now you are welcome into Staffordshire.
The Compleat Angler – Isaac Walton

A careful examination of Viator's bridge in Milldale shows that the parapets were added later. Bridges often had no or very low sides to allow laden animals to cross them. The conversation is from a book called *The Compleat Angler* by Isaac Walton and Charles Cotton. Let's look a little more about the background of Isaac Walton and Charles Cotton, who were the writers of the dialogue.

Isaac Walton was born in nearby Staffordshire in 1593, which was in the reign of Elizabeth I. He lived in London, mainly around the Fleet Street and Chancery Lane area, for most of his life. Despite the times in which he lived, he died aged 90. This means that he would have survived through troubled times, especially in London, with the Civil War, the Plague and the Great Fire of London.

The Compleat Angler, which Isaac subtitled *The Contemplative Man's Recreation,* was first published in 1653. It is a placid book, as much about contemplation and relaxation as about fishing. It is set on the River Lea in the north east of London. Isaac writes about the stretch between Waltham Abbey and Tottenham. His book is based on a discussion between an Angler (Piscator), a Hunter (Venator) and a Falconer (Auceps). They debate as to which is the best of the three sports. As was the custom at the time, the book went through several editions with various amendments with extra bits and pieces added, for example, letters of commendation.

Charles Cotton was much younger than Walton, he was born in 1630, and so Isaac would have been into his fifties before regular correspondence between them would have started. Walton is thought to have invited Cotton to add to the original book. Cotton lived at Beresford Hall, near to the River Dove, a few miles further up stream from Milldale. The hall is now in ruins but a small fishing house, which belonged to Cotton, can still be seen from the riverside path. Cotton added his part to *The Compleat Angler* in about 1676. It follows the same idea as Walton in that it is a discussion. However, this time it is between a country gentleman proficient in the Art of Fly Fishing, (Cotton) and a traveller who becomes his pupil.

While Isaac and Charles collaborated on this book, which has the distinction of being one of the country's most printed works, each of them had their own life, tales and other publications. We saw that Charles Cotton was a poet with his verse about the football match, but let's start with Isaac Walton. Despite coming from an innkeeper's family he was a deeply religious man and, after settling in London, he was encouraged to write the biographies of some of the leading religious men of the age. His first work was about John Donne who was a poet and priest, and this book received praise from Charles I.

Following the Restoration, Isaac then continued the biographies with Richard Hooker and George

Herbert, both religious divines of their time. Isaac was persuaded by his friend, Gilbert Sheldon, who we met in Snelston, to write Hooker's life. Gilbert was, at the time, Archbishop of Canterbury. His sickly predecessor had written a life of Hooker, but Gilbert wanted Isaac to write a fresh volume to correct some serious errors in the previous book.

Charles Cotton had a great respect for his friend and so he wrote a poem that was dedicated to him. The title is self-evident. The poem, *The Retirement. To Mr. Izaac Walton* by Charles Cotton includes some references to the Dove.

O my beloved Nymph fair Dove;
Princess of Rivers! How I love
Upon thy flowery Banks to lye,
And view thy silver stream,
When gilded by a Summers beam,
And in it, all thy wanton fry
Playing at liberty:
And, with my Angle upon them,
The all of treachery
I ever learnt industriously to try.
The Retirement: To Mr Isaac Walton – Charles Cotton

However, Charles Cotton was more than just an additional writer for Isaac Walton. He is known for translating the works of the French 16th century writer, Michel de Montaigne, into English. De Montaigne was a prolific French Renaissance philosopher who was a courtier at the Court of France. He is renowned for introducing the essay as a literary form, and compiled a series of these in which he represents his view on social philosophy. Charles translated all 19 volumes of de Montaigne's essays in 1685, about 120 years after they had been written.

In 1664 Charles published *Scarronides*, a popular work, which ran to 14 editions. It is based on the epic poem written by Virgil in the first century BC. It tells the story of the journey from Greece to Italy and the events on the way. Cotton produced his version as a burlesque which is an exaggerated parody on the original verse.

Cotton inherited the family home above the Dove in Beresford Dale in his twenties along with various legal problems from his father, who was a captivating character. He was born in Sussex and moved in the highest social circles. There are several poems dedicated to him by the leading writers of the day. Charles Cotton senior knew the literati of the day, including Ben Jonson. It would be through his father that we can assume that Isaac Walton and Charles Cotton met.

Charles travelled to France and Ireland but generally pursued his writings and country pursuits. Finances became difficult for him and sometimes it is believed he wrote purely to earn money. His liking of social and drinking occasions probably didn't help, but following the Restoration it had become

Milldale and Viator's Bridge

common in aristocratic society.

One book that he published anonymously, but has later been attributed to him is *The Compleat Gamester.* This took a similar presentation theme to *The Compleat Angler* but covered a variety of games, both indoor and outside, many of which have stood the test of time and are popular today, such as whist, cribbage, chess and backgammon. *The Compleat Gamester* starts with an epistle to the reader.

Reader,
I was once resolved to have let this ensuring treatise stepped naked into the world, without so much as the least rag of an epistle, to defend it from the cold welcome it may meet within its travels; but knowing that, not only that custom expects, but necessity requires it, give me leave to show you the motives inducing to this publication. It is not (I'll assure you) any private interest of my own, that caused me to venture on this subject, but the delight and benefit of every individual person; delight to such who will pass away their spare minutes in harmless recreation.
The Compleat Gamester – Charles Cotton

Charles' explanation of the rules of many of the games are difficult to follow but there are various asides which make for interesting reading.

A Scottish Holiday

Let's leave Dovedale with a final tribute to old Isaac. This comes from a nineteenth century Scottish advocate, Henry Glassford Bell. He was trained in Edinburgh, but became one of the foremost citizens of his day in his native Glasgow, as Sheriff of Lanark. Besides his legal duties, he also had a period as the editor of *The Edinburgh Literary Journal,* and was well known in the literary world. His only major prose work was *Mary Queen of Scots,* but he did produce some volumes of poetry. Judging by their content, they were often written when away from his native country and on holiday. When he visited Derbyshire, one of his poems was called *In Dovedale:*

Isaac! still thou anglest near me
By the green banks of thy Dove,
Still thy gentle ghost may hear me
Breathe my reverence and love.
In Dovedale – Henry Glassford Bell

We now take the short steep climb up the hill and our destination is Alsop. The limestone edge path gives good views over the valley which leads to Alstonefield, the home village of Charles Cotton. We soon arrive at what was the Alsop-en-le-Dale railway station. The old railway track has now been converted into a walking and biking route, called the Tissington Trail. We take the path across the dale to the small village of Alsop-en-le-Dale. This village is centred around the quaint Norman Church and Alsop Hall. The church just peeks out from the trees as we descend into the dale. When we stand on the tranquil lane, between the church and the hall, there is a great impression of timelessness. While the hall may have changed a bit with the years, the two magnificent buildings have stood firmly looking towards each other for close on a thousand years. The Alsop family lived in the Hall from after the Norman invasion until the seventeenth century, when it was sold to creditors. And

The hamlet of Alsop-en-le-Dale with the dormer window of Alsop Hall

it is both, the church and the hall, that bring us to an author who was here a few decades short of five hundred years ago.

Rude and Uncivilised

Rude and uncivilised is how Thomas Becon described the Peak of Derbyshire, but he was pleasantly surprised when he arrived in Alsop-en-le-Dale. Thomas was born in 1511, which was two years after Henry VIII came to the throne. He chose a life in the church and was ordained in 1533. He became increasingly intense in the Protestant religion and by 1540 he had fallen foul of the church authorities and the King. His progression in the church was dependent on the beliefs of the monarch of the times. When Edward VI came to the throne, he became the Chaplain to Thomas Cranmer, the Archbishop of Canterbury, but that didn't last long and the new Queen Mary soon banished him. Eventually, he was restored as Canon of Canterbury Cathedral when Elizabeth took the throne.

So what caused this fluctuation in his fortunes? He gradually developed more and more Protestant views and, therefore any attempt to prescribe what and how he should preach, ended in his rebellion and with his ejection from roles. This is what happened in 1540. Henry VIII decreed what and how religion should take place, but it was not sufficiently Protestant for Thomas. It was not only his sermons, but he also published religious works, and it was his books and pamphlets that caused him problems. He was arrested and forced to recant his views in 1540. We will then let Thomas take up his own story of when he went to Alsop Hall and found some of his own books in the library. In order to avoid persecution, and to be able to carry on preaching, he published some of his work under the pseudonym Theodore Basil.

After I had taken leave of my most sweet mother, and my other dear friends, I travelled into Derbyshire, and from thence into the Peak, whither I appointed my books and my clothes to be brought. Mine intent was, by exercising the office of a schoolmaster, to engraft Christ and the knowledge of him, in the breasts of those scholars whom God should appoint unto me to be taught. I found them of very good wits and apt understandings. Coming to a little village, called Alsop in the dale, I chanced upon a certain gentleman, called Alsop, lord of that village, a man not only ancient in years, but also ripe in the knowledge of Christ's doctrine. After we had saluted each other, and taken a sufficient repast, he showed me certain books, which he called his jewels and principal treasures.
The Jewel of Joy – Thomas Becon

Some of the books shown to Thomas were written by Theodore Basil.

We leave the old small village of Alsop, with its church, hall and farms, to cross the dale to another village, where antiquity again comes to the fore. Tissington is one of the most picturesque villages in the Peak District. While it is easy to say that the old hall and the church dominate the centre of the village, it is the overall layout that makes it very special. The wide road in front of the hall, with the church raised on the other side, leads to a triangle of green with a nearby mere, set with a traditional cottage background. The houses and cottages are totally in keeping with this quiet and quintessentially English village. To add to the tradition, the Fitzherberts of the old hall still play a very active role in the village and the surrounding countryside. A celebratory festival, in which Tissington has always taken the lead, is the annual well dressing. Each of the wells in the village is decorated with a picture that is created from petals and small flowers. These are held in a clay base so that they can be raised vertically behind the wells. Each of the pictures are designed afresh each year and normally follow a biblical theme which is often combined with local or national celebrations for that year.

Two Brothers

Tissington Hall is a fine Jacobean house set in the midst of its own extensive estate. It fronts the road through the village. It is still a family home for the Fitzherberts. It was built, by the family, in about 1617 when King James was on the throne. Tissington is one of the four estates that have belonged to the Fitzherbert family, which gives them a long and complicated history spread over the last six centuries.

The original Elizabethan manor in Tissington was probably next to the church, but at the beginning of the seventeenth century the hall, as it is today,

Tissington Well Dressing

Tissington Hall – the home of the Fitzherbert family since the 17th century

was built opposite. The Fitzherbert family became a well-known part of the national history of the United Kingdom through Maria Fitzherbert. She secretly married the Prince of Wales, but they both knew, that for a number of reasons, the marriage would not be approved by the government of the country. Unfortunately for us she did not come from the Tissington branch of the family.

However, William Fitzherbert had more compliant dealings with George III, who was the father of the Prince of Wales, and William rose through the Royal court and became a gentleman usher to the King. For his services he received a baronet, which was the first title to come to the Tissington branch of the family. Sir William interests us particularity, for as well as his royal duties, he was also an author. His work was entitled *Maxims and Reflections* and was published in 1784. It is a series of 439 short statements about maxims for living and refers to specific groups of people. We will skip over those comments that William wrote about women as these are somewhat derogatory. Although his views of his fellow man are not always that complimentary:

We see children constantly quitting the playthings they have, and crying for those out of reach, or in their playfellow's hands. Do not men, in their pursuits, act like children.
Maxims and Reflections – Sir William Fitzherbert

And finally let us see his humour when he makes a light-hearted attack on the country squire.

An old-fashioned country squire and his horse if he could talk, would both converse upon exactly the same topics, and be the fittest company for each other; oats, hay, straw, fences and turnpike roads would be their favourite subjects, and perhaps the horse would be the most conversant on every one.
Maxims and Reflections – Sir William Fitzherbert

William Fitzherbert's younger brother, Alleyne, born at Tissington, was also very successful in the service to his country. He became a diplomat, with one of his assignments being in North America, and was given the title Baron St Helens. It is after him that Mount St Helen's in the United States of America is named. He also represented his country in Ireland and Spain with his last assignment being in Russia. We must not underestimate the value that was put on such services. In the current times, large salaries and pensions command much attention, but there were substantial emoluments in the Georgian period. Alleyne retired with a pension of £2300, which is the equivalent of about £150,000 today. But it is not his work for the monarch and government that interests us, it is the way in which he supported his cousins.

A Drunken Gambling Vicar

Whilst Alleyne became a rich man, he did not forget a part of his family that had fallen on difficult times. His aunt, Anne Fitzherbert, had married a rector from Cheshire and after his untimely death,

Alleyne's cousins needed somewhere to live. He bought back, into the Fitzherbert family, the house at Somersal Herbert that had been sold when the male line had died out. He allowed his cousins to live there rent free for their life time. Two of them, Frances and Maria, were destined to live a quiet life there, but their circumstances changed.

Their brother Shallcross Jacson took holy orders, and was, for a period of time, vicar at the church in Ellastone, where we started *The Literary Way*. But his pious life did not last long as he became increasingly indebted due to horse racing and drinking. He would eventually become personal Chaplain to Alleyne Fitzherbert, Baron St Helens, and it was probably through that office that he came to Tissington in 1818 to preach the sermon at the celebration of the well-dressings. Alleyne's other cousins Maria and Frances also stayed regularly at Tissington Hall. Shallcross's debts were large, totalling about £1700, the modern equivalent of £110,000. In order to help their brother, Frances and Maria turned to writing. In keeping with the times, they published anonymously. Frances Jacson produced five novels of which *Rhoda* was favourably compared with Jane Austen's *Emma* that was published about the same time. This is the opening to Rhoda.

'Stir the fire, Rhoda and then.. '
'There! — who could have done it better ? And now, my dear Rhoda, for the tale of other times.'
'Once upon a time,' said the old gentleman, fixing his eyes upon his youthful companion, with an expression of mingled affection and pity. 'Once upon a time, there was a certain young man and a certain young woman, who loved one another so well, that they forgot that there was any body else in the world — they forgot too that any body else could ever come into the world. — So they married; and never recovered their recollection, until the young man, on the close of a hard fought day, was brought back to a miserable hut, mortally wounded, and the young woman, having received his last sigh, breathed her's also, at the moment when she gave being to a female infant.'
Rhoda – Frances Jacson

The anonymous attribution of *Rhoda* led to the work being ascribed to other authors until the late twentieth century. It received praise at the time and, while it is a lengthy story about her journey through life, it is represented with characters who do not fit the usual stereotypes. Rhoda comes from a humble background and achieves success in society, but it is tempered with self-doubt and whether she is giving in to avarice.

Frances's sister, Maria Jacson, dedicated her writing to her great interest, plants and gardening. She corresponded with Erasmus Darwin on botany matters and she produced four books including *The Florist's Manual*, which emphasised the developing interest of having a well-stocked garden at home and the need for the owners of the house to understand about plants as well as the gardeners.

To the Pastrycook

Let's turn to another minister of the Church, but this time one that had an unblemished record in his private life, who in 1773 wrote an unlikely book. It was very loosely based on the idea of Cervantes' *Don Quixote*, which is broadly considered to be a masterpiece of literature. *The Spiritual Quixote* was written by Richard Graves. The source of his inspiration, *Don Quixote*, was a satire based on ordinary people and the realism of what they did. The 'hero' in this famous Spanish book is a country gentleman, who becomes obsessed with the notion of chivalry and sets off on a number of adventures with that theme.

Richard Graves was born in Gloucestershire in 1751. His father was a well-educated local vicar and ensured his son received a classical education, which resulted in Richard going up to Oxford, and later, becoming a Fellow of All Souls College. He became interested in medical matters, and was going to follow that as a career, until he had a serious illness. This resulted in him reconsidering his future direction, and he turned to his father's role and took holy orders.

Richard produced several works, many of an ecclesiastical nature, but *The Spiritual Quixote* is the one for which he is known. He based his book on a light satire on Methodism, which he saw as a threat to the English church. The nature of his book is given in the subtitle which reads, *The Spiritual Quixote, of the Summer Rambles of Mr Geoffrey Wildgoose, A Comic Romance.* It is the story of a man, Geoffrey Wildgoose, who suddenly decides to become an evangelist and sets out on his light romantic ventures. He takes, as a companion, the local cobbler, who is only too pleased to get away from his nagging wife.

The valley that we have just left, Dovedale, would have been very familiar to Richard Graves as he stayed at Tissington Hall, with the Fitzherbert family for three years and, at the time, the estate reached as far as the Dove.

Sometime after he went to reside with Mr. Fitzherbert, at Tissington in Derbyshire, who had a donative in his gift, and was desirous of the company of a clergyman. In this house, Mr. Graves enjoyed the advantage of elegant society for nearly three years. While making a tour in the north, he accidentally met with a relation at Scarborough, Dr. Samuel Knight, archdeacon of Berkshire, by whose recommendation he obtained a curacy near Oxford; which, at this time, became necessary, as he had come into office in his college, and was obliged to reside within a convenient distance. For this purpose he lodged with a gentleman farmer in the neighbourhood, whose youngest daughter, a very amiable young lady, so far captivated him, that he resigned his fellowship and married her. This incident, with some fictitious circumstances, is supposed to be related in the present work, in the history of Mr. Rivers.
Life of the Author, The Spiritual Quixote – Richard Graves

Let us leave Richard Graves with a brief look at

his humour. *The Spiritual Quixote* has a dedication. There is no indication why this was chosen but it does show Richard's style and approach to his work.

TO MONSIEUR PATTYPAN,
Pastry-cook to his most sacred Majesty King George II.

Sir,
Though a stranger to your person, I am no stranger to your ingenuity and your profound skill in your profession. I have often amused myself with some of those elegant compositions with which you daily entertain the public. I have long been acquainted with the virtues of your diet-bread; am a great friend to your wigs; and think myself under great obligations to your admirable puffs.
As I am convinced, therefore, you will make a proper use of my works; will do justice to their merit, and cover their defects: that by the well known goodness of your taste, you will preserve them from the attacks of the sourest critics; and by the sweetness of your disposition, defend them against their bitterest enemies: if you are not over-stocked with waste-paper by my brethren of the quill, I beg leave to dedicate these few sheets to your service; and am,

Sir, Your devoted humble servant
Richard Graves
The Spiritual Quixote – Richard Graves

Let us rest awhile at the old Tissington Rail Station

As we leave Tissington we can rest a little with a cup of tea at the old railway station, which is now on the walking and biking path of the Tissington Trail. We began this chapter at the entrance to Dovedale and since then have ambled through some of the best landscape that England has to offer. The walk has combined the splendour of the limestone dale of the Dove, with the timeless picture of Alsop and a baronial finish in the Jacobean village of Tissington. Isaac Walton belongs to the same period as the origins of Tissington Hall, while his young friend, Charles Cotton, came from a neighbouring estate. Churchmen are often cited on *The Literary Way* and we met two devout examples in Richard Graves and Thomas Becon who produced contrasting works. Our third representative from the church had to rely on his sisters' writings for support, but he did, in his religious guise, preach the sermon for the renown well dressings. We also introduced the first of our women writers, Eliza Cook, from the Victorian period who rose from poverty and earned her living from the pen. We shall on future walks come across other women in the same sphere as Eliza, and they will be joined with some Victorian men who also rose from impoverished means and scribed about working class issues of the day.

Horse Tales

Tissington to Brassington through Bradbourne

Bradbourne Church: the churchyard has the grave of Nat Gould

This is the only walk that is dedicated to a single author, but fortunately for us, he was a very interesting character. He was a prolific author, who rose to the peak of his popularity among the soldiers of the First World War. He was a native Mancunian, but gained fame and fortune in the horse racing world of Australia, however, he always believed his real home to be the small village of Bradbourne.

We take our leave of Tissington and join a footpath across the estate land, with its dry stone walls and rolling landscape. On our right we pass a mound, which is the abandoned medieval village of Lea Hall. As we approach the slope down to Bradbourne Brook, we take the footpath to the left. Just further along, the road has a ford to cross the stream. There are not many fords around in modern times and it is interesting to see a number of cars turn back when they realise that the water isn't always just a trickle. As we cross the fields we can see the old mill nestled down by the roadside.

The Magic of Sport

It is not much further and we walk up the hill and enter the small sleepy village of Bradbourne. It is just off the main road and so preserves the atmosphere of peace and tranquillity. Along the road into the village, there is a shallow dale to our right which is backed by a rough grassed slope, which is called Haven Hill. The tower of the church has been visible for a while, but we must look to find the entrance to the church grounds as it is set back from the road. Bradbourne is an ancient village with its registration in the Domesday Book, although the stump of the cross in the church grounds is believed to date from several hundred years earlier.

A characteristic feature of these very old villages, as we saw at Alsop, is the close proximity between the

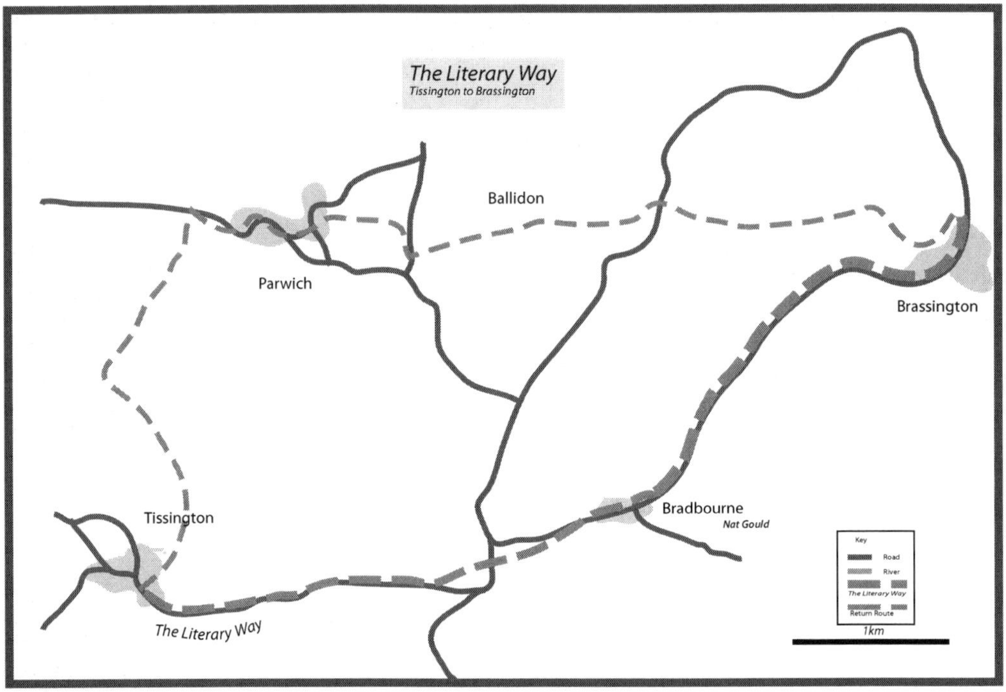

The Literary Way – Walk Five – Tissington to Brassington

Walk Directions

Tissington to Bradbourne (2.26 miles)

Take the lane leaving Tissington past the old railway station
Follow the lane across the estate land
As lane slopes downwards, the splash comes into view
Take the footpath on the left across the field
Bradbourne Mill is the building near the end of the lane
Cross the main road and follow the path
Go over a stile and arrive in Bradbourne near the church
After the church, Haven Farm is at the road junction

Bradbourne to Brassington (2.0 miles)

Carry on ahead on the lane to Brassington
Pass Parkgate Farm
Enjoy the views across the countryside from the lane
Follow the lane into Brassington
The Olde Gate pub is on the right
The church is on the left
Take the downhill lane to the main road
Turn left for the Old Smithy

Brassington to Tissington (5.61 miles)

Turn left to follow the lane behind the church
Take the footpath to the right around the craggy hill
At the cross-paths turn left and join The Limestone Way
The path joins a lane. Carry on ahead
Pass the ridge and furrow and Rainster Rocks on the right
At the end of the lane cross to the path opposite
As the path swings around the hill bear left on the path towards the gate
Pass through the gate, the path passes to the left of the chapel
On the road turn left and sharp right onto the footpath
Join another lane and then turn right and take footpath on left
Enter Parwich and go straight ahead past the church
Follow the road around the village green
Leave Parwich on road to Alsop-en-le-Dale
After the road turns right take the second path on the left
This is a green lane
Follow the lane and join the path across the fields
The path then goes down into the valley and up the other side
At the top of the slope join the Tissington Trail
Turn left and return to Tissington

Distance: 9.88 miles Ascent: 1384ft

lord of the manor's house to the church. Bradbourne is no exception here with the Elizabethan manor walls forming the edge of the church grounds. The door in the wall made it is easy for the local aristocracy to go to church.

There is a man buried in this churchyard who was a prolific author. Most of his novels were not about the Peak District, but were set in the horse racing world. Perhaps the best way of describing him is as an Edwardian Dick Francis. He wrote his first novel while working as a journalist in Australia. It was published in 1891, when he was aged 34. By the time of his death, aged 62, he had written 130 books, with more than twenty of them being released after his death.

Nathaniel Gould, known as Nat, was born in Manchester, but both his mother's and father's family were from the Derbyshire farming communities. After his education, Nat chose to go to Derbyshire to work on the farm of his relatives, first at Pilsbury, and then he came to the village of Bradbourne. From his earliest times in this village, he particularly took to horses and used every opportunity to work with them. He would only spend a few years here, but throughout the rest of his life, he always regarded Bradbourne as his true home, as we can see from his autobiographical writing, *The Magic of Sport.*

Bradbourne, figuring under the name of Millbourne in my novel "Hills and Dales" is perhaps the one place in England that I look back to as my old home and village. In Australia, up country, in the cities, amid the riot of press work and the racecourse, travelling up the Blue Mountains or the ranges of Queensland, sweltering under the burning sun, I have often thought of the village on the hill, Bradbourne, the sweetest little spot in all the lovely countryside of Derbyshire. The memory of it never left me; it came across the thousands of miles of ocean like a breath from the dear old hills.
The Magic of Sport – Nat Gould

It is in the first line above that he introduces us to one of the few novels he wrote that wasn't about horse racing. In 1897, this story, based on Bradbourne, was published called *Horse or Blacksmith.* While the book was well received, the critics did not like the title and so, in subsequent editions it was called *Hills and Dales.* The opening paragraph shows a very close resemblance to Bradbourne.

Zachary Peach was a very old man; he claimed to be the oldest inhabitant of the little village of Millbourne, and no one disputed his right to the title. Millbourne is a picturesque village in Derbyshire not many miles from Ashbourne. A long white road runs through Millbourne and it branches off from the main road to Buxton. Travellers passing along this road, in days gone by, were bought to a stop at the bottom of Mill Hill by an old-fashioned toll-bar, and payment was demanded before they could drive through on their way. Mill Hill was a pretty rustic lane, but to the ordinary mind there could be no adequate reason why it should be guarded by a toll-bar, which gave it almost as much importance as the main road. The village of Millbourne was not visible from the highway. When the top of mill hill was reached the road ran on level for some distance, so that the village, although standing on high ground, was hidden from travellers in the valley.
Horse or Blacksmith – Nat Gould

Nat had been well-educated and, prompted by his mother, who thought he could do better than just working on a farm, took an opportunity to apply for a job working on a newspaper in Newark, Nottinghamshire. This experience, and no doubt the wanderlust of a young man, took him to Australia where he developed his journalistic career and began to write fiction. He spent just over a decade in Australia and became a leading journalist on the horse racing scene. By the time he returned to Eng-

Bradbourne Manor

land he was writing novels full-time. As they were based on horse-racing, he chose to live in Middlesex so that he was close to several of the major race-courses. He never returned to live in Derbyshire but, following his death, he was brought back to Bradbourne.

The film industry was in its infancy around the time of the first world war, but growing in popularity. Eight of his novels were made into films, the first in 1911 and the last in 1920. This is a quite remarkable achievement when one thinks it is during a period of early silent films. So let's look at the start of one of his books that he wrote after he had returned to England. It begins in the next county, Nottinghamshire. It is *Rider in Khaki* and was first published in 1918. The opening chapter is called, *Will He Marry Her?*

"Do you think he will marry her?" asked Harry Morby.
"Does anybody know what he will do," replied Vincent Newport, discussing their host Alan Chesney, of Trent Park, a beautiful estate in Nottinghamshire, close to the Dukeries, Sherwood Forest, and the picturesque village of Ollerton. In the billiard room they had just finished a game of a hundred up, it was an even battle but Morby won by a few points; they were Chesney's friends, captains in the same regiment—the Guards—from which Alan Chesney resigned his commission some twelve months ago. Why he resigned was best known to himself; they had not heard the reason; nobody in the regiment appeared to have any idea.

"She's a splendid woman," said Harry, with a sigh.
"Granted, perhaps one of the most conspicuous of the reigning beauties. It may not be a question of will he marry her, but whether she will have him if he asks her," answered Vincent.
Harry Morby shook his head. "She'll marry him right enough. Why not? By Jove, Vin, what a handsome couple they'd make!" he said.
"Yes, but I doubt if it would be a happy union," said Vincent.
"Good Lord, man, why shouldn't it be? They'd have everything they wanted: money on both sides, estates close together, many things in common, love of racing, sport in general, hunting in particular; they're made for each other."

"What about temperaments?"
"All right in that way. No doubt there'd be some friction at times, but very few married people go through life without jars."
Rider in Khaki –Nat Gould

The Rider in Khaki is set during the First World War and the heroism and descriptions used, show why Nat Gould's books became very popular with the troops. A little further on *The Literary Way,* we will encounter D H Lawrence. We can then see how he refers to the Nat Gould novels. We leave the church and continue along the road to the junction. On our right is the Haven Grange farm, where Nat Gould developed his love of horses. We go straight on and we are taking the quiet lane along a small ridge that leads to Brassington. Despite the reference to a blacksmith in the novel, Bradbourne, during his days, never had a farrier. So it would be along this same lane that Nat would take the horses to the nearest blacksmith in Brassington.

Brassington has its origins in the lead mining industry, which is a traditional industry that goes back to Roman times. The White Peak Limestone has been mined in 'rakes', which are long mines either on the surface or underground that follow the ore as it spread through the limestone. This village is very typical of the area. Old houses date back to the early seventeenth and the tradition of building with the local grey limestone continued throughout the centuries. As with many villages it is mentioned in the Domesday Book meaning that is has been a settlement for at least a thousand years. The village is dominated by the church on the hill, with two of the oldest buildings in the village standing out, and they are the Tudor House on the main road and the Olde Gate pub. Just up the road from the Tudor house is the old Smithy.

Let us rest awhile at Brassington

Nat Gould comes across in *The Magic of Sport* as a relaxed man who enjoyed many sports, but he chose his life to be set around horses. Let us get Nat to introduce us to other writers who we will meet on our route, including one in the next chapter. As as young journalist in Newark, he was often sent to report on speeches made by national figures visiting the area, such as the Prime Minister William Gladstone. He heard all of the leading politicians of the day, but singled out John Bright as being the most powerful orator. We will meet John later in our walk.

D H Lawrence spent a period of his life in Australia and its during this time that he comments on Nat, who had become very much of an institution there. Fortunately for our purposes D H Lawrence's comments come through a semi-autobiographical novel he wrote during his period away from Europe.

Caves and Down Under

Brassington to Cromford through Ible and Matlock Bath

Harboro Rocks, where Daniel Defoe found a family living in a cave

Whenever anyone goes into a bookshop there is always a section labelled, *Classic Writers*. Many of the authors that are found under the classic heading have enduring qualities that have lasted the test of time. Five names on this walk can be found on those elite shelves. We start with a man who had a most amazing life and literary output at the end of the seventeenth century and the first two decades of the eighteenth century. He farmed cats, became bankrupt, but wrote a novel that is still widely read today and that has been a favourite in schools for many years. We will let his eloquence describe a journey that he made throughout the country. It has been hinted that its purpose was as much as a spy as for the gentleman's pleasure.

The early twentieth century brings us an enigmatic writer who caused controversy both in his books and his private life. Like so many of the writers we have come across, he was poor and, at times, found it difficult to make ends meet. He lived for a short period just near T*he Literary Way* and one of his short stories is based on our route. This walk has a touch of the international about it, first,with connections to Australia, and then with a visiting American writer, who took a diplomatic post in England and we garner knowledge of his thoughts through his journals, which recorded his visits to different parts of the country.

We finish the chapter with writers that were very closely linked. Scratched words on a window pane would, for most of us, constitute graffiti, but in this case, it is a memento of one of England's leading poets. The wife of his great friend, wrote a novel in the early nineteenth century when she was about 20 years old. It is on all of the classic bookshelves and to give an indication of its gripping nature it has formed the basis of 78 films. Writers are often associated with hotels, and on this walk we have more than one, who either stayed on our route, or used it for a location in a literary work.

The countryside on this walk is very varied. We start on the rolling landscape of the White Peak, with attention paid to the dolomitic crags and scars that rise from the more gentle carbon-rich lime-

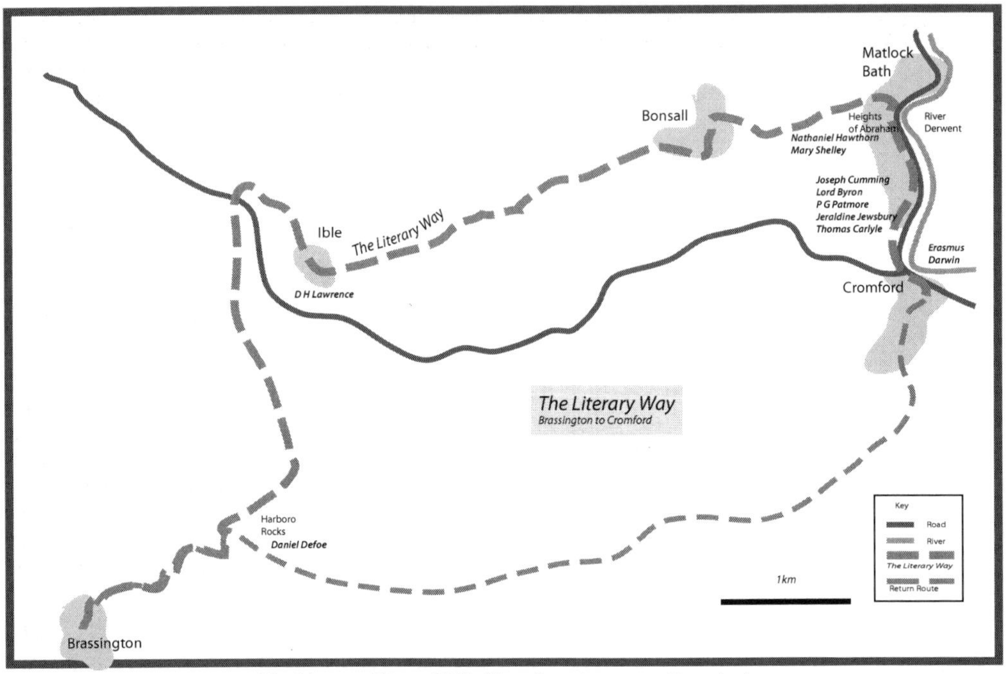

The Literary Way – Walk Six – Brassington to Cromford

Walk Directions

Brassington to Harboro Rocks (1.21 miles)

Take the main road north from Brassington
Then take the first road on the right
Follow it round the bend and take the footpath on the left
When you reach the lane, turn right and then take the next footpath on the left
The path winds through a works
Cross the High Peak Trail and enter Harboro Rocks
The cave is on the left side of the path

Harboro Rocks to Ible (2.41 miles)

Return to the path and continue across the rocks
The path goes downhill towards the farm
Go past the farm and turn left onto the wide track
Ible is visible on the opposite side of the valley
At the end of the track the path bears right
It crosses the field diagonally
It comes out of the fields by the crossroads at Grangemill
Cross the road and take the road to Winster
After a few yards turn right
Then turn right again towards Ible

Ible to Matlock Bath (3.34 miles)

Pass through Ible and take the footpath to left at the end of hamlet
Follow the path across numerous small fields
It will eventually lead onto a small track
Take the path (Limestone Way) on the left
Enter Upper Town and take the main road through this part of Bonsall
Go past the Barley Mow pub and turn left at the end of the road
Turn up past the market cross and take the lane past the church
The road bends to the left and eventually becomes a track
Take the path straight ahead as the track bends to right
Follow it over the hill and down though the woods
Turn left to the Heights of Abraham entrance
Then take the footpath opposite to the entrance down to Temple and New Bath hotels

Matlock Bath to Cromford (1.26 miles)

Go past the New Bath Hotel and join the main road, turn right
After a few hundred yards on the left is Arkwright's Masson Mill
Continue on the main road
Cross the road at the traffic lights and go towards Cromford
Take the first right turn to Scarthin Pond

Cromford to Brassington (5.31 miles)

Walk round Scarthin Pond and return to the main road
Turn right up the hill
Pass the close of workers cottages
Take the next footpath on the left
It goes up between the houses
Cross the first lane
On the second lane turn left then right back on to the path
It then becomes a lane. Cross the cattle grid
Take the path as it skirts the edge of the field to the right
Follow the path up through the woods and join the High Peak Trail
Turn right towards Middleton Top
Continue on the High Peak Trail until Harboro Rocks
Retrace the route to Brassington.

Distance: 13.5 miles Ascent: 2303ft

stone. The area, particularly around Brassington, was mined for lead for many centuries and we will cross the grassed waste heaps from those intense manual workings. We climb to one of the highest points locally before descending into the narrow ravine of the Derwent Valley.

Living in a Cave

The rolling countryside of the White Peak became most evident on our walk from Bradbourne to Brassington. The dry stones walls, often in eccentric lines, framed the coarse grass of the sheep fields, with scattered trees dotted along their edges. The White Peak gradually becomes more undulating, and just to the north of Brassington, we cross the High Peak Trail, which is another of the disused railway tracks that has been converted to a footpath and bridleway. In front of us, small spiky crags rise from grassy mounds.

These rocks are called Harboro Rocks and are made of the more resistant dolomitic limestone. There is a cave in these rocks which has a notable place in literary history. For the information we must turn to a famous English author but the location is not in one of his novels. Let's look at this man, who was not only a novelist, but a spy, and was reputed to be one of the first true journalists.

One of the most easiest recognised titles in English literature, and one that has been read in schools by millions of people, is *Robinson Crusoe*. The author Daniel Defoe is equally well-known. However, I think it will surprise many to realise just how long ago Daniel lived. He was born in London in about 1660, which puts him there as a child during the Great Plague and Fire of London. As with so many of the other writers we have mentioned he had an amazing output, as he wrote more than 500 publications including books, pamphlets and journals. He finished up in jail on more than one occasion and also had to contend with a large family and lack of money.

One of his most noted works, after his novels, is *A Tour Through the Whole Island of Great Britain* which he produced between 1724 and 1727. Its strength, and usefulness in history, is that it provides a view of Britain just as the industrial revolution was about to start. We will soon go, on *The Literary Way*, to one of the most famous sites in the world for the industrial revolution, but for now let us return to Daniel Defoe.

He wrote little before the age of thirty-five as he tried his hand at a variety of businesses, none of which turned out to be successful. At one time he was a hosier and later was very heavily involved in brick making as a pantile merchant near Tilbury on the Thames. One of his more unusual commercial attempts came when he kept a civet cat farm.

The cave where Daniel Defoe found a family living

Even today civet cats are known for their musk, which forms the stable part of a perfume. However, Daniel's attempts at business came to a head when he was made bankrupt and, for a short time, put in jail.

Daniel, and some of his friends, decided to undertake a tour of the British Isles and they visited each region of the country in turn. During the period they were in Derbyshire, the group asked for some information about a legend based on a Giant's Tomb. They sought guidance from some local people and so Daniel, and his companions, followed the directions to near Brassington and arrived at Harboro Rocks.

When we came close up we saw a small opening in the rock, the noise we made brought a woman out with a child in her arms and another at her foot.
A Tour Through the Whole Island of Great Britain – Daniel Defoe

Defoe's company then asked her about the famed Giant's Tomb.

She said that if her husband had been at home he might have shown us it. I snatched at the word home!
Says I, 'Good wife where do you live?'
'Here sir', she says, and points to the hole in the rock.
'Here!' says I, 'and do all these children live here too?'
'Yes, sir' she says, 'they were all born here'.
'Pray how long have you dwelt here?' said I.
'My husband was born here', said she, 'and his father before him'.

'Will you give me leave,' says one of our company, 'to come in and see your house, dame? '
'If you please, sir,' says she, 'but tis not a fit place for such as you to come into', calling him, your worship, forsooth; but that by the by.

I mention it to show that the good woman did not want manners, though she lived in a den like a wild body. However, we alighted and went in. There was a large hollow cave, which the poor people, by two curtains hanged cross, had parted into three rooms. On one side was a chimney, the man, or perhaps his father, being miners, had found a means to work a shaft or funnel through the rock to carry smoke out of the top, where the giant's tombstone was.

The habitation was poor, tis true, but things in it did not look so like the misery as I expected. Everything was clean and neat, though mean and ordinary. There were selves with earthen ware, and some pewter and brass. There was, which I observed in particular, a whole flitch or side of bacon hanging up the chimney, and by it a good piece of another. There was a sow and pigs running about at the door, and a little lean cow feeding upon a green place just before the door and little enclosed piece growing good barley; it being then near harvest.
A Tour Through the Whole Island of Great Britain – Daniel Defoe

Harboro rocks, and Daniel Defoe will not detain us any longer and as we cross to the far side of this outcrop we can see a small settlement perched on the opposite hill. In between us and that hamlet is a deep wooded valley, called the Via Gellia.

A Wintry Peacock

We are nearing the end of our transverse of the

The hamlet of Ible used by D H Lawrence in a short story

White Peak but before we do, we shall visit this hamlet on the facing hill, which even in the modern day, gives a good appearance of being isolated. When we planned the route of *The Literary Way*, we wanted to visit many of the locations either on foot or by car to decide whether we should include them. On one very cold weekend, that had seen some light snow, we set off by car to find the hamlet of Ible. We would point out that at the time we had not read the particular story associated with this hamlet. The significance of this cold and bleak weekend will become clear in a short while.

First of all, we had to resort to the trusty Ordnance Survey map as the satellite navigation in the car couldn't find our desired location. Finally, we found a turning off the deep valley of the Via Gellia, near Cromford. The steep bending road had only enough room for one car and as we got further away from the main road we noticed grass growing up the middle of the lane. Eventually we arrived in the hamlet which incidentally didn't have a sign post announcing its name, and is principally a group of farms, although in the distant past it had a manor.

We shall now introduce one of the early twentieth century's most controversial authors. D H Lawrence was born in 1885 in Eastwood near Nottingham. He was the son of a local miner and his mother came from the Derbyshire town of Wirksworth, which is a few miles from where we are now. David Herbert Lawrence died, aged 45, in 1930. It wasn't only David's books, such as *Lady Chatterley's Lover*, that caused controversy. He became the centre of attention and ostracism when he eloped with the wife, Frieda, of one of the German professors at the University of Nottingham. This was just before the First World War and they moved to Cornwall. But because of her German accent, they were treated as though they were spies and eventually forced to leave. No doubt they would have been treated even worse if the local people had known that her family name was von Richthofen. Frieda was a relative of the famous German flying ace, the Red Baron.

With nowhere to go after their treatment in Cornwall they returned to Derbyshire and settled in a cottage near the hamlet of Ible.

David wrote 12 novels between 1911 and 1928 with the last being *Lady Chatterley's Lover*, which for many years, was not widely published, and at one time was banned under the obscenity laws. He also wrote a considerable amount of poetry and short stories. In his later life, he transferred his interests to painting.

Mountain Cottage, where he lived for a short while, is just off the Via Gellia. Not far along the other side of the dale is the road that leads to Ible. The short story that is set here both in Ible, and at Mountain Cottage, is called, *The Wintry Peacock*. These are the opening lines:

There was thin, crisp snow on the ground, the sky was blue, the wind very cold, the air clear. Farmers were just turning out the cows for an hour or so in the midday, and the smell of cow-sheds was unendurable as I entered Tible, I noticed the ash-twigs up in the sky were pale and luminous, passing into the blue. And then I saw the peacocks. There they were in the road before me, three of them, and tailless, brown, speckled birds, with dark blue necks and ragged crests. They stepped archly over the filigree snow, and their bodies moved with slow motion, like small, light, flat-bottomed boats. I admired them, they were curious. Then a gust of wind caught them, heeled them over as if they were three frail boats, opening their feathers like ragged sails. They hopped and skipped with discomfort, to get out of the draught of the wind. And then, in the lee of the walls, they resumed their arch, wintry motion.

The Wintry Peacock – D H Lawrence

The man in the story is stopped by a young woman, living on a farm, and asked to translate a letter. The man soon works out the letter is to her husband from his mistress in Belgium, and so he misrelates the story to try to ease her pain. As their conversation develops, a peacock comes up to the woman and she strokes it. A few days later, during a period of heavy snow the man finds the peacock, cold and wet, near his cottage. He knew it was the one who was treated as a pet by the young wife. He tends for it overnight and carries it back the next day. The story closes after the man meets the errant husband and explains about his letter translation.

Let's move with D H Lawrence to the other side of the world. He and Frieda visited Australia in 1922 and as a result, Lawrence wrote a novel called *Kangaroo*. It was published in 1923. It is of interest to us for two reasons. First, it was semi-autobiographical, as the two leading characters, Richard Somers and his German wife Harriet, correspond very closely to David and Frieda. One section of the book describes their time in Cornwall during the Great War which mimics David and Frieda's stay in that county. The second reason for the interest in this book is that it contains references to Nat Gould, who we introduced in Bradbourne.

In *Kangaroo* Richard and Harriet have gone into a local library to borrow books.

'Y'aven't got a new Zaine Greye, have yer?" She spoke in these tones of unmitigated intimacy to the white–moustached librarian. One would have thought he was her dear old dad. Then came a young railway man who had heard there was a new Nat Gould.

'But,' said Somers, as he and Harriet went off with a Mary E. Mann and a George A. Birmingham, "I don't wonder they can't read English books, or only want Nat Gould. All the scruples and the emotions and the regrets in English novels do seem waste of time out here.'

Kangaroo – D H Lawrence

It is interesting to speculate that as D H Lawrence lived near Ible in 1918 which is very close to when, in 1919, Nat Gould died and was buried in a village a few miles away. We wonder from the description in *Kangaroo* whether Lawrence realised that Nat Gould was buried in a nearby village close to the time they were in the locality.

The steady incline, across the grassy lead mine wastes, brings us to the village of Bonsall, with its stepped market cross, picturesque church, and quaint pubs. After which the upward progress continues and we enter the woodland that embraces the top of the hill. As we descend the other side of Masson Hill, we reach the road and it is only a few steps to an entrance to The Heights of Abraham. Within this leisure park, there are two caverns which are open to the public as well as a cable car to journey to the valley floor, for now we are on the upper slopes of the Derwent Valley. So it is time to go underground again. But let us do so with one of the best known of the American writers.

The Liverpool Consul

Nathaniel Hawthorne was born in Massachusetts in 1804. His dark romanticism writings are portrayed through a representation of evil and temptation within the backdrop of Puritan New England. Nathaniel was best known as a short story writer but he also wrote eight novels of which *The Scarlet Letter* is the most well known. He only moved into non-fiction once, and that was to write a biography of his friend, Franklin Pierce. In 1853, following the election of his friend as President of the United States of America, Nathaniel was rewarded with the post of American Consul in Liverpool, England. It was near the end of his period of service of four years in that role, when he undertook a tour of England, which brought him to Matlock. His tour journals were not written with a view to publication, and therefore he is quite open and honest in his opinion. He was a very shy man and requested his friends not to write his biography, even after his death.

The village of Matlock is situated on the banks of the Derwent, in a delightful little nook among the hills, which rise above it in steeps, and in precipitous crags, and shut out the world so effectually that I wonder how the railway ever found it out.
Indeed, it does make its approach to this region through a long tunnel. It was a beautiful, sunny afternoon when we arrived, and my present impressions are, that I have never seen anywhere else such exquisite scenery as that which surrounds the village. The street itself, to be sure, is commonplace enough, and hot, dusty, and disagreeable; but if you look above it, or on either side, there are green hills descending abruptly down, and softened with woods, amid which are seen villas, cottages, castles; and beyond the river is a line of crags, perhaps three hundred feet high, clothed with shrubbery in some parts from top to bottom, but in other places presenting a sheer precipice of rock, over which tumbles, as it were, a cascade of ivy and creeping plants.
It is very beautiful, and, I might almost say, very wild; but it has those characteristics of finish, and of being redeemed from nature, and converted into a portion of the adornment of a great garden, which I find in all English scenery. Not that I complain of this; on the contrary, there is nothing that delights an American more, in contrast with the roughness and ruggedness of his native scenes, to which, also, he might be glad to return after a while.
Passages from English Notebooks – Nathaniel Hawthorne

The whole area has many natural caves and many more mines. Often the caves have been used as entrances to the lead mines. The number of caves open to the public has varied considerably over the years. Part of the popularity, in the nineteenth century, can be ascribed to visits by Victoria, first, when she was a princess, and then as the Queen. She went down the Cumberland Cavern, which is now no longer accessible, but was on the present site of the small children's amusement park of Gulliver's Kingdom.

The Modern Prometheus

The caves of Matlock Bath provide an intriguing link with a book that most would not associate with the area. Before we deal with the book, we want to explain a little about the author and her background which is really quite intriguing and full of literary connections. When we were in Mayfield, near Ashbourne, we discussed how Tom Moore wrote the biography of Lord Bryon, with the help of Mary Shelley.

It is now that we want to focus on Mary, who was born in 1797. She was named Mary Wollstonecraft Godwin and was the daughter of the radical thinkers Mary Wollstonecraft and William Godwin.

Let us take William first. He was very actively involved in political writing. He was closely aligned, and associated, with Thomas Paine, whose book, *The Rights of Man,* featured very heavily in both the French and American revolutions. In Ashbourne, we also mentioned the Lunar Society, a group of intellectuals, formed by Erasmus Darwin, who would help shape the industrial revolution. One member of the Lunar Society was Joseph Priestley, the person who separated oxygen into a pure state. He was also a radical political writer associated with Godwin and Paine.

Mary Wollstonecraft was attracted to these meetings. She was very much a radical woman and would go on to write a book, that is seen as a singularly important milestone in the history of women's liberation, *The Vindication of the Rights of Women,* which was published in 1792. It is easy to imagine that it created a great deal of controversy.

Mary Wollstonecraft was a woman given to passion in her relationships. Her first love was Henry Fuseli, who painted *The Apotheosis Of Penelope Boothby*, who was the five-year-old daughter of Brooke Boothby, that so tragically died. Mary Wollstonecraft's second lover was Gilbert Imlay. It was a tempestuous affair, that produced a daughter but no marriage. It would cause social rejection for Mary in later times when it became widely known that they had never married. When Imlay deserted her, she tried twice to commit suicide. For the second attempt she walked in the rain until her clothes were sodden and then turned and stepped directly into the River Thames. However, she had been spotted and a passer-by pulled her from the river. George Eliot came to know of this suicide attempt and included it in her last novel, *Daniel Deronda,* which was published in 1876.

Mary then went on to marry William Godwin. So it is with this parental background that daughter Mary was born into the household of Mary and William. But tragedy would strike as Mary would die within ten days because of complications in the birth of her daughter. After his wife's death, William carried on with his radical ideas and this would bring him into contact with Percy Bysshe Shelley, who harboured similar political leanings. By the age of 17 daughter Mary was infatuated with Percy and the feeling was reciprocated. However, Percy was married, but in late 1816, after the suicide of Percy's first wife, they married.

By this time William Godwin had remarried and Mary now had a half-sister, with whom she got on well, called Claire Clairmont. As part of their first year of marriage, Mary and Percy spent time in Switzerland with Claire and Lord Byron, who was Percy's friend. Byron was already having an affair with Claire and this continued whilst they were in Switzerland, much to the chagrin of Percy and Mary. The liaison finally resulted in the birth of Allegra, who Lord Byron took with him to Italy and placed her with nuns for her upbringing, and in the process treated Claire very badly. Little Allegra died as a young girl, and the treatment of her and her mother by Byron caused rifts with Percy and Mary.

But we get ahead of ourselves, so let us return to the foursome holiday in Switzerland. It was during this period, and at the age of 19, that Mary Shelley would conceive the idea for her most famous novel, *Frankenstein*. This is from Mary's Introduction, and it should be remembered that it was published within five years of *Pride and Prejudice.*

The circumstance on which my story rests was suggested in casual conversation. It was commenced partly as a source of amusement, and partly as an expedient for exercising any untried resources of mind. Other motives were mingled with these as the work proceeded. I am by no means indifferent to the manner in which whatever moral tendencies exist in the sentiments or characters it contains shall affect the reader; yet my chief concern in this respect has been limited to the avoiding the enervating effects of the novels of the present day and to the exhibition of the amiableness of domestic affection, and the excellence of universal virtue.

The opinions which naturally spring from the character and situation of the hero are by no means to be conceived as existing always in my own conviction; nor is any inference justly to be drawn from the following pages as prejudicing any philosophical doctrine of whatever kind.
Frankenstein – Mary Shelley

The Old Well at Cummings which is all that remains of the main Old Bath Hotel

The book was published anonymously, as was common for women writers, when Mary Shelley was twenty years old. The preface was written by her husband Percy and the dedication was to her father William Godwin. The introduction also shows the links, and her understanding, with some of the writings of Erasmus Darwin.

So how is the book mainly set in Switzerland linked with Matlock? As the story develops so there is a frantic sinister journey to escape as far away as possible from past evil deeds. In hoping to avoid pursuit, the characters travel to England.

We left Oxford with regret and proceeded to Matlock, which was our next place of rest. The country in the neighbourhood of this village resembled, to a greater degree, the scenery of Switzerland; but everything is on a lower scale, and the green hills want the crown of distant white Alps which always attend on the piny mountains of my native country. We visited the wondrous cave and the little cabinets of natural history, where the curiosities are disposed in the same manner as in the collections at Servox and Chamounix. The latter name made me tremble when pronounced by Henry, and I hastened to quit Matlock, with which that terrible scene was thus associated.
Frankenstein – Mary Shelley

It is not known which caves Mary Shelley was referring to, but those in this vicinity are likely to be favourite as they were closest to the fashionable places to stay when visiting Matlock Bath. And it is now an opportune time to visit the old hotel area perched on the side of the hills, which had been made famous during the Victorian years by its many visitors.

Cumming's Hotel

The hotels in Matlock Bath have changed since their zenith in the nineteenth century. The largest at the time was the Old Bath Hotel and so let's start with a writer who was born there. It is common in the area for hotel names to change, and they often took on the name of its owner, and so, the Old Bath became Cumming's Hotel for a period. It was here, in 1812, that Joseph Cumming was born. He went to Cambridge, and after taking his masters degree, he also took holy orders. A few years later, he moved his home in order to take up a teaching post. It would be that location that would stimulate his interest, and produce, as a result, most of his life's publications. He had settled in the Isle of Man and went on to produce nine major archaeological and geological works about the island. This is the preface to *The Isle of Man; Its History, Physical, Ecclesiastical*

The following work originated in the desire expressed by some friends, whose judgment I value, that I would place before the public in a popular form the substance of my memoirs upon the physical history of the Isle of Man, which have appeared in the numbers of the Quarterly Journal of the Geological Society of London.

I was the more inclined so to do from observing that a deficiency existed on matters connected with natural history in all works upon the island hitherto published, and from finding that on one subject, its geology, peculiar circumstances enabled me to supply information not possessed by any other.
The Isle of Man; its History, Physical, Ecclesiastical – Joseph Cumming

Joseph returned to England, taking professorial posts, and finally finishing as a clergyman at Bethnal Green in London, which is where he died aged 56.

Graffiti Window

The current Temple Hotel, was originally part of the Old Bath Hotel. A particular window in this establishment has been made famous. It is the graffiti of the lines of a poem etched into the window, in the dining room, by Lord Byron who was a frequent visitor to Matlock Bath. He came to this spa in the attempt to court his first love Mary Chaworth. Byron had a physical deformity to his foot that prevented him dancing as he would have liked.

In the dances of the evening at Matlock, Miss Chaworth, of course, joined, while her lover sat looking on, solitary and mortified. It is not impossible, indeed, that the dislike which he always expressed for this amusement may have originated in some bitter pang, felt in his youth, on seeing "the lady of his love" led out by others to the gay dance from which he was himself excluded.

On the present occasion, the young heiress of Annesley having had for her partner (as often happens at Matlock) some person with whom she was wholly unacquainted, on her resuming her seat, Byron said to her, pettishly, "I hope you like your friend." The words were scarce out of his lips when he was accosted by an ungainly-looking Scotch lady, who rather boisterously claimed him as "cousin," and was putting his pride to the torture with her vulgarity, when he heard the voice of iris fair companion retorting archly in his ear, "I hope you like your friend."
Letter and Journals of Lord Byron with Notices of his Life – Thomas Moore

By this time Byron was convinced he was in love with Mary Chaworth, the first realisation of which happened down a cave, but not one in Matlock Bath. We shall have to wait until later on *The Literary Way* to discover where. He was only fifteen at the time but Mary was two years older and never really took any interest in him. It could have been just their respective ages as to why she wished to avoid him, but there had been an incident in the history of their families that could have coloured her mind.

Mary Chaworth came from an old established family on the Annesley estate in Nottingham, which is very near to the ancestral home of Lord Byron. The poet Lord Byron was the sixth in line of the noble family. He inherited the title when he was ten from his uncle the fifth Lord Byron. Some years before, the fifth Lord Byron had killed his cousin and neighbour, William Chaworth, in a duel. When the future poet inherited the Newstead Abbey, the sword that had killed William Chaworth was still hung on the wall.

Even though he was young, Byron was developing his first poetry and, at the age of 17, privately published some poems. One of these was dedicated to Mary Chaworth, who eventually persuaded her parents to let her marry the man of her choosing,

In later years, when writing *Childe Harold's Pilgrimage* Byron did not forget the impression of Matlock Dale.

The sky was changed! and such a change ! Oh, night,
And storm, and darkness, ye are wondrous strong,
Yet lovely in your strength, as is the light
Of a dark eye in woman! Far along
From peak to peak, the rattling crags among,
Leaps the live thunder! Not from one lone cloud,
But every mountain now hath found a tongue,
And Masson answers through his misty shroud
Back to joyous Tor, who calls to him aloud.
Childe Harold's Pilgrimage – Lord Byron

Romance of the Week

But before we leave the vicinity of what was the Old Bath Hotel let us look at part of the opening chapter of an 1844 book entitled, *Chatsworth or The Romance of the Week.* It is a series of stories told by people in Chatsworth, but our interest lies in the narrator's description of the journey from London to the country house, which is a few miles further up the Derwent Valley.

Peter George Patmore, or as he was usually known, P.G. Patmore, was a periodical journalist based in London and mainly specialised in articles about old masters and various other paintings. However, on the title page of his book called Chatsworth, it does not give an author's name. It reads *Chatsworth or The Romance of the Week, edited by the author of Tremaine, De Vere etc*

If we let our minds drift back to Okeover Hall, on the River Dove, where Robert Plumer Ward lived, and we noted that he wrote, *Tremaine* and *De Vere.* So how do we sort out this confusion of anonymous books. For P.G. Patmore the writing of articles was not his only work. For the publisher Henry Colburn, Peter was also an editor and especially helped new writers to get their work up to publishable standards.

Robert Plumer Ward was one such author who he helped and, in the end, they became good friends. Robert, as we saw, wished to remain anonymous and while this continued, the literary scene in London detected the style of Peter and assigned him as the author of *Tremaine.* The book, *Chatsworth or The Romance of the Week,* came from the same publishing stable and so the owner was happy to go along with the attribution. To return to *Chatsworth:*

On opening their eyes, shaking their ears, and looking immediately around them, our aerial travellers will find themselves on a little patch of smooth-shaven turf, enclosed by a low, light, iron railing; dotted with diminutive flower beds, that look as if they had been cut out by a pastry-cook's pie-mould; furnished here and there with green garden-chairs; and finished in the centre by a baby fountain, falling into what may be mistaken for a moderate-sized punch-bowl, — its edges glittering with moss-grown spar, its surface floating a single water-lily, and its shallows gay with gold and silver fish.

Saxton's Hotel which is now the New Bath Hotel

A glance upward discloses the truth: we are standing on the terrace in front of The Old Bath Hotel, at Matlock Bath. It may please us, presently, to enter for a moment the obsolete halls of Dame Cumming; for they are classical ground: but metal more attractive than all the classics in anti-Christendom awaits us where we stand. Turn your back then, reader, on yonder old fashioned boarding-house, which the Wizard of the North has preserved from demolition by writing his magic name on one of its window panes, and where the beautiful Lady of Annesley made herself and her lover immortal by writing her's on the heart of the boy Byron.
Chatsworth – P G Patmore

We will leave P G Patmore standing on the terrace admiring the famous window, while our footsteps lead us down the hill to the New Bath Hotel which features, under its old name of Saxton's Hotel, in a ground-breaking novel for its day.

The Acting Half-Sister

The Half-Sisters was written by Geraldine Jewsbury in 1848. While we were in Dovedale, we introduced the poems of Eliza Cook, who adored the actress Charlotte Cushman.

In Geraldine Jewsbury, Charlotte found another great devotee. Geraldine followed the trend among the circle of the actress friends and often dressed in men's clothes. However, there did develop a clear rivalry between Geraldine and Eliza Cook for Charlotte's attention.

The *Half-Sisters* was published very close to the release of *Jane Eyre* by Charlotte Bronte, but the approach was different. In the *Half-Sisters,* Geraldine explored women's role in society from two different perspectives. One of the half-sisters was the wife of a wealthy industrialist and lived in a substantial mansion, while the other came from the much lower perceived status of the acting profession. Not only did Geraldine base the actress in the story, called Bianca, on Charlotte Cushman, but the name she chose was the first major role that Charlotte played in England.

The other sister in the story was called Alice, and it was she that appeared in the scene set at Saxton's Hotel in Matlock. Mrs Helmsby is Alice's mother, and Alice is not yet betrothed to the wealthy industrialist.

Good Mrs. Helmsby and Alice journeyed en route to Matlock, one fine afternoon, about ten days after the dinner-party.
"I hope, Alice, we shall find Saxton's a comfortable house, and that the beds will be well aired: that is the great drawback in travelling; one can never feel quite safe. Well, I must say, that really is very pretty, indeed. Look, Alice, at those white houses, upon those rocks, nearly hidden with the trees."
The Half-Sisters – Geraldine Jewsbury

Later on during the visit to Matlock, Alice goes to the nearby Romantic Rocks to read. The rocks are within the wooded area currently called Upper Wood. The whole area contained far less trees and woods in the nineteenth century. The book that she takes to read was by Germaine de Staël and it became a very influential book of the time.

One day Alice had taken her book — it was a volume of "Corinne," which she was reading for the first time — and had clambered up to the spot called the "Romantic Rocks" in guidebook parlance; they resemble an immense mountain shivered into a fantastic skeleton, and covered with a tanglement of shrubs, and creeping plants. Seated in a cleft of rock, so narrow that she could scarce see the sky above her for the ivy that hung across, she was quite unconscious how the time flew by. The first reading of " Corinne" is an epoch a woman never forgets, and Alice never lifted her head till she had come to the last line in the last page of the volume.
The Half-Sisters – Geraldine Jewsbury

Geraldine wrote six novels for adults, and two for children, and her writing skills were greatly admired. She also worked in the publishing business and rejected a writer that we shall shortly come across further down the valley. Despite the rejection, the author went on to become extremely successful and produced ten times more novels than Geraldine.

The First Celebrity Couple?

The infatuation of Geraldine with Charlotte nearly led to a rift between Geraldine and her best friend Jane Carlyle, but despite some sharp rebukes the friendship survived for Jane's lifetime.

.......Geraldine by the way is all in a blaze of enthusiasm about Miss Cushman the actress – with whom she has sworn everlasting friendship at Manchester.... Ever since her letters have been filled with lyrics about this woman – till I could stand it no longer – and I have written her such a screed of my mind as she never got before – and which will probably terminate our correspondence – at least until the finale of her friendship with Miss Cushman
To her sister Jeannie Welsh – Jane Carlyle

In the introduction to *The Half-Sisters,* the dedication is to Jane. A great deal of information of this period of history is learned from the letters of Jane and her husband Thomas Carlyle, who was a leading Victorian intellectual and essayist. He not only wrote a great deal of social commentary, but he also had a deep interest and knowledge in German philosophical idealism, especially the work of Fichte.

Jane and Thomas's letters totalled over 3000 and there were a large number to and about Geraldine Jewsbury. But first let's get the view of Charlotte Cushman on Jane and Thomas Carlyle. The extract comes from a biography of Charlotte written by one of her friends just after her death in 1876.

It was at this house she first met Mrs. Carlyle, that wonderful woman, who was able to live in the full light of Carlyle's genius and celebrity without being overshadowed by it; who was in her own way as great as he, and yet who lived only to minister to him.
Charlotte Cushman : Her Letters and Memories of her Life – Emma Stubbins

Thomas Carlyle also visited Matlock Bath. Our walk from The Temple Hotel to the New Bath would go along Temple Terrace and it was here in 1847 that Thomas Carlyle stayed and wrote to his brother, John. He first explains that they prefer private accommodation rather than the hotels.

The three Hotels are all fine airy houses, seemingly the best in the place; and Matlock is not Malvern for noise, but a comparatively very quiet place, tenanted by invalids, manufacturing ennuyés, and people generally who make no great din. However we did get private lodgings; moderately successfully, and without any difficulty

To his brother, John – Thomas Carlyle

Thomas then goes on to describe Matlock Dale, in which he makes a comparison with Milk Water, which is a river in Dumfries, near where he was born.

I will not trouble you with much description; but take this in the way of scientific increment of knowledge, if you like. The thing called "Matlock Dale," about the middle part of which we stand here, begins as I understand somewhere below Matlock Village northwards, and ends at the south about Cromford (aforesaid), some two miles in all; and is a great yawning chasm, rent across a range of limestone Hills, watered by the flow of the river Derwent, a green rather foul-coloured stream, which may rank about the size of Milk Water.

Both sides of this said dale are very precipitous, and as is usual in fine limestone country, very vegetative, fond of producing trees, bushes, ivy, grass, wherever there is the smallest opportunity for a root. Both sides are precipitous, but the west, especially hereabouts, is most so, indeed almost quite sheer, just opposite our windows, a sheer whitish wall of rock, winding about, perhaps near 200 feet high, and all along well mantled with wood &c: our village again stands altogether on the western side of the river; stands, or rather hangs; for you never, in this country, saw human houses so situated; all stuck along the steep, connected by zigzag paths, shrouded in wood, overlooked, they too, by bare cliffs;—at night with their lit windows you might think them caves of the Troglodytes, by day they are as bird-cages, each hung by its nail on the green wall. The only platforms of any extent (and they not of much) are occupied by the hotels, three in number;—and a small patch of street, for one little while, attaches itself to the carriage road, which runs close by the river, hewn out in many parts,—very far below where I now write. Such is Matlock Bath; a place for lounging; and for bathing in three lukewarm Springs (properly tanks, where you use them), not warmer I think than about 60° of Fahrenheit; pale-greenish in colour, mawkish-insipid in taste.

To his brother, John – Thomas Carlyle

The Love of Plants

From the New Bath Hotel it is a short journey down to the main road to find a large five-storey redbrick building, which has its origins defined on its front in large letters. Richard Arkwright built this mill in 1783 to harness the River Derwent for the water power needed to drive the spinning machines. The original mills, just down the road, were built earlier and we will visit them shortly. The Arkwright mills, along with those at Belper and Lea, are a World Heritage site as they were key locations in the establishment of the industrial revolution. Erasmus Darwin visited Masson Mill, no doubt as the guest of the Arkwrights, which enabled him to write the following lines in the *Love of Plants* section of *The*

Masson Mill built by Richard Arkwright in 1769

Scarthin Pond and its bookshop

Botanic Garden.

So now, where Derwent rolls his dusky floods
Through vaulted mountains, and a night of woods,
The nymph, Gossypia, treads the velvet sod,
And warms with rosy smiles the watery god;
His ponderous oars to slender spindles turns,
And pours o'er massy wheels his foamy urns;
With playful charms her hoary lover wins,
And wields his trident, - while the monarch spins.
The Love of Plants – Erasmus Darwin

We follow the main road for a short time and then turn to Cromford, After that there is an immediate right turn, and we enter Scarthin, with its mill pond for the yet unseen mill. The wonderful old bookshop overlooking the pond was used in the Anand Tucker's Film, *When did you last see your father?* starring Jim Broadbent, Colin Firth and Juliet Stephenson.

Let us rest awhile at Scarthin Pond

Caves have formed an important part of this chapter, and to which, we add the springs that flourish from those same rocks which started the spa business of the hotels, then we have the basis for many of the literary works of this chapter. We have looked at novels, short stories and travelogues, as well as letters and diary entries. All these literary forms have given us a great insight into the work of some of the leading names of literature. When we return to Daniel Defoe, in *The Literary Way* he will be in a much more sceptical mood about Derbyshire.

D H Lawrence has certainly shown his quixotic character. The short tale at Ible along with his novel *Kangaroo* show the complexity of this man whose native county Nottingham is nearby. We have tried to give a tantalising peek at the fascinating, but labyrinthine relationship that surrounding Charlotte Cushman, the poet, Eliza Cook, and the novelist, Geraldine Jewsbury, which has been enriched by them all knowing the Carlyles. Added to these literary strengths, we have the contrasts between the open rolling limestone moors near Taddington with the precipitous cave-rich valley of the Derwent.

We have ended this part of our journey in Cromford, which grew as a result of the growth of Arkwright's mills, but we will continue with the same industrial period in the next walk, when we visit another part of the world heritage site.

A Dark Wood, Dark Deeds and a Lamp

Cromford to Matlock through Lea, Holloway and Dethick

The end of the Cromford Canal near Arkwrights's Mills

A story from a dog's point of view was not normal late Victorian fare, but a visitor to Derbyshire wrote a nine-volume novel about this subject, which begins in the local area around Cromford. She was an eccentric author, rejected by Geraldine Jewsbury in her role as a publisher's reader, but became one of the most popular authors for a period. Her sixty books allowed her a lavish lifestyle, but in the end she died in poverty.

Imagine you are a small child of eight or nine and your only way to school and back home again is through a dark wood. Not only was this true for a local author, but she would capture that same sense of childhood fear some thirty years later as she turned to writing, following the tragic suicide of her husband. Her books became such an established part of every childhood, that it is said, that the Queen read them to her own children.

Sir Richard Arkwright is the renowned founder of cotton mills and is a name that many people remember. But it would be his son that would go on to form the family dynasty, and take the family business in a different direction. If you will excuse the pun, there is an everlasting yarn about another part of the World Heritage site, and the story is even more remarkable, because it has run for over two hundred and twenty five years. Again it is a father and son combination that achieved success.

We will then come across a lady from a well-to-do family, known very well to our industrialists, who lived in a large house and who wrote about how to treat patients. The words and sentiments expressed in the book are what we would expect to be commonplace in modern times, but when they were written, they were new and the nursing profession had hardly started.

A small collection of buildings around a small church, that stands proudly on a rise over the fields of flowing grass, produced a man who would be horribly executed when he was twenty-five years old. But by that time, he was assured a place in one of the best remembered royal rivalries in the history of this country.

On this part of *The Literary Way* we turn away from some of the more popular tourist areas, briefly embrace the legacy of the Industrial Revolution, and then rise up on to an undulating stretch of countryside with quiet walks, sleepy lands and some wonderful distant views.

Fame and Fortune at the Greyhound

However good the bookshop at Scarthin, Cromford has a much greater place in history on the world stage. It is a large village that was built by the Arkwright family for the workers in the mills. The Scarthin pond, in the heart of this village, was built to serve the mills, which are just around the corner close to the River Derwent. The village has many

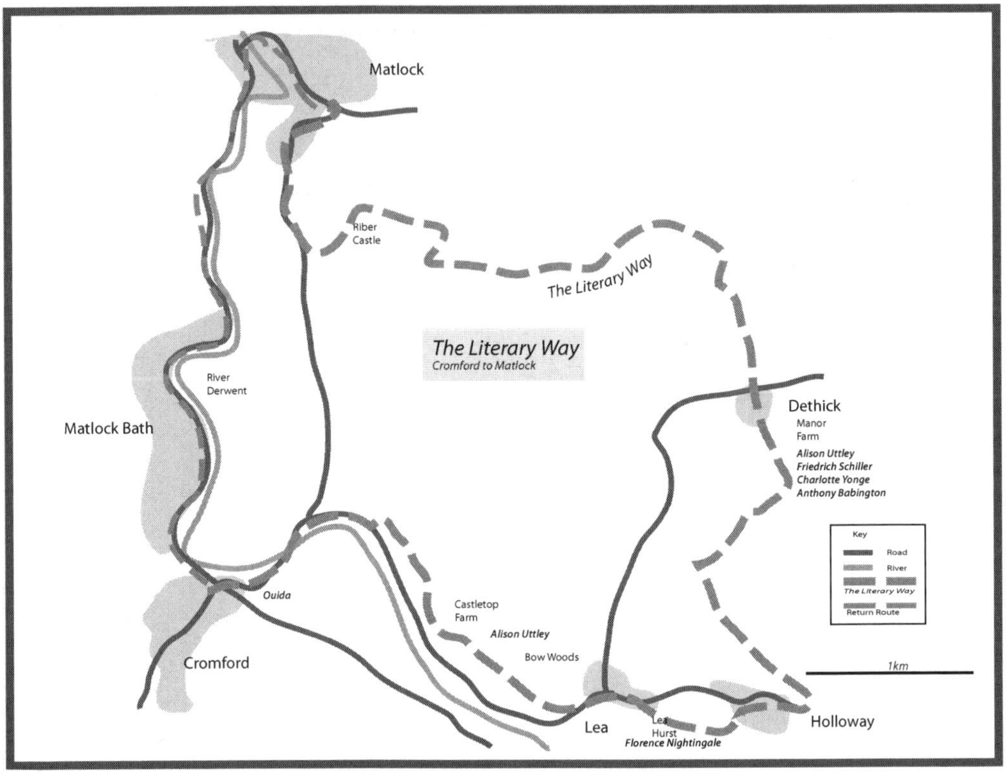

The Literary Way – Walk Seven – Cromford to Matlock

Arkwright's Mill overlooked by Rock House

listed buildings as a result of the heritage, and a walk up the hill is rewarded with the setting of some splendid workers cottages.

The market square is dominated by the *Greyhound Inn* and it will provide us with a hint of what we have to come later on *The Literary Way*. Sir Richard Arkwright's son, also called Richard, asked the Duchess of Devonshire to leave a note to explain how she would repay a loan. Unusual you might think? Richard Arkwright junior inherited his father's business, but chose a change of career. He decided to sell many of his businesses and entered into Government Bonds with heavy investments in land and property. He was very successful and eventually took over the ownership of a bank. He was far richer than his father and, when he died, he left a legacy of £3.25 million pounds. So it is not just the twenty-first century that sees huge sums for some individuals. In today's money the bequest would be worth about £235 million.

We rejoin the Derwent Valley, along which runs the busy A6 from London to the northwest of England. We can look up the main road to the north and can see Arkwright's Masson Mill. Up on the hill in front of us is Willersley Castle, but it was originally called Willersley Hall, which is a more appropriate name, even though it has architectural rounded towers on its multifaceted facade. It was built in the 1780s as the home of Richard Arkwright senior, but was not finished in time for him to move in, and it was his son who lived there. We walk down the road, and after passing the mill manager's house and the Counting House on the opposite side of the road, we reach the mills. High upon the rocks is the aptly named Rock House, which is where Richard Arkwright senior lived, while establishing the mills. If we turn into the mill complex and stand on the bridge over the leat, we get a feel of the scale and gloom of these buildings. Imagine being a cotton

Walk Directions

Cromford to Lea

Leave Cromford by crossing the main A6 and taking the road to Lea
The original Mills are on the left, and on the right is the canal basin
We follow the road over the bridge with a view of Willersley Castle
After the railway station, we take the footpath on the left
When we reach a cross of paths we turn right into the wood
The path goes through the wood, across a field and joins a lane
We turn left, and at the left bend there is the track to Castletop Farm
The path goes straight on into Bow Woods
At the end of the woods, it is Lea Mill, and the Smedley Works

Lea to Dethick (2.3 miles)

We follow the road past the mill (not under the arch)
On the hill there is a footpath to the right which we take
It crosses a field and in the next field hugs the wall
Inside the wall is Lea Hurst, Florence Nightingale's home
The path continues to the deer fence and we take the path to the left
We are on a minor road and we then take a path through the housing on the right
We cross the road and then there is a steep path through the woods
When we come out on the road, turn right and take the first left
This is the quiet Long Lane with many distant views
As we descend towards Holloway take the footpath on the right along the wall
It passes the playing fields
It comes out on a lane and we turn left
At the bottom turn right through the estate
At the junction turn left and immediately onto the right footpath between the houses
It comes out in a small park
Turn right on the road and on the left we take the footpath
It dips into a valley and then climbs over the fields
We then reach Dethick

Dethick to Riber (1.64 miles)

Pass through the church grounds and follow the footpath to the road
Take the footpath opposite and cross two fields
The path forks to the right to meet the lane
We turn right on to the lane
At the junction turn left and follow the lane
After the junction on the right we take the footpath on the right
This leads across the fields towards Riber Hall
Turn right on the lane in front of Riber Hall and follow it around to the left

Riber to Hall Leys Park, Matlock (0.92 miles)

Take the lane down the side of the cottages and join the footpath
Riber Castle can be viewed behind us
There are extensive views over Matlock
Take the path straight ahead down the steep hill
It eventually comes out on the road, where we turn right
Walk along the road to the church and take the path down the far side of it
At the bottom turn left into Hall Leys Park

Hall Leys to Cromford (2.65 miles)

In Hall Leys Park cross the bridge over the River Derwent
Walk to the junction and turn left.
Follow the road out of Matlock to Matlock Bath
Go past Masson Mill and return to Cromford

Distance: 9.58 miles Ascent: 1597ft

worker used to plying your trade by a small cottage window and then being moved to these edifices of automation. The three and four-storey dour buildings give a hint of the obscurity and hard labour that was forced on the workers within them.

Opposite to the mills is the beginning of the Cromford canal, which was the main form of transport in original days of the Industrial Revolution. The canal goes south from Cromford to join the Trent Navigation system and the canal structures of midland England. The area now has extensive open views and we might want to sit by the canal to consider our next writer. Precise information about the location of her Derbyshire references are difficult to determine, but we have chosen this location for a number of reasons. Let us first introduce her, and in doing so, draw out the references to where we are now.

The Love of Dogs

I am only a dog.

I find in all autobiographies which I have ever heard read that it is considered polite to commence with self-depreciation. But for all that I do not consider myself the inferior of any living creature: I never heard of any autobiographies that did consider himself so. According to their own account they are all 'incompris' and I suppose I was also; for I was always held in contempt as a dumb brute. Nobody, except that wise woman Rosa Bonheur, ever discerned that animals only do not speak because they are endowed with a discretion far and away over that of blatant, bellowing, gossiping, garrulous Man.
Puck – Ouida

The above extract is taken from the start of the novel, *Puck*, by Marie Louise Rame. Marie was born in Suffolk in 1839 and had a French father and English mother. But hers was no ordinary writer's career and she became as well known for her eccentric ways, as she was for her writing. She considered herself more French and continental than English, and after her father disappeared under mysterious circumstances, he went to France never to return, she had her mother as her constant companion on her travels.

She held very firm views on many matters both politically and socially and these included the protection of animals, especially dogs. She was friendly with her cousins, the Lockwoods, and visited them many times in Derbyshire. Her book, *Puck*, begins in Derbyshire, although her preferred setting for her other novels was in Europe. Her book starts with Ben, who is a quarryman, and his concern for the new puppy. An interesting link with another writer in *The Literary Way* is at the end of the introduction to *Puck,* Ouida references one of her preferred French writers, Jean-Jacques Rousseau, who we met in Ellastone.

Marie lived the last thirty years of her life in Italy, and while she often wanted to return to England, she would not leave her dogs and could not bring them with her because of rabies laws. In all, she wrote 40 novels as well as many short stories which she considered herself very good at, but that, in general, English writers were very poor at. She frequently wrote to major newspapers on the current issues of the day, but shunned any invitation to supply autobiographical information. In fact, she frequently wrote that she should only be known by her pseudonym, Ouida. The origins of the word are believed to be her childish attempts to pronounce her own name Louise.

Her lifestyle became more and more bizarre as she progressed in the literary world. During her most famous period, she would stay for extended periods, four months or more, at the famous Langham Hotel in London, where a loyalty scheme was named after her in the 21st century.

She wrote many letters about the protection of animals and she corresponded on this subject with a writer we shall meet later on *The Literary Way,* Henry Salt.

The original owner of Puck was a quarryman, and a look around the hills here show that quarrying is of prime importance to local commerce. The book also mentions the River Derwent and lead mining. The latter we already know to be dominant in this area for many centuries. In her book called *Strathmore* she refers to the 'Black Rocks of Derbyshire', which are part of the large hill to the south west of the canal basin. Ouida always wanted to offer her view on social matters. This extract is when she describes a woman she knew from Derbyshire.

I once knew a perfectly well-bred person who yet could neither read nor write. I can see her now in her little cottage in the Derbyshire woods on the brown, flashing water of the Derwent River (Darron, as the people of Derbyshire call it), a fair, neat, stout old woman with a round face and a clean mob-cap. She had been a factory girl in her youth (indeed, all her womanhood had worked at the cotton-mill on the river), and now was too old to do anything except to keep her one-roomed cottage, with its tall lancet windows, its peaked red roof, and its sweet-smelling garden, with its high elder hedge, as neat and fresh and clean as human hands could make them.
View and Opinions – Ouida

Her money management was very poor and she was frequently in debt and evicted from the houses in which she lived with a variety, and often a large number, of dogs. She was a very popular writer and would often seek publishers advances before even the book had been started. She held a very high opinion of herself, but she also had many friends and admirers who were prepared to help her. She died in Italy in 1908.

Alison's Route to School which she re-tells in The Country Child

Alice Jane Taylor

So we leave the canal and after passing Cromford station we turn up into the woods. A path through the woods and across a field brings us out on a track near to Castle Top Farm. It was at this farm, in 1884, that Alice Jane Taylor was born. She had a long life and lived to the ripe old age of 92. She went to secondary school further up the Derwent Valley at Bakewell, where she received a good education. Just after the turn into the 20th century she went to University in Manchester where she studied physics. She chose teaching as a career, and as a result moved away from her home in Derbyshire, but her fond childhood memories of her native county always stayed with her.

Tragedy struck her family life when she was widowed in her late forties. It was then that she took to writing. It is perhaps not surprising that her first books resulted from her acquaintance with children. She slightly changed her first name and used her married surname. The name Alison Uttley soon became recognised as a well-known author. She is most famous for the books that she developed early in her writing life, and these focused on animals, especially *Little Grey Rabbit*. In all, she would write over one hundred books. At least two of her novels were set locally to Cromford, *The Country Child,* which is a fictional account of her childhood, and her book called *The Traveller in Time,* which is set in the nearby farm complex of Dethick, which we shall shortly visit.

But let's return to her own youth. Her farming parents were keen that she had a good education and that meant that she had to attend the local primary school. We will now trace the route, which is along *The Literary Way* that would take her to school and formed the opening to *The Country Child*. Let's get a feeling for the life of Alison Uttley near the end of the nineteenth century. But before we do, we take the path past Castle Top Farm and into Bow woods. This was her route to school.

In the story Susan is a little girl of about 9 years old. The book opens with the chapter entitled *Dark Wood*.

She walked along the rough path, casting fearful glances to right and left. She never ran, even in moments of greatest terror, when things seemed very near for They would know she was afraid and close round her. Gossamer stretched across the way from the nut bush to the bracken frond, and clung to her cold cheeks. Her step was strangely silent, and a close observer would have seen that she walked only on the soil between the stones of the footpath. A mis-step made her iron heel catch a stone, and the sharp ring alarmed a blackbird dipping amongst the beech leaves, but it frightened the child still more. She gasped and held her breath, listening with all her senses, her heart beating in her throat.
The Country Child – Alison Uttley

A little later on in the book, when she is at home on the farm, she looks at her library which consists of four books. It is interesting to note that one of those books was *Robinson Crusoe,* which gives us a coincident link with the previous chapter and Daniel Defoe. Before we consider her work, *The Time Traveller,* which is set a little further along *The Literary Way* we will encounter two families who became, not only important locally, but also made a significant mark nationally and internationally.

Two Hundred Years of Fashion

As we leave the end of the Bow Wood we come out to Lea Bridge, just near the small village of Holloway. Immediately apparent on our left is an industrial premises. It carries the sign which shows us that it is part of the World Heritage site of the Derwent Valley Mills. However, this site is clearly different to Arkwright's mills just along the road at Cromford. A quick look at the complex shows that it is still fully operational. John Smedley's factory has been on this site since 1784 making over 225 years of production of cotton and woollen knitwear. Its products can be found either on-line or in high quality high street stores. For the original business name and its products to survive since the early part of the industrial revolution is a truly remarkable achievement, especially when one thinks of the turmoil in the clothing industry and what has happens in any decade let alone two centuries. What really raises this achievement to the highest levels is that the company still works from the same mill.

The company was founded in the late 18th century by John Smedley and Peter Nightingale. The latter is a name that we shall re-visit shortly. The mill site

Smedley's Mill – over 225 years of production

was typical of many that were established at the time, in that it was next to a stream with a good flow of water, which would provide the needs for the industry. The business has always been managed by successive generations of the Smedley family and continues to operate, not only from Lea Mill, but from other factories as well. The founder had a son, also called John. We shall find out more about John, junior, later in the nearby Derwent Valley where he made such a lasting impression, but for now we can say that it was his enterprise that changed the faltering business into a long-term successful one.

The Medical Needs of the Army

We move further along the valley and we take a footpath near to Lea Mill. After crossing some fields, we come to a large house which was built by Peter Nightingale, the partner of John Smedley. It passed from Peter to William Nightingale via his mother. The house we are looking at is called Lea Hurst and was the home of one of most iconic and inspirational figures in English history.

To William and Fanny Nightingale, a daughter was born on the 12 May 1820 in Florence, Italy. They named their daughter after the city. They were a successful family and had sufficient income to own several residences in different parts of the country. Against her family's wishes Florence took a great interest in helping the poor and the sick. She gained the knowledge of the time in hygiene and sanitation as she visited and helped in hospitals in this country and in Europe.

Her fame came when she went to the Crimean peninsula to help the wounded soldiers, and that is where she gained the name, 'The Lady with the Lamp'. Even after her return, she worked tirelessly on the reform of the medical services in the Army. What is little known about her, is that she authored several books and pamphlets on medical matters. In the English educational system we become aware of the work and person of Florence Nightingale from an early age. Later on in life, we see her referred to many times as a result of anniversaries and other retrospective views of events in history. In all of this familiarity, one thing that we never expected to hear was Florence Nightingale's voice. But we were wrong. It came as a surprise to visit the British Library at St Pancras in London and find an exhibit, which was a sound recording of her voice.

Let's see how the inspirational nurse was commended by her sovereign. Queen Victoria's letter to her, was included by Lytton Strachey in his biography of Florence. Strachey first, puts the letter in context, and then quotes from it. Scutari is the hospital for the Crimean War in which Florence worked.

It was not until July, 1856 — four months after the Declaration of Peace—that Miss Nightingale left Scutari for England. Her reputation was now enormous, and the enthusiasm of the public was unbounded. The royal approbation was expressed by the gift of a brooch, accompanied by a private letter.

"You are, I know, well aware," wrote Her Majesty, "of the high sense I entertain of the Christian devotion which you have displayed during this great and bloody war, and I need hardly repeat to you how warm my admiration is for your services, which are fully equal to those of my dear and brave soldiers, whose sufferings you have had the privilege of alleviating in so merciful a manner.

"I am, however, anxious of marking my feelings in a manner which I trust will be agreeable to you, and therefore send you with this letter a brooch, the form and emblems of which commemorate your great and blessed work, and which I hope you will wear as a mark of the high approbation of your Sovereign!"

Florence Nightingale – Lytton Strachey

As an aside at this point, Lytton Strachey is characterised in a book by one of the twentieth century's most famous authors. The inspiration for the story was found when the author visited a friend on *The Literary Way.*

But for now let us return to the Lady with the Lamp. Florence Nightingale had strong views on the role of women, as well as the development of the care of patients. Let's leave Florence with her views on what she became famous for, namely nursing. She wrote *Notes on Nursing, What it is and What it is not.* This was published in 1860 when Florence was 40 years old. This quotation is taken from the Preface.

The following notes are by no means intended as a rule of thought by which nurses can teach themselves to nurse, still less as a manual to teach nurses to nurse. They are meant simply to give hints for thought to women who have personal charge of the health of others.

Notes on Nursing, What it is and What it is not – Florence Nightingale

The Time Traveller

We leave the view of Lea Hurst and pass through the small village of Holloway. It is then across the fields to Dethick, which is a collection of buildings now consisting of three farms and a church. The building on our right was formerly Babington Manor and is now Manor Farm. This towered church, which could stand proudly in the centre of any village, has virtually no catchment area. Yet the manor and the church would play a part in a significant event in the history of this country. For that event we must return to Elizabethan times.

Queen Elizabeth I had a significant problem that threatened her reign. Her father Henry VIII had set up the Church of England by breaking away from the Pope and the Catholic Church because of his marriages. Up to that time the populace of the country were Catholics and there was a lot of resentment at the time that Henry had taken such drastic steps, including the dissolution of the monasteries. Elizabeth fully supported her father's church and was intent in making the Protestant church stronger. But the difficulty she had, was her cousin Mary, Queen of Scots, who was a staunch Catholic and regarded by many the rightful queen, not only of Scotland, but of England.

Elizabeth and her advisers feared a plot to assassinate her. Their problem was that Mary had done nothing wrong, but she still posed a focus for unrest in the realm, so she had been placed under 'house arrest'. Elizabeth asked some of her advisers to confine Mary in a restricted manner, but that she was not to be put into prison. She moved around the country and was resident in difference places at times. One of her 'keepers' was the Earl of Shrewsbury, whose wife Bess would go on to build Chatsworth and establish the Cavendish dynasty with its extensive house and estates. Mary was also held in Sheffield Castle.

Messages of support were smuggled into Mary. Elizabeth's spies and loyal aristocrats kept careful watch on anything that could associate Mary with a plot to kill Elizabeth. If that happened, Mary could be charged with treason and executed. A further complication was that Catholic Spain was sabre-rattling against the Protestantism in England. Would-be Catholic plotters could always ensure clear support for their ideas and promises of riches and elevation if they succeeded. The stance taken by Spain would result in them sending the Spanish Armada.

It is against this background that Thomas Babington, a 21-year-old, swore that he would do his utmost to place Mary on the throne of England. Thomas lived in the building on our right, the former Babington Manor. The plot was discovered and Thomas Babington was cruelly executed. It would lead in a complex set of links to the implications that Mary supported the plot and she too was executed. Mary, Queen of Scots has been a story that has enthralled people for centuries, and because of its intrigues and behaviours it has featured heavily in fictional literature. We are going to find a number of instances on our journey of how fiction has been woven with facts, and this story is one of the most renowned.

Earlier in this chapter we passed Castletop Farm where Alison Uttley was born. So let us take Alison as our first link between Dethick, Anthony Babington and Mary, Queen of Scots. One of Alison Uttley's most successful books is called *The Time Traveller*. It is about a young girl who lives with her poor family in London in the early twentieth century. She is in poor health and so the parents decide to send her to an old aunt and uncle who live on Manor Farm, which in the novel is called 'Thackers'.

In exploring the big old house she finds she has the power to step back in time. She enters the house just before the Babington plot where she meets Anthony and the household as it was in Elizabethan times. Alison Uttley's childhood home was a farm a short distance away and she had a friend at Dethick and would regularly visit there. In the introduction to *The Time Traveller* she shows how she became interested in Dethick and the Babingtons.

All my early years were spent at the farm across the hill-side from the small manor-house I have called 'Thackers' in my story, and I often climbed to the crest and looked down the well known fields to the church tower with its emblazoned shields which rose from among the barns and haystacks of Anthony Babington's birthplace. My father talked of Anthony Babington as though he had recently lived in the old farmhouse of his neighbour.

A grassy path across the fields leads to Dethick Church

He spoke of secret passages underground which he had entered in his own childhood. The tunnels had been filled in but the memory remained. Country tradition is strong and they said that Anthony Babington tried to help the Queen of Scots to escape from Wingfield along these hidden galleries to the little manor farm. The unsuccessful plot took place two years before the great plot which shook England and brought the Queen to the block and Babington to the gallows.
The Time Traveller – Alison Uttley

In *The Time Traveller* Penelope and her aunt and uncle are about to start a journey in the pony trap when the little girl is sent upstairs to fetch a rug to cover them from the wind.

Upstairs I went again, but when I got to the landing I looked at the closed doors and did not know which one was Aunt Tissie's, for there was something strange and unfamiliar about them. I hesitated and opened a door, and then stopped short, for in the room before me, down a couple of steps, were four ladies playing a game with ivory counters. They sat around a table and a bright fire was burning in the open hearth. They were young and pretty, except an older woman whose expression was cold and forbidding. Their dresses were made of stiff brocade, and their pointed bodices were embroidered with tiny flowers. On their heads they wore little lace caps, and I saw golden hair poking out from her headdress. Each wore a narrow lace tucker around her neck, and rings glittered on white hands that threw the dice. All this I saw in the moment I stood transfixed at the door.
The Time Traveller – Alison Uttley

Penelope rushes out and becomes a little lost on the landing with the confusion of doors when her aunt comes to find her.

"Aunt Tissie I opened a door and saw some ladies sitting in a room. Who were they?" I whispered, shy to speak about it as if I had done something amiss.

She started, 'You saw them? You've seen them?' She looked at me with astonishment and then drew me into her arms. Down below in the yard I could hear Uncle Barney thumping and banging his whip end, impatient to be off, but my aunt took no notice.
"It's the secret of Thackers," she said very quietly. "They lived here once, my dear, and some say they live here now. I've never seen them, nor has Uncle Barnabus, but my own mother saw them when she was a child."
The Time Traveller – Alison Uttley

The Courting of Anthony Babington

Charlotte Yonge was born in 1823 and so was a contemporary of Eliza Cook. However, she had a very different life, although they did have a number of things in common. Both had a large output of writing, although Charlotte produced novels rather than poems. Also, both ran their own periodical magazine.

Where Charlotte's life was different was that she virtually never left her home county of Hampshire. She dedicated herself to supporting young women through her commitment to the church. Early in her career she produced a best-selling novel called, *The Heir of Redclyffe,* which was a romantic story with a Byronic lead, which she wrote when she was 25 years old. In its day it rivalled the works of Dickens and Thackeray, although it is little known today. It made her sufficient money, not only to be able to live comfortably, but to also fund some missionary ships. She not only produced nearly 50 novels, but plays and collections of stories as well as many religious commentaries.

It would be over thirty years later, and many other books before she would produce *Unknown to History,* which is about Mary, Queen of Scots. She blends her own inventions with the historical facts and follows Mary from when she is in the custody of the Earl of Shrewsbury. Anthony Babington is part of the Earl's household and has been there since he was a page-boy. He grew up with a girl who is now under the care of Mary. He is keen to marry her. In the selection we have chosen, Richard is one of the nobles caring for the Scottish exile.

"Young man," said Richard, "listen to friendly counsel, and meddle not in perilous matters. I ask thee not whether Dethick hath any commerce with Wingfield; but I warn thee earnestly to eschew beginning again that which caused the trouble of thy childhood. Thou mayst do it innocently, seeking the consent of the lady to this courtship of thine; but I tell thee, as one who knows more of the matter than thou canst, that thou wilt only meet with disappointment."

"Hath the Queen other schemes for her?" asked Babington, anxiously; and Richard, thinking of the vista of possible archdukes, replied that she had; but that he was not free to speak, though he replied to Babington's half-uttered question that his son Humfrey was by no means intended.

"Ah!" cried Antony, "you give me hope, sir. I will do her such service that she shall refuse me nothing! Sir! Do you mock me!" he added, with a fierce change of note.

"My poor lad, I could not but laugh to think what a simple plotter you are, and what fine service you will render if thou utterest to the very last person who should hear them! Credit me, thou wast never made for privy schemes and conspiracies, and a Queen who can only be served by such, is no mistress for thee. Thou wilt but run thine own neck into the noose, and belike that of others."

"That I will never do," quoth Antony. "I may peril myself, but no others."

"Then the more you keep out of secrets the better. Thou art too open-hearted and unguarded for them! So speaks thy well-wisher, Antony, whose friendship thou hast won by thine honourable conduct towards my rash boy, though I tell thee plainly, the maiden is not for thee, whether as Scottish or English, Cis or Bride."

So they parted at the gate of the park, the younger man full of hope and confidence, the elder full of pitying misgiving.
Unknown to History – Charlotte Yonge

Mary, Queen of Scots in German

One of Germany's leading nineteenth century playwrights was also poet, philosopher and historian. His name was Friedrich von Schiller. He was born in 1759 and a few years before his death he composed a play called *Mary Stuart.* He portrays her as a victim, which was very much in keeping with his social philosophy writings. Lord Burleigh, also

Manor Farm, the home of Anthony Babington

known as William Cecil, was one of Queen Elizabeth's advisers. In this scene they are discussing Babington.

Mary: Upon this statute, then, My Lord, is built the verdict of my judges ?

Burleigh: (reading) Last year it was enacted, "If a plot henceforth should rise in England, in the name or for the benefit of any claimant to England's crown, that justice should be done on such pretender, and the guilty party be prosecuted unto death."

Mary: Lord Burleigh, I can well imagine that a law expressly aimed at me, and fram'd to compass my destruction, may to my prejudice be used. O! woe to the unhappy victim, when the tongue that frames the law shall execute the sentence. Can you deny it. Sir, that this same statute was made for my destruction, and nought else?

Burleigh: It should have acted as a warning to you: By your imprudence it became a snare. You saw the precipice which yawned before you; Yet truly warn'd, you plung'd into the deep with Babington, the traitor, and his bands of murderous companions were you leagued. You knew of all and from your prison led their treasonous plottings with a deep-laid plan.

Mary: When did I that, my Lord? Let them produce the documents.

Burleigh: You have already seen them: They were, before the court, presented to you

Mary. Mere copies written by another hand; Show me the proof that they were dictated by me, that they proceeded from my lips, and in those very terms in which you read them.

Burleigh: Before his execution, Babington confessed they were the same which he received.

Mary: Why was he in his lifetime not produced before my face? Why was he then dispatched so quickly that he could not be confronted with her whom he accused?

Burleigh: Besides, my Lady, your secretaries, Curl and Nau, declared on oath they are the very selfsame letters which, from your lips, they faithfully transcribed.

Mary: And on my menials' testimony, then, I am condemned ; upon the word of those who have betray'd me, me their rightful Queen, who in that very moment when they came as witnesses against me broke their faith.

Burleigh: You said yourself you held your countryman to be an upright, conscientious man.

Mary: I thought him such; but it is the hour of danger alone which tries the virtue of a man.
Mary Stuart – Friedrich Schiller

Let us leave the Babington Plot with his own words. This is the plea for mercy that he wrote to Elizabeth, who rejected it, and had him executed.

Most gracious Sovereign if either bitter tears, a pensive contrite heart or any dutiful sight of the wretched Sinner might work any pity in your royal breast I would wring out of my drained eyes as much blood as in bemoaning my dreary tragedy should lamentably betray my fault and somewhat no doubt move you to compassion but since there is no proportion betwixt the quality of my crimes and any human commiseration.

Show sweet Queen some miracle on a wretch that lyeth prostrate in your prison most grievously bewailing his offence and imploring such comfort at your anointed hands as my poor wife's

Riber Castle, the home of John Smedley

misfortunes doth beg my child innocence doth crave my guiltless family doth wish and my heinous treachery doth least deserve. So shall your divine mercy make your glory shine as far above all princes as my most horrible practices are more detestable amongst your best subjects whom lovingly and happily to govern I humbly beseech the mercy Master himself to grant for his sweet son's sake Jesus Christ.
Plea for Mercy – Anthony Babington

We take our leave of Dethick and pass over the footpaths and quiet lanes to the hamlet of Riber. On our approach to the buildings there is one that stands out as having a long history. Riber Hall is a seventeenth century building with many other associated buildings of the same age. The hall's entrance from the narrow lane is very uncharacteristic of grand houses, but the quaint rounded steps, with gates and railings and the near background of the leaded and mullioned window, yield a view of Babington's times. There is little doubt that the main hall and the nearby buildings are left from another age, untouched as the centuries have rolled past them.

A Smedley Legacy

It is a building that we cannot yet see that is Riber's most famous landmark. If we make our way past the hall and turn left at the end of the lane and follow the path we walk down the side of Riber Castle. As we clear the woods we are also greeted with a spectacular view of the Derwent Valley and Matlock.

The four towers of Riber Castle dominate the sky line and can be seen from practically all of Matlock in the valley. It was build by John Smedley the son of the founder of Lea Mill. It was completed in 1862 and became his home. He lived here until he died and it remained the home of his wife until her death. It then passed from the family and had a very chequered history until the present day. We leave the house and pass down the footpath taking the route that leads us to the road into Matlock, which we enter through the Hall Leys Park, a century old town centre park.

Let's rest awhile in Hall Leys Park

The River Derwent flows through this municipal park that has been updated and adapted to modern living, but has also retained its traditional flower borders and boating lake. Near to the Derwent are the markers for previous flood levels. The river in those periods of spate would have been above a person's head if they had been in the park at the time. These were real floods that have been documented, but in the next chapter we will come across a fictional account of the Derwent bursting its banks.

At the Cromford end of our walk in this chapter we celebrated the long existence of the John Smedley production and at the end we have seen the eccentric castle that he build, but there is still more of him to come after he went through a life-changing experience. The Smedley's partner family, the Nightingales, gave the nation one of its most noted heroines and the small hamlet of Dethick has played its part on the national stage both in fact and fiction.

Boys, Trees and Water

Matlock to Darley Bridge through Two Dales

The River Derwent flows under Matlock Bridge

The title of this walk gives a potent mixture for fun, and we have a wonderful rogue who would certainly have taken the opportunity to fall into the river and get wet. A life-changing event totally redirected one man's ambitions, and through his actions, it brought a story writer to Matlock who, while he was here, worked on a famous boys' novel based in his home country of Scotland. The literary world benefited, because he went against his father's wishes, who wanted him to go into the family profession of building lighthouses.

Our focus on water is not only the Derwent but also its therapeutic properties. We also introduce two of the leading romantic poets. One had a poem commissioned by the offer of money. He accepted, but Tom Moore, Byron's biographer from Ashbourne, refused to respond to the financial enticements. Our second Romantic poet visited the area several times, but his role on this walk was to praise a poet whose name is far less well-known. And finally, what better subject can there be for a customary poem than a yew tree in a churchyard.

Matlock is a small town at the northern end of the limestone gorge through which the River Derwent flows. The immediate entrance to the gorge has High Tor to the east and a very steep wooded slope to the west. It leads in a mile or so to Matlock Bath and then onto Cromford and the Arkwright Mills. To the north, the valley opens out to a much gentler vista and this part of the Derwent is known as Darley Dale.

Praise from a Poet

Before we leave the centre of Matlock let's look at the River Derwent that flows through the town. In many places it is not obvious, but the park has a good stretch of it and it passes under the main bridge in the centre of the town. Also, if we follow it south towards Matlock Bath again we can walk alongside the river. The reason, for focusing on the Derwent, is to join with Samuel Taylor Coleridge and appreciate a poem written about the town of Matlock and the River Derwent. Let us look at the beginning of the seventeen verses.

Matlock, amid thy hoary-hanging views,
Thy glens that smile sequester'd, and thy nooks
Which yon forsaken cragg all dark o'erlooks.
Monady written at Matlock – William Lisle Bowles

William Lisle Bowles was the son of a vicar and after attending Oxford, he took holy orders. He was born in 1762 and wrote poetry from an early age. He was thought by some to have changed the

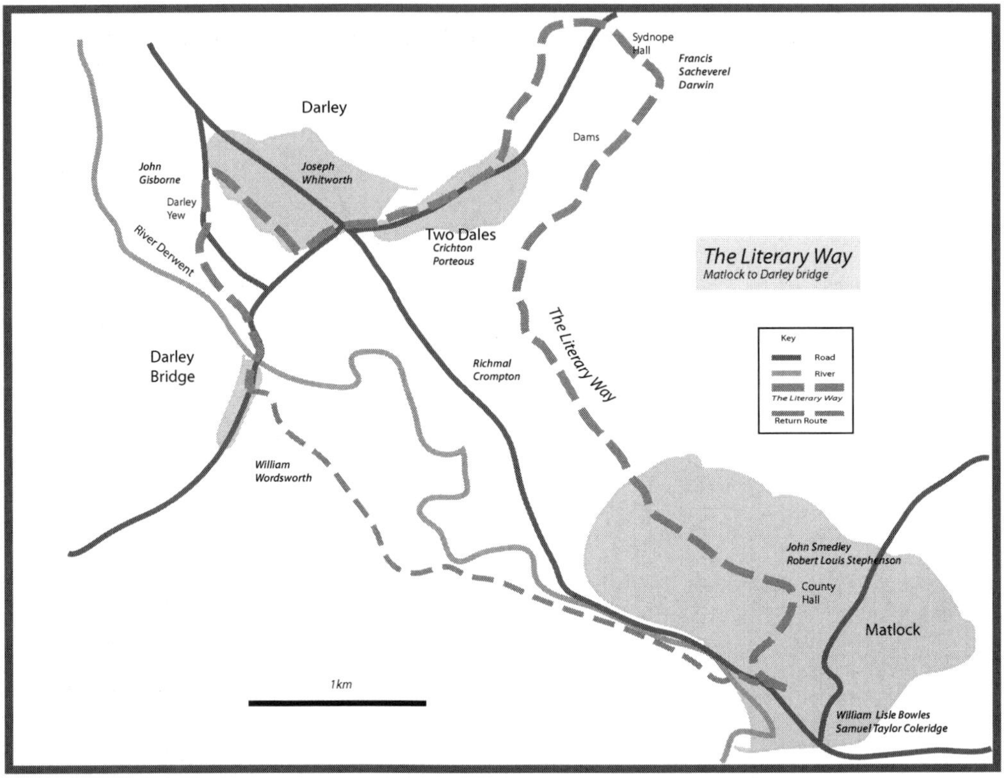

The Literary Way – Walk Eight – Matlock to Darley Bridge

style of poetry of the time, with the *Monody, written at Matlock,* being one of the examples that earned him praise. It was written in 1791 when he was on a tour of the north of England and foreign lands after having his proposal to a young lady rejected. One who praised his style and went on to become one of England's most notable poets was Samuel Taylor Coleridge, who visited Matlock in August 1796, and it prompted him to write a sonnet about William, who he considered to be one of his 'greats'.

My heart has thank'd thee, BOWLES! for those soft strains,
To Bowles – Samuel Taylor Coleridge

Thomas Bowles took up his living in Wiltshire. One of his fiercest critics was Lord Byron, which was interesting as Thomas Bowles' neighbour and good friend became Thomas Moore who we met at Mayfield on *The Literary Way* and was Lord Byron's biographer.

A Dedication to Help

Let us leave the centre of Matlock and take the road up towards the hill overlooking the centre. We are going to go past the building that stands dominantly on the hillside overlooking Matlock. It is now County Hall, but it was built for a completely different reason. We must again return to John Smedley and learn a little more about why he designed and constructed this building.

Lea Mill which we passed on *The Literary Way,* on the last walk was founded by John Smedley, senior and Peter Nightingale. The business, whilst initially successful, ran into difficulties more than once. John Smedley had a son, born in 1803, also called John Smedley, and he is the person who built what is now County Hall. The son came into the textile business at a young age and it was his idea to convert the cotton machinery at Lea Mill to take wool.

In the next 16 years, which unfortunately included the death of his father, he built up the mill into a very successful business. In 1847, at the age of 44, he married Caroline Hayward, but the same year his life would change forever.

Whilst on honeymoon he contracted a fever and this would have a significant effect on him. During the next three years, he became weaker and lacked the energy to carry on running his business. After trying the standard drugs of the period, he went to Yorkshire for water therapy. This he believed changed his life. The illness disappeared and he returned to his full energy and determination to complete tasks. The water-cure had given him a new lease of life. The textile business had been run

Walk Directions

Matlock to Sydnope (3.36 miles)

We leave the park in Matlock and take the road up to County Hall.
We pass behind the former Smedley's Hydro and turn left.
The road goes straight ahead along the valley
We stay on the road ignoring any turns that go downhill
At the fork we take the right road (Farley Hill) for a short distance
And then the left fork. This keeps us going along the side of the valley
The main road begins to dip down and we take the cul-de-sac in front of the houses
It eventually becomes a path
The path forks and we take the left fork down the hill by the fence
At the bottom we take the path up past the dams
We follow the east side of the water until it leads us to a footbridge
We have passed the reservoirs and cross the stream using the bridge
The path climbs up out of the valley and we come to an open field
Sydnope Hall can be seen on the right

Sydnope to Two Dales (1.28 miles)

We cross the field and go right of the farm and come out on to the road
After turning left we cross the road and take the next turning on the right
At the end is a T-junction onto a track, we turn left
We continue on this track until it meets the main road
We turn left and immediately right
This allows us to walk along the loop of lane through Two Dales

Two Dales to Darley Bridge (1.7 miles)

We come out again on the main road and turn left down the hill
The road now has a pavement.
It takes us down to the main road through the valley
We cross diagonally to the Whitworth Institute.
It is then a gentle stroll past the main building into the park.
We follow the edge of the lake going away from the road
There is a footpath exit from the park which we take.
It runs along the edge of the railway line
We come out in Churchtown
We cross the level crossing and visit the Darley Yew
After leaving the churchyard we go back onto the road and turn right
In a short distance there is a footpath on the right which we take
We walk across the meadows and past the cricket ground
When we reach the road we turn right and have good view of Oker Hill
We then reach Darley Bridge

Darley Bridge to Matlock (2.48 miles)

We cross Darley Bridge and take the lane immediately to the left
After a short distance we turn right onto a footpath
The footpath leads us up onto Oker Hill.
In several places we can see the single Sycamore
(The public footpath does not pass the tree)
As we descend from the highest point we go straight ahead at the path junction
We come out at the junction of two roads
We carry straight ahead along the road
After a short distance we take the footpath on the left
This crosses a field and passes close to the river
Follow the path past the works and continue on it to Matlock Centre

Distance: 8.82 miles Ascent: 1149ft

successfully by his managers during his illness and instead of returning to full-time work, he was determined to give the benefit of the hydro treatment to as many as possible. He set about it in his old style of hard work and started by making the treatments available for his staff at the mill.

John Smedley did not rest just with the hydro hospital at the Lea Mills works. In 1853, he bought a house on Matlock Bank, which became the foundation of his hydro. He was determined to help as many as possible, so the facility was open to all. Over the next twelve years it was extended extensively as he bought up surrounding land. No expense was spared in the increasing elaborate provisions, which had a strict regime, not only of hydro treatments, but of diet and recuperative living.

Alcohol was banned and the whole operation, conducted jointly with his wife, was run under strict religious principles. Caroline and John not only developed the hydro, but also the treatments that were on offer. At first John was highly critical of many existing medical practices, but in the end, became more reconciled with them, and the hydro was eventually run by a doctor.

John was an eccentric man and very firmly believed in his own capabilities and convictions. As well as the medical profession, he also had a very long running disagreement with the established church. Unlike many others that had similar problems with the establishment, he was never sufficiently comfortable to join one of the nonconformist groups. He backed up his view on religion by both preaching himself and building chapels and schools for several local communities in the neighbourhood of Matlock and Lea Mill.

By 1864 the Smedley hydro was very well established. John and Caroline lived in Riber Castle with a clear view across to Matlock Bank and the dominating building, the Hydro. John not only dealt with the practicalities of running the hydro, but wrote an extensive book, over 440 pages of small print and detailed information about hydrotherapy. It was a successful book as it reached a seventh edition and a circulation of 35,000. Let see how John Smedley describes the effect of his own return to health.

County Hall which is the old Smedley Hydro

I returned to Lea Bridge (seventy miles), and sat up part of the same night burning my foolish ballads and light books, upon which even clergymen had with me often wasting precious time. I locked up my extravagant plate, ornaments, equipage, &c, until I could give them away or sell them for the benefit of religious societies, which I did shortly after. I then brought my wife from Cheltenham, and we commenced our new and better work.
Practical Hydropathy - John Smedley

Smedley's Hydro in Matlock remained open until the 1950s. After its closure it gained its current role of County Hall. Before we move on further on *The Literary Way*, we will look at a famous book that was partly written whilst the author attended the hydro.

Kidnapped

In 1886, Robert Louis Stevenson stayed at the Smedley Hydro in Matlock with his father who was very unwell. He had begun the story *Kidnapped* during the previous year and, whilst faltering a little in his effort, he was writing it during the period he was at the hydro. It was published in a boys magazine over a period of months later in that year. Robert was 36 at the time and had three years earlier published one of the books for which he is renowned, *Treasure Island*. Just before the release of *Kidnapped* perhaps his most well-known work, the novella, *The Strange Case of Dr Jekyll and Mr Hyde* was published. So in the three years he produced three works which would establish his literary reputation although, like many writers, he has been in and out of favour.

Robert was born in Edinburgh into a family of engineers, who specialised in building lighthouses, but he disappointed his parents by choosing a different profession. He did study law, but never practised, as his heart was into writing. He wrote 13 novels and many other short stories, poems and travel books. Like his father he suffered a great deal of ill-health, particularly with his chest and breathing, so much so that he was lucky to survive on a number of occasions. He remained undaunted by his illnesses and was determined to travel. He visited America and then decided to sail around the Pacific Islands. Whilst in Hawaii, he became friends with the King of Hawaii and finally settled in the Samoan Islands, which is where he died aged 44.

Kidnapped is an historical novel set in the Scottish Highlands with the fiction being intertwined with real events and people. So as to give a flavour of the book let's consider the words near the opening.

"Very well, Davie. Then it behoves me to tell your fortune; or so far as I may. When your mother was gone, and your father (the worthy, Christian man) began to sicken for his end, he gave me in charge a certain letter, which he said was your inheritance.

"So soon," says he, "as I am gone, and the house is redd up and the gear disposed of (all which, Davie, hath been done), "give my boy this letter into his hand, and start him off to the house of Shaws, not far from Cramond. "That is the place I came from," he said, "and it's where it befits that my boy should return. He is a steady lad," your father said, "and a canny goer; and I doubt not he will come safe, and be well liked where he goes."
"The house of Shaws!" I cried. "What had my poor father to do with the house of Shaws?"
Kidnapped – Robert Louis Stevenson

The book is an adventure for the young man who confronts difficulties and people determined to stop him achieve what is rightfully his. Following on from the success of *Kidnapped,* Robert Louis Stevenson produced a sequel entitled, *Catriona,* which continues Davie's adventure.

Let's leave the Hydro with John Smedley and Robert Louis Stevenson and take Smedley Street towards Upper Hackney which overlooks Darley Dale. Farley Lane leads up on to the hills and plateau above Darley Dale, but we take some minor roads and lanes which will take us towards the moors above Two Dales. As we walk along this road we can see between the houses below.

The sweep of the Derwent valley is at its best as the summer sun enhances the many shades of green in the trees and grasses. On the far side of the valley there is a hill that stands out and on its summit is a single tree. There is a story to be told about this sycamore, but we shall leave it to one of the country's most significant Romantic poets to explain it to us in verse a little later as we get closer to it.

As we progress along the road we need to keep glancing down until we catch the sight of a large complex of buildings which was, for many years, a school and has now become a retirement village.

A Wonderful Rogue

It is common in the teaching profession for teachers to return to the school in which they were educated. But very few then go on to become famous authors. One such woman was the daughter of a clergyman, and up to the age of fourteen, went to school in Warrington, Lancashire.

The school moved to Darley Dale in 1904, and Richmal moved to. She took an instant liking to her surroundings, and her novel, *Anne Morrison,* illustrates her school days in the Peak. She would go on to write 49 non-children's books, which were either novels or collections of short stories. Her writing career started in 1923 and would last until 1960, but her books have lived on for future generations. Following her school education, she obtained a scholarship in London and became a teacher. She returned initially to Darley, but would later move to south-east London where she died in 1969. However, it would not be her 49 books for which she became very famous, but a series of short stories and novels set around one character. And what a wonderful character he was! He would appear in 41 books written and published between 1922 and after her death in 1969.

Richmal Lamburn chose to write using her middle name, Richmal Crompton. We are, of course, referring to the lovable young rogue defined by the first title, *Just William.* He was what every boy aspires to. A rascal who gets into trouble but always comes out tops in the end. Her books allowed Richmal to retire from teaching. Her works were translated into many languages and became a standard library books and presents, for more than one generation of boys.

This extract is from the first story in *Just William,* which launched him into the limelight. William has been treated by his aunt to a trip to the cinema and some sweets. He is now returning home.

Once outside, he glanced cautiously around and slunk down the road in the direction of his home. Then he doubled suddenly and ran down a back street to put his imaginary pursuers off his track. He took a pencil from his pocket and, levelling it at the empty air, fired twice. Two of his pursuers fell dead, the rest came on with redoubled vigour. There was no time to be lost. Running for dear life, he dashed down the next street, leaving in his wake an elderly gentleman nursing his toe and cursing volubly. As he neared his gate, William again drew the pencil from his pocket and, still looking back down the road, and firing as he went, he rushed into his own gateway. William's father, who had stayed at home that day because of a bad headache and a touch of liver, picked himself up from the middle of a rhododendron bush and seized William by the back of his neck.
Just William – Richmal Crompton

Let's pass on along the lanes and take the route up through Holt Wood and along the delightful footpath that follows the trees that line the dams in Sydnope Valley. Through the lush vegetation we can just catch sight of the tranquil waters behind the dams. A glimpse of the dam shows us that they are no longer used, as rivulets of water stream down their slopes. They were originally built to drive the textile factory at Two Dales a little further down the valley.

We continue to climb the path until we have cleared the top dam and can see on the opposite slope a neat little waterfall. Soon after we can cross the top of the valley and come out into the high fields, which then stretch upon to the moors.

The Turkish Chameleon

We broach the top of the woods and then we come in sight of Sydnope Hall. One of the friends for *The Literary Way* is Erasmus Darwin, who we have already met several times. The Hall that we can see is where one of his sons, Francis Sacheverel Darwin, lived for many years. Francis followed his father in many ways. His natural love of plants inspired him and he also chose the medical profession.

After qualifying as a doctor, and at the age of 22, he set off with four other young men to explore Spain and the eastern Mediterranean, but particularly to go into areas where the British had not been before. Of the five that set out, Francis was the only one to survive. Whether losing his friends or other reasons overtook him, but once he had returned home he never travelled again. Initially, he followed his father, and set up medical practice in Lichfield, but soon moved to Sydnope Hall. After a period here he moved to his final home, Breadsall Priory in south Derbyshire.

Francis kept a succinct journal of his exploits in Spain, Greece and Turkey. It was for his private information, but some years later, it was published by a member of his family. It makes fascinating reading.

A young man, aged 22, completes his studies and goes abroad. We are sure you are thinking that it is very reminiscent of the modern notion of the 'gap' year. However, modern travellers do not generally encounter murder, the plague, sinking and hostile ships, and pirates or privateers. Francis set out on his travels in 1808. This is an entry during the following year. A janizary was a Turkish soldier.

Fri 29 September 1809 Brusa
We parted from our friends at Brusa, and set out for the plains of Troy and Smyrna; and as the road was much infested by robbers, it was necessary to take another guard besides our own janizary. We therefore decided to have a Bayracta – as all the country fears him, being an executioner. There is something very impressive in the extraordinary quiet and silent demeanour of these people... We desired the interpreter to enquire how many people he had beheaded in his time, and to this he made no reply. One of the janizaries, however, told us he had decapitated four persons the day before our arrival.
Travels in Spain and the East, 1808-1810 – Francis Sacheverell Darwin

Another young man, about the same age as Francis, also had similar ambitions for travel. Lord Byron also journeyed around the Mediterranean with his friend John Hobhouse. This was Lord Byron's first trip to Greece, after which he would return

Sydnope Hall, the home of Francis Darwin

to England. It was his second trip from which he never returned. Unfortunately Francis left very little detail of when he met Byron in Smyrna, which is on the west coast of Turkey. For on that particular day, Francis was more interested in recording his encounter with a chameleon than giving an opinion about Lord Byron.

A Love of the Countryside

As we passed through Bradbourne we discovered it was the place that Nat Gould called home. He had began working on a farm, but then moved into the newspaper industry. Some fifty years later Leslie Porteous, who came from Manchester, took up farm work on the edge of the Peak District. His family was set on him joining his uncle's very profitable business of cotton trading, but he chose the hard work of a farm.

After a few years, like Nat Gould, he moved into the world of newspapers, eventually rising to become the assistant editor of the northern Daily Mail. By the age of 38, he decided to concentrate on being a freelance writer. He had moved to the village of Combs, near to the small town of Chapel-en-le-Frith. His intention was to settle in the Peak District, which had been an area he had liked from the days of his school holidays. His first book, which is mainly autobiographical, started with his fascination with farming and was called, *Farmer's Creed*.

By the end of the Second World War he had moved across the Peak District to Two Dales, near Matlock. By the time he finally retired from writing he had produced 31 books, which were a mixture of novels and books about the Peak District. He is known for some of the best descriptions of the Peak. Several of his novels were set in and around the Derwent Valley. Two Dales was formerly known as Toad Hole. Leslie chose as his writing name, Crichton Porteous. The introduction to *Broken River* by Crichton Porteous says:

At one time the Darent River broke its banks nearly every winter, but since the huge new dam had been built, all the people in the valley felt safe. Then one August in a terrible storm, the river began to rise with terrible haste, it rose higher than any previous record, and remained at that height.
Broken River – Crichton Porteous

This book is one of the later ones in *The Literary Way* being published in 1956. The dam referred to is the Ladybower Dam which was built in the 1930s and 1940s.

An Inspirational Engineer

As we look at the buildings along the road through Darley Dale one name stands out. Both the old Mechanics Institute, and also the hospital, carry the name, Whitworth. They are named after Joseph

Whitworth who was born near Manchester, but would eventually settle in Darley Dale. He and his wife funded local causes especially in the areas of education and health. Joseph lived near the main road in Stancliffe Hall with his second wife. He never forgot his home of Manchester and the Mechanics Institute he founded there went on to become part of the university, and is now called the University of Manchester Institute of Science and Technology (UMIST).

Joseph moved from being a mechanic in a factory to a member of the Royal Society, and he would create a legacy that would last until this day. He made his fame and fortune through mechanical engineering. His work, although varied, would be focused on precision engineering. He would introduce a range of techniques, which would help machines to be built accurately and to within very fine tolerances. His reputation rapidly grew, and by 1858, when he was in his fifties, he was admitted as a member of the Royal Society. He had already developed screw-making equipment that would precisely remake the same threads consistently. The development of this standard was encapsulated throughout the industry, and is still referred to today, with modern screws being designated Whitworth threads. Here is what Whitworth in his book entitled, *Miscellaneous Paper on Mechanical Subjects published in 1858* had to say in the Preface about screws.

The paper on screw threads was read at the Institution of Civil Engineers, in London, in the year 1841; since that time the systems has been generally adopted in this country, and is becoming extensively used in America and other countries.
Miscellaneous Papers on Mechanical Subject – Joseph Whitworth

The Great Exhibition in 1851 was a show-case for Joseph Whitworth and impressed all that visited his stand with his precision engineering and increased accuracy of measurements. By then he was moving in higher circles and Prince Albert was particularly keen to see his work and help promote it, along with the rest of British industry. One fascinating meeting took place during the exhibition, that was recorded in John Bright's diary. We will meet John in a quiet dale later on the walk, but for now we can say that he was one of the leading politicians of the day.

Met also Chas. Dickens, and was introduced to him by Paxton. It was in the little room where J. Whitworth was exhibiting the machine for measuring the millionth of an inch. Dickens's face scarcely indicates the possession of the powers of the mind he has displayed, tho' it is intelligent in expression, and pleasant to look upon.
Diary – John Bright

Joseph Paxton was the man who built the Crystal Palace, and we shall say more about him at Chatsworth.

The Darley Yew

John Gisborne moved with his family from Blackpool to Darley Dale in 1818. He was 48 years old by then and had previously lived at Wootton Lodge near Ellastone which was near the beginning of *The Literary Way*. In 1792, he married Millicent Pole and it is here that we have another connection with Erasmus Darwin, because Millicent was his step-daughter by his second marriage.

John was a devout man, with sufficient money to allow himself to dedicate his time to good causes, and to supporting those less fortunate than himself. Millicent had previously become ill, which is why they moved from Wootton to Blackpool, as the location was recommended because of the sea air.

John and Millicent moved to Darley Dale when her health improved. John Gisborne spent much of his time visiting the poor of the area, but decided to write a long poem while he was resident at Darley. He had already completed a topographical poem called *The Vales of Wever* with its dedication to the Rev John Granville of Calwich Abbey, while living at Wootton Hall. His poem *Reflections: A Poem Descriptive of Events and Scenery Connected with Different Months of the Year,* takes a number of different events and local themes that he relates to months of the year.

St Helen's parish church in Darley dates back to the 12th century and its churchyard contains the Darley Yew. It's vast trunk shows its considerable

Darley Church with the old yew near the door

The hemispherical sycamore on Oker Hill

age, however, it is difficult to establish with such trees their true age due to a hollowing process. Their longevity is ascribed to that, when they split with age, they do not seem to become infected. The Darley Yew is near the front door of the church. In John's *Reflections* this is how he described the tree.

Nor shall thy reverend Yew, the Sire who holds
His sceptre verdant through the changeful year,
Unnoticed stand. She has beheld, like three,
Thousands entomb'd within his shadow; heard
For ages past the sobs, the heart fetch'd groans
Of parting anguish ere the grave was closed,
And drank the mourner's tears!
Reflections – John Gisborne

The Brothers

We leave the churchyard and take the path to the riverside until we reach the old Darley Bridge. It is a 16th century packhorse bridge over the Derwent. After passing over the bridge we can see on our left a small elongated hill with a single sycamore on the summit. This is Oker Hill, and has been made famous in a poem, written in 1838, by William Wordsworth who went to the same college, St John's in Cambridge, as John Gisborne.

Wordsworth was travelling through the area when he wrote a sonnet about a local fable. Two brothers each planted a sycamore tree on the top of Oker Hill. The brothers separated and one went away, and soon died, as did the tree he planted. William called the poem, *A Tradition of Darley Dale*, Derbyshire. How it came to publication is interesting.

A combination of an ambitious publisher, with new techniques, and a man who wanted the best, led to the development of a literary annual that first saw the light of day in 1828. The intent was to financially persuade some of the most acclaimed names in literature to contribute poems and stories. This the owners thought could be achieved by offering large amounts of money, and to a great extent they succeeded.

The first edition, published in 1829, was to become renowned because of the contributors. However, one person that money couldn't buy was Thomas Moore, who we met in Mayfield. He turned down £700, the modern equivalent of £47,000, to edit the edition. I think we will agree that is a lot of money at any time. He did, however, contribute poems.

Mary Shelley and Samuel Taylor Coleridge contributed, and also Sir Walter Scott wrote some short stories. Wordsworth accepted the offer of the fees and one of his contributions to the edition was *A Tradition of Darley Dale.*

'Tis said that to the brow of yon fair hill
Two Brothers clomb, and, turning face from face,
Nor one look more exchanging, grief to still
Or feed, each planted on that lofty place
A chosen Tree; then, eager to fulfil
Their courses, like two new-born rivers, they
In opposite directions urged their way
Down from the far-seen mount. No blast might kill
Or blight that fond memorial;--the trees grew,
And now entwine their arms; but ne'er again
Embraced those Brothers upon earth's wide plain;
Nor aught of mutual joy or sorrow knew
Until their spirits mingled in the sea
That to itself takes all, Eternity.
A Tradition of Darley Dale – William Wordsworth

Let's rest awhile at Oker Hill

In the short distance from Matlock to Darley Bridge we have been able to cover literature in many and varied forms, with a close juxtapositioning of the Romantic notions of Lisle Bowles and the scientific intents of Joseph Whitworth. Benevolence has also been to the fore in our walk, with the writing of John Gisborne and the lasting legacy of the Whitworth's name in many places. On this walk we again came into contact with the Darwin family, but this time it wasn't Erasmus, but his son and step-daughter.

The walk along the upper edges of the Darley valley and its tributaries give some first-rate views over the countryside both near and far with the single sycamore of Oker Hill, in Wordsworth's sonnet, capturing our attention on most of the route.

The wooded walk up to Sydnope Hall, and the Church set in the meadows, with the revitalised steam engines chugging past, show how good it is to get away from the main road.

Seventeenth Child

Darley Bridge to Birchover through Winster

Market House, in the centre of Winster

Can you imagine what it must be like to be the seventeenth child within a family? One such person is the first author on this walk. However, he had no regrets at being one of a multitude and he took his father's outlook on life, believing that hard work would bring its rewards. In this he wasn't mistaken, for he combined strenuous efforts with talent in many fields, to leave us a rich legacy. His eldest brother was 17 years older than him, and so he had not only his father, but his big brother as a role model, and it was that relationship that determined the first steps in his career. After that, he went from strength to strength and all the writing about him compliments him on his good nature and extensive hospitality.

By coincidence, the author in the next chapter shared many of the same passions and interests, although they were very different men in their nature. So for these two walks we are turning the clock back to the Victorian times and entering the world of the antiquary. We also introduce a working female Victorian writer, who made her way in the world from humble beginnings. She was a prolific writer and became learned in history and archaeology, but her forte was the writing of novels centred on children.

The local area is rife with sites of antiquity. There are many tumuli, and other ancient sites, some of which are shrouded in mystery. We will pass by some of these sites on these two walks and try to understand the passions they drove in our authors.

We leave the Derwent Valley and follow the route through a gentle and shallow dale. The characteristic dry stone walls and green fields show that we are returning to the Carboniferous Limestone country. The dale takes us towards the small, but very picturesque village of Winster, but we immediately notice that this village is not the same as many on the White Peak plateau. Most of the villages we have walked through have two-storey small cottages made from the local stone. Winster is different in that many of the houses along the main street are three-storey and they represent a mixture of different styles. There are numerous alleys and tracks, which often lead through to a group of asymmetrically arranged small cottages.

The impressive main street is dominated by the Market House, a fine old building effectively set in the street rather than along the edge of it. It is now in the care of the National Trust. At the far end, the Dower House appears to terminate the road, but it slips past it through tight corners. Near to the

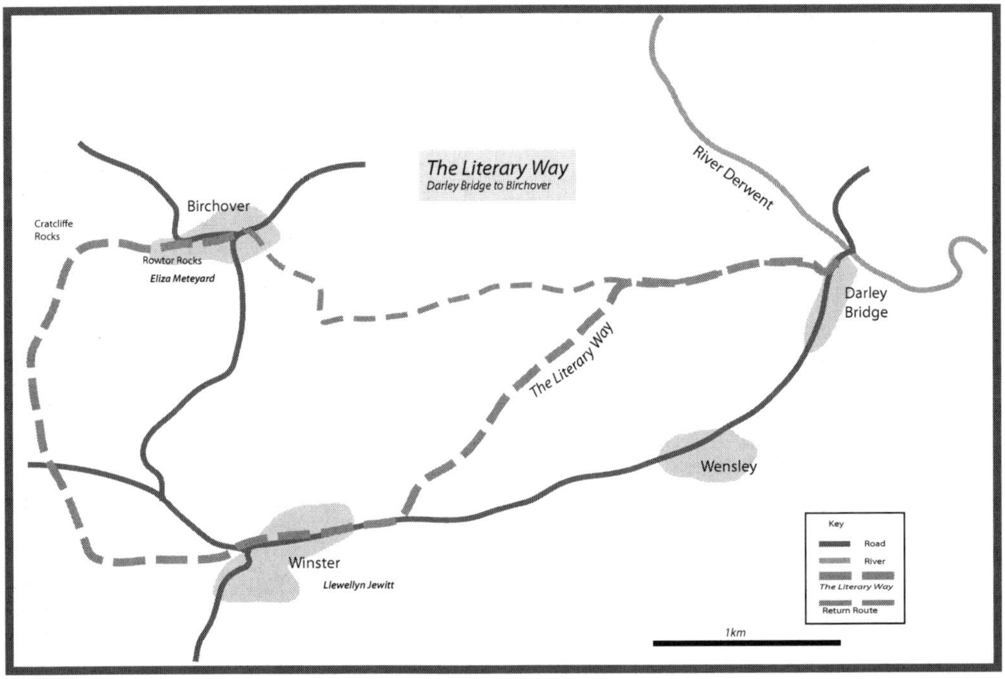

The Literary Way – Walk Nine – Darley Bridge to Birchover

Walk Directions

Darley Bridge to Winster (2.29 miles)

We cross to Darley Bridge and pass the first few cottages
After the bends, we take the first turning on the right
As the lane passes through the woods we take the left track
When the track takes a sharp right we take the footpath to the left
Shortly after we take the left of the two paths
At the next path junction we take the right
We are then following the path through the woods
The path runs parallel to the stream
We emerge from the woods and follow the path across the fields
It goes diagonally and finally reaches the road
We turn right as we are now on the edge of Winster
It is a short distance to the centre of Winster

Winster to Birchover (2.11 miles)

We walk through Winster
We can note Winster Hall and the Market House on the main road
Facing us at the end of the street is the Dower House
We take the left turn and then go along the footpath into the churchyard
We walk through the churchyard and take the path out the far side
It passes through a small wood and after a field joins a road
We join the path on the opposite side of the road.
Then there is a path junction. We take the left path to Elton
The path becomes a lane and we come out onto the road
We cross this road and take Dudwood Lane opposite
We follow it to the end of the lane where it joins the main road
The path to the left takes us up to Cratcliff and Hermit's Cave
After visiting these we retrace our steps to the road
We then take the footpath opposite
It climbs steeply across the field and then goes around a hill
It turns to a track and leads us past the Vicarage and church into Birchover.
The Druid Inn is on our left and Rowtor Rocks are behind it
We continue our walk through the village and pass the Red Lion

Birchover to Darley Bridge (2.42 miles)

Just past the Chapel in Birchover we take the footpath to the right
It winds round some buildings and then crosses fields
After about the fifth field there is a path that crosses in front of us
We turn right along the path on the far side of a wall
(The track appears to continue but is only for farm access)
At the bottom of the field we cross the stile
It is a small green lane
We turn left and follow the lane.
It will take us back to Darley Bridge
The last section of it retraces the first part of the outward route.

Distance: 6.82 miles Ascent: 1008ft

Market House is Winster Hall, which is our focus of attention and where our author lived.

Making an Impression

Llewellyn Jewitt was born in 1816, but it would be 52 years before he would settle in Winster Hall. He then played an active life within the community, particularly by sponsoring the first water supply for the village.

Let's look how the seventeenth child can make an impression. His father was a school teacher and travelled widely in the Midlands in search of the best jobs for him and his family. He came from a large family in Sheffield and was due to follow the traditional cutlery apprenticeship, but he extended his learning with the intention of taking a teaching role. After some success in Sheffield, he decided to open his own school, but his only access to the right kind of premises and catchment area was in Chesterfield, which is about 12 miles from Sheffield where he and his family lived. He wasn't daunted by the prospect. Very early every Monday morning he would set out on foot to stride out the miles to his school. On Saturday he would return to his family. This arrangement was necessary as he could not afford to move his wife and family to Chesterfield. His wife obviously fully supported him because she would also walk to Chesterfield and back so that they could spend some time together.

The teacher-father inspired his offspring with a sense of learning. Llewellyn excelled and he would also gain a great deal from his eldest brother, Orlando, who was seventeen years older. He became very interested, and then very skilled at engraving, and Llewellyn would follow him and become very skilled at drawing and engraving to allow images to be printed. He clearly had talent in the arts and many of his books contain elaborate sketches. This he combined with goods skills in writing which would allow him in his later life, while at Winster Hall, to produce a number of books with sketch illustrations.

The writing came after he was employed by an engraver to contribute to a number of magazine and periodicals. It was the combination of writing and engraving that gave him the edge over others. While living in London he became a newspaper reporter, but his engraving skills gave him an advantage in doing his job.

Winster Hall, the home of Llewellyn Jewitt

Three-storey cottages in the village of Winster

In today's world when a story needs to be covered, say a major economic event or county show, the newspaper would send along a reporter and a photographer. In Llewellyn's day there was no photography, so the next best thing was to have a sketch of the scene or new equipment, and this is why he was so useful. He could report the story, and do the sketch for the engraving, which would produce the line diagram.

When he was 43, his career took a change of direction as he became senior librarian in Plymouth, where he stayed for four years before returning to Derbyshire and, with yet another change of career direction, as he became the editor of the *Derby Telegraph*.

He was also actively involved in the County Museum and the Natural History Society, which during his involvement merged with Derby Philosophical Society that had been founded by Erasmus Darwin.

Ceramics

Llewellyn's lasting legacy is an extremely well researched book entitled, *The Ceramic Art of Great Britain*. The depth of these volumes, which run to over a thousand detailed pages, is appropriately summed up in the subtitle:

The Ceramic Art of Great Britain: from prehistoric times to the present day: Being a history of the ancient and modern pottery and porcelain works of the kingdom and their production of every class.

The Ceramic Art of Great Britain – Llewellyn Jewitt

Llewellyn also continued the ceramics theme in another book, which was a biography of the Wedgwood family, especially Josiah, the founder of the pottery dynasty. Llewellyn gives a detailed account of the life and work of Josiah Wedgwood from his early beginnings, when he had succumbed to smallpox and was crippled, through to his successful business that made pottery for royalty. We have mentioned before in several places Erasmus Darwin. One of Erasmus' sons we heard of in Darley Dale, whilst another became a doctor in Shrewsbury. We will leave it to Llewellyn to explain the relationships:

On 3rd of January 1795, Josiah Wedgwood died. By his wife, he had a family of eight children. The eldest, Susannah, baptised at Burslem, on the 2nd January 1765, married Dr Robert Darwin, son of Dr Erasmus Darwin, was the mother along with other sons and daughters of Charles Darwin, author of the Origin of Species.

The Wedgwoods – Llewellyn Jewitt

So the famous Charles Darwin had a paternal grandfather in Erasmus Darwin and maternal grandfather Josiah Wedgwood.

Antiquities

Llewellyn had a great interest in antiquities and this was fostered during his friendship with Thomas Bateman, a Peak District man, who we will meet shortly. It was during his prolific writing period, while at Winster, that he wrote several works about archaeology, such as: *Graves, Mounds and their Contents: A Manual of Archaeology as exemplified in the Burial of the Celtic, Romano-British and Anglo-Saxon period.*

Half-Hours Among Some English Antiquities was the title of another of his works that was written at Winster Hall. This book ran to a second edition and to give some idea of the detail, it is illustrated with 320 engravings. This book was Llewellyn's attempt to popularise antiquities. The preface to the first edition reads.

In the preparing this little manual I have endeavoured so to popularise the subject treated upon in its several chapters as to prevent them becoming 'dry' or wearisome to the reader. Whilst thus endeavouring to make then acceptable to the younger student, however, my object has been to impart such a tone to the 'half-hours' as will make the volume acceptable to those of more matured study, to whom it may, I trust, serve as a text-book for occasional reference.
Half-Hours Among Some English Antiquities – Llewellyn Jewitt

In addition to the antiquities, Llewellyn took a keen interest in historic houses. He wrote books, again with a large number of illustrations, about the stately homes of England and separate books about Chatsworth House and Haddon Hall, as they were both within easy reach of Winster. As typified by his roles in historical and museums societies, he took a great interest is his adopted county of Derbyshire. This is exemplified in a 'lighter' work as he draws together the traditional ballads and songs of Derbyshire.

We have selected one that was written by Leonard Wheatcroft in 1672, who was a teacher at Ashover which is a Derbyshire village. It is entitled, *An Elegy upon the Death of all the Greatest Gentry*. We have chosen a verse that refers to a place where we have visited so far on *The Literary Way*. It is Oker Hill that Wordsworth some 150 years later would describe. Berchoret is the old name for Birchover, a village close by Winster.

As I on Oaker-hill one-day did stand,
Viewing the world which I could not command,
I turn'd my face tou'rd Berchoret partly west,
To view where Greaveses us'd to have their nest ;
But out, alas ! I found they were all gone,
Not one was left to rest against a stone.
An Elegy upon the Death of all the Greatest Gentry – Leonard Wheatcroft

Private Poetry

Llewellyn, as we have seen, used his journalism and drawing skills combined with his historical knowledge to produce and edit many works. He rarely went that step further to enter the field of creative writing. When he did so it was only to produce a private publication with a circulation of 25.

Winster Church, the final resting place of Llewellyn Jewitt

It was a book of poetry which he called *Antennae*. It was dedicated to his family and friends and held a collection of poems of about 160 pages, mainly dedicated to 'poetic' subjects such as the seasons, and aspirations.

There is one poem that stands out as it is about a person that we have already mentioned on *The Literary Way*, and she would have been very much in the news as a local heroine during Llewellyn's time. It is, of course, Florence Nightingale. The poem comprises of 51 four line verses. The first half of the poem sets the scene of battle and conflict, so let's look at when he introduces Florence:

Woman to that scene of carnage,
To that field besmeared with gore,
Wends her quiet, gentle passage,
Lands upon that distant shore

As an angel fresh from heaven
Lights upon this sinful earth,
And refreshes by her presence
Those erewhile doom'd to pain and death,
Florence Nightingale – Llewellyn Jewitt

Llewellyn was well liked by his friends and known for his hospitality and clearly enjoyed inviting people to stay with his family. As we can see he grew in many directions throughout his career and became very respected both in terms of his archaeological knowledge as well as his succinct and illustrated way of writing.

Llewellyn was 70 when he died not long after being given a civil list pension. His wife had died a few months earlier. It is appropriate to finish our visit to Winster, Llewellyn's resting place, with a view of the church and its surrounding cemetery.

We then follow the path through the churchyard and over the fields to the ancient routeway called Portway. The lane continues after the Elton road down to the main road, where we can make a minor excursion to see a fascinating carving in the rock, at Hermit's Cave. It is estimated that it was carved around the fourteenth century. Hermits, at that time, often offered guidance to travellers and as a result local churches and manors would give them alms for their watchfulness. We then return to the road, and cross it, to join the path to Birchover. We round the hill and begin to come down into Birchover. We pass the vicarage and a small church. At the end of the lane we come out by the Druid Inn, and as the name suggests, it resounds with mysteries from the past. Just before the Druid Inn is the stile into Rowtor Rocks.

As we wander around these rocks with their captivating features and look at the view across the White Peak from them, let us understand a little background before we introduce our next author. The Vicarage that we have just passed was built on the site of the old Rowtor Hall, which had been built in the mid-1600s by Thomas Eyre. Later he added a private chapel, which is now the church. The hall had become derelict over the years and remained so for many years well into the nineteenth century. There are various rock carvings in Rowtor Rocks including 'armchairs' where it is believed Thomas would sit to write his sermons.

Lillian's Golden Hours

There is a Victorian children's book that uses Rowtor Rocks as one of its key settings. The book was written by Eliza Meteyard and published in 1857. Let's look at Eliza and then see how she placed Rowtor Rocks in her story.

She was born in Liverpool, but by the age of 17 she would be living in London. She worked for a short while for her brother, but she was determined to earn her own way in the world, so she set about writing for a living. One of Eliza's many fellow authors was Mary Howitt, who was a prolific writer in her own right and a good friend of Charles Dickens. We will find her involvement in *The Literary Way* when we are in Eyam. In Mary's autobiography, compiled by one of her family after her death, there is a letter from Mary to one of her friends. In the letter there is a reference to *The Doctor's Little Daughter* which was written by Eliza as a semi-biographical novel about her childhood.

Miss Eliza Meteyard, too, is with us. She is now a sufficiently old friend of ours for us all to feel perfectly at ease one with another. She has her work as well as we. Poor dear soul! she is sitting by me at this moment with her lips compressed, a look of abstraction in her clever but singular face, and her hair pushed back from her forehead, while she is busy over a story about a Bronze Inkstand, which she hopes to make a very fine one. A good creature is she! She has just published a most interesting juvenile book, called 'The Doctor's Little Daughter.' It is her own early life. Out of the money thus obtained, she has provided for and sent out a young brother to Australia; while for another she is striving in another way. Indeed, she is both father and mother to her family; yet she is only seven-and-twenty.
Mary Howitt – An Autobiography

As we know, Eliza Cook, who wrote about Dovedale, came from a poor family, and was determined to keep away from poverty by writing. Eliza Cook was two years younger than Eliza Meteyard. The two Elizas knew and supported each other in their writing. In fact, when Eliza Cook started her Journal the first article, excluding her own writings, was *Three Hyacinths before Heaven* by Silverpen. The pseudonym belonged to Eliza Meteyard.

Eliza Meteyard was a prolific and focused writer of children's and adult fiction as well as some notable factual books, such as, *The Life of Josiah Wedgwood: From his Private Correspondence and His Family*. She also wrote another book about the younger Wedgwoods, and a manual for collectors of Wedgwood. Her connections with the Wedgwood family, who we remember were joined in marriage to the Darwins, led to her sponsorship and success in obtaining a civil list pension. It was Charles Darwin who led the sponsorship that finally earned her a state pension.

In her fictional writing, she found suitable places to include her understanding of pottery making and the collection of valuable pieces. Her love of animals also comes across in her work, especially the children's novels which feature not only little girls, as the principal characters, but they have a full menagerie of pets. She also became very knowledgeable about antiquarian and prehistoric matters as we shall see on the next walk.

So let us turn to the children's tale set at Rowtor Rocks. The principal character in the book is the little girl called Lillian, who is the daughter of the local squire, and they live in the main house of the village. Our focus of attention is called Quarr rocks in the book and the ruined house that stands below them. This is part of Eliza's introduction to *Lillian's Golden Hours.*

The well-known Rowtor Rocks, in Derbyshire, and the Ruined House of Eyre at their base, are the true scene of this story, and gave me its first idea. I conceived that the former, with their natural passages and cavernous hollows,— and the latter, with its mournful century of ruin, made together an admirable locality for a child's story, as affording that due amount of romance which at once interests, and is effective as means for the instilment of educative truth. Apart from this, the story is purely ideal; and the general scenery that of the moorlands of Yorkshire.
Preface Lillian's Golden Hours – Eliza Meteyard

Within the novel there are various descriptions of the rocks, their caves and underground passages. They are introduced during a carriage ride.

The carriage winding round the side of these towards a low wall of stone, the Ruined House of Quarr, in all its solitude and desolation, came in view. A. garden fenced in by the wall, lay in front of it at the bottom of this garden were some neglected marish fishponds surrounded by leafless alders; at a little distance in a sort of paddock, stood an old grey lichen-covered chapel, and at the rear of the ruined hall, the narrow wall continuing, divided a strip of ground covered with turf, low shrubs, and ruins, from a bridle-road which ran at the foot of the rocks.
Preface Lillian's Golden Hours – Eliza Meteyard

Let's rest awhile at Birchover

There could not have been a better neighbourhood for Llewellyn, the founder and lifelong editor of the antiquarian journal, *The Reliquary*, to live. We have said that he and his family enjoyed hospitality and Llewellyn frequently invited learned and interested friends to a stay so that they could spend some days

Rock Armchairs, Rowtor Rocks

Rowtor Rocks

opening tumuli and other burial mounds belonging to the prehistoric inhabitants of these hills and dales.

It is towards some of these that we will head on the next walk. Eliza Meteyard turned herself into a professional writer and shows her skills in the varying areas of children's stories, adult novels and a number of non-fiction works, as well as numerous articles under her non-de-plume 'Silverpen'.

On this walk, we have covered two authors, the first Llewellyn because he lived in Winster for the latter part of his life, and the second Eliza, who wrote a book about Rowtor Rocks, which are about a mile away from Winster Hall.

Uncannily they were both born in the same year. Just a coincidence you might think, but in 1865 they both produced an in-depth book about the life of Josiah Wedgwood including his private correspondence. Also both books were dedicated to the same person, William Gladstone the future Prime Minister, but that is less remarkable as he had just opened the Wedgwood Centre in Burslem.

We can only find one reference, in Llewellyn's diary, to them ever meeting and that was two years before the Wedgwood books. It is brief and fairly uninformative.

1863 October 8th. — Went to see Eliza Meteyard (Silverpen). She was delighted to see me, and I staid some time with her.
The Life and Death of Llewellyn Jewitt – William Goss

The Barrow Knight

Birchover to Middleton-by-Youlgreave across Stanton Moor

Grey Tower built in celebration of the 1832 Reform Act

The Church Farm clock has a beautiful chime that makes you stop and listen. It is in the picturesque village of Middleton-by-Youlgreave. Our theme of the last walk, an author fascinated by antiquities, continues here, but what a different character! There are some people who stand out in a crowd of contemporaries because their interest turns into a passion, and he was one such man.

In the 1840s it took time, money and a great deal of ingenuity to be passionate about archaeology and so, on this walk we will try to understand the man who put so much drive and energy into his dedication for uncovering the knowledge of past times. A visiting Victorian journalist, unusually a young woman, visited the village for a factual interview and left with the inspiration to write a novel about what she had seen.

With these two walks about antiquities the most appropriate route is through the countryside that is littered with them, some of which have been clearly explained, while other have engendered mysteries. We will see cairns and laid out stones that have been there for centuries, but our first stop will be a gritstone tower. Antiquities are fine and honourable, but there is nothing like some scandal.

Reform

On Stanton Moor, a short distance from Birchover, is the Earl Grey Tower. This edifice was built by the local landowner to commemorate the passing of the 1832 Reform Act, which was a major step in changing the franchise districts in this country. The old 'rotten' boroughs, which only had a few people under the direction of a landowner, were abolished and the growing cities given far more of the elected members of parliament. But it is to the eponymous Charles Grey, the second Earl Grey, who was Prime Minister, when the Reform Act was passed, that we want to pay our attention.

As well putting his name to the tea, although its real origins are somewhat unclear, he was also a well-known name in London society.

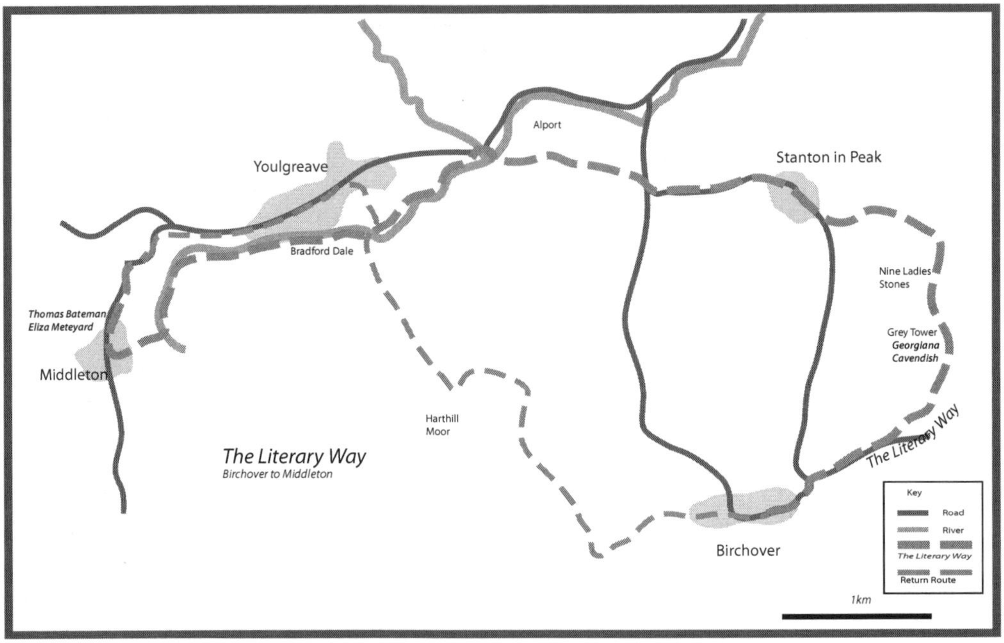

The Literary Way – Walk Ten – Birchover to Middleton-by-Youlgreave

Middleton Hall where Thomas Bateman's grandfather lived

Walk Directions

Birchover to Stanton-the-Peak (2.41 miles)

We take the road east from the Red Lion in Birchover
The road climbs the hill, turn right at the junction
There is a footpath on the left after the quarry
We take the path and then the right fork on the path
The path takes us to the Grey Tower
We pass the Tower and reach the Nine Ladies Stones
After the Stones we continue on the path to the road
We turn left onto the road and walk down to Stanton-the-Peak

Stanton-in-Peak to Alport (1.38 miles)

We continue on the road through Stanton
We pass the grounds of Stanton Hall
At the main road junction we cross and take the path opposite
This joins a quiet lane and we turn left
In a short distance we take the path to the right and leave the lane
The path diagonally crosses two fields
It then enters Alport and joins the road

Alport to Middleton (2.08 miles)

In a very short distance there is a footpath in front of us
We take it and cross the stream
We join the road and at the junction take the left path
This is the riverside path and we follow it to the footbridge
We then cross the stream and stay on the stream side path
We are now on the north side of the stream
Further on we recross the stream to the south side
We follow the wooded valley past the dams
At the end of the valley we cross the stream and take the right path
This leads us into Middleton
At the top of the path we enter the village square
Middleton Hall is along the left road from the square
We proceed to our right along the road
We pass the Chapel and Castle Farm
After the wooded bend is Lomberdale Hall.

Middleton to Birchover (4.08 miles)

We pass Lomberdale Hall and continue on the road until Youlgreave
At Youlgreave we turn right at the church towards Bradford Dale
We cross the stream at the bottom of the hill
Just after the small building there is a footpath on the left which we take
It crosses several fields in a south-easterly direction.
As we reach a steep part of a field the path bears to the left
The path divides and we go straight ahead over the wall
This takes us past Castle Ring and Harthill Moor Farm
We follow the path to the lane and join the path opposite
This crosses the fields towards the rocks called Robin Hood's Stride
We follow the path through the rocks and down to the road
We join the path opposite and it takes us round the hill and into Birchover

Distance: 9.94 miles Ascent: 1691ft

One of the centres of attraction of the fashionable sect was Devonshire House in London, with the hostess being the young Georgiana, Duchess of Devonshire. Charles Grey joined the throng and then pursued the married Georgiana relentlessly. Finally, he achieved his ambition, but it did not work out well for the Duchess as she became pregnant by Charles in 1791. When the Duke of Devonshire found out, she was sent away to mainland Europe to have the baby and it was taken away at birth and given to the Grey family to raise.

However, it was not Charles Grey that would be responsible for the baby, for he was soon committed to be married. He married Mary Ponsonby and they had sixteen children. The Duchess of Devonshire's illegitimate baby was Eliza Courtney. Georgiana could only occasionally see the child, who was not told who her mother was until after Georgiana's death, but she did write some poems about the enforced separation. Eliza Courtney went on to marry and named her first daughter, Georgiana. Sarah Ferguson, the Duchess of York is a descendant of Eliza Courtney.

And yet remote from public view
A flower there is of timid hue,
Beneath a sacred shade it grows,
But sweet in native fragrance blows.
From storms secure, from tempests free,
But ah! too seldom seen by me.
For scarce permitted to behold
With longing eyes each grace unfold.
My bosom struggles with its pain
And checks the wishes form'd in vain ;
Yet when I perchance supremely blest,
I hold the floweret to my breast,
Enraptur'd watch its purple glow
And blessings (all I have) bestow.
The gentle fragrance soothes my care
And fervent is my humble prayer
That no dread evil may beset
My sweet but hidden violet.
To Eliza Courtney – Georgiana Cavendish

We introduced the same Duchess of Devonshire at Cromford, where she was sought by the banker Richard Arkwright Junior, but we will save more details about her, including her authorship of a novel, until we reach Chatsworth.

As we leave the Earl Grey Tower we pass the Bronze Age Nine Ladies Stone, which English Heritage manage as a national monument. We then pass through Stanton-in-Peak and towards the confluence of the Lathkill and Bradford at Alport. We then enjoy the delightful walk, past the small dams with their metal sluices, along Bradford Dale.

Ten Years Digging

Middleton-by-Youlgreave is an old quaint village unspoilt by the modern trappings of the twenty-first century. As we come into the village near the church, we can hear the delightful chimes of the Church Farm clock, and we come out into the central square of the village. The limestone cottages neatly line the periphery, with the large buildings, and their mullioned windows, giving the historical ambience, which is complemented by the sleepy nature of this settlement. The village stands on a rise above Bradford Dale, along which we have just walked.

The man who is the focus of our attention in Middleton is Thomas Bateman, but before we look at the activities of Thomas, let's put him in the context of the village for which he and his family have left a clear legacy. He was born into a Derbyshire land- owning family, one of whose family seats was Middleton Hall, which is just along the road north west from the square in the village centre. Thomas's father died early and he was raised by his grandfather who lived at the Hall.

Around 1820 a lot happened for Thomas's grandfather. Not only did he have the benefit of his new grandson Thomas, but he also re-built Middleton Hall. As we have seen at Snelston and Ilam, it was a popular time for building, and as with the other two villages, he reshaped and remodelled some of the buildings in the village itself. This included the building of a Congregational Church just off from the village square. The living was determined by the grandfather who actively supported this church. However, the church itself does not have a graveyard with the exception on one elaborate railed grave. This is the resting place of Thomas Bateman who would only be 39 when he died.

Although he had a short life, it was one in which he packed a great deal and was not without its controversy. We can see the ambitions of Thomas early on, when at the age of 24, he decided that he would build his own hall in the village. Just out on the Youlgreave road is Lomberdale Hall.

Thomas's father, before his own early death, developed a keen interest in archaeology and opened a few of the local prehistoric burial mounds, with which the local area abounds. His young son accompanied him on some of the digs and was obviously taken with the excavations. His interest gradually increased, until it became his overwhelming passion particularly between 1848 and 1858, when he opened hundreds of barrows.

Let's first look at his archaeological work. His major writing for this period was a book entitled *Ten Years Diggings in Celtic and Saxon Grave Hills.* He confined himself mainly to local Derbyshire barrows, but he did have two loyal helpers who independently completed some excavations in nearby Staffordshire and near York. All the significant finds from all three counties were taken back to Lomberdale Hall, where Thomas displayed his collection. As was very much a tradition of the time, Thomas's book was dedicated to the local nobility, and in this case to Lady Adeliza Norman who was the daughter of the fifth Duke of Rutland.

Let's look at his approach to his digging at the local mound at Kenslow Barrow, which is near the road to Elton, and about a half a mile from Middleton. The opening of this particular barrow commenced on 1st February 1848. The previous opening in 1821 was by his father William Bateman.

We commenced re-opening the barrow upon Kenslow Knoll, which was formerly investigated by Mr William Bateman, in 1821, when it appears that the primary internment was discovered, and besides it, some other relics which indicated that there might still remain additional deposits in that part of the barrow that was not then disturbed. By taking a wide trench through the middle of the barrow from the outer edge , it became apparent that its convexity had chiefly been preserved by a border of large limestones placed with great regularity on the surface of the natural soil.
On clearing the area within them, many pieces of calcined flint and animal bones were picked up; also a splinter from a stone celt, a round piece of slaty sandstone that had been burned, and a crescent shaped ornament of bone having two perforations: the latter is precisely like the one found at the prior opening, and give the idea of a large canine tooth of a wolf split down the middle, being convex on one surface and level on the other, although in reality it is cut out of solid bone.
Ten years Diggings in Celtic and Saxon Grave Hills – Thomas Bateman

Thomas's methods came in for fierce criticism. It was said that he was too keen and his methods lacked a systematic approach. His work was at the time when the extensive opening of barrows was only in its infancy. Today's methods are vastly different, with much more care taken in the recording of the approach and details of the finds. Even so, Thomas became a celebrity in the archaeological circles, and a leading member of national bodies that were established around that time. However, he was his own individual man and often shunned attending conferences where he had been asked to speak. Also, he had a number of acquaintances he met through his digging, but many of these did not stand the test of time and he was often less than amiable towards visitors.

One such person he fell out with over some national society matters was the Reverend Stephen Isaacson. During any dig, various visitors and notaries were often present. Thomas would be supervising the excavation, but in keeping with the times, it would be the labourers who would be doing the physical work. This left time for the watchers to amuse themselves when nothing of interest was taking place. Extensive lunches and shelter would often be provided by people from the estate.

During one such period of inactivity, during a dig on the Staffordshire border at Wetton, Stephen Isaacson wrote a light poem about Thomas

Bateman and his digging, *Barrow Digging by the Barrow Knight*. It was a title by which Thomas would come to be known. When a dig was imminent, then all the notaries that were due to attend would assemble the night before at Thomas's Lomberdale Hall for dinner and to discuss the approach.

Till chat enthusiasm gave,
They'd a barrow digging go,
For each hillock sure must proved a grave,
Each pile of earth a low.

Quickly bring the barrow-tools,
Pick, shovel, scratcher, rules
Exhibit the deposit box
Which mine key alone unlocks.

Your lady beg to walk up hither
Tomorrow spite of wind or weather,
We take the field intent to hit on
Remains of Saxon or of Briton.
Barrow Digging by the Barrow Knight – Stephen Isaacson

Will he inherit?

The nearest town to Middleton is Bakewell and Thomas had a very mixed relationship with the people in that town. Before he built Lomberdale Hall, when he was a young man, he went to live in Bakewell. This caused his grandfather a considerable amount of distress because he lived with a local woman. But the old man would not be defeated, and when he finally died in his eighties, he left a caveat in his will. It was spelled out very clearly. If he did not cease his relationship with the local woman, within three months, then he would be disinherited from the entire estate, which was of a considerable size.

Thomas therefore made events happen very quickly. He proposed and was accepted by the daughter of one of his workers. It was the man who normally led the logistical operations and directly managed the physical digging. What happened to his previous lover is not known. The executors of his grandfather's will, accepted his marriage, and he inherited Middleton Hall and the estates as well as keeping his own, Lomberdale Hall. The building of his hall also caused controversy in Bakewell. The old church was in danger of collapse and it needed to be rebuilt. It is unclear how Thomas obtained a number of relics and stones from the church, and many criticised his underhand methods, but many of the church keepsakes were built into the fabric of Lomberdale Hall. At one point Thomas extended Lomberdale Hall just so that he could exhibit more of his collection, which gradually extended from the artefacts he had collected personally, to other historical goods and documents. The scale of his collection meant that he entertained many visitors who came to his house, as one would go to a museum.

Dora and Her Papa

We have learned in the last chapter about the writ-

Middleton Chapel, built by the Bateman family

ings of Eliza Meteyard. Her interest in historical information developed when she visited Middleton to meet with Thomas Bateman. It was a journalistic meeting, and whilst there Eliza observed Thomas and his family.

Many of Eliza's fictional works focused on servants and workers. She knew that Thomas had married one of his worker's daughters and felt that, with a few modifications, it would make a good story.

Dora and Her Papa was published in 1868 and featured Dora as a young child, who goes everywhere with her widowed father, who is an archaeologist. In the same village, there is a niece who acts as a working companion to her old aunt. The niece takes an interest and becomes friends with little Dora. The book fits into children's range of books that were written by Eliza. She used her knowledge of Thomas Bateman and his methods in the story. In this extract father and daughter are going on a barrow dig.

A cloth had been spread on the sward, and on it set cold meat, pasties, bread cheese and beer. Old David laid aside his notebook and ink-horn and carved for the men; whilst away in the tent, which had been set up in a green hollow, Mr Flaxdale and his friends and Dora dined too. As the little girl looked sleepy when her dinner was done, and the gentlemen had yet to smoke cigars and drink their wine, her papa made her up a nice little bed with carriage cushions and coats and placed her therein most tenderly, promised not to let the diggers proceed until she awoke; for Dora was very anxious to see what other curious things had been buried in this old cairn – hallowed by the solemn passage of some many years

Dora and Her Papa – Eliza Meteyard

Lomberdale Hall, the home of Thomas Bateman

Early Death

Although Llewellyn Jewitt and Thomas Bateman would be born within four years, and knew each other very well, because they shared the same enthusiasm for the remains of ancient cultures, they were never to be neighbours. The Barrow Knight from Middleton died early at the age of thirty-nine. Llewellyn did not move into Winster Hall until after Thomas's death. However, in the year before Thomas suddenly died, Llewellyn had launched the *Reliquary Journal – A Depository of Precious Relics – Legendary, Biographical, and Historical.*

The opening year saw five articles by Llewellyn, three by Thomas and two by Eliza Meteyard. It would be the second volume of the *Reliquary* that would carry the lengthy obituary of Thomas Bateman written by Llewellyn.

Since the publication of the last Reliquary the literary and antiquarian world has sustained a severe and irreparable loss in the death of that well known antiquary Thomas Bateman Esq of Lomberdale House, and Middleton Hall, in the county of Derby; a gentleman whose name has for years been "as familiar as a household word" to the learned men of all counties, and whose Museum of Antiquities – unrivalled in many if its branches by any collection in existence – has been constantly referred to and made use of by eminent writers in every branch of history and antiquities. Knowing Mr Bateman intimately as a truly dear and personal friend for many years, it is indeed to us a matter of the deepest pain to announce his decease.

The Late Thomas Bateman Esq of Lomberdale House, and Middleton-by-Youlgreave – Llewellyn Jewitt

Let's rest awhile in Middleton

The walk through the village of Middleton reflects on Thomas Bateman. There is the old Hall where the grandfather lived, who so nearly cut Thomas out of his inheritance. We then encounter the Chapel with Thomas's grave and his memorial behind it. As we neared the edge of the settlement we reach Lomberdale House, which he built. But the fortunes he built were not to last long, for his son would lose all his money and estate and the collection would be sold off.

Eliza Meteyard, closely associated with both Llewellyn Jewitt and Thomas Bateman, was a hard-working writer who earned her living from her works, which spanned serious historical articles to children's novels. But *The Literary Way* is not finished with Eliza Meteyard yet, as she will be with us to help us unravel where history and fiction merge.

A Gothic Elopement

Middleton-by-Youlgreave to Haddon Hall

Haddon Hall – the home of Dorothy Vernon

What can be better than a good walk through one of the most picturesque dales in the Peak District National Park to a castellated manor. In addition, the historic house is rife with literary connections, and has a wonderful mixture of fact and fiction.

On this walk there is still more. From the quiet dale, and the medieval house, we have links with the USA that span from the puritans of the seventeenth century to the flamboyance of the twentieth century. But we begin with a man who was sent to jail for his beliefs and who lived in an isolated dale, at an outpost of an old abbey. One of his friends, with whom he exchanged letters regularly, became one a founding father of the United States of America. The freedom of speech exemplified by the new nation percolated down to the prisoner's descendants, one of whom, became one of Parliament's most powerful orators, and was remembered over a hundred years later by an American President.

A quaint village overlooks a dale and has a fine old church with an interesting sundial, which links us back to the seventeenth century and one of the fishing friends that we met on *The Literary Way*.

We leave Middleton-by-Youlgreave along the road past Thomas Bateman's Lomberdale Hall. Our route goes up and across the fields towards a farm and behind it to the wooded valley. A steep tree-covered slope takes us down into Cales Dale, and shortly, we will follow the stream in this delightful dale, but first, we follow the path up the other side until we reach One Ash Grange Farm, which is about one mile outside of the small village of Monyash.

A Pioneering Preacher

We must go back a good while in history to understand the origins of One Ash Grange. It was originally a Cistercian Monk's building for Roche Abbey, which is situated near Doncaster. Between 1100 and 1538 monasteries flourished in England and they held a large amount of land. Roche, compared to many, was relatively small, but still held

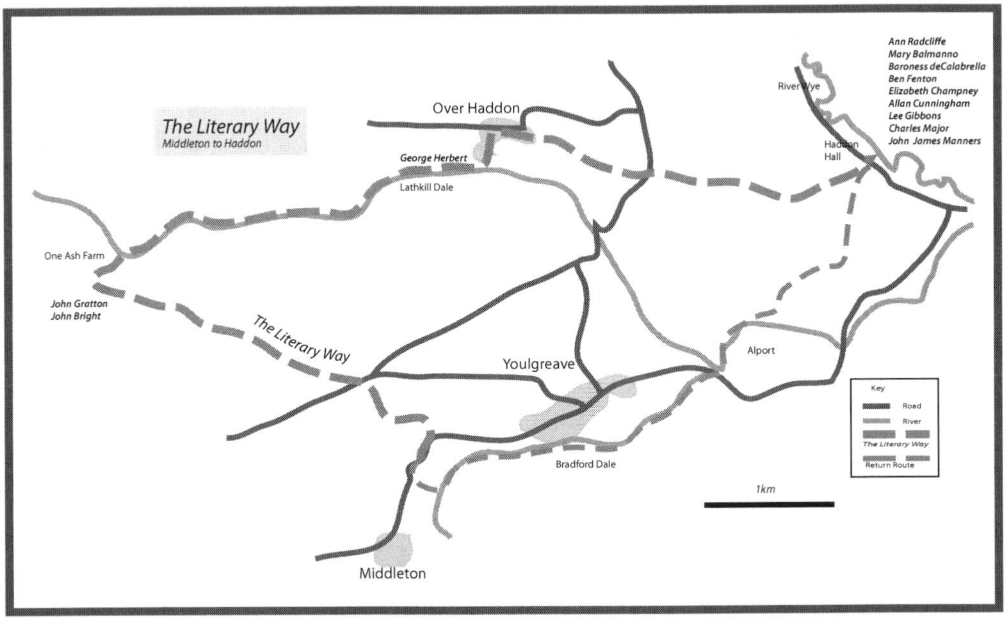

The Literary Way – Walk Eleven – Middleton-by-Youlgreave to Haddon Hall

Tufa Falls in Lathkill Dale

Walk Directions

Middleton to One Ash Grange (2.14 miles)

On the bend of the road just past Lomberdale Hall we take the footpath on the left.
It crosses a small field and comes out on a lane, we turn left
A little way along the lane, just past the bend, there is a footpath on the right
This takes us across several small fields to a lane where we turn left
At the road junction the path goes straight ahead (It is the Limestone Way)
We aim for the farm, the path goes round the buildings and through the wood
The path bears right diagonally across the fields
It then takes a sharp drop into Cales Dale
We go down the path to the footbridge over the stream
One Ash Grange is at the top of the path opposite

One Ash Grange to Over Haddon (2.42 miles)

We retrace our steps to the bottom of Cales Dale and turn left
This takes us down the path towards Lathkill Dale
As it opens up, there is a footbridge, which we cross and turn right
The screes slopes are very evident here
The path takes us along the north bank
The tufa falls are on the right (they may be dry in summer)
Bateman's House is on the right over a footbridge
The ruined Engine House is on the left
We come to the first house and a road
We take the road to the left uphill
This brings us into Over Haddon
The church with its sundial is on the right

Over Haddon to Haddon Hall (1.94 miles)

We turn right through Over Haddon and take any of the right side roads
This leads us past the pub, The Lathkil Hotel
We pass the pub and take the footpath straight on
Ignore the path to the left and carry on across the fields
It reaches a lane which we cross
Then there is a small field and another track which we cross
The path then skirts the wall on the left
We cross the stile and a small field, and another stile
The path then crosses the field diagonally, aim just right of the trees
We join a track and turn left
We then get the first sight of Haddon Hall
The track takes us down to the Hall

Haddon Hall to Middleton (3.4 miles)

We leave the Hall and re-cross the road.
In front of us is the track on which we arrived
At 45 degrees to the left is another path which we take
It goes up the hill across the fields
The stile is in the very top corner of the field
The path then goes diagonally across the next field
Aim for the left edge of the woods
Follow the path to the right around the edge of the woods
After the first field the path goes along a fence which is the edge of the quarry
Follow the path through the woods
The path goes diagonally down hill across the field
It then straightens in a small valley which takes us down to the road
We come out on the road and turn right along the pavement
This brings us into Alport
We take the riverside path on our left
This is the Bradford Stream
We follow the path through Bradford Dale back to Middleton

Distance: 10.4 miles Total Ascent: 1655ft

over 120 different sites throughout the Midlands and one as far away as Sussex. In 1538, Henry VIII abolished the monasteries and the land was transferred to the Tudor monarchy.

We will stay with the religious theme, for in 1642, John Gratton was born, and in his twenties, he moved to One Ash Grange. However, his taken religion was of a very different form to the monastic system, although he was as devout as the monks. John rejected the local Anabaptists and became an evangelical convert to the Quakers and began to travel widely in the local area. But his evangelical calling wasn't popular with the authorities. Even with the more relaxed attitudes of the Restoration period, the same time as William Congreve explored with his plays, John Gratton was a step too far, and he was imprisoned for his nonconformist approach. This is what he wrote from Derby jail where he described himself as a prisoner for the sake of truth.

Dear brethren,
I can truly say I am with you in spirit; and my love springs freshly to you, and I should be glad to be with you personally, but could not get leave; so as a token of my dear love and true unity unto you and with you, it was in my heart thus to write. In this I remain your dear friend and brother.

Everlasting praises be given to our God forever. Amen.
Written in Derby jail, where I am a prisoner for the Truth's sake.

John Gratton
22nd of the Third month, 1683
Journal of the Life of John Gratton – John Gratton

John became a significant character in the Quaker Movement of the time and one very close religious colleague was William Penn, who was one of the founding fathers of the United States. The state of Pennsylvania was named after him. As we can see from one of the letters from William, it is about wishing John to get well after an illness and suggests his own medicine.

William Penn to John Gratton
To William Storr in Chesterfield for J. Gratton Darbyshire.

Lond. 21.6.95.
Dr John, My unfeigned dear love salutes and embraces thee. Know, I had both thy dear letters at my coming to Town, and still hold my resolution, if the Lord will, in a month or 6 weeks, if I can, and I hope by that time to be at liberty. My way will be from Bucks to Northampton and so the road to Notts, of which may inform thee. I rejoice thou art better. If thou canst, drink Garlic boiled in milk, or an handful of Ivory shavings — boiled in clear

Bateman's House with its underground view of draining the lead mines

white wine posset, drink it, and, then drink the posset drink (a pint). I hope thy jaundice will be cured. So with my dear love to thee, thyn and Friends, I close, with deep owings of my dear love, and prayers for thy preservation I am Thy assured friend.
W. P.
To John Gratton – William Penn

John moved from Monyash in the last period of his life to be cared for by his daughter, Phoebe. We can note, with interest, that her married name was Bateman which, of course we have come across in Middleton. One famous descendant of John Gratton was John Bright, who although several generations later, named his new house in Rochdale in memory of Monyash and John Gratton. It is claimed that he frequently visited his relatives in Monyash.

He gave it (his Rochdale house) the name of One Ash, in honour of an ash-tree which was a conspicuous feature in the garden, and in memory of his favourite ancestor John Gratton.
The Life of John Bright – George Macaulay Trevelyan

John Bright was part of the new commercial class that had arisen in the wake of the Industrial Revolution. Originally he was a factory owner from Rochdale, but later he was elected to Parliament as an MP. He became famous as one of the orators who campaigned for the abolition of the Corn Laws, which established tariffs for the price of wheat. Those on the side of the workers in the factories believed that, if prices were allowed to fall, then the working people would have more income to spend on clothes and other essentials. To be against the Corn Laws at the time, was to support the notion of Free Trade.

John Bright campaigned for a long time until the laws were successfully repealed. Whilst famous in his own time, along with his colleague Richard Cobden, he is perhaps little known today, until he was brought to much higher recognition by Ronald Reagan, when he was President of the United States. The President in a speech said that Richard Cobden and John Bright were two of the most important advocates of free-trade in the history of commerce. As we know from Darley Dale, John Bright was a lifelong friend of Joseph Whitworth, and as a speech maker greatly impressed Nat Gould.

We leave One Ash Grange and begin what is a fascinating walk along Lathkill Dale. It is important to look for the details of the past as well as the creatures and flora of today. The high limestone crags are becoming more noticeable by this time. As the valley deepens even more, there is, on our left, a high and very majestic limestone crag with the layered beds of limestone and numerous scree falls of rocks and boulders. As we reach the point, where another valley joins from the left, the nature of the landscape changes quite considerably. We are now walking along the valley floor with the river on our right. This is another of the examples of limestone water flows. If the river is full, see if you can work out where all the water comes from. It is not obvious. There is a small spring, but it is not sufficient to give the amount of water in the main river. It is an area of several intermittent streams that, dependent on the rainfall, either flow on the surface or make various subterranean routes.

The valley is heavily wooded on both sides. The path takes us through the woods. This is a remarkably different scene at each season in the year. During winter and spring, the river is dominant. This is typified as it flows over a small natural waterfall. It is about two metres high, but is the width of the river. It is made of a resistant rock called tufa, which is a calcareous deposit from the shoreline of an ancient lake. During a dry period the waterfall, if it exists at all, is covered with vegetation.

The remaining weirs, and other water features, are all man-made. In some places, there are small dams that form typical millponds behind them, and in other places there are small sluices. During the winter months many of the trees have lost their leaves and so we can see further, both down and across the valley. The contrast, is at the end of a normal summer period, when the valley is luxuriant and the path in some places follows a tree-lined tunnel. The waterfall and weirs have practically dried up and there is a bed of vegetation that entirely covers the upper stretches of the water in the river.

It is hard to believe that this valley was almost completely clear of woodland during the peak of lead mining in the eighteenth century. If that seems surprising, it is thought that the valley was cleared in prehistoric times, about 4000 years ago, but woodland had regained the area by the seventeenth century. The main lead vein called Mandale Rake is further along the valley and there are various remnants of the attempts to mine the area, including the channels, called soughs, which were used to try to drain water from the working areas. Before we reach the remains of the Mandale Rake activities, there are some relics of mining in Palmerston Wood. The mine here not only found lead, but also produced chert, a flint-like mineral.

We then catch sight of the remains of a small house on the other side of the river. It is called Bateman's House and is a former lead agent's house that has been built over the pumping system for draining the workings. It is possible to descend steep steps to see down into the shaft with the water flowing at the bottom. It is quite eerie in the small rock cavern which, even in the height of summer, is cold and damp. The only sounds which echo on the rocks are the flowing water that we can see below.

We pass many caves and old shafts on our way along the path and there is one final dramatic structure that we come across. It is the old Engine House for the mine. It is a large structure tucked away from the valley floor and is now well set with the luxuriant green growth around it.

We eventually reach the first house in the valley and it is at the bottom of a lane that comes down from Over Haddon. A climb up the road takes us to the small village of Over Haddon and to its church. There is an inscription on the sun-dial on the south facing wall.

Sundial

The inscription is the last verse in a poem called *Mattens* by George Herbert. It was part of a larger collection of his poems published in about 1640, called *The Temple*. The full collection went through thirteen editions by 1680. George Herbert was born in 1593 and after a short, but distinguished spell at Cambridge University, he became an MP. But with the accession of Charles I, in 1625, he decided to enter the clergy and eventually gained a living near Salisbury. Most of his poetry is devotional and he was the subject of a biography by one of the characters we have already encountered on the walk, Isaac Walton. He was always in weak health and died aged 40. Here is the full Mattens poem.

I cannot ope mine eyes,
But Thou are ready there to catch
My morning soul and sacrifice:
Then we must needs for that day make a match.

My God, what is a heart?
Silver, or gold, or precious stone,
Or starre, or rainbow, or a part
Of all these things, or all of them in one?

My God, what is a heart?
That Thou shouldst it so eye and wooe,

Over Haddon Church Sundial with the George Herbert verse

Powring upon it all Thy art,
As if that Thou hadst nothing else to do?

Indeed, a man's whole estate
Amounts, and richly, to serve Thee:
He did not heav'n and earth create,
Yet studies then, by Him by Whom they be.

Teach me thy love to know
That this new light that now I see
May both the work and the workman show
Then by a sunne-beam I will climb to thee.
Mattens – George Herbert

We leave Over Haddon by going past the pub and taking a path across the fields towards the small hillock. Having crossed by the tumulus we descend along the path into the Wye valley.

Gothic

The first glimpses are the crenellated tops of a building. Trees surround it, but the parts of it that we can see make us think of a castle. Let's set the scene with William Adam, whose book, *Gem of the Peak*, details a day out in early Victorian times, about 1837.

The sun was fast declining in the 'far west' when we attained the eminence near Haddon. This relic of by-gone age, with its weather-beaten towers and battlements, we observed peering from amidst the thick foliage, its numerous turrets and windows gleaming in the sun light; and being in part strongly shaded by its umbrageous envelope, it presented a fine object for the pencil. The situation of Haddon is pre-eminently beautiful. It stands on a shelving, a rather elevated mass of the finest limestone, overlooking the entire dale and its meandering and lovely Wye, backed by extensive woods and surrounded by majestic trees. At first sight it has more the appearance of an old fortress than what it really is, a Hall, chiefly in the Elizabethan style, and without any effectual defences, as we shall show by the following remarks, which we beg to make while we contemplate this interesting structure - a structure which assisted the imagination of Mrs Radcliffe in its wildest flights, when writing the Mysteries of Udolpho.
Gem of the Peak – William Adam

The view of the hall gradually disappears into the trees as we go further down the hill. Haddon Hall is a fortified medieval manor house dating from the twelfth century, and is the home of Lord Edward Manners, whose family have owned it since 1567. The house is part of the estate of the Duke of Rutland.

The gate-house which is hidden behind the bushes on the far side of the road, gives us entry into the Hall's grounds. The main tower is on a slight rise to our right. After we have passed over the bridge, the stable block is directly in front of us and to our left is a cottage embellished with wisterias and fronted with topiary.

An immediate impression on passing through the tower gate and into the bare flagged courtyard is that this building will be very different to many historic houses that are open to the public. Its bleakness gives the idea of what it would have been like to live here, when it was at its prime. The chapel

The Courtyard at Haddon Hall

and the kitchens we found the most fascinating, for they demonstrate the Hall's feeling and ambience.

Inside the main door from the courtyard, we go down a narrow passage to the kitchens. The troughs, ovens and well-worn work surfaces are clear evidence of a formerly busy working kitchen, but they hold the realism of the working methods and conditions that were prevalent over the centuries. The Chapel, one of the oldest parts of the Hall, is entered from the corner of the courtyard. The whole of this small Chapel gives a feeling of great antiquity and, with the dates ascribed to it being fourteenth and fifteenth century, one can begin to understand the barrenness and harshness of those days. The contrast with the Chapel is the far more recent Long Gallery. This is much lighter and airier and is where the ladies of the house would take their exercise during the inclement weather. Let's continue our impression of Haddon Hall and pick up on William Adam's reference to 'Mrs Radcliffe.'

Horace Walpole, in 1764, published *The Castle of Otranto,* which was to define a new Gothic genre in literature. It would go in and out of literary fashion as times changed, but there has always been a dedicated few who follow it.

By coincidence, in the same year as the genre was defined, Ann Ward was born. By her mid twenties, she had taken her married name of Radcliffe, and developed the form of the Gothic novel. She took isolated Italian castles and gave them a mixture of the sinister and supernatural. To this she added innocent young women and the subsequent romances. It is thought that she did not travel to the mountains of Italy where *The Mysteries of Udolpho* is set but used a combination of her imagination and the English settings that she had seen.

Anne Radcliffe had many connections with Derbyshire and she visited the area many times. There is no direct evidence about her visiting Haddon, but she certainly visited the county, and her mother is buried at Wheston, near Tideswell, which is about ten miles from Haddon. She saw many castles and houses in the south of England, where she lived, and quite possibly blended several of them together to reach the images in her book. This is one of her descriptions.

The sun had just sunk below the top of the mountains she was descending, whose long shadow stretched athwart the valley, but his sloping rays, shooting through an opening in the cliffs, touched with a yellow gleam the summits of the forest, that hung upon the opposite steeps, and streamed in full splendour upon the towers and battlements of a castle, that spread its extensive ramparts along the brow of a precipice above....
The Mysteries of Udolpho – Ann Radcliffe

The Romance of the Forest, published in 1791 and *The Mysteries of Udolpho,* 1794, established her as a leading writer of her time. As we see in many areas of literature, names and genres can become almost forgotten in future generations, but were the height of popularity at the time and many would have an indirect lasting effect. Anne Radcliffe, although not well-known today, has had a significant impact on writers in different areas that came after her. The Romantic poets, including, Byron drew from her work. In contrast, Jane Austen offers a parody on *The Mysteries of Udolpho* in *Northanger Abbey.* The heroine of the story has been reading Anne's novel, when she is invited to Northanger Abbey and builds the picture of a dark and sinister Gothic location. Another famous writer who clearly respected the work of Ann was Sir Walter Scott.

It is easy to see how, when standing in the courtyard, with its flagstones, grey walls and turreted towers, it inspired Anne. Especially when this is combined with the view of the house as it emerges from the trees, when seen from the hill opposite.

A Local Lass

William Adam goes on to quote 'the beautiful and touching lines' from the magazine *Bijou* in 1828. It should be taken in the context that Haddon Hall was unoccupied for most of the nineteenth century, and it therefore benefited from missing out on the early nineteenth century changes that we have become aware of at many of the country seats on our journey.

Haddon, within thy silent halls,
Deserted courts, and turrets high,
How mournfully on memory falls
Past scenes of antique pageantry.
Haddon Hall – Mary Hudson Balmanno

Mary Hudson was born in Matlock, just down the road from Haddon in 1802. She married a Scottish historian, Robert Balmanno, from Aberdeen and moved to the United States of America where she settled with her family for the rest of her life.

The poem, *Haddon Hall,* appeared in the *Bijou* Magazine in 1828, under the pseudonym initials HB. Her husband Robert is credited with supplying some of the illustrations for the magazine, which contained contributions from some of the leading writers of the time, such as Samuel Taylor Coleridge and Robert Southey. Perhaps as a result of Robert's involvement it also had many aspects about Scotland.

Mary continued a light Scottish theme, when in 1858, she published *Pen and Pencil,* which was a collection of engravings, poems and articles, with the first chapter focusing on Mary, Queen of Scots. As with many publications of the day, the list of those who subscribed to it is contained at the front and this included both the Duke of Rutland and the Duke of Devonshire.

In *Pen and Pencil* Mary Balmanno included both a

The medieval Chapel at Haddon Hall

descriptive account of Haddon Hall and the poem *Haddon Hall* that she had released thirty years earlier. Mary also produced a memoir and selected works of Thomas Moore who lived on *The Literary Way* at Mayfield.

The Italian Baroness

Catherine Ball Hughes is not normally the type of name we would associate with an Italian baroness. You might well think she married into the title, but no, Catherine did have three husbands, but none of Italian descendent. After the death of the last of them, she brought a property in Italy and with it a title. After that she was known as Baroness de Calabrella. She came from a rich family and was a self-styled socialite in the court of the Prince Regent, who then became George IV. She was also an author of many titles, one of which was *Haddon Hall.* It is an unusual book, in that following the introduction, where a group of people meet at Haddon Hall, each tells a story. The first one sets the tone and it's about a knight's tournament, but it has no direct connection with Haddon. It is similar in style to P G Patmore's *Chatsworth,* which we introduced at Matlock Bath. The stimulus for the stories come from a set of drawings and engravings.

It is, then, to Haddon Hall, with its noble recollections, its happy associations, and the still happier promises and prophecies of what may belong to its future destiny, — that we desire the reader to accompany us in imagination, while we endeavour to place before him, in a light worthy their unequalled beauty, results of the pictorial art which nothing but scenes and social institutions like those of Haddon in the olden time could have inspired, and which, in the presence of more modern localities and associations, would lose half their interest, and all that dignified propriety and appropriateness which are the crowning graces high art.
Haddon Hall – Baroness Calabrella

A Tourist from Sheffield

Benjamin Fenton was a merchant from Sheffield and his father was a colonel in the local volunteers. Ben wrote only occasional verse and the poems were often published in a local magazine. His sole collection, simply entitled *Poems,* was published in 1843. He lived in Sheffield and many of the works are the result of his visits to different locations and his observations.

In his book there is a poem entitled *Haddon Hall.* The reason for him writing this poem he gives as a preface to the work.

The Author of the present lines had gone with some near relatives to visit the scenes of which they are the recordance. He had been so often within the walls, that whilst his party, to whom it was new, explored the interior, he remained to perambulate without; he did so, till, weary of waiting, he bethought himself of scribbling, on the ruins around, a sonnet – usually understood to consist of fourteen lines.

How far, what he them commenced, has swelled beyond his original intention, the piece will shew. He offers no excuse; they who were with him, wished him to print the lines, to put them in a more legible form, and he has been obedient to their wish. Those who like the subject, may probably excuse the lines; those who like neither, will of course, in the reading, deem their time misspent.
Haddon Hall – Benjamin Fenton

Two of our last three contributors have been local people, Benjamin Fenton came from Sheffield, just to the north east of the Peak District, and Mary Balmanno came from Matlock, but moved to the USA, and it's now time to pick up another thread of our American theme.

The Vassar Girls

Elizabeth Champney graduated from Vassar College in the USA in 1869. The College still exists today and is a top co-educational liberal arts college, situated in the Hudson Valley to the north of New York City. It was founded 1861 as a women's college.

Lizzie, as she preferred to be known, toured Europe extensively and wrote 'travelogue novels' about the experience of three young American ladies following similar tours. The books cover many parts of Europe and also include visits to South America. She also wrote a number of 'romance' books. The touring books were known as the "Three Vassar Girls" novels.

In 1884 she wrote, *A Holiday Excursion of Three College Girls through the Mother* Country. In addition to her view of Haddon, we shall also let Elizabeth

Champney tell you the story of a famous elopement that took place from Haddon Hall.

The King of the Peak, the last of the name of Vernon who owned the castle, had two daughters, Margaret and Dorothy. Margaret was betrothed with her parent's consent to the son of the Earl of Derby; but Dorothy had formed an attachment, for some reason not approved by her father, for young John Manners, son of the Earl of Rutland. On the very night of the marriage of the elder daughter, John Manners, who had been lurking about the place for some days in the disguise of a forester, caused his horses to be brought to the confines of the park, and just when the merriment in the castle was at its height, when the beacons blazed on the turrets, the tables in the great hall groaned with wassail, and the minstrels were playing their gayest wedding march, Dorothy, stealing out of the banqueting hall, joined her lover at the foot of this terrace.

Holiday Excursion of Three College Girls through the Mother Country – Elizabeth Champney

This has introduced the famed elopement which many associate with Haddon Hall. As with many of these old stories, the exact facts can often be questioned, but it does add to the Gothic nature of the Hall.

The Love Steps of Dorothy Vernon

Before we continue with our trans-Atlantic theme let us return to our antiquarian writers in this country. We have already said, on *The Literary Way,* that Eliza Meteyard contributed to Llewellyn Jewitt's first edition of *The Reliquary,* the antiquarian journal. Her very first article was called *The Love Steps of Dorothy Vernon.*

In modern-day parlance we would call the article a dramatic reconstruction interpreting such facts as are available. However, along with Eliza and Llewellyn, let's not be too pedantic about the mixture of fact and fiction as it is such a wonderful story that still endures to this day. The opening of Eliza's contribution sets the tone. It was written in 1860.

Three centuries are nearly past and gone, three hundred gilded summers have waned into russet autumns – and autumns brought their winters rough and cold – and yet no drear oblivion has fallen on a sweet old story; it is as new as though of yesterday, and hallows Haddon Hall.

The Love Steps of Dorothy Vernon – Eliza Meteyard

Two Kings of the Peak?

Eliza was not, however, the first writer to dramatise the elopement of Dorothy Vernon. About 1820, there were two publications, one a journal article and the other a novel in three volumes, and both were called *The King of the Peak.*

Let's look at the journal article first. It was written by a Scot who had an interesting career. Allan Cunningham wrote his interpretation of the story of Dorothy, in an article called *The King of the Peak,* which was published in *The London Magazine.*

Allan was born in a remote part of southern Scotland, and it was under the influence of his father, who had been a neighbour of Robbie Burns, that he gained an interest in poetry. At first, he com-

Haddon Hall Kitchens

bined writing a few verses with an apprenticeship as a stone-mason. But like many young men, the bright life of London attracted him, and so at the age of 26, he moved to the city, where he was fortunate to change careers, and he became a journalist. This lasted for four years and then he took the role of the clerk of works at the studio of the sculptor Francis Chantry. It was a job he would keep for the next 26 years.

During that time he also published several novels and non-fiction works such as, *The Lives of Eminent British Painters, Sculptors, and Architects.* Allan's apprenticeship as a stone mason stood him in good stead and it is believed that he assisted Francis on some of his works. Francis was a prolific sculptor and there are many key examples of his works in the major cathedrals and squares in this country and abroad.

So how do we get a Scotsman, his employer, a famous sculptor, linked with Haddon Hall. Francis Chantry was born into a family lacking money in the village of Norton, which at that time was in Derbyshire, about four miles outside of Sheffield. It has now been subsumed as part of the City.

Although Francis went to London as a young man, he retained a friendship in Sheffield which would have brought him to Haddon. His friend was Ebenezer Rhodes, who was at one time a Master Cutler, and later the editor of the *Sheffield Independent*, but, above all, he is known for one book called *Peak Scenery,* which was published in 1819. And as you might well have guessed, the drawings for the book were completed by Francis Chantry and they include a very notable one of Haddon Hall. This is the dedication at the beginning of *Peak Scenery:*

The author cannot close these introductory observations without acknowledging his obligations to Mr. Chantry, the artist, whose Sketches of the Peak Scenery of Derbyshire, so essentially contribute to illustrate and embellish the following pages. Remote as this interesting part of the kingdom is from his present residence, he has repeatedly visited it, uninfluenced by considerations of expense, for the purpose of making a series of drawings for this production, which have been gratuitously presented to the writer, as a token of his friendship, and a mark of his attachment to his native county. To say more on this subject might be useless; to say less would be ungrateful.
Peak Scenery – Ebenezer Rhodes

Allan Cunningham produced poems and articles on a regular basis during his period with Francis. We have chosen a short extract, from *The King of the Peak,* to show what Haddon was like at the time.

Those who have never seen Haddon Hall, the ancient residence of the Vernons of Derbyshire, can have but an imperfect notion of the golden days of old England. Though now deserted and dilapidated — its halls silent — the sacred bell of its chapel mute — though its tables no longer send up the cheering smell of roasted boars, and spitted oxen — though the music and the voice of the minstrel are silenced, and the light foot of the dancer no longer sounds on the floor — though no gentle knights and gentler dames go trooping hand in hand, and whispering among the twilight groves — and the portal no longer sends out its shining helms, and its barbed steeds; — where is the place that

Long Gallery, Haddon Hall

can recall the stately hospitality and glory of former times, like the Hall of Old Haddon ?
The King of the Peak – Allan Cunningham

Allan's *King of the Peak* appeared in the magazine a month after a poem about the same topic, the elopement of Dorothy Vernon, which was called *The Seven Foresters of Chatsworth,* again written by Allan. Not much unusual about that you may think, but let's now look at the Preface of the other *King of the Peak,* by Lee Gibbons.

In February, 1822, having a mind to fix upon some work of this kind, I visited Haddon and the adjacent country, to lay in a stock of materials, and returned to my cottage with a tolerable budget full of particulars. On entering my study, I found on the table The London Magazine for that month, which, as I then thought, unfortunately, contained an article, a poem, and a very fine one, called "The Seven Foresters of Chatsworth," which embraced my very subject. I found, on perusing it, which I did several times over, and every time with renewed pleasure, that the author had forestalled part of my tale, that he had visited and beautifully described my scenery, drawn some of my characters, and altogether had written a much finer ballad than any which had appeared in modern times. In faith, Sir, this discovery staggered me no little, and I began to be somewhat mortified, not only that my subject was pre-ingrossed, but that I had been at the expense and trouble of a journey at that time of the year, which was likely to be of no service.
The King of the Peak – Lee Gibbons

However, the reticence expressed by Lee did not hold him back for long, as his three-volume version was published the following year in 1823.

Just to add to the mystery a little more, Lee Gibbons was a pseudonym and while there are a couple of likely names for the real author, it has only recently been clarified. We will return to Lee later on *The Literary Way.*

When Knighthood was in Flower

Let's return to our trans-Atlantic theme to meet an American writer, who also used the events of the elopement of Dorothy Vernon in one of his novels. Charles Major was born in Indianapolis in 1856, and to put this date into a historical context, the Crimean War ended in that year, and in the United States, tensions were becoming strained. These would lead to the American Civil War by the time Charles Major was five years old. In adult life, he became a successful lawyer, but his interest was always in literature and so, in 1898, he published his first novel.

It was set in the times of Henry VIII, and was entitled, *When Knighthood was in Flower.* It would go on to make his name famous throughout the United States. It was a romantic novel and the readers took a liking to it. This made it a good subject for the growing theatrical audiences and it was turned into a play and performed on Broadway.

Charles, following his first success, carried on his historical romantic theme, and in 1902, *Dorothy Vernon of Haddon Hall,* was published. It is a good swashbuckling story with Charles adding extra characters to the main historical participants. He also made some changes to the historical facts, for example, he portrayed Elizabeth I and Mary Queen of Scots visiting Haddon, which did not actually take place. In the epilogue to his book he does detail the changes he made to historical events and the extra characters he added.

In this scene, from *Dorothy Vernon of Haddon Hall,* Dorothy's father had imprisoned her and so she put on the clothes of one of her male friends:

Dorothy's disguise was so complete and her resemblance to me had been so well contrived that she met with no opposition from the guards in the retainer's room nor from the porter. She walked out upon the terrace where she strolled for a short time. Then she climbed over the wall at the stile on the back of the terrace and took her way up Bowling Green Hill toward the gate. She sauntered leisurely until she was out of sight of the Hall. Then gathering up her cloak and sword she sped along the steep path to the hill crest and thence to the gate.
Dorothy Vernon of Haddon Hall – Charles Major

The book was a success and was again performed on the stage, starring Bertha Galland in the leading role. Further posthumous success would come for the author, when the book was made into a film in 1924. The film was entirely made in Hollywood and was directed by Marshall Neilan, who was a top director for many years. It starred the famous Mary Pickford in the leading role. Mary was not only a renowned actress, but she has had a lasting legacy in the film industry as she was one of the film stars who started the United Artists company. Also, she was one of the founders of the Academy of Motion Picture Arts and Sciences, which is now known for its awarding of the annual Oscars. Her second marriage was to Douglas Fairbanks and both of them became part of the Hollywood legend of film stars.

Diva

The source of Dorothy Vernon's elopement as a basis for dramatic productions was not confined to Charles Major and Mary Pickford. In London, in 1892 an Opera opened at the Savoy Theatre, it was called *Haddon Hall* and loosely followed the story of the elopement, although the writer Sydney Grundy moved the rendition forward by 100 years to the age of the cavaliers, and made some other changes to the family structure.

The music for this light opera was composed by Arthur Sullivan and this was his first work after his collaborations with Gilbert. Grundy would have been a natural choice, after Gilbert and Sullivan had separated, as he was already a successful writer of a number of plays. The opera ran for 208 performances with the soprano, Lucille Hall, playing the role of Dorothy Vernon.

Haddon Hall comes very much alive in the many

instances where it has been used as a period location in modern films. In the BBC production of Jane Eyre (2006), it was Thornfield Hall. The film of the same name by Franco Zeffirelli was also shot at this location in 1996, as was the 2011 version with Judi Dench. *Pride and Prejudice* (2005) was partly filmed at Haddon and in previous televisions shows *The Prince and the Pauper* and *Moll Flanders* it was also used as a set.

John Manners on John Manners

We have not, by any means, included all the poems and references to Haddon Hall and the Dorothy Vernon elopement. Both the hall and the fable intermixed with facts have inspired writers across the centuries. Whether Haddon is unique, may be doubted, but it is certainly an inspiring Gothic manor, that is so different from many of our country houses.

You will remember from the story of the elopement that it is John Manners who is courting Dorothy Vernon, so it is very apt to finish with a poem written by John Manners. Unfortunately it is not the one who stole across the plains of the Wye to secretly meet with Dorothy. It is the John James Manners who, on the death of his elder brother, became seventh Duke of Rutland. He was born in 1818 and, being the younger son, would not expect to inherit the title. After Eton and Cambridge, he chose a career in politics being elected to Newark along with William Gladstone. Whilst his political career did not emulate his polls partner, he held a number of offices and was awarded a knighthood for his services, especially as Postmaster-General. He succeeded to the Dukedom 18 years before his death in 1906.

He published two books of poems, the latter being *English Ballads and Other Poems* in 1850, which contains the poem, *The Legend of Haddon Hall.*

The King of the Peak in his gallery sate,
In his wonted pomp and pride,
And he looked on the terraced gardens below,
And the maid who stood by his side.

But his look it was stern, his brow it was bent,
As he gazed on her pale wan face;
Oh! why on those youthful features fair
Should sorrow have left its trace?
The Legend of Haddon Hall – John Manners, Seventh Duke of Rutland

Let's rest awhile at Haddon's Stable Block

Haddon Hall is one of the highlights on *The Literary Way* and is one of the richest spots on our route for literary prowess. Most of the works are based on Dorothy Vernon and John Manners. The extra mystique that is engendered, given the scantiness of true information, has only added to the stories with writers all taking their own perspectives. The supposed elopement is a grand story and as we have seen set near to the time of Mary, Queen of Scots and in the reign of Elizabeth I, both of which add to the grandeur and setting of the story.

Also let us not forget the reflection of individualism at the remote One Ash Grange. John Gratton spoke out against the laws of the lands in adherence to his beliefs and his descendant campaigned for the repeal of laws, which he saw restricting the working class. By the time John Gratton was born, our religious divine whose verse adorns the aesthetic memorial sundial at Over Haddon, had completed his life's work. Adding to the literary variety we have seen on this walk we have also been privileged with a wonderful stroll through the national nature reserve of Lathkill Dale.

Satanic Mills in Arcadia

Haddon to Hassop Station through Monsal Dale

The Old Bridge at Bakewell over which Celia Fiennes would have travelled

The mills in William Blake's emotive poem, *Jerusalem*, conjure up foreboding images of cruelty, the lack of hope, and dark deeds. Mills were at the centre of the industrial process, during the nineteenth century, and the other great commercial push was the railways, which snaked their ways across the nation.

We're at the heart of the National Park, and one section of this walk has been described as the mythical Arcadia or pastoral paradise. We are going to let the literary contributions of this walk describe the juxtapositioning of evocative scenery and some nineteenth century controversies.

It wasn't easy travelling across the country in the later 1600s, but one intrepid lady made a tour with just a single servant. We are going to have her description of the time. We are joined again by Lord Byron, whose friend became a vicar in a parish on our route, and he attempted to save his Lordship's marriage.

The spa baths in our market town provide us with their superintendent who, was not only one of the earliest geologists, but also developed a business around the newly formed science. In a quaint village, not far away, we meet the geologist's uncle, whose marble works stimulated a poem by a local candle maker. The rocks theme continues, with a poem by our *Literary Way* friend, Erasmus Darwin, on a discovery that helped his friend Josiah Wedgwood.

A much quoted location for one of the most well-known books in English literature is on our route, although there is scepticism from many scholars as to whether the town was the location that has been ascribed to it. A famous pudding emanates from the hotel where this lady stayed. Also the hotel has a strange poem carved into a stone in its fabric. Within the same small town there is an interesting old house that has a clear connection with the antipodes. Our walk finishes with a short story commissioned by one of the most famous names of Victorian literature.

On *The Literary Way* we left Haddon Hall, which is a little less than two miles from Bakewell, and took the riverside path. It is the opposite direction to which John Holland walked in 1823. He was from Sheffield, and with three of his friends, was walking towards Haddon. His poem, which takes its name from the house, has a description of the walk included in the first part. Let's see if we gained the same view along the banks of the Wye:

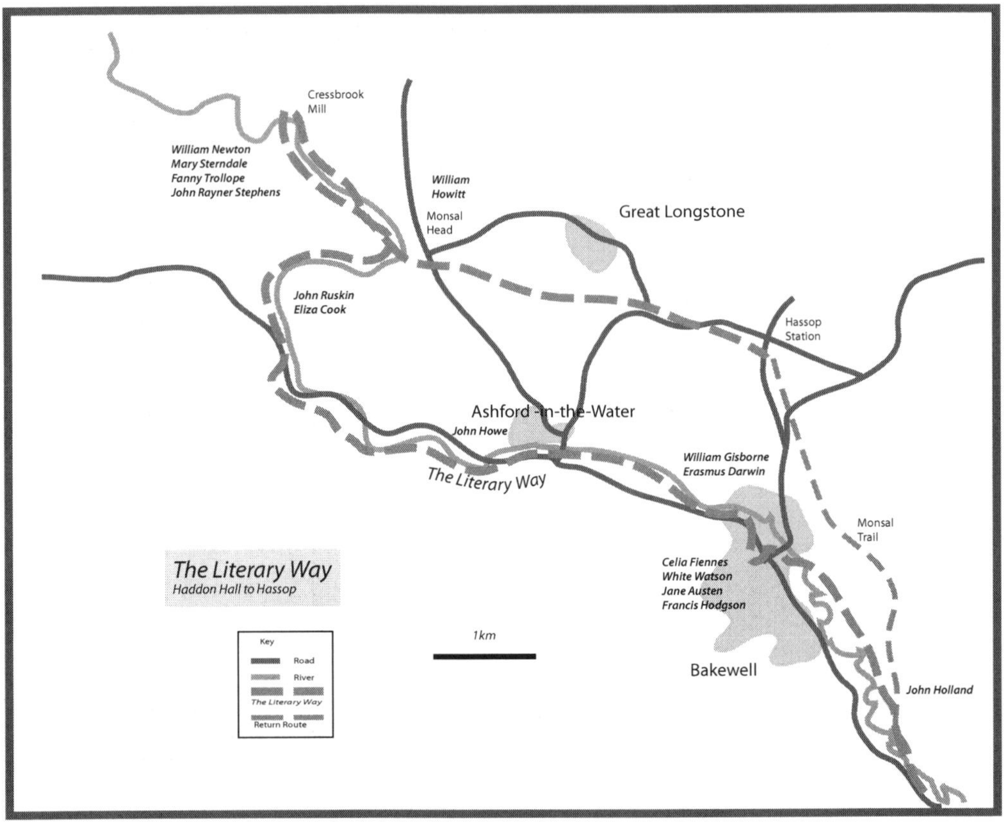

The Literary Way – Walk Twelve – Haddon to Hassop Station

The New Bridge crosses the River Wye in Bakewell

Walk Directions

Haddon Hall to Bakewell (1.9 miles)

We turn right outside of Haddon Hall along the pavement of the A6
In a few yards we take the footpath on our right.
We cross the river and follow the path, which comes out onto a lane.
We turn right for a short distance and then take the first path left
The footpath divides but both follow the river to Bakewell (The one to the right is easier in wet weather)
We cross the fields and come into the Agricultural Centre grounds
We pass the main building on our right and cross the river
We are now in the centre of Bakewell

Bakewell to Ashford-in-the- Water (2.16 miles)

After crossing the new bridge we turn right along the riverside
Turn left at the road and walk down through Bakewell
The gardens are on our right and the Rutland Arms is in front of us
At the far end of the gardens are the old Spa baths
Go up the street to the left of the Rutland Arms to the Bakewell Parish Church
We can then visit the Bakewell Museum behind the church
Take any of the steep roads down hill
Turn left when you reach the A6 and cross to the other side
We pass the old mill. Carry on until you see the small bridge
Cross the old packhorse bridge and just ahead is Holme Hall
On our left is Richard Arkwright's house
If we go along in front of the cottages we reach Lumford Mill where we return to the main road
We then take the next footpath on the right and go along the river to Ashford-in-the-Water
As we arrive in Ashford we take the old road into the centre of the village

Ashford-in-the-Water to Cressbrook Mill (4.66 miles)

We go past the Ashford Arms and the Bull's Head
At the end of the street we turn left
Here we have the picturesque sheepwash bridge which we cross
On the main road turn right, and take the lane on the left
Follow it as it passes the meander loop with the old limestone works
Take the first path on the right
Stay to the right when it divides and walk along the riverside
It then leaves the river and goes up through the woods
Climb the stile and turn right down towards the car park
Go through the car park, cross the road and take the riverside path
Follow the riverside past the weir and under the Headstone Viaduct
Not far after the viaduct we cross the river on the footbridge
It brings us out on to a lane and we turn left
Walk along the lane until you reach Cressbrook Mill

Cressbrook Mill to Hassop Station (3.53 miles)

Walk past Cressbrook Mill and take the footpath to the riverside
It passes behind the mill and we come out at Water-cum-Jolly
Turn left and cross the footbridge near the mill and weir
Follow the path up the hill and join the Monsal Trail
Turn left and follow the trail back towards the viaduct
Cross the viaduct under Monsal Head and walk through the tunnel
Carry on along the trail past the back of Thornbridge Hall
Go past the old Great Longstone station
Continue along the trail until you reach the old Hassop Station

Hassop Station to Haddon Hall (3.11 miles)

Continue along the trail past the old Bakewell Station
At the end of the trail follow the footpath that goes ahead
Along this track take the footpath to the right
Cross the field and turn left onto the footpath
Go to the end of the field and retrace steps to Haddon Hall

Distance: 15.4 miles Ascent: 1479ft

O what a lovely river is the Wye!
Curving and glittering through the emerald meadows,
While the blue heavens are mirrored in its bosom,
And when bright inverted summer sun-bright
Seems pillowed there in his meridian glory;
Haddon Hall – John Holland

After we left Haddon Hall, we gradually came into wide open parkland, the flood plain of the River Wye, and finally came towards the town itself. Bakewell is an old small town, just too large for a village, but it has a compact feel to it. One feature of its long history has been its relationship with the River Wye that flows through it. This relationship can be seen at different periods, by the three bridges that cross it. The bridges are almost exactly evenly spaced in time, which is about three hundred and fifty years apart.

At the end of the meadows we pass the agricultural market and cross the new bridge, built at the end of the twentieth century, over the River Wye. We have a really good view of Bakewell's oldest bridge which is further up-stream. We turn along the river path and walk towards the old bridge. It is almost seven hundred years old and, whilst modified to some extent, it has been at the core of Bakewell for a very long time, and so it is likely that our next writer crossed this same bridge.

Side Saddle

Let us introduce our quite intriguing traveller. She is Celia Fiennes, who was born in Wiltshire in 1662. She made many tours throughout different parts of England and often travelled only with her servant. She took pride in being able to stoically endure the difficulties presented by a women travelling virtually alone. She never intended publishing her travelogues as she considered them for family reading only.

In the succeeding centuries the works were drawn together in a volume called, *Through England on a Side Saddle in the Time of William and Mary*. We can see from the period of her travels, it was not long after the Restoration, so she was in the same period as William Congreve, Daniel Defoe and John Gratton, and true to the time, her father had been a Roundhead Colonel in the English Civil War. She offers an intriguing view of the places and houses she visited. This is what she had to say about Bakewell,

Thence we came to Bankwell(Bakewell) a pretty neate market town, it stands on a hill yet you descend a vast hill to it, which you would think impossible to go down and we was forced to fetch a great compass, and by reason of its steepness and hazard of the Wayes, if you take a wrong way there is no passing - you are forced to have guides as in all parts of Darbyshire, and unless it be a few who are use to be guides the common people know not above two or three miles from their home, but they of the country will climbe up and down with their horses those steep precipices; there are many fine springs of water purling out of the rocks these hills.
Through England on a Side Saddle in the Time of William and Mary – Celia Fiennes

The centre of Bakewell has changed considerably since Celia's time with the current layout of Rutland Square and the Hotel being completed in the nineteenth century. The town is built on a slight rise at the side of the valley. Let's turn down the main street and after the shops on our right are the town's gardens. As we stroll around them, which is always pleasant at any time of the year, at the far end, we reach the bath house. It was built when spa waters were in vogue, although, given the water here was very tepid, it did not catch on as well as rival towns such as Buxton and Matlock Bath. Our interest lies in a man who was superintendent of these baths for many years.

Superintendent of the Baths

Although not a native of Bakewell, one man who lived here for many years was a geologist named White Watson. His uncle developed what was to become the famous black marble near Ashford-in-the Water, which is only a few miles up stream from Bakewell. This is where White probably got his enthusiasm for rocks. His unusual first name is his mother's maiden name. White Watson combined his interest in geology, with being the Superintendent of the Baths. Because of his knowledge of rocks he also became a monumental mason. He was born near Sheffield in 1760 and lived until he was 75.

Geology was very much in its infancy at the time White Watson began his studies. For example, Charles Lyell who is often credited with the foundation of systematic geology was born 35 years after White. White only published a few works, but these were taken up by subscription by most of the eminent people of Derbyshire at the time.

One innovative method he used was to create a model of the landscape. A typical example of this is from Buxton to Bolsover, which is a distance of about 38 miles. He would collect samples from rock strata along the line and construct them into a framed model.

A Delineation of the Strata of Derbyshire by White Watson is not easy reading and one suspects the gentry bought the book for their libraries. White Watson's name lives on, as it was accorded to a fossil found in the rocks of the Peak. The fossil is a trilobite, now extinct for millions of years, called Griffithides whitewatsoni. There is an interesting comment made by White in the introduction to his book. It appeared he had been duped by a fellow geologist. They had planned to jointly publish some work based around White's specimens, but when it came to the public's attention 'Mr Martin' had removed practically all references to White.

Yet now, in 1810, the first volume being published the entire Mr Watson's name, as proposed of the work, is withdrawn, and though the whole of the original specimens, from which the figures are take, nine excepted, are still in his possession.

The Author most willingly refrains from making any reflections on this behaviour, however painful to his feelings, since it relates to a person who has already gone to the land where his ear is equally insensible to the reproaches of injured friendship, as it is to the applause from which his abilities so justly merit.
A Delineation of the Strata of Derbyshire – White Watson

Lambton

If we re-trace our way out of the gardens, then we will come to the hotel that is on the roundabout. It is the Rutland Arms. It has become well known, because it is claimed that Jane Austen stayed here when writing *Pride and Prejudice*. Whether the market town of Lambton, in the novel, is based on Bakewell is often disputed. However, with the close proximity of Chatsworth, which serves its worth as Pemberly, the home of Mr Darcy, it is easy to see the links.

In the novel Elizabeth is accompanying Mr and Mrs Gardiner for a holiday in Derbyshire, where Pemberley, the home of Mr Darcy, is situated. Let suppose for a moment that Jane Austen did envisage Bakewell as Lambton, and we'll let her take up the story.

It is nor the object of this work to give a description of Derbyshire, nor any of the remarkable places through which their route thither lay; Oxford, Blenheim, Warwick, Kenilworth, Birmingham etc, are sufficiently known. A small part of Derbyshire is all the present concern. To the little town of Lambton, the scene of Mrs Gardiner's former residence, and where she had lately learned that some acquaintance still remained, they bent their steps, after having seen all the principal wonders of the country; and within five miles of Lambton, Elizabeth found from her aunt that Pemberley was situated. It was not in their direct road nor more that a mile or two out of it.
Pride and Prejudice – Jane Austen

The Rutland Arms & Bakewell Church

Hotel Poem

We will not leave The Rutland Arms Hotel for the moment as it has two interesting features. It is claimed to be the home of the famous Bakewell Pudding, which was created by a mishap in the kitchen. But more intriguing for us it has a poem engraved on its brickwork:

Here's to one who took his chances
In a busy world of men
Battled luck and circumstances
Fought and fell and fought again
Won sometimes but did no crowing
Lost sometimes but did not wail
Took his beating and kept going
Never let his courage fail

He was fallible and human
Therefore loved and understood
Both his fellow men and women
Whether good or not so good
Kept his spirit undiminished
Never let down on a friend
Played the game till it was finished
Lived a sportsman to the end.
Rutland Hotel

This poem seems to have had many forms and these two verses are often the last of four. The words are slightly changed in some versions, when the last line does not refer to a sportsman, but just uses the reference to man. There are many ideas to where it might have originated, but there is no clear indication of an author. It's quite intriguing as to how it came to be on the wall of the hotel.

The Bakewell Parish Church dedicated to All Saints stands proudly on the hill overlooking the main part of the town, which nestles in the valley. And we now have the climb up to the church, which was partially rebuilt in the nineteenth century with a few stoneworks appearing at the Lomberdale Hall of our antiquarian, Thomas Bateman, who we met at Middleton on *The Literary Way*.

Poet, Critic, Friend and Teacher

In 1816, a new vicar was appointed to the parish of Bakewell. The living was the gift of the Lord of the Manor, the Duke of Rutland. This is how the new incumbent received comments following his letter of thanks:

July 18, 1816.
Sir, I can assure you that it was wholly unnecessary for you to take the trouble of making a formal acknowledgement of the trifling service which it has been in my power lately to render you; and indeed I have my reward in the conviction which I feel, that in being the cause of your promotion to the vicarage of Bakewell, I am doing an essential benefit to the interest of religion by placing so excellent an incumbent in a living where such a character is highly desirable.

I have the honour to be, Sir,
Your most obedient and humble servant,
Rutland.
To Francis Hodgson – Duke of Rutland

Francis Hodgson was 35 years old when he was appointed to Bakewell. He had been educated at Eton, a school to which he would return, after his period in Derbyshire, as the Provost. At Cambridge he met, and became very good friends, with Lord Byron, and after his Lordship's death, Francis had extensive correspondence with Thomas Moore who lived in Mayfield. During the first years in the town Francis attended principally to religious matters and so wrote very little. Before we relate a letter from Byron's wife to Francis, let's put Lord Byron's wife into context.

Lord Byron married Anne Milbanke when he was 27, but by this time he already had a considerable past. He had a tempestuous affair, which lasted for a few months, with a married woman, Caroline Lamb. This will grip our attention at Chatsworth as it has many connections with the famous house and its inhabitants. He was heavily in debt, had frequent severe swings of mood, as well as a number of casual sexual encounters. And there was an even more damming social rumour that was spreading at the time.

Lord Byron had not been brought up with his half-sister Augusta Leigh, and they only met as adults, but they spent a lot of time together and then Augusta became pregnant. Despite a lot of Byron's documents being destroyed, many historians do believe that he fathered Augusta's child, Elizabeth Medora. It was soon after this that Byron courted,

The packhorse bridge which leads to Arkwright's Cottage and Holme Hall

and eventually married, Anne.

It wasn't to be a happy marriage, and it only lasted a year, before she left him taking the baby from the marriage with her. There was antagonisms between the two and it is doubtful whether Anne every got over the marriage although, ironically, she did have a on-off friendship with his half-sister Augusta Leigh.

The baby from the marriage was called Augusta Ada. She never met her father, who died when she was nine, but in adult life she became very fond of him and was buried with him at Newstead Abbey. Anne, Byron's wife, was a very gifted lady and, when young, had a tutor who developed her talents. Unusually for her time, she took a firm interest and developed her skills in mathematics. That interest and capability passed to her daughter, who was known as Ada. She worked with Charles Babbage, who invented the first mechanical computer, and in doing so, it is claimed she became the first computer programmer, although it does seem that her overall contribution was quite small. However, the major computer language, Ada, was named after her.

And so to return to Francis Hodgson, the vicar of Bakewell. His closeness to Lord Byron can be seen in the extract from the following letter he received from Lady Byron.

Dear Sir,—I feel most sensibly the kindness of a remonstrance which equally proves your friendship for Lord Byron and consideration for me. I have declined all discussion of this subject with others, but my knowledge of your principles induces me to justify my own; and yet I would forbear to accuse as much as possible. I married Lord B. determined to endure everything whilst there was any chance of my contributing to his welfare. I remained with him under trials of the severest nature. In leaving him, which, however, I can scarcely call a voluntary measure, I probably saved him from the bitterest remorse.
To Francis Hodgson – Lady Byron

Before moving to Bakewell, Francis had produced a number of small publications, including a translation from Latin of the *Satires of Juvenal*, and *Lady Jane Grey - A Tale,* with miscellaneous poems in English and Latin. In 1818 he produced his longest work entitled *Friends*. It comprised four volumes and is set in both Wales and Canada. After 1818 his main publications were of a religious or educational nature, although he did produce many reviews of literature.

The church is set on the hill overlooking Bakewell, and it is a steep hill, as we find out when we walk down to the road. We turn left along the Buxton road, and go past the old mill. Shortly on our right is a footpath over the old packhorse bridge, which is our third bridge of Bakewell and was probably built away from the town centre so as to avoid the tolls.

Gisborne, New Zealand

As we cross the bridge we catch a glimpse of a fine old Jacobean building, Holme Hall. It was built in 1622 by Bernard Wells whose daughter, Mary, married into the local Derbyshire family, the Bradshaws. This must have made an interesting life for her, as her brother-in-law, John Bradshaw, was the President of High Court of Justice for the trial of

Charles I. It was his judgment which resulted in the execution of the King.

The house, in the mid-seventeenth century, moved into the Eyre family where it stayed for 150 years before being bought by Thomas Gisborne. It is his third son, William, who would eventually inherit the house, who interests us. He was born in 1825, and at the age of 17, he emigrated to Australia and, after a few years, he moved on to New Zealand, which is where he made his mark. His career started in the civil service, but then he moved into politics. The town of Gisborne that is in the north-east of New Zealand is named after him. In later life, he returned to England and after he re-settled in this country, he wrote a book entitled, *New Zealand, Rulers and Statesmen, 1840 – 1885.* Let's just give a taste of this work with the opening lines:

The birth of New Zealand as a British Colony was strange and troublesome. Mrs Mother-Country, as represented by the Colonial Office, did not seem glad that a colony was born into the world. Outside Downing Street, however, preparation had long been made for this event. Captain Cook, the great English navigator, had, for all practical purposes, discovered New Zealand in 1769; and in the same year he took possession of the islands in the name of King George the Third. Moreover, when New South Wales was declared, in 1878, a part of British dominions, New Zealand, though not named, was within the proclaimed boundaries.

New Zealand, Rulers and Statesmen, 1840 – 1885
William Gisborne

Circling Chertz Betwixt

Directly behind Holme Hall, the land is rich with an unusual rock type, which surprisingly gave rise to a short poem. Chert is a micro-crystalline rock, one variety of which is called flint. In the land near Holme Hall there are some rich beds of the rock, which often only occur in a thin and fragmented way. The mineral rights were shared by the owners of Holme Hall, and the adjacent land, which belonged to the Duke of Devonshire.

Josiah Wedgwood was forever working on ways to improve his pottery and he discovered that chert made the best grinding tool for the production of the clay. Therefore, he sought the best and most workable deposits in the UK, which were found in mines behind and adjacent to Holme Hall. As we have already learned, Erasmus Darwin and Josiah Wedgwood were good friends and Erasmus has included a few lines in *The Botanic Garden* about chert.

In the lines below, kaolin is the weathered granite, and is normally referred to as china clay. Etruria was the site of Josiah's works in the Potteries.

Gnomes: as you now dissect with hammers fine,
The granite-rock, the nodul'd flint calcine
Grind with strong are, the circling chertz betwixt,
Your pure kaolins and petunteses mixt;
O'er each red saggar's burning cave preside,
The keen-eyed fire-nymphs blazing your side;

Holme Hall behind which were the chert mines

Sheepwash Bridge, Ashford

And please on Wedgwood ray your partial smile,
A new Etruria decks Britannia's isle.
Charm'd by your touch, the flint liquescent pours,
Through finer sieves, and falls in whiter showers;
Charm'd by your touch, the kneaded clay refines,
The biscuit hardens, the enamel shines.
Botanic Garden – Erasmus Darwin

There is a row of cottages that are close to the pack-horse bridge, and near Holme Hall, the end one of which, has a plaque denoting that Richard Arkwright lived there. Richard was the son of Sir Richard, the founder of the Cromford Mills. Lumford Mill Cottages were built for the Arkwright mill a little further upstream. It was a mill that Richard, junior, kept in the family after selling many of those that his father founded.

We then have a pleasant walk along the Wye to the very scenic village of Ashford-in-the-Water. William Wordsworth entered the same village on fifth November 1830, this is how he described it in his diary:

A solitary equestrian entering the romantic little town of Ashford in the Waters, on the edge of the wolds of Derbyshire, at the close of day, when guns were beginning to be let off and squibs to be fired on every side.
Diary – William Wordsworth

This quiet village has benefited from the diversion of the main road away from the centre. The former coaching inn, the Ashford Arms, leads us toward Greaves Lane. Candle Cottage was built on the site of an old candle making factory, which was a thriving industry before gas lighting. Our attention here lays with a young man who was an apprentice tallow maker. He also became the local poet. His name was John Howe. An article on John, and his poetry, was written for Llewellyn Jewitt's *The Reliquary* by Thomas Brushfield, who was a local Justice of the Peace and a friend of Llewellyn and Thomas Bateman.

John clearly studied well because, in a letter to his daughter, who was in service in Manchester, he writes about poets who have lived in straitened circumstances and often died in poverty. The list, including Greek, Roman, as well as British poets, is extensive and demonstrates his wide knowledge of poetry.

Let's rejoin the old main road through the village. We go towards the church and then come to one of the most photographed scenes in Derbyshire. It has appeared in countless books and calendars, and it is the old sheepwash bridge over the River Wye. After crossing the bridge and taking the main road to Buxton for a few yards, our route goes up the lane to the left and then on to a footpath on the right, which will takes us through Great Shacklow Wood.

Black Marble

Just near where we take the footpath off the lane, the River Wye has a pronounced meander and in the neck of that feature was Henry Watson's black marble works. He was the uncle of White Watson, the geologist who lived in Bakewell, and he patented machinery for working the local black marble. The market for his work was greatly helped by the local Lord of the Manor, the Duke of Devonshire, who at the time, owned most of Ashford.

John Howe in his poem *Monsal Dale* describes the works.

And turning left to the left, by Cliffend green,
We first admire the curious machine.
Here grating saws divided the ponderous blocks,
(Hewn from the quarries of neighbouring rocks,)
And here engine's retroactive power
Sweeps the rude marble's rugged surface o'er,
Till polish, by another process brought,
Gives elegance, surpassing even thought,
Fit to a adorn the palace and the dome,
The poor man's grave-stone, or the rich man's tomb.
Here stalactites are, by artist's aid,
Wrought in all forms that fancy e'er portrayed;
And, when thus manufactured, may conduce
Either to luxury or real use.
Monsal Dale – John Howe

At the end of the wood we re-cross the road and can walk along the side of the Wye through Monsal Dale. Eliza Cook, who we met in Dovedale, also visited Monsal Dale and penned her views in her poem, *Derbyshire Dales.*

And Monsal, thou mine of Arcadian treasure.
Need we seek for "Greek Islands"and spice-laden gales,
While a Tempe like thee of enchantment and pleasure
May be found in our own native Derbyshire Dales
Derbyshire Dales – Eliza Cook

What a delightful walk this is. As we stroll through the dale alongside the river, with its gushing weir, the countryside, with no village or road in view, is picturesque. It is hard to imagine that just around the corner in this arresting dale is controversy. Not only that, but it is not just one problem, but two significant disagreements, both of which started in the 1800s, and still have resonance today. As we wind round with the river, there will soon appear in front of us a huge railway viaduct, where the line emanates from the rocky hillside Headstone tunnel.

Fors Clavigera

John Ruskin was an extremely talented Victorian gentleman, whose extensive travels, brought him a significant understanding of art and architecture. Undoubtedly he was a polymath, at various times writing and lecturing on geology, botany, art, architecture and society. He became a noted philanthropist and promoted the setting up of communes. His ideas for these were taken up internationally, and he founded his own one just outside Sheffield.

He established the Guild of St George which still exists today. It has many international branches and is focused on education. John became well-known as an art and architecture critic and wrote copiously about the revival of the Gothic influences in buildings. He also became the University of Oxford's, first Slade Professor of Fine Art.

The initial part of his career focused on drawing, art and architecture, and it was in later life, that he transferred his attention to social issues. He believed that traditional methods were being undermined by machinery and that technological developments were losing touch with their social situation. His private life has been the subject of much

Monsal Dale Weir situated in Eliza Cook's Arcadian paradise

Headstone Viaduct, Monsal Dale from Monsal Head

speculation. He did marry, but it was annulled after six years because of non-consummation. In his latter years, he suffered from mental health problems and this added to the speculation about his relationship with one young woman in particular.

John selected the viaduct and its railway in Monsal Dale as a major issue in one of his works. *Fors Clavigera,* written in 1871, which comprised a series of open letters to the workmen and labourers of the country. In his work he addresses many of the social issues that he saw as affecting society.

Our selection not only encompasses his views on the railways, but about the new growth of telecommunications by cable, and the invention of the camera. It is quite a remarkable passage, given how much all these technologies developed.

That telegraphic signalling was a discovery; and conceivably, some day, may be a useful one. And there was some excuse for your being a little proud when, about last sixth of April (Coeur de Lion's death-day, and Albert Durer's), you knotted a copper wire all the way to Bombay, and flashed a message along it, and back. But what was the message, and what the answer? Is India the better for what you said to her ? Are you the better for what she replied?

If not, you have only wasted an all-round-the-world's length of copper wire, — which is, indeed, about the sum of your doing. If you had had, perchance, two words of common sense to say, though you had taken wearisome time and trouble to send them; — though you had written them slowly in gold, and sealed them with a hundred seals, and sent a squadron of ships of the line to carry the scroll, and the squadron had fought its way round the Cape of Good Hope, through a year of storms, with loss of all its ships but one, — the two words of common sense would have been worth the carriage, and more. But you have not anything like so much as that to say, either to India, or to any other place.

You think it a great triumph to make the sun draw brown landscapes for you. That was also a discovery, and some day may be useful. But the sun had drawn landscapes before for you, not in brown, but in green, and blue, and all imaginable colours, here in England. Not one of you ever looked at them then; not one of you cares for the loss of them now, when you have shut the sun out with smoke, so that he can draw nothing more, except brown blots through a hole in a box.

There was a rocky valley between Buxton and Bakewell, once upon a time, divine as the Vale of Tempe; you might have seen the Gods there morning and evening — Apollo and all the sweet Muses of the light — walking in fair procession on the lawns of it, and to and fro among the pinnacles of its crags. You cared neither for Gods nor grass, but for cash (which you did not know the way to get); you thought you could get it by what the Times calls "Railroad Enterprise." You enterprised a railroad through the valley — you blasted its rocks away, heaped thousands of tons of shale into its lovely stream. The valley is gone, and the Gods with it; and now, every fool in Buxton can be at Bakewell in half an hour, and every fool in Bakewell at Buxton; which you think a lucrative process of exchange — you Fools Everywhere.

Fors Clavigera – John Ruskin

We will leave you to make up your own mind about the impact of the railway on Monsal Dale as you amble along the riverside, which will take us on our way to the second controversy. We pass under the viaduct and follow the river, crossing it near the farm which is painted in the colour of Chatsworth.

The Minstrel of the Peak

We take the quiet road upstream along the valley and it is not long before an immense building appears in front of us. For its size, it is remarkably well hidden in the valley, but it really does dominate when we are down next to the river. It is now a set of apartments, but was once the huge cotton mill, called Cressbrook. Needless to say, it was originally built by the Arkwright family. Our particular interest, however, lies not with the cotton tycoon, but with one of the carpenters that worked on its building. Before going into the controversy, that this woodworker caused, we would point out, that less than a mile further up-stream, is another very similar building, called Litton Mill.

Our walk heading was *Satanic Mills* which comes from the poem by William Blake, and although he probably wasn't referring to industrial cotton mills, it certainly has its applicability as we shall see. Contrast that with the section title, *Minstrel of the Peak,* which appears to give the impression of happiness and all that is good. So how do we reconcile the two? The answer is in one man, called William Newton. He is the carpenter that we referred to. William was born, in 1750, about five miles away, on a farm near the hamlet of Abney. After having worked for Richard Arkwright, as a craftsman, the latter appointed him as manager after the mill was rebuilt following a fire. However, this was only possible because he was lent some money by his sponsor. The investment made him a rich man.

The benevolence came from Anna Seward who we will meet in her home village of Eyam later on *The Literary Way.* Suffice to say, at this point, that she was well known in literary circles, being the biographer of Erasmus Darwin and her own biography was written by Sir Walter Scott. As William was born within the same parish as Anna, once she had discovered some of his poems, she promoted his work to a wider audience.

It was Anna Seward who named him 'The Minstrel of the Peak'. Much of his work did not survive, but one poem shows his humanitarian values. Up to 1834, the courts would often display the body of a murderer in public, on a gibbet, which was supposedly to deter similar crimes. It was frequently applied to highway men after they were executed.

In 1818 the last gibbeting took place in Derbyshire at Wardlow Mires, which is about halfway between Abney, where he was born, and William Newton's Cressbrook Mill. This is William Newton's poem on the gibbet, which many credit with helping to bring to an end the practice in Derbyshire.

Art thou, my son, suspended here on high,
Ah! What a sight to meet a father's eye!
To see what I prized most, what most I loved,
What most I cherished – and once approved,
Hung in mid air to feed the nauseous worm,
And waving horrid in the midnight storm.
If crime demand it, let the offender die,
But let no more the Gibbet brave the sky;
No more let vengeance on the dead be hurl'd,
But hide the victim from a gazing world.
The Supposed Soliloquy of a Father, Under the Gibbet of his son, near Wardlow – William Newton

Crossing the River Wye near to Cressbrook Mill

Cressbrook Mill where the orphans from London were sent to be under Richard Newton

John Holland provided us with a description on our walk from Haddon to Bakewell and this is how he describes meeting William Newton:

When we last met a little more than a year ago he appeared venerable in years with locks white and floating in the breeze, his poetical feeling was not extinct and some latent sparks of that enthusiasm remained with which he many years ago sung:

I love to wander on the mountain's brow
Amid the terrors of the howling year
When neither moon nor twinkling stars appear
But deepest darkness hides the scene below
When winter's fierce conflicting tempests blow
And all the arrowy winds a loud career
Congenial to my soul the tempests roar
Which lifts the mind above this earthy sod
Calls forth my powers obedient to adore
The cause of nature for that cause is God
William Newton – John Holland

When we started *The Literary Way* we visited Snelston where Michael Sadler was born. In the early 1830s he campaigned to reduce the child labour in the mills. In the late 1820s, when Michael was raising awareness of the misuse of young labour, William Newton, our Minstrel of the Peak, was the manager in charge of Cressbrook Mill. Both of the mills in the Wye valley required large number of workers, and there were no nearby towns, as happened with many of the Lancashire and Yorkshire mills, so labour had to be brought in.

Orphans, and other children without families, were under the direction of the parish. It only needed a churchwarden to sign the indenture for them to be apprentices, in which role they would remain until they reached the age of majority, 21. Children could expect to be under the direction of the mill masters for seven years, and in many cases even longer. Cressbrook and Litton Mills took apprentice orphans from the major cities, including London and Bristol. It is not difficult to see how child abuse would happen and why Michael Sadler wanted action.

But were things different at Cressbrook? They certainly were if we accept the views of Mary Sterndale, in her work *Vignettes of Derbyshire,* written in 1824. Mary was a Sheffield writer and she penned several novels and travel commentaries. *Vignettes* is about various trips she made into the Peak District.

At Cressbrook mill constant and regular industry is enforced but no unnatural labour. Their hours of work and necessary relaxation are kindly and judiciously arranged the former never exceeding what ought to be exacted from those in their station of life and of their tender age, their food is of the best quality and amply dispensed they have eight hours uninterrupted sleep in comfortable beds and airy rooms the utmost decorum is maintained between the boys and girls but if a brother and sister be amongst the number the affectionate relationship is kindly encouraged the relatives of the children are allowed to come to the House.
Vignettes of Derbyshire – Mary Sterndale

Mary carries on with similar lines for the rest of that chapter. She mentions William Newton and his family several times and praises their commitment. But before we take all of what Mary has written as correct, let's look at another book, this time a novel, that fictitiously refers to a mill in a deep valley.

The title of the book is *The Life and Adventures of Michael Armstrong, The Factory Boy.* It was written by Fanny Trollope, who wrote about fifteen major works, many of which were controversial, but all focused on aspects of society. We pick up the story when Michael is on his way to the mills.

....they gradually approached the level of a stream running through so very narrow valley, as in many places to afford barely space enough for the road between the brook and the precipitate heights which shut it in. On reaching this level, the road, which for the last quarter of a mile had seemed to be leading them into the little river itself, turned abruptly, and by an angle so acute, following the indented curve of the lofty hill, that they speedily appeared to be shut in on all sides by the towering hills that suddenly, and as if by magic, reared themselves in every direction round. It is hardly possible to conceive a spot more effectually hidden from the eyes of all men than this singular valley. Hundreds may pass their lives within a few miles of it without having the least idea that such a spot exists.
The Life and Adventures of Michael Armstrong – Fanny Trollope

Michael has now arrived a the mill and is taken inside.

But the master of the ceremonies at this feast of misery bore a huge horsewhip in his hand, without which indeed, it is said, he seldom appeared on the premises, and with it an eye that seemed to have the power of quelling with a single glance the will of every little wretch it looked upon.
The Life and Adventures of Michael Armstrong – Fanny Trollope

Fanny was diligent in her research and visited many mills. The book was finally published in 1840. She puts an interesting footnote to the description of the Deep Valley Mills of Derbyshire.

The real name of this valley (which most assuredly is no creation of romance) is not given, lest an action for libel should be the consequence. The scenes which have passed there, and which the few following pages will describe, have been stated to the author on authority not to be impeached.
The Life and Adventures of Michael Armstrong – Fanny Trollope

Fanny's novel of factory life is taken to be one of the first industrial novels and it certainly raised controversy. She was accused in leading reviews of inciting people to burn down mills and factories. The Luddite riots had burnt factories and destroyed equipment in the same communities in living memory and many saw Fanny as an agitator.

Let's conclude our section on Cressbrook and William Newton with the account of one of the apprentices at Cressbrook Mill, when William Newton was there. The account appeared in a periodical called *Stephens Monthly Magazine,* which was produced by a Methodist minister who campaigned for the working class and the needs of poor children. His name was Joseph Rayner Stephens and he espoused his independent views and spent some time in jail because of his campaigning.

During the time I was at Cressbrook, Mr Newton would not have had less than four hundred apprentices. .....Then he ordered the watchman to strip us, made us mount on one another's backs, and would himself flog us with these hazel sticks across our bare buttocks and loins till he cut the flesh and made the blood flow. He also made us flog one another, and would stand over us to see that we laid on; and if we did not lay on hard enough, he laid on us himself.
Stephens Monthly Magazine – Joseph Rayner Stephens

The mill pond, formed on the River Wye, behind Cressbrook Mill

So why were the views of Mary Sterndale so far out? Mary was a friend of Anna Seward, who was the sponsor and loanee of William Newton and no doubt wanted to do the best by her friends. It was common for mill owners to say conditions were good and many kept most details secret for fear of reprisals, if any information got out. On other social matters, Anna Seward offered the view that she would leave conduct and decision-making to true Christian gentlemen. So we think we had two women who wished to see the best and believed what the Newtons told them although it was very far from the truth.

Let's move on from Cressbrook Mill. We go past the mill on the footpath and it brings us out in Water-cum-Jolly, which is a pooled area of the River Wye, backed by steep white cliffs. We pass over the footbridge by the mill weir and climb the steep path up to the Monsal Trail, where we turn towards Bakewell. It isn't long before we see the valley, and the mill, from a different perspective. We are going over the Headstone viaduct, and through the tunnel, but before we do we can see the buildings at Monsal Head, which is on the road from Ashford-in-the-Water to Tideswell, where many of the unfortunate orphans are buried.

Household Words

In 1850 Charles Dickens started the periodical, *Household Words,* and published it every week for nine years. It only cost tuppence and thereby ensured a wide readership. Charles invited friends and authors he knew to submit poems or short stories. William Howitt, who we will meet with his wife Mary, at Eyam wrote a short story, in three chapters, called *The Miner's Daughter.* It is set in the area in which we are walking with the Bull's Head as the pub on Monsal Head. This was its name when William Howitt would have visited the area.

We are at the Bull's Head, a little inn on that road. There is nothing to create wonder, or a suspicion of a hidden Arcadia in any thing you see, but another step forward, and—there! There sinks a world of valleys at your feet. To your left lies the delicious Monsal Dale.

The Miner's Daughter – William Howitt

Let us pass through the Headstone Tunnel on the Monsal Trail. We soon go by the back of the stately home, Thornbridge Hall. One of the more eccentric owners had his own station built a few yards from the one that serves Great Longstone village.

Let's rest awhile at Hassop Station

The old Hassop station allows us to rest and reflect on the controversies that we have met in this chapter. The child labour debate of the 1820s and 1830s was somewhat typified in Cressbrook, where we found the different views put forward. We think there is little doubt, that it was a cruel time for those poor orphans.

Judging by the number of people who take pictures of the Headstone Viaduct, set in Monsal Dale, many obviously do not think that it spoils the view.

John Ruskin has been our leading writer in this chapter and we shall meet him again as a young boy underground. Francis Hodgson, Lord Byron's friend, gave us more information about his life and his wife. We also introduced that intrepid traveller from the late seventeenth century, Celia Fiennes, who give us some fascinating observations. There have also been three instances of how the local geology has inspired writing.

The countryside since leaving Haddon has been nothing short of magnificent. We have had the bustling Bakewell, set beautifully on the River Wye, with its dominant church watching over the country market town. The Sheepwash Bridge, at the appealing Ashford-in-the-Water, is the high point in this tranquil, unspoilt village, with its rows of traditional cottages. Many writers have ascribed the term, Arcadia, or pastoral paradise, to Monsal Dale and the River Wye valley, and it is certainly one of our favourite walks.

Sylph, Leviathan and Families

Hassop Station to Chatsworth

Chatsworth House with the Emperor Fountain

We will leave the isolated old station at Hassop to go to a house which is one of the gems of the nation. The sheer opulence of Chatsworth captivates all who visit it. And that has been the same for centuries. In the course of constructing *The Literary Way* we have read many extracts from biographies and travelogues. Chatsworth appears as a destination for visitors since the seventeenth century, and apart from a period in the 1950s, it seems to have always been willing to show off the accumulations of art, books and sculptures that have been gathered over the years.

As we might expect, it has been the focus for some keys writers and literary works. Our oldest literary paragon in this country seat, a name still read today, arrived at the house just as the major building work was being finished in the very early 1600s. At the other end of the scale we have a fascinating read in the twentieth century. In between, we have scandal that rocked society when, amongst others, the Duke and Duchess of Devonshire were portrayed, not at their best, in a novel. And as one more taster for this chapter we have a *menagè a trois* and gambling debts that went into millions of pounds.

We follow the Monsal Trail towards Bakewell and then take a path which leads us to a road. The quiet lane sharply bends through the woods, and then we reach Ball Cross farm, and in a nearby field is an earthworks site of antiquity. Soon after we begin to descend and we take the track on our right. This will take us through the only street in the Chatsworth estate village of Edensor.

Blotting Paper

Edensor's common characteristic is the warm yellow coloured stonework. As we walk down the lane we can see the markedly different designs of the houses, which take their inspiration from many different periods, but have a unity across them as they were built at the same time. The model villages at Snelston and Ilam were built in the 1820s and it was around that time that the sixth Duke of Devonshire began a substantial building programme at Chats-

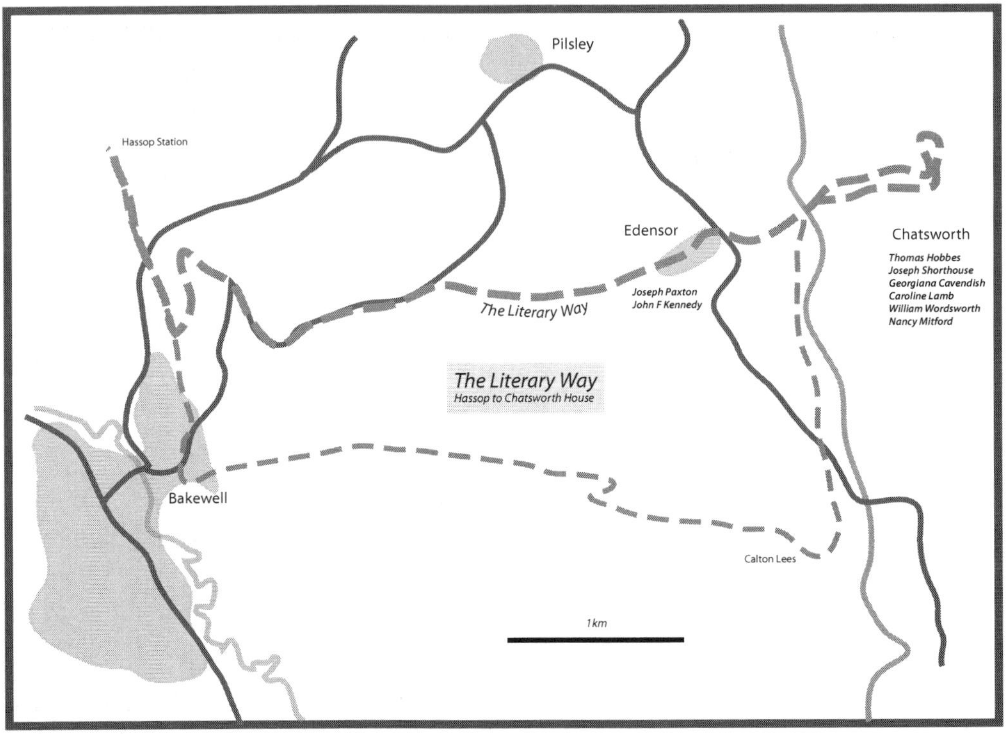

The Literary Way – Walk Thirteen – Hassop Station to Chatsworth

Edensor Church with Paxton's Grave in the left foreground

Walk Directions

Hassop Station to Edensor (3.01 miles)

We take the Monsal Trail towards Bakewell
After about half a mile we take the footpath on the left
It goes up the hill where it swings around to the right and joins a track
We go right on the track, and join the road at a hairpin turn
We take the left lane and go towards Ball Cross Farm
The lane takes us past the farm.
Just after the steep gradient there is a track to the right which we take
This is the road through Edensor
The church is near the bottom of this estate village

Edensor to Chatsworth House via Hunting Tower (1.57 miles)

We leave Edensor and cross the road and join the path
This takes us to the main bridge over the Derwent
We carry straight on and go past the house towards the farm yard
The road to the right near the entrance of the farmyard takes us up to the Hunting Tower
We retrace our steps and visit the garden and house

Chatsworth House to Hassop Station (5.46 miles)

Leave the house and cross the main bridge.
Immediately turn left and follow the river's edge
It will pass two weirs
Take the path up by the old corn mill to the Garden Centre
Go into the car park and take the lane past the Garden Centre
The lane bears to the right where we take the path to the right to Calton Pastures
The path goes past Calton Houses after which we turn left across the field
We pass the mere and go around the patch of trees.
Immediately in front of us the path goes into the woods.
Follow the path down through the trees and across the golf course
(Don't forget to ring the bell)
Follow the path over the Monsal Trail and down into Bakewell.
Turn right on the lane and at the end turn right up towards Bakewell Station
Join the Monsal Trail and return to Hassop Station

Distance: 10.0 miles Ascent: 1496ft

worth, which included the new model village. The old village, built of local traditional stone, was down towards the river with some buildings straddling along the banks to the old corn mill.

There were three men involved in the design and development of the new Edensor. The first was the sixth Duke of Devonshire, often known as Hart. He employed an architect, John Robertson and the third man was the Duke's Head Gardener, which is whom we wish to concentrate on first, for he turned out to be far more than a cultivator of plants.

One of the Duke's London residences was Chiswick House. He had lent part of the grounds to the Royal Horticultural Society, but still enjoyed walking in the gardens. On several occasions he met a young gardener and he was so impressed with him, that he offered him the head gardener's job at Chatsworth. This started a life time business relationship and friendship. Joseph Paxton had a passion for hard work. We shall see some of his notable works in Chatsworth's garden, but we will also explain why he became so famous. After Joseph came to this stately home he quickly made changes to the gardens but also, with the Duke's agreement, took on the design of other gardens and public spaces.

Whilst he had no formal architectural or engineering training, his projects became more and more ambitious. It was a period of great railway building, and Joseph became involved in many successful business ventures concerning the railways. His wife began to deal with the daily matters at Chatsworth. Paxton's most noticeable achievement in the gardens is unfortunately no longer there. It was located at the site of the current maze, and was called the Great Conservatory.

Paxton was ambitious in his design and building, and he used the Conservatory at Chatsworth as the first step to a grander plan. The small wall on the outside of the maze was the foundation wall for the Great Conservatory, through which a carriage could be driven.

In 1851, the Government had planned the Great Exhibition which was to take place in Hyde Park. A Royal Commission was appointed to manage the design of a building which was to house the exhibition. The eminent group had problems in finding a solution which was cost-effective and could be built in time. Joseph, was by then a Director of the Midland Railway, and he visited London and obtained agreement to submit his own design. It had to be completed in a short time scale and so he drafted his idea while in a meeting. It was sketched out on the blotting paper that was in front of him. It was developed over the next few days into a formal design. The blotting paper is now in the Victoria and Albert Museum.

He had designed the building using a modular approach. He knew that railway companies could make the iron girders and supports necessary for the overall framework, which would support the weight of the glass. It was built in a little over six months and was nicknamed by the *Punch* Magazine, "The Crystal Palace". It was a huge structure. To be the first to build such a structure and to complete it in about six months would make modern builders envious. To give the exhibition its full name it was, *The Great Exhibition of the Industry of All Nations.* Needless to say Joseph Paxton became a

A Cottage in Edensor with a build date of 1839

celebrity in his own right.

The driving force behind the exhibition was Prince Albert, Queen Victoria's Consort, and therefore Joseph Paxton was knighted. As we saw in Darley Dale, Joseph Whitworth, the precision engineer, came to international prominence at the Great Exhibition.

Joseph Paxton continued his many jobs but never left Chatsworth, even though, later in life, he became the MP for Coventry. In yet another business venture Joseph and his partners set up a national newspaper, *The Daily Chronicle* and he appointed Charles Dickens as editor, although he did not last very long in the job. However, this is how Charles Dickens described the construction of the Crystal Palace:

Two parties in London, relying on the accuracy and good faith of certain ironmasters, glass-workers in the provinces, and of one master carpenter in London, bound themselves for a certain sum of money, and in the course of four months, to cover eighteen acres of ground with a building upwards of a third of a mile long (1851 feet- the exact date of the year) and some hundred and fifty feet broad. In order to do this, the glass maker promised to supply, in the required time, nine hundred thousand square feet of glass (>400 tons). The iron-master passed his word in like manner, to cast in due time 3300 iron columns; 34 miles of guttering tube, 2224 girders. The carpenter undertook to get ready within the specific period 205 miles of sash-bar; flooring for a building of thirty-three millions of cubic feet; besides enormous quantities of wooden walling, louver work and partition.
Household Words – Charles Dickens

Paxton's major contribution to authorship was through the publication of books and magazines on gardening, the first of which was the *Horticultural Register* in 1831. It is interesting to note that the first article in the Register was a *Description of a House for Forcing Vines in Pots* by Mr Stafford, who was the head gardener to Richard Arkwright at Willersley Castle, Cromford.

The church dominates the village of Edensor and we can see it in its full glory, situated on raised ground, overlooking the park which spreads out along the River Derwent in the front of Chatsworth House. Let us go into the graveyard of St Peter's Church. One of the largest memorials, and probably the one that captures the first attention, is not one of the Cavendishes, the family name for the Duke of Devonshire, but it is the grave of Sir Joseph Paxton.

Kick and Jack

The title of this walk includes the simple word, families. It is not only the Cavendishs that we want to allude to, but also a famous American family. The 1940s were a pivotal time for the world. For half of that decade, war affected everyone. Just before the war, in 1938, a new US Ambassador was appointed to the Court of St James in England. His name was Joseph Kennedy. He was already a very successful business man with a strong Catholic background. Joe and Rose Kennedy had nine children. One of their daughters, Kathleen, known as Kick, came to England twice during the Second World War, the second time in the service of the Red Cross.

William Cavendish was the eldest son of the tenth Duke of Devonshire and therefore held the title of the Marquis of Hartington. Despite opposition from her mother, Rose, Kathleen Kennedy married William Cavendish in 1944. It was expected that, after the death of his father he would become Duke, and therefore Kathleen would become the Duchess of Devonshire. Four months after the marriage tragedy would strike when William was killed in action while with the Coldstream Guards. Another tragedy would strike a few years later when Kick was killed in an airplane crash in France.

The subsequent events of the Kennedy family became known globally. Kathleen's brother became the President of the United States of America. In 1945, John F Kennedy, known in the family as Jack, visited Europe. In his diary, he wrote about the tenth Duke of Devonshire, who was his sister's father-in-law. It would be very interesting to know how JFK might have reflected on his words in the 1960s when his family became so dominant in the USA. The words also present an interesting perception of Eastbourne. Compton Place was one of the properties owned by the Duke of Devonshire.

June 29, 1945
Kathleen and I went down this afternoon to Eastbourne in southern England to Compton Place. Eastbourne is a small village and Compton Place is in the centre of it, though for its quietness it might be in the middle of a large forest. Its owner, the Duke of Devonshire, is an eighteenth century story book in his beliefs - if not in his appearance. He believes in the Divine Rights of Dukes, and in fairness, he is fully conscious of his obligations - most of which consist of furnishing the people of England with a statesman of mediocre ability but outstanding integrity. David Ormsby-Gore maintains that in providing the latter service the aristocracy, especially the country squires, really earn their sometimes extremely comfortable keep...
Although the Duke is an anachronism with hardly the adaptability necessary to meet the changing tides of present day, he does have great integrity and lives simply with simple

pleasures. He has a high sense of noblesse oblige, and it comes sincerely from him.
Prelude to Leadership – John F Kennedy

Jack Kennedy remained friends with the Cavendishs and when he visited England, he came to Edensor to Kathleen's grave. This journey to Chatsworth was a few months before he was assassinated. A plaque on Kathleen's grave, in Edensor churchyard commemorates the visit.

Let us take our leave of St Peter's Church and cross the park to the main Chatsworth House. As we approach the bridge, with the house on the other side of the river, we can see on the wooded hill behind the house, the Hunting Tower. It is situated in Stand Wood, and the tower is often called The Stand. Having set the scene, and before we go into the House and Gardens, we are going for a stiff climb up the hill. It is also time to turn the clock back, to near the period when the present house started its life. On our left after the bridge is another feature left from the early days of the house. Queen Mary's Bower was once an island in one of the original lakes of the house. It takes its name from Mary, Queen of Scots who was kept at Chatsworth for a period when Queen Elizabeth had asked the Earl of Shrewsbury to supervise her.

We follow the signs to the farm and adventure playground, but we take the road to the right up the hill. You might wonder why we want to start at the Hunting Tower? It's one of the few parts that is unchanged from the original days of Chatsworth. The Hunting Tower on the top of the hill, overlooking the House, was completed in 1580. Bess of Hardwick, who was the main driving force behind the construction of Chatsworth, was 53 at the time. She would live until she was 81. It would be in the year she died, that a young man just out of Oxford, would come to the Cavendish family to tutor her grandson.

Social Contract

That fresh young man was called Thomas Hobbes. He went on to become a leading political philosopher, whose work is still studied today. He is renowned for his laying of a major milestone in the foundations of political philosophy. He conceived the idea of a social contract, which is effectively an agreement between people that must be in place for a society to function. Thomas was born in 1588, which is the same year as the Spanish Armada, and he lived approximately the same life span as Isaac Walton and died when he was 91. This was a grand old age given the political turmoil of the period, including, the English Civil War and the prevalence of disease, such as the plague.

His long life was even more of a considerable achievement given that he managed to alienate both sides during the English Civil War. His writings were denounced as unacceptable, both to the Parliamentarians and to the Royalists. At one stage he fled to France, where he tutored the future King Charles II. When the war was over, and the monarchy had been restored, he was allowed to live on with the Devonshires, provided he did not publish further writings. The Earls of Devonshire, as they were until the end of the 17th century, owned two

The Bower was originally an island and was built before Mary, Queen of Scots was kept at Chatsworth

The Hunting Tower was a feature of the first Chatsworth built by Bess

major houses in Derbyshire. These were both the work of Bess. So she not only built Chatsworth, but she had constructed Hardwick Hall, which still stands. There is the ruin of the first hall and next to it is the current hall. Hardwick Hall can be seen from the main north-south motorway (M1) just south of Chesterfield. The Cavendish family moved between the houses on a regular basis and therefore so did Thomas.

Thomas Hobbes was described in a Victorian novel, written by Joseph Henry Shorthouse, in 1880. The story is set in the time of Charles I. It is an intriguing story written in the late nineteenth century about events 240 years earlier. The tale centres around John Inglesant, who was the second twin, and so is shown no favours, as he would not inherit. His father is at the Royal Court and so the boy is given to the Jesuits to raise. They do so with the purpose of him being able to understand the delicate religious line between, the monarchy of Protestant England and, the drift towards Catholicism. The English Civil War then erupts and John Inglesant is involved in battles, but also in the machinations of religion between the different parties.

Joseph Shorthouse was a Birmingham Quaker who became a member of the Church of England. *John Inglesant* was his first book and it made him famous Thereafter he mixed with senior politicians and writers of his day, including William Gladstone and Matthew Arnold. Our interest in this book is that it paints a picture of Thomas Hobbes. Devonshire House was one of the Cavendishes' London residences. Near the beginning of the book, when he is still in the company of a Jesuit, they go to meet Thomas Hobbes.

The Jesuit took him one day into the city to Devonshire House, where, inquiring for Mr. Hobbes, they were shown into a large handsome room full of books, where a gentleman was sitting whose appearance struck Inglesant very much. He was tall and very erect, with a square mallet-shaped head and ample forehead. He wore a small red moustache, that curled upward, and a small tuft of hair upon his chin. His eyes were hazel and full of life and spirit, and when he spoke they shone with lively light; when he was witty and laughed the lids closed over them so that they could scarcely be seen, but when he was serious and in earnest they expanded to their full orb, and penetrated, as it seemed, to the farthest limit of thought. He was dressed in a coat of black velvet lined with fur, and wore long boots of Spanish leather laced with ribbon.

John Inglesant – Joseph Shorthouse

Thomas Hobbes did not restrict himself to philosophy and, as with many men of his era, he wrote on a large number of matters, but for now let us see how he describes Chatsworth.

On the English Alps where Darbie's Peak doth rise
High up in hills that Emulate the skies,
And, largely Waters all the Vales below
With Rivers' that still plentifully Flow,
Doth Chatsworth by swift Derwin's Channel stand,

Fam'd for its pile, and Lord, for both are grand.
Slowly the River by its Gates doth pass
Here silent, as in Wonder of the place.
Chatsworth – Thomas Hobbes

But let us end with Thomas by looking at his most famous work, which was called, *The Leviathan* or *The Matter, Forme and Power of a Commonwealth Ecclesiastical and Civil.* It was published in 1651. *The Leviathan* is not an easy read. We have chosen the introduction, in which Hobbes draws analogy between the man and the state.

Nature (the art whereby God hath made and governs the world) is by the art of man, as in many other things, so in this also imitated, that it can make an Artificial Animal. For seeing life is but a motion of Limbs, the beginning whereof is in some principal part within; why may we not say, that all Automata (Engines that move themselves by springs and wheels as doth a watch) have an artificial life? For what is the heart, but a spring; and the nerves, but so many strings; and the joints, but so many wheels, giving motion to the whole Body, such as was intended by the Artificer?
The Leviathan – Thomas Hobbes

The *Leviathan*'s strength as a political work is that it goes on to define the nature of a social contract and discusses the way in which countries and people should be managed. Thomas is still regarded as a first-rate philosopher.

Let's close with a little mention of his autobiography, which was somewhat of a challenge for people of any historical period, including the present day. He wrote it, at the age of 84, in Latin rhyming couplets.

From the Hunting Tower, we get good views over both Chatsworth House and its estate. And as a little advance information for one of the later periods of Chatsworth. While we are near the Hunting Tower, we could go for a walk around the man-made Emperor's Lake. This stretch of water is the source for many of the nineteenth century features in the garden. This Emperor's Lake, the Swiss Lake, and the nearby woods, form a wonderful spring amble with the bluebells spreading out in the dappled sunshine of the trees.

The New Duke

But let's move on in place and time. We'll come down from the Hunting Tower and go into the gardens to see one of its most famous features, the Cascade. At the top of this large stepped water feature is Cascade House. It was designed to be part of the fountains and on special occasions the full water features are turned on including the jets from the floor. In summer, it becomes a paddling pool for the children and many adults! The Cascade was finished in the 1690's and the Cascade House added a little later, which certainly must make it one of the oldest paddling pools in the country.

A lot has happened between the Hunting Tower being built and the Cascade being finished. The English Civil War has been and gone. Chatsworth

The Cascade from Cascade House

The Grotto designed for Georgiana by White Watson

survived despite being the centre of action at different times. The Plague of 1666 had affected a village only a few miles away, and the Chatsworth physician became involved in controlling its spread. William and Mary had come to England and to the throne. This affected Chatsworth. The Fourth Earl had earnestly supported William and Mary, and for services rendered, he became the First Duke of Devonshire. In the late 1680s, the First Duke began rebuilding and he extensively changed the house. Celia Fiennes, who we met in Bakewell describes in her journals the gardens of Chatsworth as they were then, but they have been extensively changed since she was there.

The Sylph

As we entered the gardens we passed the stable block, which is an immense structure. It now houses the restaurant, bar and shop. A walk through the garden takes us to the grotto area, which was originally developed at the same time as the stable block.

In our journey through history we stop about the time of the American Declaration of Independence, in 1776, which as we have seen before, is slightly after the visits of Rousseau to Dovedale and when Johnson had achieved his fame with the English dictionary. About this time the house had one of its most noted characters, Georgiana Cavendish. She was the wife of the Fifth Duke, and mother to Hart, the Sixth Duke who substantially added to the House itself and re-built Edensor.

Devonshire House, in London, was one of the prime centres of the very fashionable social scene. Georgiana was the consummate hostess, but as we learned when we were on Stanton Moor she was seduced by Earl Grey and was sent away to France to have the illegitimate baby. In another strange turn of her life, she introduced her friend, Elizabeth Foster, to her husband. Nothing unusual about that you may think, but he took Elizabeth as his mistress. It was not uncommon during marriages of the time, although normally the affairs were conducted with discretion. But not so in this case. She moved in with Georgiana and they lived as a threesome, with Elizabeth having two illegitimate children by William. This arrangement lasted until Georgiana's death and afterwards the Duke married Elizabeth.

Apart from the unusual living arrangements and other affairs, a key part of society of the time was gambling. In this Georgiana revelled but she was also unsuccessful. In an attempt to keep her gambling debts unknown to her husband she would often borrow money, which is why Richard Arkwright wanted a repayment of a loan. He left his note to Georgiana at the Greyhound Hotel in Cromford.

Georgiana would send begging letters to some of the most eminent men in society, including the Prince of Wales. After her death her husband found out the true extent of the gambling debts, which in modern-day estimates appears to be in excess of £3 million pounds. She managed to run up such a large amount because of the generosity of her banker, who went on to establish a famous name in the banking world, Coutts.

After her death, her husband did not clear the debts and so when his son, Hart, the sixth Duke inherited the debts and their interest were still there. He finally took action, and in the end, he sold one of his estates, Londesborough in Yorkshire, to pay them off. Georgiana was seen as one of the most beautiful and leading women in society, but was often parodied in magazines as a result of her conduct. In order to support her friends in elections she would kiss prospective voters, which was very much against the norms of society at the time. Georgiana was portrayed in the film *The Duchess* by Keira Knightly.

Whilst women of this period wrote a large number of letters, they did not write books, as this was seen to be a man's task. This challenge was taken up by women in two ways. A contemporary of Georgiana's, but from a different class in society, was Mary Wollstonecraft, Mary Shelley's mother, who during this period wrote, *The Vindication of the Rights of Women*, which we have previously introduced in *The Literary Way*. This targeted middle class women, and stated that it wasn't necessary to be the weak females, and that they were equal and entitled to the same education as men.

Georgiana dealt with her desire to write a book through anonymity. Another woman, who lived at the time, also wrote anonymously, but she was later recognised as the author, Fanny Burney. She wrote *Evelina* against all the expectations of her father and society. Fanny Burney's father was a regular correspondent and good friend of Samuel Johnson. We have seen that, even in a much later period, many women writers published their work anonymously or under a pseudonym, as with George Eliot and Currer Bell, who we shall come to later on our journey.

Fanny Burney's *Evelina or The History of a Young Lady's Entrance into the World*, was published in 1778. It is written as a series of letters, some of which are quite long. One wonders about the coincidence that Georgiana published an anonymous book in 1779, which was also about a young lady entering society. It was also constructed from a series of letters. We have selected a small extract from, *The Sylph*, by Georgiana. The leading lady in the book is writing to her sister.

To Miss Louisa Grenville
Surrounded by mantua-makers, milliners and hair dressers, I blush to say I have hardly any time to bestow on my dear Louisa. What a continual bustle I do live in, without having literally anything to do! All these wonderful preparations are making for my appearance at court; and, in consequence of that, my visiting all the places of public amusement. I forsee my head will be turned with this whirl of folly, I am inclined to call it, in contradiction of the opinion of all mankind - If the people I am among are of any character at all, I think I may comprise it in a few words: to me they seem to be running about all the morning, and throwing time away, in concerting measures to throw more away in the evening. Then as to dress, to give an idea of that, I must reserve the line of an old song. 'What was our shame is now our pride'. I have had a thousand patterns of silk brought to me to

Chatsworth House from across the Lawns

The Duck Pond where Georgiana's great-great-grandneice, Princess Diana, held a tea party

make choice, and such colours as yet never appeared in a rainbow.
The Sylph – Georgiana Cavendish

Georgiana had a complex life with intriguing relationships. At one time, she was away from England. This is the last part of the poem, *The Passage of the Mountain of St Gothard,* which was published in 1799. It is about her longing for home, Chatsworth, and to be re-united with her children.

Hope of my life! dear children of my heart!
That anxious heart, to each fond feeling true,
To you still pants each pleasure to impart,
And more – O transport – reach its home and you.
The Passage of the Mountain of St Gothard – Georgiana Cavendish

Let us return to the theme of families. Georgiana, in her day, was the belle of society. At the top of the garden is the Grotto which was built for her; it has since been remodelled and it is now topped with an old wooden structure resembling a bandstand. It overlooks one of the largest ponds in Chatsworth, and it is one of our favourite places to enjoy the wonderful gardens and watch the coots and moorhens moving in the rushes. Our links here extend to White Watson, the mason and geologist from Bakewell. He was paid £66 for the design of the grotto.

Further down the garden, and nearer to the main house, is a small circular pond with the duck fountain at its centre. On the grass near to the pond is a small plaque that says that Diana, Princess of Wales, held a garden party there for the charity Barnados, in 1986. What is the connection between these two women? They both come from the same family. Both Georgiana and Diana were Spencers from the Althorp estate. Diana was Georgiana's great-great-grandneice. And while their characters are entirely different, they were united in the major impact they had on society at the time.

A Lock of Pubic Hair

If Georgiana's conduct, at home, and in society, seems outlandish, it appears timid when compared to her niece, Caroline Lamb. William Lamb was a rising politician in London and would go on to be the significant Prime Minister, Lord Melbourne, who guided the young Queen Victoria through the first years of her reign. William, had not inherited the title, when in 1805, he married the 19 year old Caroline Ponsonby. By 1807 they had a son and later a daughter, who died young. Having recovered from two difficult childbirths, Caroline rejoined the elaborate society of the day, which had just seen the death of her aunt Georgiana.

Caroline had known her aunt very well because she spent a lot of her life as a child at the Cavendishes' homes. Children, at the same age as her, included the two illegitimate offspring of Elizabeth Foster, and Hart, who would become the sixth Duke of Devonshire. Her return to society captured the attention of Lord Byron, who was mainly in London at the time, but had not yet established his poetic career.

Initially she played hard to get, but then succumbed and became his mistress. They ignored the normal discretions and their tempestuous affair became common knowledge. The exchange of locks of hair between lovers was common at the time, but a new twist was given to the momento by the increasingly erratic and possessive Caroline. She sent Byron a lock of her pubic hair with a note:

I asked you not to send blood but yet do – because if it means love I like to have it – I cut the hair too close and bled much more than you need.
To Lord Byron – Caroline Lamb

When Byron tried to finish the affair she continually pestered him. In modern day parlance she would, no doubt, be arrested for stalking. She wrote to Byron's publishers and forged his signature. One of Caroline enjoyments was dressing up and so she would don the dress of a page boy, which allowed her to gain secret access to Byron's house.

Having set the scene for an unusual literary work let's return to Chatsworth, which was famous for its celebrations in the country and now under the charge of Hart, the Sixth Duke. As we learned Hart and Caroline were children together, and with the feeling he had for her, it was surprising they didn't marry. On the breakdown from her affair with Byron, her family, including Bart, went to Ireland to be away from society. Bart had recently inherited his title, and it was one of his first trips to the Irish part of the Cavendish estate, Lismore Castle.

The castle was originally an Abbey, that received royal favour, when Henry II stayed there in the twelfth century. It was to this ancient abbey, that had been partially developed into a castle, that Hart and Caroline went, and it inspired Caroline to write.

In 1816, when Caroline was 31 she published her first novel. She set it in Ireland during the Irish Rebellion of 1798, which was in living memory of many. It was a vituperative novel with the central characters easily recognised as Byron, in the title role of Glenarvon and Caroline herself as Calantha. While it was published anonymously, the parody of the Whig society, of which she and Byron were part, was easily recognised. It is a Gothic novel, which is full of passion, love and death, with an underlying trace of masochism. Caroline also included a detailed representation of her family and her close friends.

The Duke and Duchess of Devonshire, in whose houses she had been raised, play a leading role, and also Bart who was her friend and tried to help her following the breakdown of her affair. Even her husband was depicted in the book, as well as Georgiana, and Byron's wife. All her family and friends had passed on from her affair by then, and the book opened new wounds and poured scorn on their lives and society. Caroline was blackballed from society for a while, but some, such as her husband and Hart, stayed loyal to her. One of the main locations for the book is an abbey castle.

Castle Delaval, the property of that nobleman, was situated in a valley sheltered from every keen blast by a dark wood of fir and elm. The river Elle, taking its rise amidst the Dartland Hills, flowed through the park, losing by degrees the character of a mountain torrent, as it spread itself between its rich and varied banks in front of the castle, till it joined the sea beyond the Wizzard's Glen. The town of Belfont stands close upon the harbour, and from one of the highest cliffs, the ruins of the convent of St. Mary, and a modern chapel may yet be seen, whilst Heremon and Inis Tara, raising their lofty summits, capped with snow, soar above the clouds.
Glenarvon – Caroline Lamb

Caroline even used the love letters that Byron had written to her in the book.

The Literary Duke

Hart certainly supported and enjoyed the company of literary people during his time at Chatsworth. William Thackeray stayed briefly during the period he was writing the serial, *Vanity Fair,* as magazine articles. This was just after Charles Dickens had stayed. Charles had asked Hart for his help in putting on a charity performance, and Hart generously allowed the use of the theatre at Devonshire House in London for a royal performance in front of Queen Victoria.

Chatsworth was open to visitors during the nineteenth century and on one occasion Elizabeth Gaskell was visiting with her daughter, and was, to her surprise, invited to stay that night. The Duke by this time was in a wheel-chair and Sir Joseph Paxton

Emperor's Fountain

discreetly helped in the host's role.

In 1830 William Wordsworth visited Chatsworth and composed his description of the house in a sonnet which was published in 1835

Chatsworth! thy stately mansion and the pride
Of thy domain, strange contrast do present
To house and home in many a craggy rent
Of the wild Peak; where new-born waters glide
Through fields whose thrifty occupants abide
As in a dear and chosen banishment,
With every semblance of entire content;
So kind is simple Nature, fairly tried!
Yet he whose heart in childhood gave her troth
To pastoral dales, thin set with modest farms,
May learn, if judgment strengthen with his growth,
That not for Fancy only pomp hath charms;
And, strenuous to protect from lawless harms
The extremes of favoured life, may honour both.
Chatsworth – William Wordsworth

Hart also was generous and willing to financially help some writers. The poet and critic, Leigh Hunt, who was a friend of Shelley and Byron, fell on hard times, and although he didn't know him, Leigh wrote a begging letter to Hart who responded with £200. Hart never married although he did have a long term mistress. He was also very popular at the court of the Prince Regent, and he reluctantly took on royal duties.

Francis Hodgson, Byron's friend, left the vicarage at Bakewell and became Archdeacon at Derby which was before he moved to Eton. While he was at Derby, Hart appointed him to the Perpetual Curacy of Edensor and they became good friends.

The Emperor's Visit

The Emperor's Fountain near the House is our next stopping point. It was named after the Emperor of Russia, and it was built by William Paxton in 1843, but the Emperor never saw the fountain. Hart and the Russian Prince had met in London in their youth and became firm friends. Some years later Hart represented the British monarchy at the coronation of the Russian Emperor in the Kremlin in Moscow. When a formal visit was planned to England, Hart hoped and expected that the Emperor would come to Chatsworth, but the visit never occurred and they met at Chiswick House.

We have mentioned Joseph Paxton previously as being involved in the design and building of the village of Edensor. He had come to Chatsworth as a gardener and had gradually taken more responsibility for major projects. One example was the Emperor Fountain, which he designed. This included the piping of the water from its source, which is a man-made lake on the top of the hill. This was a monumental work for its time.

Incidentally the normal height of the fountain is lower than its original design. On special occasions the valves are fully opened and it can rise to 200 feet.

21st Century Chatsworth House

Let's consider the introduction given by the 11th Duke of Devonshire, Andrew Cavendish, who died in 2004.

The first thing that springs to mind when I think of Chatsworth is surprise that I live here at all. I came as a child, always at Christmas when my grandfather was alive and, being a younger son never expected that Chatsworth would one day become my home. But my brother was killed in Belgium in 1944. When my grandfather died in 1938, my father moved in until the war broke out, and the house became a girl's school until about a year after the war. My parents were planning to return to Chatsworth when my father died in 1950. My wife and I were then faced with raising the money for death duties and any idea of living at Chatsworth was quite out of the question for several years. The fact that we moved back there in 1959 is entirely thanks to my wife. In the end I listened to her advice rather than that of my financial advisers.
Guide to Chatsworth by Andrew Cavendish, 11th Duke of Devonshire

Andrew's brother, as we learned at Edensor, was married to Kathleen Kennedy. Andrew also took a bride during the war years and, as indicated above, she played a major role in the transformation of the house from the 1950s to what it is today. Deborah has written many books in recent years, but in keeping with our stated intent of not considering contemporary works, we have not included them. However, we will refer back to a book, written in 1940's, in which Deborah is portrayed. In the chapter title, we emphasised families and as, not only Deborah, but her sisters and parents were represented in the novel, we need to explain a little about this phenomenal family.

Everyone More Foolish Than The Last

The words in the title of this section were said by Lord Redesdale about his daughters. And so we must apologise to Deborah as she was the youngest of the six. In truth, it certainly cannot be applied to her, but the sisters, with practically all of them making headlines at sometime, had tempestuous times with each other, but often found reconciliation in the end. Constantly in the headlines, their father, at times, despaired of them. They were known as the Mitford sisters, and they all entered the social whirl between the wars as debutantes, and they would be known to the rich and famous through the world, for vastly different reasons. All six were undoubted beauties and their elegance was always with them.

The eldest, born in 1904, was Nancy who became the celebrated author and it is her books *The Pursuit of Love* and *Love in a Cold Climate,* in which her family is portrayed. They are light-hearted books and depict a family between the wars which is exactly what the Mitford family were. Nancy had an unsuc-

The maze: the outside walls give the size of the original Great Conservatory built by Paxton

cessful marriage and, in later life, moved to Paris to be with her lover, who at one time was General de Gaulle's chief of staff.

Pamela was born three years later, and was the sister who generally lived out of the headlines. She married and then divorced one of the country's leading scientists and that was when John Betjeman fell in love with her, but nothing finally came of the relationship. Thomas, the only son, of the seven children, died in action in the Second World War. The fourth born would be one of the most independent minded and one of the most controversial.

Diana Mitford's wedding, into the Guinness Empire, became the celebration of 1929, but her marriage failed four years later, when she took up with the fascist Black-shirt leader Sir Oswald Moseley. Despite the many recriminations and pleas from family and friends she stayed with him for the rest of her life, which involved being locked in Holloway during the Second World War.

Unity Mitford was attracted by fascism of a different kind. When in Germany, she became infatuated with Adolf Hitler and finally met him and probably became his mistress. She was clearly in favour, as she, her mother and Deborah took tea with him one afternoon. The Mitfords were very fond of Germany and the declaration of the Second World War greatly affected Unity, so much so, that she attempted suicide by shooting herself in the head. Surprisingly, she didn't kill herself. Hitler sent her to a hospital in Switzerland from where she was collected by her mother and Deborah. The second youngest was Jessica who eloped in the 1930s and took the communist side in the Spanish Civil War. Then she later moved to America.

We think that from the six daughters we can see enough political intrigue, but there was even more through relationships and marriages. The Mitfords were cousins of Winston Churchill, and following Deborah joining the Cavendish family the Kennedys became friends and Andrew's uncle was a minister in the government, Harold Macmillan.

There is a photograph in existence of Aunt Sadie and her six children sitting around the tea-table at Alconleigh. The table is situated, as it was, is now, and ever shall be, in the hall, in front of a huge open fire of logs. Over the chimney piece plainly visible in the photograph, hangs an entrenching tool, with which, in 1915, Uncle Matthew hacked to death eight Germans one by one as then crawled out of the dug-out.... In the photograph Aunt Sadie's face, always beautiful, appears strangely round, her hair strangely fluffy and her clothes strangely dowdy.
The Pursuit of Love – Nancy Mitford

Uncle Matthew and Aunt Sadie were the portrayal in the novel of Nancy's mother and father, Lord and Lady Redesdale.

The River Derwent from the Bower

Let's rest awhile on Derwent's banks

As we sit at the edge of the meandering Derwent it gives us chance to reflect on our visit to Chatsworth. The Reverend Francis Hodgson, became a good friend of Hart, and when Francis marries for the second time we shall come across him again on *The Literary Way.*

The life style of our larger than life ladies, Georgiana and Caroline, would even make some of our modern pop stars look timid in comparison. We saw another saga in the life of Byron, who we are meeting through his friends and lovers. Undoubtedly, he was a charismatic figure and the demonic and flawed Byronic anti-hero has lived on from his time in so many forms of literary tribute. We found the relationship between Hart, the Bachelor sixth Duke and his gardener Joseph Paxton fascinating. While they became firm friends and travelled extensively together, Joseph never attempted to be anything but a respected employee even after he was knighted for his role in the Great Exhibition.

At Chatsworth, as in many other locations the climax of visits and events, are celebrated after dark. In modern days we use fireworks. Joseph wanted Queen Victoria's visit to be spectacular, so, in the 1840's he lit the conservatory with 15,000 lamps and then lit the grounds and cascade with thousands of Bengal lights. His ultimate compliment for the display came from the normally unforgiving Duke of Wellington, who commented that Paxton should have been one of his generals. In modern times Chatsworth has figured in many films with recent notable ones being, *The Wolf Man, Pride and Prejudice* and the *Duchess,* which is about Georgiana.

The Victorians

Chatsworth to Curbar Gap through Baslow

Thatched Cottages in Baslow

On this walk we will join three Victorians who had such vastly different lives and interests. One gave his name to technology, which became commonplace in households in the 1960s and his wife wrote a fascinating biography of this man and his inventions. To tempt us even further, many of us still have, in our houses today, something that he devised. Of the other two men, we shall meet on this walk, one was a local poet from Sheffield, whereas the other strode on the national stage and many believed that he should have been the Poet Laureate.

Our walk initially borders the Derwent, but after Bubnell and Baslow we go up onto the gritstone ridges for some wonderful views. The East Moors which we cover, on this walk and the next, give such striking contrasts. On the western edges, overlooking the Derwent Valley, the late August sun gives us a stunning purple landscape as the heather flowers in profusion. Contrast this with a cold windy winter's day on Big Moor with the marshy grasses whistling in the swirling air and we have the most bleakest of landscapes.

We leave the majestic Chatsworth and take the path along the river, past Queen Mary's Bower, and through the revolving gate close to the village of Baslow and follow the path a further few hundred yards. We pass a very pretty row of thatched cottages and turn left over the stream bridge and come out into the Goose Green area of Baslow. Just on the other side of the green is the main road, on which heavy weekend traffic arrives from both Chesterfield and Sheffield. We turn towards the church and go down between the church and the Rutland Arms to the River Derwent. Once away from the main road it is a quiet and picturesque village. The old bridge, with its ancient toll booth, makes a good setting as does the weir a little upstream. The hamlet of Bubnell is on the far side of the bridge from Baslow.

Fair Baslow!

John Hall was a business man, born in 1824, who lived at Norbury which, at the time, was outside of Sheffield, but is now part of the conurbation. John wrote poetry that was mainly published in the local newspapers and the occasional magazine, with one of his first published works being in Eliza Cook's Journal. He chose to draw together his poems for his family and published a private edition of his works in 1877. The poems represent places that he visited and major events in his life. He called his collection of poems, *Thoughts and Sketches in Verse.*

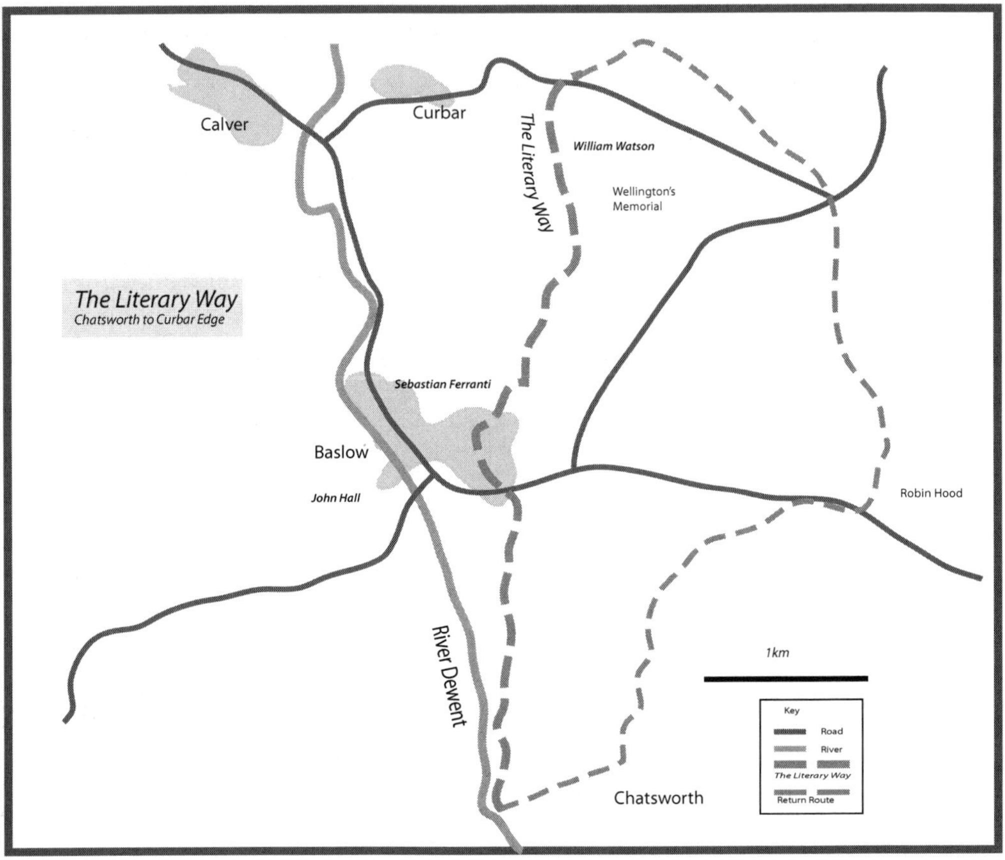

The Literary Way – Walk Fourteen – Chatsworth House to Curbar Gap

The first poem in the book is dedicated to Baslow. It is about three pages long so let us take the summarised view at the end:

Such are the charms which thou canst boast,
Fair Baslow! - such thy beauteous host;
And long as Nature shall dispense
The bounteous gifts of Providence
Long as the trees put on their green,
And landscapes glow with summer's sheen
While rivers murmur as they run,
And fountains sparklet in the sun,
And mountain heath and garden bloom
Their tints perennial resume,
Thine e'er shall be a chosen seat
A fond Arcadian retreat
A cherish'd, honour'd, favour'd spot,
By none who know thee e'er forgot;
A land of luxury and ease,
Of joy and hope, of health and peace!
Thoughts and Sketches in Verse – John Hall, J.H.J

As we return to the main road, a little along the road on our right is Baslow Hall, which is not visible from the road. It is now a reputed restaurant and small hotel. One man who lived there from 1913 was an electrical inventor, who would see his company continue his innovative approach. It would later grow into a large corporation which manufactured power supply electrical equipment, computers and defence electronics. His name was Sebastian Ziani de Ferranti.

Inspired Electronics

Sebastian Ziani de Ferranti was born in Liverpool in 1864 and moved to Baslow Hall in 1913. He grew his business from a small firm to a multinational corporation within his lifetime. For many of the generation that were around when televisions became common place in the home, the name Ferranti will easily resonate. Of course, television was added to an established portfolio of electrical products, already produced by the corporation.

Sebastian himself, and the original direction of the company, focused on the provision of electricity. Even in his schools days, he had a fascination with inventions, especially concerning engines. As a young man his inventive mind turned to electricity. He was the pioneer of high voltage systems and how they could be cascaded down to the local levels necessary for widespread electrical lighting. He was the inspiration behind the building of Deptford

Walk Directions

Chatsworth to Baslow (1.57 miles)

We leave Chatsworth along the banks of the Derwent
We go north past the cricket ground and follow the path to the end of the open estate
Go through the twirling gate and follow the path past the thatched cottages
Turn left to Goose Green
Turn left onto the main road and then right at the roundabout
The church is on the left, a little path takes you down to the riverside
Go past the church and view the weir from the bridge by the Rutland Arms
Baslow Hall is further down the main road on the right
Little of it is visible from the road

Baslow to Curbar Edge Car Park (2.46 miles)

Retrace your steps to the mini-roundabout by the church
Take the left road and follow it up through the cottages and houses of Baslow
Keep on the road which begins to climb and the houses gradually end
The road becomes a track
Follow it uphill. You will reach the gate to the Open Access land
Go through the gate and bear right to the Wellington Memorial
From the memorial head for Eagle Stone (it is a squarish shape in the middle of the heather)
Pass Eagle Stone and continue along the edge and enjoy the fine views
At the end pass through the gate and turn right to go to the car park

Curbar Edge Car Park to Chatsworth (4.52 miles)

A path leaves the car park across the moors (near where it joins the road)
Follow the path which dips down and then rises along a wall.
At the end of the wall a path crosses in front of us, turn right
Follow this across the moor until it comes out near the road junction
Walk to the crossroads. Diagonally opposite is a path
Take the path which leads to the craggy outcrop
As you approach the rocks, branch off to the left along the path
This takes you up onto the edge of the rocks
There you will find Nelson's monument and his ships' names carved into the rocks
Go past the named rocks and take the path down from the edge
There is a main path under the edge. Turn left.
Follow this until it comes out on the main road near the Robin Hood pub
Turn right and go past the pub.
On the left-hand side of the road is a footpath
Follow this which dips down over the stream and then climbs the other side
Follow this path along the edge
It eventually turns inland and will arrive at a large stile over a wall
On the other side of the wall on your left is a track
Take the track through the woods until you reach the Hunting Tower
Descend from the Hunting Tower to Chatsworth

Distance: 8.54 miles Ascent: 1282ft

Houses, stream and bridge in Baslow

Curbar Edge with an abandoned millstone

power station, which was the first in London to provide mass lighting. He also developed the meters for measuring electrical usage. The Ferranti meters have had over a hundred years of service and have the very familiar small dials, each with a single hand, and a revolving disc showing electricity is being used. Ferranti's work has had its impact on each and every one of us. We now take for granted the national grid electrical system, for which he laid the foundation. Sebastian died in the 1930s, but his pioneering spirit continued in the Ferranti Company. The second commercial computer in the world, the Ferranti Mark I went on sale in 1949, which was in the very earliest days of computing.

Ferranti and his family lived at Baslow Hall and, from 1918, gradually introduced electricity. His biography was written, in 1934, by his wife. This is what she had to say about the introduction of electricity into Baslow Hall. The description below was installed between 1921 and 1925:

It is necessary to give some account of the electrification of Baslow Hall, for the problem connecting it, occupied my husband's spare time during our first years there. Panel heating with thermostatically operated pumps and valves to control the house temperature was fitted throughout.... An electric laundry was also installed with washer, ironer, electric clothes drier and airer.... Practically every labour saving or other device which contributed to comfort was fitted at Baslow including wireless to all rooms, floor polishers, vacuum cleaners, bed warmers and airers, ultra-violet ray apparatus, every example of electric cookers and heaters, electric vacuum clothes brushes, refrigerators etc....

The Life and Letters of Sebastian Ziani Ferranti by G Ferranti & R Ince

After our brief look round Baslow it is now time to take the steady climb up onto the gritstone edges, which have been evident since we first saw them behind Chatsworth. From the Rutland Arms we go back towards the centre of Baslow, but we turn left at the mini-roundabout. We're now going to follow this road up, through this quiet part of Baslow, until it becomes a track. It gradually gets steeper. Eventually we reach a gate that indicates that it leads to the Open Access of the moorlands.

The Iron Duke Memorial

If we go through the gate and take the path to the right, we are heading towards a monument that looks out over the valley back towards Chatsworth. When we reach it, we discover that this three metre obelisk is dedicated to the Duke of Wellington. The 'Iron Duke' was a soldier and a statesman. We can see Chatsworth House in the valley and the Duke visited there and he was impressed by the work of Paxton. One of the waterfall features, in the Rockery, built by Paxton, is named after the Duke of Wellington.

This obelisk on Curbar Edge was erected by a local man from Baslow. The First Duke of Wellington, Arthur Wellesley, lived from 1769 to 1852. He was one of the leading military figures of the nineteenth Century. His most noted achievement is a history legend. It was his leadership of the forces that defeated Napoleon at the Battle of Waterloo. He had become a Duke two years before the famous battle, following recognition of his previous military expertise. He went on to become Prime Minister on two separate occasions.

These gritstone moorlands are so different to the limestone on which we have been walking. The moors have many significant archaeological sites. This is because prehistoric farmers were the last to farm these high hills. All subsequent farming involved the removal of the valley forests and the development of many centuries of cultivation on the valley sides and along the floor. Our route takes us across the moor towards the large smoothed rock that stands high above the heather. It is Eagle Stone, not because it looks like an eagle, but it is thought to be a derivation of Eccles stone, which is of religious significance. As one would expect, it tends to have various stories associated with it, such as, a local young man must climb it before his proposal of marriage will be accepted.

Nearly the Poet Laureate

We have been walking along Baslow Edge which becomes Curbar Edge. In a newly formed 1894 Literary Periodical called, *The Yellow Book,* there was a sonnet by the poet, Sir William Watson. He was a great supporter of Lord Tennyson as the Poet Laureate. When Tennyson died in 1892, William was mooted as a successor to him as, at the time, he was the leading poet in the land. William was 34 when the Laureate, who had held the post for 42 years, died. However, William had taken an interest in South Africa and expressed his opposition to the sabre rattling as the prelude to the Boer War. In the eyes of many politicians, it made him unsuitable for the role and so the post went to someone else. As we stroll along the millstone grit edges towards Curbar Gap and Curbar Edge, we look down on the Derwent Valley as it stretches from Calver to Baslow. William Watson wrote a sonnet entitled *Night on Curbar Edge.*

No echo of man's life pursues my ears;
Nothing disputes this Desolation's reign;
Change comes not, this dread temple to profane,
Where time by aeons reckons, not by years.
Its patient form one crag, sole-stranded, rears,
Type of whatever is destined to remain
While yon still host encamped on Night's waste plain
Keeps armed watch, a million quivering spears.
Hushed are the wild and winged lives of the moor;
The sleeping sheep nestle neath ruined wall,
Or unhewn stones in random concourse hurled:
Solitude, sleepless, listens at Fate's door;
And there is built and 'stablish over all-
Tremendous Silence, older than the world.
Night on Curbar Edge — William Watson

Let's rest awhile at Curbar Gap

The area through which we have come in this chapter, Baslow and the gritstone edges, inspired all three of the men in this chapter in different ways. Sebastian decided to build his house here even though he was working in the cities of Manchester and Sheffield. William Watson travelled around the country, as was common for a man of his status, but he was sufficiently pleased with the area when

Open Stretches of heather moorlands on Curbar Edge

The path at Curbar Gap

he stayed nearby to turn it into verse. Finally, John Hall was a businessman who took his relaxation by journeys from Sheffield into the Peak District and favoured Baslow and the Derwent Valley.

The Sage

Curbar Gap to The Grouse through Millthorpe

Towards the Cordwell Valley and the home of Edward Carpenter

We are going in pursuit of a sage. Our main writer on this walk left the hurly-burly of city life to move to the quiet and solitude of the Cordwell Valley, but he often didn't manage to achieve that tranquillity, because he became a writer that everyone wanted to meet and they were prepared to travel thousands of miles to talk with, and to listen to him. He was a Cambridge graduate, who took holy orders but left the south of England, his birth place and family home, to build a house on the fringes of the Peak District.

His writings are not easily accessible, due to the complexity of his thoughts, but he gathered friends and like-minded people near him. Some were permanent residents and other visitors. He wrote and received letters from the famous the world over. His relationships with both men and women make a compelling study.

Among those who came to the quiet village, was a London loving playwright of the twentieth century, and a second man who had many times been described as the master English novelist of the same century.

Another man who shared similar political feelings had a completely different mission in mind. He was one of the pioneers of opening up the countryside for walkers. He did such a magnificent job, that in the 1940s, the Ramblers Association, bought and presented him with a hill-top in the Peak District. And finally we have two women. One created a famous novel, now a classic, about South Africa and the other was a campaigner for the rights of women to have the vote, and she was also a novelist. One of her books was read to an assembled group of friends in our sage's cottage.

We leave Curbar Edge and head across the moors on a path almost parallel to the road. In winter this is really a windswept and desolate moor. It is a winding path that picks its way across the boggy parts of the moor with its accompanying reed grasses. We turn left along the main road for a short while and then take the lane towards Shillito Woods. It is a quiet road and we can stroll happily along looking out at the distant views. We turn right in front of Shillito Woods and then after a few fields, take the first left lane towards Unthank. Its a longish walk of a few miles from Curbar to our destination, beyond Unthank, but it is worth it as we shall see.

We begin to descend and we are heading down into the verdant valley that we can see in front of us. It is quiet and well-sheltered, especially when compared to the open moors from which we have come. We pass the old Unthank Hall and some farms. Where the lane takes a sharp turn to the left we go

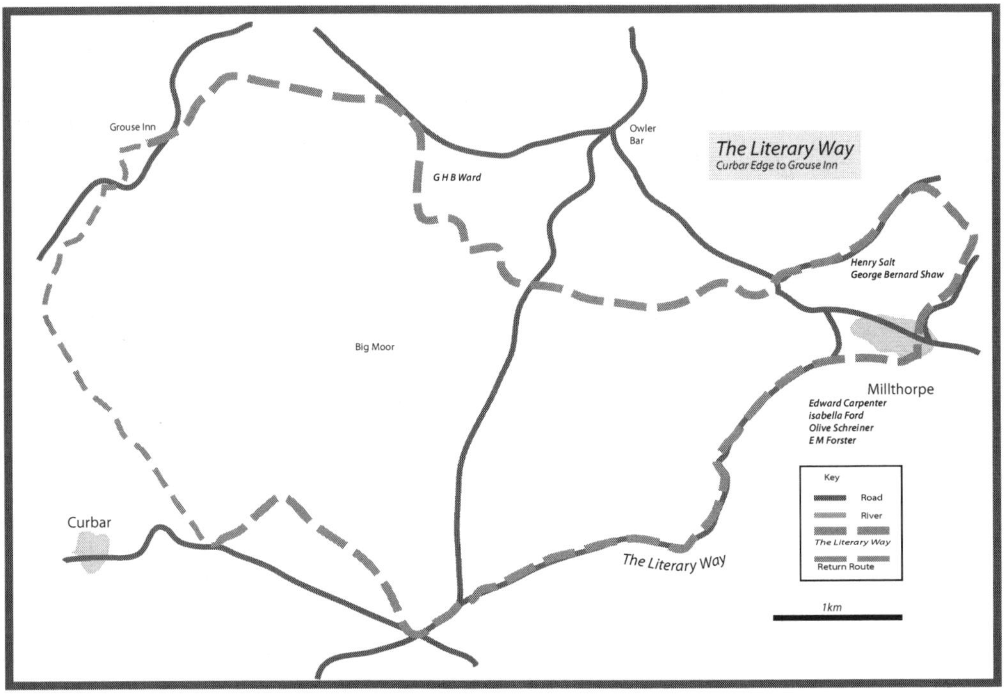

The Literary Way – Walk Fifteen – Curbar Edge to The Grouse

Edward Carpenter's Cottage

Walk Directions

Curbar Gap to Millthorpe (4.63 miles)

A path leaves the car park across the moors (near where it joins the road)
Follow the path which dips down and then rises along a wall.
At the end of the wall a path crosses in front of us, turn right
Follow this across the moor until it comes out near the road junction
We turn left for a few yards and take the lane on our right
This quiet lane takes us towards Shillito Woods
At the junction before the woods we turn right
There is a good view across the fields to the Cordwell valley below
We take the next turning on our left which leads us past Unthank Hall
When the second sharp left bend is reached take the footpath straight ahead
Follow it across the fields and then Edward Carpenter's hut can be seen in the garden
The path comes out on a lane and we turn left across the splash.
At the top of the lane is the Royal Oak pub
We turn left to reach Edward Carpenter's house and then retrace our steps to the crossroads

Millthorpe to Big Moor (4.78 miles)

We turn left after the pub
About half a mile up the lane is Cartledge Hall where Murray Gilchrist lived
We take the path opposite to the Hall and cross the fields
We come out at the top of Horsleygate Lane
We turn left down the lane to Little Orchards
This is where Henry Salt lived and where George Bernard Shaw stayed when he visited
Just past Horsleygate Hall we take a path on our left
It passes around the back of an Equestrian centre and comes out on the main road
The path continues on the opposite side of the road
Follow it as it bends round the trees until you come to a cross of paths
Take the path furthest right and follow it through the woods
At the fork of the path take the left hand way
This bring us out on to a green lane
Turn right and walk to the top of the lane
Cross the main road and enter Big Moor through the gate.

Big Moor to the Grouse Inn (1.34 miles)

Follow the path ahead until it joins a track and turn right
At the track junction turn left towards the solitary house
Follow the track to the right of the house and join the path that runs parallel to the track
Rejoin the same track and head towards the road
Just before the wall turn left along the path and over the brook
This is now on G H B Ward's route
The footpath then angles away from the road and goes up the heather slope
When you reach the cross path at the top go straight ahead towards the lodge
As you near the lodge take the path to the left
It goes parallel to the top of the rise
When you reach a track turn right and go down hill to the road
Turn left along the verge to reach the Grouse Inn

Grouse Inn to Curbar Gap (2.64)

Walk past the Grouse Inn and turn right down into the car park just after the pub
Turn left at the bottom, and follow the track
Cross the road and rejoin the track
Follow the track along Curbar Edge back to Curbar Gap

Distance: 13.4 miles Ascent: 1780ft

straight on along the footpath. We are now going along the side of the valley and we need to keep a careful eye to the left. At the bottom of the slope is a stream and on the far side appear some houses with largish gardens. We are looking for a small hut, it looks a little like a small summer house, near to the stream and at the bottom of the garden.

Towards Democracy

We can now see the small village of Millthorpe straddled along the Cordwell valley. This stream-side hut and its local countryside became a centre of literary pilgrimage in the late 1890s, and early twentieth century. Edward Carpenter was a prolific writer who became resident in Millthorpe. He was a pioneer of socialism in England and was one of the founders of the Fabian Society. He is perhaps best known today as one of the first gay activists and this is reflected in many of his socialist philosophy writings.

It is interesting to compare Edward with our last notary, The Duke of Wellington. Two completely different characters who had an outlook on life that was poles apart. They will never have met as Carpenter was only eight when Wellington died in 1852, but in their time, both would move in the highest circles in England and personally know many famous leaders and authors.

Edward was a man who put considerable thought into his writings and attracted many people into his sphere of influence. Several of the people he met, and corresponded with, came from completely different background. Isadora Duncan, the American dancer, who moved to Europe, aspired to the same principles as Carpenter. As many will know, she moved to Russia to join the social and political revolution there. Carpenter was initially inspired by the writings of the American poet, Walt Whitman. They would become friends and meet on several occasions.

Edward was a founder member of the Fabian Society, which is an intellectual socialist movement. It still operates today and is given the press label, 'think-tank'. It was founded in 1884 and soon became driven by Sidney and Beatrice Webb. This led to the rapid attraction of new members, includ-

The ford at Millthorpe

ing some famous playwrights and novelists of the twentieth century, such as George Bernard Shaw, Oscar Wilde, HG Wells, Virginia Woolf and Edith Nesbit, who wrote *The Railway Children*. The political activists that became part of the Society included Emmeline Pankhurst and Ramsey MacDonald. And here is link with a writer we have already met on *The Literary Way*. Alison Uttley, the children's writer, was a friend of Ramsey MacDonald and his wife. They enjoyed Alison's company for many years, but did not see her in a political light, although Alison had socialist inclinations at the time.

One political agenda, that was pioneered by the Webbs, and for which Edward had a lot of support, was the growth of co-operatives. They took on many forms and many have commercially stood the test of time until the modern-day. The idea of a commune had already been taken up by one who Edward greatly admired, John Ruskin, who established one a few miles from Millthorpe. It was nearing the end of its existence when Edward Carpenter stayed there before he built his house at Millthorpe. Although he never tried to establish a formal commune, Edward did buy the land and built his house with a view to self-sufficiency and he certainly started with the notion of creating a market garden. It was successfully run for a short while by one of his associates, but he paid less and less time to it as his volume of writing increased.

To return to our location overlooking the valley with Edward Carpenter's back garden and the streamside hut. Whilst it was a large house, for many years, he had another family staying with him. In the latter years, it would only be his partner, but by then, he was famous and inundated with visitors. So he used the hut in the garden to gain solitude for his writings. Let's follow the path until it comes out on a lane and then we turn down into the village and over the footbridge by the water splash. As we reach the main road we turn left past the pub, the Royal Oak. It was where George Merrill, Edward Carpenter's long-term partner frequented as he was reputed to be a man who liked his pint. Edward was known to play the piano there during the Sunday night singalong.

Carrying on along the road and we come to the front of what is now called Edward Carpenter House, but when it was built, in 1882, it was called Millthorpe Cottage. It was the year after he moved in that he wrote the work which was to make him famous. It was called *Towards Democracy*. Unlike many political writings, such as Hobbes' *Leviathan*, it does not seek to build a reasoned and logical argument for the nature of man and society. Instead Edward's approach was a mixture of the poetical, the transcendental, and the totality of existence. It has its roots in Walt Whitman's approach. It is written in a series of verses in poetic style mixed with prose, here is the opening of the first edition:

The sun, the moon and the stars, the grass, the water that flows round the earth, and the light air of heaven:
To You greeting. I too stand behind these and send you word across them.
Freedom at last!
Long sought, long prayed for — ages and ages long: the burden to which I continually return, seated here thickbooted and obvious yet dead and buried and passed into heaven, unsearchable;
[How do you know indeed but what I have passed into you?]
And Joy, beginning but without ending — the journey of journeys, Thought laid quietly aside .
Towards Democracy – Edward Carpenter

Its publication, led to its widespread reading and established Edward Carpenter as a leading thinker of the time. As people discovered his writing and his way of life, so a visit to Edward at Millthorpe came on to many people's agenda.

Leaves of Grass

Let's look at how a former curate of the Church of England became a gay activist, and incorporated into his writing eastern mysticism. Edward's early life followed a relatively conventional pattern. He was born in a good part of Hove, Sussex and attended Brighton College before going to Trinity Hall, Cambridge. At University he showed his talent and was offered a fellowship to stay on. He was a little reluctant because a condition of the fellowship required him to be ordained. However, he was persuaded and took up the academic role and became a curate in the Church of England.

So what made such an impact on him to completely change his life? He said that it was the poems of Walt Whitman. His major work *Leaves of Grass,* is a Romantic appeal to all people, coupled with the explicit expressions of feelings. Edward gradually moved into a lifestyle which was so radically different from his upbringing. He left his middle class roots and first moved to be at the heart of the working class in Leeds, and then to Chesterfield.

He finally settled at Millthorpe, which is just outside of Sheffield, and at the edge of the Millstone

Royal Oak, Millthorpe where Edward Carpenter played the piano for Sunday night singalongs

Grit, that forms the hills which separate the East Midlands plain from the White Peak of Derbyshire. He became increasingly radical, as he studied the views of Engels and had extensive contacts with labourers and the working class, as he was one of the pioneers of evening classes. Sheffield, by this time, had become the major iron and steel town in England. Added to his increasing political polarisation, he became a greater advocate of sexual freedom. By now, he was settled on the small-holding at Millthorpe, which he ran and shared with a range of people.

His views on sexual freedom continued and he fully acknowledged his homosexuality. He visited India in pursuit of the mysticism he sought, and when he returned in 1891, George Merrill moved into his home in Millthorpe. Merrill had come from one of the poorest parts of Sheffield and had had no formal education. Their relationship endured even though, four years after coming together, there would be Oscar Wilde's trial, after which the law was changed outlawing homosexuality. However, it did not stop Edward and George's relationship continuing in the seclusion of Millthorpe.

As a philosopher, Edward was also known for his 1889 publication of *Civilisation, its Cause and Cure,* in which he outlines his view of the disease of civilisation and seeks the cure through closer association with the land and the inner self.

We find ourselves to-day in the midst of a somewhat peculiar state of society, which we call Civilisation, but which even to the most optimistic among us does not seem altogether desirable.
Civilisation, its Cause and Cure – Edward Carpenter

Edward had very many uninvited visitors who had come to hear him reading from his works and to see his lifestyle. He also invited many of his friends and members of the societies to which he belonged. He does say that although the place was very busy at times, he could find peace and quiet in Millthorpe, because of the distance from the nearest railway station, which was about four miles. Also, he was not a recluse and, not only travelled to London regularly, but often went abroad.

Edward's output of works was prolific. Whilst he wrote many full length works, he was better known for articles, speeches and other varied contributions to the social topics of the day. He also had a wide breadth of interests and approached his chosen lifestyle from a number of different perspectives. He wrote about love, sex, eastern mysticism as well as police, prisons and punishment. His first major work was produced in 1870 and the final one in 1924, which was five years before his death. His chosen poetic style of *Towards Democracy* is also reflected in other poetry such as one entitled *Memory.*

An African Farm

There would be many women who would intellectually engage with Edward. Before his publication of *Towards Democracy,* and his subsequent high profile, he became aware of a newly published book about individuals and women in society. It had the unlikely background of being written from an isolated farm in South Africa. It was published in 1883 and was called *The Story of an African Farm.* It was written by Olive Schreiner, but the first edition was published under the male pseudonym Ralf Irons. She became a prolific writer on individualism and the importance of friendship. She moved to London for a number of years, but never really settled in one place and journeyed around a great deal. She became very close friends with Edward and stayed in a cottage in Millthorpe for a number of months during her period in England. Olive was also instrumental in helping Edward sort out some of his complex relationships that he developed, particularly when one of the his first loves, George Hukin, decided to get married. This is how she describes meeting Edward:

The first time I met Carpenter was in London about 1883, at a meeting of a society which we had then newly formed for the purpose of attempting to arrive at some method of carrying out practically the ideal of a simplified and socialised life. He was then somewhat under forty. What struck me, as I looked across the table, was the curious light upon the face. The features themselves, not small and not very regular, were forgotten; only the expression remained with one.
Edward Carpenter – The Man and His message – Tom Swan (who quotes from Olive Schreiner's Diary)

Olive and Edward would remain friends for the rest of Olive's life. She returned to South Africa just before her death in 1920, at the age of 65.

On the Threshold

Isabella Ford came from a very different background from Olive, but was equally determined about women's rights and socialism. Her father was a forward looking solicitor from Leeds, where Isabella lived for all her life. She soon became involved in the Independent Labour Party. In the 1900s she would become a suffragette, but abhorred the violence in the movement and distanced herself from them. She was highly articulate and, as she could speak French and German, often represented socialists, women, and trade unions at international meetings. Through her speeches and writing she became known to Edward and they became friends.

As with Olive, she helped him in some of his relationships and the two women also became good friends. She was a frequent visitor to Millthorpe and was regularly invited by Edward. She was in Millthorpe, at Edward's cottage, shortly after the publication of her book *On the Threshold.* Evenings at the cottage were often spent reading or listening to music.

On one occasion Isabella read her newly produced book to them. The novel is about two young women who tire of their lower middle class life in the provinces and go to London with the idealist notion of changing the world. The book is a gentle one about their trials and tribulations and Isabella uses some of the speakers to put forward her views on society. The principal mouthpiece in the novel for these views bears many characteristics of Edward Carpenter.

I and my friend Kitty Manners had come up to London one January to study art, of course somewhat against the wishes of our parents, for parents in my young days regarded any kind of study, or student life, for their daughters, with considerable aversion. Kitty was at the School of Art; I was studying music. It was the days before ladies chambers and cheap flats, so because our means were limited, painfully limited, we had settled into three small dark rooms in a street in Bloomsbury.
On the Threshold – Isabella Ford

Maurice

There were many visitors who came to Millthorpe to meet Edward and discuss his work and views on society. Edward Morgan Forster, who is best known for his works *Room with a View* and *Passage to India,* visited in 1912. He went on to become very well known in the 1930s and 1940s. He was elected to a Fellowship at Cambridge, broadcast regularly for the BBC, and wrote libretti for Benjamin Britten. In 1953 Morgan was awarded the Order of Companion of Honour and in 1969 given the Order of Merit by the Queen, despite having turned down a knighthood some twenty years earlier. At the age of ninety, Morgan died at the home of his long-term friend Robert Buckingham.

Morgan had a difficult life in many ways. While he was free from financial worries, his father died young and he remained very close to his mother throughout his life. He struggled for many years to deal with his homosexuality and his visits to Edward almost certainly helped him to come to terms with it, but it was still a long while before he settled into a discreet relationship. All of his novel writing, many of which have become celebrated, was completed in a relatively few years. In later life, he became a broadcaster and critic but he never wrote another novel after the age of forty-five.

During Morgan's visit in 1912 he paid particular attention to the relationship between Edward and George Merrill. By the following year Morgan had written a novel based on George which he entitled *Maurice*. Although it was completed in 1913 it would not be published until after his death in 1970. *Maurice* is a book that follows a man from his school days through to adulthood and his homosexual loves. The book has been subsequently, in 1987, produced as a film starring James Wilby, Hugh Grant, Denholm Elliott, Simon Callow, Billie Whitelaw and Ben Kingsley. The real life relationship between Edward and George was the bringing together of middle and working class. In *Maurice* the same theme is explored between a stockbroker and a gamekeeper. Let's take a short look at one of the meetings in the book

'Had I best be going now, sir?' Abominably shy, Maurice pretended not to hear. 'We mustn't fall asleep though, awkward if anyone came in,' he continued, with a pleasant blurred laugh that made Maurice feel friendly but at the same time diffident

and sad.
He managed to reply, 'you mustn't call me sir,' and the laugh sounded again as if brushing aside such problems. There seemed to be charm and insight yet his discomfort increased.
'May I ask your name?' he said awkwardly.
'I'm Scudder.'
'I know you're Scudder – I meant your other name.'
'Only Alec just.'
'Jolly name to have.'
'It's only my name.'
'I'm called Maurice.'
Maurice – E M Forster

When Morgan was at Cambridge he met Lytton Strachey, who we cited on *The Literary Way* as the biographer of Florence Nightingale. In a note at the end of *Maurice* Morgan says that he based the undergraduate in the novel on Lytton Strachey.

We retrace our steps past the pub and turn left and walk along the lane to Cartledge Hall. A friend of Edward's, and a fellow writer, lived in this Hall and they would often share a bottle of whisky. His name was R Murray Gilchrist and he wrote novels, short stories and travel guides. However, we will leave considering Murray, as he also lived in another village along *The Literary Way* and we shall discuss his works when we arrive there. A path takes us from Cartledge Hall, across the field, and it is a short distance to Horsleygate Lane. We can soon see the sign to a house called Little Orchards and this was the residence of another prolific writer, who was also a friend of Edward's.

A Sage at Close Quarters

Henry Salt came from a privileged background and went to Eton, and from there to Cambridge, where he excelled as a classics student. As a result he returned to Eton as an assistant master. Life was normal for a man from his background and his talents. However, he became enthralled by the writings of H D Thoreau, who advocated a simple life in country seclusion. It was then that Henry read of Edward Carpenter setting up a form of self-sufficiency in a country village. Both these writers inspired him and he chose to do the same. He received further encouragement from Edward when he met him and, in a short time, had left Eton and moved, with his wife Kate, to live in a cottage in Surrey.

As Henry developed his views on life, he began to advocate vegetarianism and the abolition of cruelty to animals. He was instrumental in setting up the Humanitarian League. In a similar vein to Edward, Henry wrote many articles and put considerable energy into getting them published. This was quite an achievement as many were against the norms of society at the time. In all his life he never gave up his causes.

He gained international recognition for his promotion of vegetarianism with the highest accolades coming from Mahatma Gandhi, who thanked Henry for his justification of vegetarianism and in introducing him to the writings of H D Thoreau. Henry produced many works during his lifetime

Cartledge Hall where Edward would share a whisky with Murray Gilchrist

which spanned 1851 to 1939. These included biographies and appraisals of H D Thoreau, Percy Bysshe Shelley and Alfred Lord Tennyson. He was among the founding members of the Fabian Society, but accepted that socialists were not good at agreeing with themselves. Henry would philosophically accept when schisms took place in new labour-focused movements. He has been credited with being one of the first writers to advocate the rights of animals. The Humanitarian League produced a controversial volume of essays entitled *Killing for Sport.*

Henry married a former colleague's daughter, Kate, who agreed with the lifestyle and principles. Eventually they would leave Surrey and London and move to Millthorpe to be near Edward. Whilst he and Kate lived at Millthorpe, one of the many works that Henry produced was *The Logic of Vegetarianism, Essays and Dialogues.* This was published in 1906. Henry explains the purpose of the volume in the Introduction.

It is the special purpose of this book to set forth in a clear and rational manner the logic of vegetarianism.
The Logic of Vegetarianism – Henry Salt

The title of this section is taken from *A Sage at Close Quarters* as it was one of the essays produced by Henry Salt. It is a description and assessment of his friend Edward Carpenter. It is a realistic account and not one seen through rose-tinted glasses. This is the start of the essay.

Some personal reminiscences of Edward Carpenter, by a friend who knew him intimately for over forty years, may hereafter be of interest, and even of value, to students of his writings, inasmuch as it is often more difficult to form a clear idea of "the man behind the book" than of the books themselves. My acquaintance with him dated from 1884; and during the next twenty-five years my wife and I were often visitors at his cottage at Millthorpe, or stayed for weeks at a time in neighbouring farm-houses; while he, in his turn, was frequently our guest in London or in Surrey, or went on excursions with us to the mountains of Wales or Cumberland. In 1910 we built a cottage at Holmesfield, within a mile of Millthorpe, and lived there for some seven years. It will be seen that I am not writing without knowledge.
A Sage at Close Quarters – Henry Salt

The essay explains that at times he could be moody and very demanding, but overall, he was a very good friend to have.

Nobel and Academy

Let's step back a little to before Henry was in Millthorpe to when his wife, Kate, would play a significant part in the development of a triangle of writers. The volume *Killing for Sport* had a preface written by George Bernard Shaw. He was both a vegetarian and a Fabian, and was to be friends with Henry for the rest of his life. GBS would, not only frequently meet with Henry and his wife Kate, but they would share many evenings of music and literature. Kate became George's unpaid secretary for a period.

There are many biographies and articles that comment on the complex relationship between Henry, Kate, Edward and GBS. One supposition, that is frequently referred to, is whether Kate and Henry's marriage was ever consummated. Certainly she confided a great deal in Edward, especially through letters before they moved to Millthorpe, but unlike many other letters between the four of them, the ones from Kate to Edward have been destroyed. While Edward and GBS weren't the closest of friends, they both had a great admiration for Kate and were good friends with Henry. They all certainly tolerated GBS's humour and did not take offence at some of his caustic comments. For example, Henry and Edward were members of the Fellowship of Life and the Fabians. George was only a member of the latter. He described the difference between the two organisations to be "sitting among the dandelions or organising change in the docks."

Another point of considerable conjecture is about a play written by GBS entitled *Candida.* It has been suggested that Edward Carpenter was a model of Morell and Kate Salt was the lead role called Candida. Let's look at how GBS describes aspects of the two characters. First the study of Morell's bookcase:

...recessed above the fireplace, is fitted with bookshelves, on which an adept eye can measure the parson' s divinity and casuistry by a complete set of Browning's poems and Maurice' s Theological Essays, and guess at his politics from a yellow backed Progress and Poverty, Fabian Essays, a Dream of John Ball, Marx's Capital, and half a dozen other literary landmarks in Socialism.
Candida: A Pleasant Play – George Bernard Shaw

Here is how GBS describes Candida:

She is a woman well built, well nourished, likely, one guesses, to become matronly later on, but now quite at her best, with the double charm of youth and motherhood.
Candida: A Pleasant Play – George Bernard Shaw

GBS never liked travelling far from London or his house in Hertfordshire, but he, for the sake of friendship, did travel up to Millthorpe and stayed near to where Henry and Kate were living. GBS was held in esteem by Henry, Kate and Edward and it is easily forgotten the extensiveness of his capabilities and high regard in which he was held in literary eyes. He is still the only person to be awarded both the Nobel Prize for Literature and an Academy Award.

Let's return to the theme of walking and look at another character from just north of this village who would share more than the love of the countryside with Edward. We leave Millthorpe by walking down Horsleygate Road and taking the path to the left. After crossing the road and following the curve of the fields we have a pleasant stroll through the woods. After we reach the lane we turn right and head for the moors. We cross the main road and go directly onto Big Moor. The path joins a track which passes the single house that is in sight. We follow the edge of the disused reservoir and take the track towards the road. However,we do not go on to the road and cross a footbridge over the stream. On a post nearby is a marker commemorating G H B Ward.

Clarion

The *Clarion* newspaper was founded by Robert Blatchford in Manchester in 1891. It was developed as a paper to represent Socialist views. It continued in production until the 1930s. Apart from espousing the political agenda it also encouraged, and established a platform, for the development of community groups. The *Clarion* was Socialism based on a sense of community rather than the Marxist interpretation. Two of the main local community groups that were formed were either choirs or cycling clubs. They would often use cycling trips into the country as a form of enjoyment, but would often distribute socialist literature when they arrived at their destination. Many of the Clarion cycling groups would visit the Peak District and, one point of call for many of them, would be one of the leading socialists in the country at the time, Edward Carpenter. Several of them would have heard him speak at meetings in Sheffield and therefore wanted to visit him. This was just one of the groups that descended on Edward.

In 1900, George Herbert Bridges Ward, usually known as Bert, used the *Clarion* contacts to invite anyone who would like to join a walk across the moors. There were a number of difficulties on walking across land at the time and the moors were particularly protected by the landowners, who wanted to use them for shooting. Bert, true to his socialist principles, believed that there should be a right for people to be able to walk the countryside paths. From these initial contacts, the Clarion Ramblers were formed, and many Clarion groups still remain in existence today. Bert lived just outside Millthorpe and shared both the walking and socialist interests with Edward Carpenter. In 1910, Bert become the founding editor of the annual handbook for Clarion Ramblers. For decades he edited the book and chaired the Sheffield Clarion Ramblers until his death in 1957 at the age of 81.

The Handbooks, not only gave directional instructions, but imparted a lot of local knowledge and information about the history of the area. This is the opening to the 1927/28 Handbook which focus on Big Moor where we are now. It was the nearest moor to Bert's house when he lived for 43 years.

It is big and brown, wide and drear, featureless and lonely, flat and boggy as any moor in Peakland, and yet, to those who know it most intimately, full of interest, and in the treading of it, verily, a big man's moor.
Clarion Ramblers Handbook – G H B Ward

In order to make the point of land access and bring it to public attention Bert organised a mass trespass of Bleaklow, in 1907 which is 25 years before the famous trespass on Kinderscout, which we shall

Bert Ward's windswept Big Moor

The way down from Big Moor

come to on *The Literary Way*. For all his work in trying to open the countryside to ordinary walkers, the Ramblers Association presented him, in 1945, four years after his retirement, with a piece of land on Lose Hill which overlooks the village of Hope in the Hope Valley. This was duly presented to the National Trust and is called Ward's Piece. Bert saw vast changes within countryside access during his life of campaigning, with the creation of many paths as rights of way and the establishment of the National Parks.

Bert did not restrict his excursion to walking in this country and he became a seasoned traveller. One particular destination inspired him to write a book about it. Bert was a strong socialist and so the book is not a travelogue, but one that addresses the political issues in Spain around about 1910. The preface explains why he embarked on this work.

My aim in the following pages is not to castigate individuals, who are to be regarded as symptoms rather than as causes, nor do I wish to toll a knell over a dead empire. My desire has been rather to point to the real causes of ills which have their roots in history, and which have been bequeathed as a dismal legacy to almost every Spanish speaking people.
The Truth about Spain – G H B Ward

From the bridge we take the path through the heather and over the top of the ridge to look down on the Longshaw Estate. The path on our left leads us down to the Grouse Inn.

Let's Rest Awhile at the Grouse Inn

The sleepy, small and remote village of Millthorpe at the beginning of the twentieth century was an unlikely place to find such literary talent and output. Edward Carpenter was the attraction, although Henry Salt and his wife Kate also drew visitors, such as George Bernard Shaw. Edward, the metaphysical poet, didn't finish his days in Millthorpe and neither did Henry, but when they were there they made an impact not just on the local area, but far and wide. Their correspondence was remarkable both in volume and the number of famous names with whom they corresponded. It is a pity most of the letters between Kate and Edward were lost as they would have shown some additional perspectives on their life style.

Edward and Henry enjoyed walking, and spent many hours on the moors and in the Peak District. The local man, Bert Ward, also a socialist, and the most forthright campaigner for access to the countryside lived nearby and clearly knew Edward very well. We saw Bert's description of Big Moor and it's good to know we are following in the footsteps of such eminent people.

The Plague

The Grouse to The Plough, Leadmill through Eyam

Plague Cottages, Eyam, which is where the disease started

The plague hit a village on *The Literary Way* almost 350 years ago and caused widespread death, but for us it has left a tremendous legacy of writing. Strangely, there is virtually no writing in the immediate aftermath of the devastation, but it has given inspiration for later writers and poets to tell the tale in their own ways.

From the same village comes a vicar's daughter, who moved in some of the highest literary circles in England. Although Sir Walter Scott was only 13 years old when Samuel Johnson died, our writer knew both men very well. She appears the epitome of a spinster from the vicarage, but all may not be as it seems! She was a copious letter writer and produced a biographical memoir of one of our friends on our journey, Erasmus Darwin, who she knew most of her life.

Of those who took the plague as their theme, we have a local historian, a novel-writing newspaper man and a poet, who was a friend of Charles Dickens.

Coincidentally the same village produced several other writers, some who were native to the area, while others had moved in. One person gives us late nineteenth century Gothic short stories, and another, poems about the local area. The latter poet had an unusual biographer. But that is not all.

We will start with a man who was a defence advocate in the House of Lords for one of the most famous trials in the constitution of this land. He went on to a successful legal career, but still managed to contribute some literary articles. His daughter became the wife of Francis Hodgson who, as we know, was Byron's friend and at one time vicar of Bakewell and latterly Curate of Edensor. Finally, on this walk we will consider a book that was somewhat of an eccentric production. Only two copies were printed.

The variety of landscapes in this chapter is extensive. The long distant views with the Derwent Valley tucked under the edge, contrast with the rolling countryside with hidden remote green valleys. The villages comprise traditional Derbyshire cottages, that have been there for centuries, and are solidly built from local stone.

We leave the Grouse Inn and take the route along Curbar Edge until there is a path on our right to allow a descent. We follow it down the hill, cross the road near the Chequers Pub, and eventually come out at the pretty Froggatt Bridge over the River Derwent. After crossing the bridge we follow the river bank towards Baslow, for a short way, until

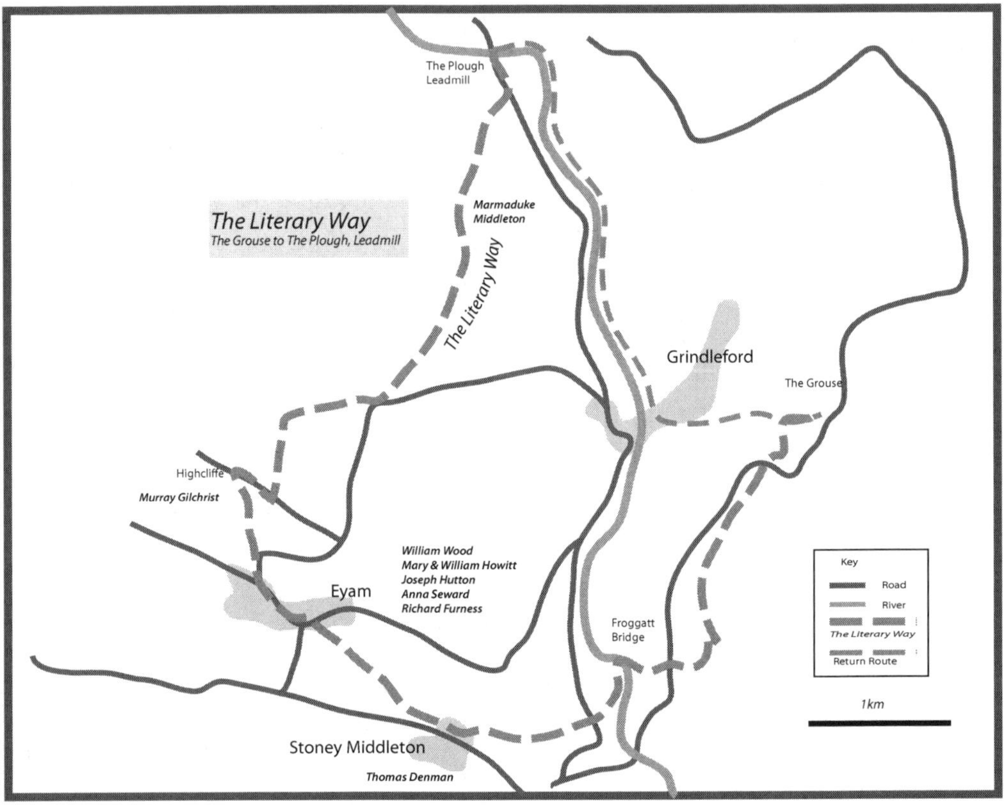

The Literary Way – Walk Sixteen – The Grouse to The Plough, Leadmill

The Bath House near to Stoney Middleton Hall and built by Thomas Denman

Walk Directions

The Grouse inn to Stoney Middleton (3.1 miles)

Just south along the road from the Grouse Inn we turn towards the car park
This takes us from the main road. Go into the small car park
At the bottom, in the woods, a path crosses. Turn left on to it.
Cross the stream and climb back to the road which we cross
Go through the gate opposite
It is now a delightful walk along the gritstone edge.
After nearly a mile there is a footpath sign down the slope
It passes under the rock faces and turns left down through the wood
Follow this, cross the road and finally come out near the river
Turn right and walk to, and then cross, Froggatt Bridge
Take the immediate left footpath on the far side
Walk with the stream until you reach a path that goes away from the river
Take the path across the fields to the road
Opposite is a track which leads to a farm
The path goes round the back of the farm buildings
On the other side of the building there are two paths
Take the left one which goes diagonally across the field
Follow this until it comes out onto a lane
Turn left to go into Stoney Middleton past the Bath House

Stoney Middleton to Eyam (1.11 miles)

Go past the church and follow the road
At the junction turn right and go virtually straight ahead along the lane past the cottages
At the junction of two footpaths take the left one
It goes up across the fields
When you reach the top and it levels out you will pass the Boundary Stone with the vinegar holes
Follow the path which goes ahead
When it joins the lane follow this and come out in the centre of Eyam
Turn left towards the church

Eyam to The Plough, Leadmill (3.68 miles)

When you have finished in Eyam take the road by the general store up past the car parks
At the bend take the cul-de-sac
Follow this track up towards the ridge
When you reach the top of the lane, Highcliffe is on your left
Turn right along the lane and take the footpath on the left
This goes near the mast
Cross the fields which have fine views and you will come out on a track
Turn right and follow the track
At the junction with the road there are two footpaths
Take the one ahead and to the left
The path comes out on a lane near to Leam Hall
Follow the lane down to the main road and turn left to reach The Plough at Leadmill and the river bridge

The Plough, Leadmill to The Grouse (3.17 miles)

Cross the bridge and take the path immediately right
Follow the river side through the fields, then a wood and then fields
You will come out on the road near the church in Grindleford
Turn right past the church and then left along the track
The path bends to the right and then enters the wood going straight uphill
Follow the path towards the Grouse Inn (straight up through the woods)
Arrive at the Grouse Inn and then return to the car park

Distance: 11.1 miles Ascent: 1882ft

we reach a footpath on our right. This takes us over a road and past a farm and brings us out on a lane which leads into Stoney Middleton. On our right is a small building with a stream emerging from the wall by the side of it. This is an old bath house and the remains of some past aspirations to be a spa. Interestingly, if you place your hand in the water you will be in for a surprise as the water is tepid and not cold as one would expect. On our left, before the church, is Middleton Hall.

Defending the Queen

If you are an advocate in the courts of London and wish to become a King's Counsel, then a career limiting move would be to challenge the King in Parliament, but that is exactly what Thomas Denman did.

George IV, when he was Prince of Wales, illegally married Maria Fitzherbert, and then shortly after completed a legal marriage to a woman he had never seen before the nuptials, Caroline of Brunswick. After nine months she had a baby and, shortly afterward, they separated. Caroline went to Europe and according to the rumours took a number of lovers. Some fourteen years later, the Prince of Wales became George IV following the death of his father. Caroline returned to England anticipating becoming Queen of England. The King was totally opposed to it and wanted her removed as his wife and Queen.

This prompted furious debates in both Houses of Parliament, and in the press and populace, as the returning Queen was seen as a symbol of the reform movement. Thomas Denman was one of the advocates that became part of the Queen's defence team. Eventually, it was settled that she would go away with a large annual annuity. At the time, it did not help Thomas Denman's career, but a combination of being a Whig MP, a leading advocate and circuit judge, meant that he became a King's Counsel and went on to become the Lord Chief Justice. He was given this leading legal role in 1832 and served for 18 years, until he resigned because of ill-health at the age of 71.

Although he lived in Stoney Middleton Hall, he took the title of Lord Denman of Dovedale because of his particular liking for the valley. Here he described, in a letter, his feelings for Dovedale. The

Stoney Middleton Hall, where Lord Denman of Dovedale lived

letter was contained in a biography of him written shortly after his death by a fellow judge, Sir Joseph Arnould.

Dovedale I traversed yesterday: all its beauties begin on my father's estate. I am sure that you never saw a more astonishing or romantic place. The descent to it is through my father's enclosures, till the ground becomes so steep and craggy as to defy all enclosures, and to be incapable of being ploughed, mown, or reaped. But there is good pasture, and the cattle acquire address and courage enough to walk among the rocks with ease, and graze with security. Some were reposing in the cool and oozy caverns, and others standing in the river.

The Dove, indeed, is not quite such a river as I should have wished for; but then I saw it at a disadvantage, for it had lately subsided from a flood to its former channel, as to want both the rapidity of a large stream and the clearness of a small one. It runs in this part of its course almost directly southward, separating Derbyshire from Staffordshire; the hills of the latter county, which form the western banks of the Dove, are higher and more wooded; those belonging to Derbyshire are bolder and more rocky, more various and grotesque.

On both sides they stand almost perpendicularly above the river, and sometimes close it in so completely that there is no path except over large stones thrown into the water.
Life of Thomas, First Lord Denman – Sir Joseph Arnould

Thomas's daughter Eliza married Francis Hodgson who had been the vicar at nearby Bakewell.

After our climb from Stoney Middleton the grass finally evens out and we follow a path that is generally straight ahead. In the middle of this open grass area there is a relatively small and low stone. This was the boundary stone that marked the edge of quarantine for the village of Eyam during the plague. The 'vinegar' holes, which are clearly visible in the rock, are where the money was left in exchange for food. We carry on straight ahead and then pick up a path between some low walls and this leads us down into Eyam.

Eyam is famous for being the village that was decimated in the 17th century by the plague that had spread from London. There are numerous indications of these past times in the village itself, in the museum, and in many books. There are also many helpful information signs dotted around the village. We follow the path as it leads us into the centre of the village. We cross the square and head along towards the church. Just past the church on the right is a row of cottages. The church and the cottages set the scene for us to examine some of the characters and writing when the plague came to Eyam.

Duty and Tragedy of the Mompesson Family

Many people know the story of the plague and how it swept through London, however, it is not generally known, except for those that have visited the village, that the plague spread from London to the small Derbyshire village of Eyam in 1665. It is, of course, speculation as to how it made its journey, but the local tailor had ordered cloth from London and he was one of the first to die. The general account of the story says that the local Rector, William

Vinegar Stone, between Stoney Middleton and Eyam

Mompesson, persuaded all the villagers to stay in isolation. Many will have wanted to leave and go to the towns, such as the nearby Sheffield, for safety. It is quite possible that the village quarantine stopped the plague becoming widespread across the northern towns of England. The results were devastating for the village and caused a high proportion of deaths. However, the disease was contained and there were no further outbreaks in the area.

The account of the plague in Eyam is taken from the physical evidence of graves and especially from the work of the local historian, William Wood, who was born in the village just after the turn of the century into the 1800s. Hence his account is a historical one which was written some 140 years after the plague itself. His most popular work, *The History and Antiquities of Eyam*, has as an explanatory subtitle, with a Full and Particular Account of the Great Plague which Desolated that Village AD 1666. The book was published in 1842 for the cost of three shillings (15p).

William's description of the plague is:

From the latter end of 1664 to December 1665, about one-sixth of the population of London fell victims to the appalling pestilence; but at Eyam, five-sixths were carried off in a few months of the summer of 1666, excepting a few who died at the close of 1665.
The History and Antiquities of Eyam – William Wood

It should be said that the figures have been disputed, but he does give us an idea of timing and the impact of the Plague that arrived at the close of one year, lay dormant for a while, and then re-appeared with vengeance the following summer. The disease is thought to have been delivered from London in a parcel of cloth for a local tailor, who lived in one of the cottages near the church.

George Vicars, then was the person who opened the terrible box. In removing the patterns and clothes, he observed in a sort of exclamation, how very damp they were; and he therefore hung them to the fire to dry. While Vicars was superintending them he was suddenly seized with violent sickness and other symptoms of the disease.
The History and Antiquities of Eyam – William Wood

Thomas Stanley had been the incumbent at the parish until his removal for Puritan views, which had been in favour when he had been appointed under the Cromwell regime. He did, however, remain in the village where he was known for over

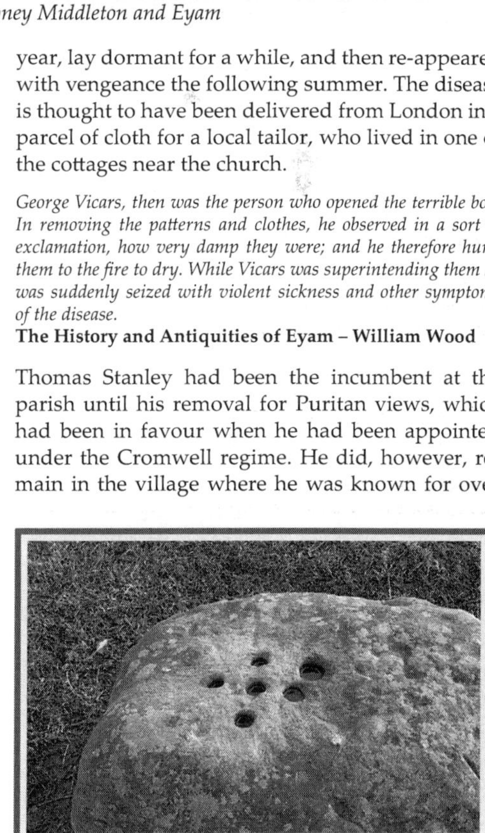

Vinegar Stone

The bank in the Delf in the foreground from which the Reverend Mompesson would preach, snow is in the bottom of the Delf

twenty years. William Mompesson had arrived with his wife, Catherine, and their children, a year or so before the outbreak. During the winter phase when the disease seemed to be reducing, the Mompesson's sent their children away to other members of the family in Yorkshire. Catherine stayed behind with her husband. The plague and the deaths grew in their intensity and this resulted in the village going into quarantine.

As part of the way in which they tried to deal with the Plague in the village, the Rector baulked against drawing a crowd into the confines of the church each Sunday. A short distance away in the village there is a deep valley, called Cucklet Delf, which has a mound overlooking it. On that mound that are some limestone arches in which it is reputed that William stood to deliver the service to the people of the village who could spread themselves out in the Delf. We leave the church with its reminders of the plague and carry on along Church Street. We turn left near Eyam Hall and left again along a footpath and in a hundred yards or so cross into the field on the left. As we walk around the field we can see the Delf and the limestones arches from which the preaching to the plague congregation took place.

William Mompesson and Thomas Stanley both survived the disease but Catherine Mompesson died. William had the task of writing to his children to tell them. This letter survived the years, and this is how it opened.

To my dear children, George and Elizabeth Mompesson, these present with my blessing.
Eyam August 31, 1666
Dear Hearts, – This brings you the doleful news of your dear mother's death – the greatest loss which ever befell you! I am not only deprived of a kind and loving consort, but you are also bereaved of the most indulgent mother that ever dear children had. We must comfort ourselves in God with this consideration, that the loss is only ours, and that what is our sorrow is her gain. The consideration of her joys, which I do assure myself are unutterable, should refresh our dropping spirits.
Letter to His Children – William Mompesson

As a modern adjunct to the history of events over three hundred years ago, *The Roses of Eyam* is a play written by Don Taylor and first screened on television in the 1970's. It is based on the village and how the plague progressed and its original stars, were Ronald Pickup, Leslie Sands and Caroline John. It has been revived many times at different theatres and has become a studied play within English Literature syllabuses.

Among the Verdant Mountains of the Peak

In 1821, Mary Botham married William Howitt and, after he had given up his business, they set forth to write together. Some were joint works and others were produced by one or the other. We introduced one of his short stories at Monsal Head when Charles Dickens, a friend of the family, had commissioned a story.

Mary and William were very productive writers covering a large range of books, over 180 between them, and also articles, poems and hymns. Among the most successful for Mary were childrens' book, and she produced the well-known rhyme, *The Spider and the Fly,* but she also learned Swedish and translated many books into English. William and Mary became well-known and respected.

Mary's poetry was compared with Keats, and both her and her husband were good friends with Elizabeth Gaskell, who sent them a draft of her first novel *Mary Barton* before publication. Mary was sympathetic to young women trying to make their way in the world, and we saw earlier, in *The Literary Way* how she befriended Eliza Meteyard. She also struck up a friendship with Charlotte Cushman, the American actress, before she became famous in England.

William and Mary moved house many times, but for a short period lived in Belper, which is in the Derwent Valley. They made frequent trips to the Peak District.

One of their first publications was *The Desolation of Eyam,* which is a long poem about the plague in this village. This is the third verse.

Among the verdant mountains of the Peak,
There lies a quiet hamlet, where the slope
Of pleasant uplands wards the north-winds bleak ;

Below, wild dells romantic pathways ope;
Around, above it, spreads a shadowy cope
Of forest trees : flower, foliage, and clear rill
Wave from the cliffs, or down ravines elope;
It seems a place charmed from the power of ill
By sainted words of old: so lovely, lone, and still.
The Desolation of Eyam – William and Mary Howitt

A Swordsman and a Painter

A local paper is called the *Derbyshire Times*, it was founded in 1854 as the *Derbyshire Times and Chesterfield Herald*. Its original owner was Francis Augustus Hatton, a printer and bookseller at Chesterfield in Derbyshire. One of his sons was Joseph Hatton, who would follow his father into the newspaper business, however, he did not become an owner, but he was a journalist and editor. At different periods in his career, he was the London correspondent of the *New York Times* and editor of the *Sunday People*. However, we have an interest in one of the 15 novels that he wrote. It is entitled *The Dagger and the Cross*, with the sub-title, *A Romance*. It was published in New York, in 1897.

If we return to the main road through Eyam and turn left, just past the turn, on the right, there is an open space in front of some cottages. It was also the site of one of the village wells. Just behind this space are the ruins of Bradshaw Hall. The book is set around Bradshaw Hall, of which only a few remains are left in the current day. The opening of the book is set in Venice with one of the key figures being a painter, discussing with a friend the escapades of a swordsman, who had the reputation as a chaser of women. The book quickly moves on to Derbyshire and the village of Eyam. The owner of the Old Hall, and his daughter, wished to decorate their house with the finest murals possible. The father wishes to rival the elegance of Chatsworth, so he had sent to Italy for the best painters and artists.

The story then takes shape as the Italian painter's entourage arrive, and a little later, the swordsman also moves into the village. Reuben Clegg is Eyam's local man in the story and he is infatuated with the daughter, Mary Talbot, of the Lord of Old Hall.

The daughter of Sir George Fanshawe Talbot (the chief personage in the village, its local magistrate and general patron), Mary Talbot, as we have already understood, was far above Clegg's station in life in an age when the different classes of the people were emphatically distinguished one from the other.
Sir George and Clegg were, however, on intimate terms, not alone because Clegg interested Sir George, and there was something to learn from him, but for the reason that to all intents and purposes he was Sir George's partner in the lead mine that had done so much toward the mending of his fortunes, not to say the making of them. The lead deposits, their extent and capability of being worked, had been entirely Clegg's discovery. The mine was one of the triumphs of the divining rod.
The Dagger and the Cross – Joseph Hatton

To add to the contrast between the local villagers and their visitors, the story is set in the year before the plague arrives. Local characters, who had key roles during the spread of the disease, are included

Eyam Church, with the Mompesson grave in the churchyard

in the story. Those mentioned include Vicars, the tailor's journey man, and William and Catherine Mompesson.

The winter passed and in the spring the new arrival in the village was Zilleto, the swordsman.

The people of the village treated the strangers with respect, but with something of suspicion, until, with the first spring notes of the thrush, the earliest primroses and the bursting leaves of the lilac, there arrived at Eyam that master of manners, that prince of good fellowship, Giovanni Ziletto, who spoke English with an accent as musical as his voice, who drank with the men at the Crown and Anchor, paid graceful court to all the women, and one night, sitting on the settle in the Crown and Anchor's timbered old house-place, produced a mandolin, and charmed every man there assembled with the fascinating spell of a modern Apollo. His songs were in a strange tongue, but they tuned men's hearts to love and chivalry and new desires. The magic of Ziletto's music seemed almost miraculous.

The Dagger and the Cross – Joseph Hatton

Having set the scene for the remainder of the book it is perhaps time to leave Joseph Hatton's Italians mixed with the villagers of Eyam before an event that we now know about.

The Swan of Lichfield

Nearly 150 years after the Plague, Eyam church, or more precisely the rectory, gave us a poet. We will let Sir Walter Scott, her biographer and literary executor, guide us through her contribution to the literary world. Anna Seward also gives us the opportunity to draw together several of the notable people in literature at the time. She provides a significant link between the two giants of English Literature, Samuel Johnson and Sir Walter Scott. The latter was only 13 years old, when the former died, but Anna Seward knew them both.

The name of Anna Seward has for many years held a high rank in the annals of British literature; and the public has a right to claim, upon the present occasion, some brief memorials of her by whom it was distinguished. As the tenor of her life was retired, though not secluded, and uniform, though not idle, the task of detailing its events can neither be tedious nor uninstructive.

The Poetical Works of Anna Seward with Extracts from her Letters and Literary Correspondence – Sir Walter Scott

She spent her early life in Eyam, where her father was the Rector. He was responsible for building the Rectory in the village. Her family then moved to Lichfield where she joined the literary circle of the town, which had already been strongly established, as it was the home of Samuel Johnson. As his fame became more widespread so people of literature had gravitated towards Lichfield. This was accentuated with the arrival of Erasmus Darwin.

Lichfield, the birth-place of Johnson and of Garrick, and, necessarily, the residence of a body of learned and well-educated clergy attached to its cathedral, had been long distinguished by its classical pretensions. These were at this time exalted by its being the residence of the celebrated Dr Darwin, who soon distinguished and appreciated the talents of our youthful poetess.

The Poetical Works of Anna Seward with Extracts from her Letters and Literary Correspondence – Sir Walter Scott

The Seward family had moved to Lichfield in 1754, when her father became a Prebendary of Lichfield Cathedral. They moved into the area, near the Cathedral, and had Erasmus Darwin as a neighbour. Anna gradually became known as 'The Swan of Lichfield'. She wrote both poetry and a poetical novel, *Louisa*. It was very popular at that time, although it is the type of work that is not in favour today. She was also a great correspondent and exchanged letters with many of the leading figures of the day.

The celebrated Dr Johnson was an occasional visitor of their circles; but he seems, in some respects, to have shared the proverbial fate of a prophet in his own country. Neither Dr Darwin nor Miss Seward were partial to the great moralist. There was, perhaps, some aristocratic prejudice in their dislike, for the despotic manners of Dr Johnson were least likely to be tolerated where the lowness of his origin was in fresh recollection.

The Poetical Works of Anna Seward with Extracts from her Letters and Literary Correspondence – Sir Walter Scott

Anna had particular praise for Erasmus Darwin's most significant poem. It was called *The Botanic Garden*. As we have seen with some of the quotations we have taken from it, it was divided in two major parts *The Economy of Vegetation* and *The Love of Plants*. The poems go beyond just flat descriptions. For example, Darwin introduces the new idea of the Linnaeus' classification of plants, and the reproduction methods that he frequently compared with humans. He also brought forth, in the poems, other scientific discoveries which he knew about through his wide range of friends.

Despite its large size and cost it did become a good seller because of the attempt to bring new discoveries in science to the reading public. Seward in her *Memoirs* offers a critique of the poems, the style and topics of which were closely aligned to her own. Seward gives the scope to her work in the Preface to the Memoirs.

My work consists of the following particulars of the person, the mind, the temper of Dr Darwin, his powers as a Physician, Philosopher and Poet; the peculiar traits of his manners: his excellencies and faults in the Petrarchan attachment of his middle life, more happy in its result that was that of the Bard of Vaucluse; the beautiful poetics testimonies of it's fervour while yet it remains hopeless: an investigation of the constituent excellencies and defects of his magnificent poem, The Botanic Garden: remarks on his philosophic prose writings; the characters and talents of those who formed the circle of friends while he resided in Lichfield; and the very singular and interesting history of one of them, well know in the lettered work, whose domestic history, remarkable as it is, has been unaccountably omitted by the gentleman who wrote his life.

Memoirs of Dr Darwin – Anna Seward

Anna Seward never married and there has been

speculation about her sexuality. She stayed at home and looked after her ailing father for many years, and by then she was of an age where marriage would have been difficult. However, she did strike up female friendships, which wouldn't have been unusual, but she was very distraught when one of her close female friends, Honora Sneyd, married. This is how she reflected when Honora was not there:

Dear Sensibility! how soon thy glow
Dy'd that fair cheek, and gleam'd from that young brow!
How early, Generosity, you taught
The warm disdain of every groveling thought,
Round sweet Honora, e'en in infant youth,
Shed the majestic light of spotless truth ;
Bid her for others' sorrow pour the tear,
For others' safety feel th' instinctive fear;
But for herself, scorning the impulse weak,
Meet every danger with unaltering cheek;
And through the generally unmeaning years
Of heedless childhood, to thy guardian cares,
Angelic Friendship, her young moments
And heedless of herself for others live.
Time Past - Anna Seward

One of Anna's more noticeable poems is the *Vale of Llangollen*. Anna dedicated this to Lady Eleanor Butler and Miss Ponsonby, who were known as the Ladies of Llangollen. They shocked society at the time by eloping together. Both Anna Seward and Sir Walter Scott visited the Ladies at Llangollen at their home.

While engaged in attendance upon her father, Miss Seward, besides other occasional pieces, published, in 1782, her poetical novel, entitled Louisa, which was favourably received, and passed rapidly through several editions. Other pieces, chiefly on occasional topics, fell from her pen some of which found their way to the public, and others are now, for the first time, printed from manuscripts. The beauties of Llangollen Vale, with the talents, virtues, and accomplishments of the ladies who have so long honoured it with their residence, claimed and obtained commemoration. Its inmates were among those whom Miss Seward valued most highly, and the regard was reciprocal.
The Poetical Works of Anna Seward with Extracts from her Letters and Literary Correspondence – Sir Walter Scott

In 1778, when Anna was forty-six, she passed through Eyam on her way to Sheffield. This is how she describes returning to Eyam.

Not two short miles from thee, - can I refrain
Thy haunts, my native Eyam, long unseen?
Thou, and thy loved inhabitants, again
Shall meet my transient gaze.- Thy rocky screen,
Thy airy cliffs I mount; and seek they shade,
Thy roofs, that brow the steep, romantic glade;
But, while on my the eyes of friendship glow,
Swell my pained sighs, my tears spontaneous flow.
Eyam – Anna Seward

Currier, Teacher and Medic

Richard Furness, born in Eyam in 1791, was a studi-

Stocks outside Eyam Hall

ous boy and when the time came for his first job he aspired to be the bookkeeper at the mill, but his family had other ideas. He was sent to Chesterfield and apprenticed as a currier, where he duly served his time as an apprentice and qualified to be accepted into the craft guild of leather makers. He began as a journeyman and set off for London. Nothing unusual we might say for a hard-working and bright young man in 1810. The difference with Richard was the additional things that he did with his time while an apprentice. The hours to do his job were long and no doubt frequently tedious. However, he would use the time, while others slept, to read. As Chesterfield was a main town, there was more reading from the library available for him than in Eyam. His interests were widespread, and this, in later times, influenced his poetry.

After his spell in London he returned to his home village and during the annual wakes week, a celebration festival, he met the woman who was to become his wife. She came from Hathersage and that is where they married against her father's wishes, but we have to assume that all was made well as he continued to live in the village. Richard's self study had led to a knowledge level that impressed many, and he soon took the local post of teacher. He also helped others and was a regular aid to the doctor in Hope, a nearby village, and began to deal with minor medical matters, leaving the doctor to focus on more complex problems.

He responded to an advert for a village teacher, and he and his wife moved to the village of Dore, a few miles over the hills towards Sheffield. Again he became a central part of the community. He remained in Dore until his death in 1857. In the following year his poetical works were published. The book also included a brief sketch of his life. The role of his biographer sheds some more information on how much Richard developed through self-study. Often the biographers of village people tend to come from the same locality and document one of the local well-known people. We have given the name and background of Richard's biographer:

G Calvert Holland M.D. Edinburgh, Honorary Physician to the Sheffield General Infirmary, Bachelier-es-lettres of the University of Paris, Formerly President of the Royal Physical and Hunterian Societies, Edinburgh

So not only was his biographer, a man of great skill and knowledge, and who made a major impact on the medical profession, but he was also of a different class in society at the time. Normally there is likely to have been very little contact between the two. In the Preface he describes Richard Furness:

The many, who have to labour for their daily bread, and who experience difficulties and hardships, may learn from the career of Richard Furness valuable lessons. He was one of their number. He came into the world to work, and he bravely did his part. By industry, perseverance, and untiring energy of purpose, he rose, if not high, above the drudgery of a manual occupation. Intent on the acquisition of knowledge, he gained it, and luxuriated in the rich possession. It scattered in his path numerous sources of happiness, and enabled him to leave a name that will long be cherished in the wild and beautiful districts of his county. His spirit was ever with its bold and picturesque scenery, and, embodied in his writings, will live associated with it to future times.

The Poetical Works of the Late Richard Furness – G Calvert Holland

From the information, given in the next quote, we can see how Richard would meet and impress the eminent man who became his biographer.

While at Eyam, but more particularly afterwards at Hathersage, he acquired considerable knowledge of the medical profession, for which he had a decided taste. A close intimacy had been formed between him and Mr. Cheetham, surgeon, of Hope, a neighbouring village. This gentleman had long rounds to take in the country, and being likewise of a very social disposition, an intelligent friend to look after urgent cases was at times extremely useful. This was the duty of the poet, who had a strong nerve for any surgical operation, and was not slow to profit from the lessons which were freely given. No wonder that leather ceased to interest, and at length was given up as unprofitable.

On these matters I may be allowed to express an opinion. As a surgeon he had considerable talent, and often succeeded in effecting important cures in cases in which clever and regularly educated practitioners had failed. In the other branch of the profession, medicine, though not equally skilful or well informed, he did great good in inflammations, fevers, and other ordinary affections.

The Poetical Works of the Late Richard Furness – G Calvert Holland

The work, for which Richard's name is mainly associated, is *Rag Bag*. The story starts with a rag collector, who has filled his bag from various houses and loaded them on to his donkey. When the animal will go no further, the contents, which belonged to people of all different classes, spill out of the bag and become a succession of speakers.

When in an instant, from my flaxen poke,
Discordant voices in loud murmurs broke;
Out swelled the bag, the motley group within,
With fury storming made the seams to grin;
They shriek'd, they howl'd, they fought in mad uproar.
Till steam and dust flew out at every pore.

Rag Bag – Richard Furness

One of the enjoyments of reading the books published centuries ago is their wonderful flowery descriptions. We had William Adam's, *Gem of the Peak*, a travel guide to the Peak, and in Eyam, some eloquent language from William Wood. As we climb up the steep slope to the north of Eyam let's enjoy William Wood's description of the hill.

A little farther north, nearly in the centre of the parish, rises Sir William – the Parnassus of the Peak; a mountain of great altitude, and honoured by numberless classical associations. From the summit of this Prince of Derbyshire Hills, the view extends over countless hills and luxuriant dales. Masson, Ax-edge, Mam Tor, Kinderscout and Stanage lift their hoary head and, beckoning to Sir William, tell in language stronger than words, of a companionship of ages. How rapturous must be the feelings of the tourist who mounts the peak of this mountain,

and with fire-kindled eye beholds on every hand the uneffaced landmarks of Nature! How joyous his sensations to perceive......
The History and Antiquities of Eyam – William Wood

We turn up the cul-de-sac called the Nook. This leads us up the ridge behind Eyam and at the top we come to Highcliffe, which adjoins the moors.

Gothic Moors

Highcliffe Nook is near the wide sweeping moor that leads to William Hill. These moors, featured in the novels of R Murray Gilchrist, who lived overlooking Eyam. In some of his writings there is the fictitious village of Milton, which is synonymous with Eyam.

The books such as *The Peakland Faggot* are short stories with each focusing on a particular character in the village. In many ways his book about Milton can be seen to be a 'soap opera' of the time. *The Last Posset* opens by introducing the character of Miss Brimble. A characteristic of Murray's writing was the use of local accents in the speech which can make for difficult reading.

"By 'r leddy," she muttered, " et 's more nor hot—et 's griddlin'. I reckon I suffer more wi' bein' fat. When that poor lad Aitchilees were a-courtin' me, we used for to think nowt o' th' climb—et were but child's play then. But I measured nineteen inch raand th' waist i' those days, an' naa I'm forty an' five inch ! Solid flesh, tho'/ she struck her bosom heavily with her closed hand; " better nor 's to be fun' naa'-days !
The Last Posset – Peakland Faggot – R Murray Gilchrist

He only lived in the village for a short period as he mainly lived in Cartledge Hall and was a friend of Edward Carpenter. Murray was born in 1867 and died aged 50. He wrote over twenty novels and many short stories, as well as some regional books about the Peak District. He was a very private person, but did support charity work and is known for his support of Belgian Refugees. As well as his writing about characters in Milton he developed another theme in which his writing returns us to the genre depicted at Haddon Hall, on *The Literary Way*, by Ann Radcliffe.

While there is the underlying common theme of Gothic, Ann developed the romance of the genre, whereas Gilchrist emphasised the horror. One of his best known work is *The Basilisk.* This is the opening few lines.

Marina gave no sign that she heard my protestation. The embroidery of Venus's hands in her silk picture of The Judgement of Paris was seemingly of greater import to her than the love which almost tore my soul and body asunder. In absolute despair I sat until she had replenished her needle seven times. The impassioned nature cried aloud:-
'You do not love me!'
She looked up somewhat wearily, as one debarred from rest. 'Listen,' she said. 'There is a creature called a Basilisk, which turns men and women into stone. In my girlhood I saw the Basilisk – I am stone.'
The Basilisk – R Murray Gilchrist

We pick up the tracks and paths towards the summit of Sir William Hill and then take the path until we reach the vicinity of Leam Hall.

Only One Poem

When a poet only publishes one poem, and that work is not well known, then it is difficult to claim

Highcliffe situated above Eyam

a place in any literary review. For this reason we would normally have excluded this writer from *The Literary Way*. But, he was quite intriguing and the reason for his poem is difficult to discern. He was an important and busy man so why take the time to write? We shall let William Wood introduce him.

Throughout the whole of this parish are scattered many elegant and substantial dwellings – some for situation and elegance are rarely to be met with at so great a distance from places of commerce. Amongst the latter description is Leam Hall, the residence of M M Middleton Esq, an old English gentleman, alike distinguished for urbanity, good sense and literary taste.
The History and Antiquities of Eyam - William Wood

Marmaduke Middleton's only book is *Poetical Sketches in a Tour of the West of England.* So why was it interesting? First, it is the background of the author. As Wood says, he was an English gentleman, in fact he was at one time the High Sheriff of Derbyshire, an ancient post at the discretion of the monarch. He lived at one of the larger estates in the parish, Leam Hall, which is high above Eyam and overlooks the Derwent woodlands. His work is about 1500 lines long and follows the title as he has snippets of poetry about a tour of the West Country commencing at Bridgewater, going to Penzance and returning to the Mendips.

Leaving at Bridgewater the usual road,
At Minehead first I take up my abode,
And spend the Sunday, where, alas, is traced,
How ruthless fires its beauties have defaced:
Here twice to church my willing steps are led,
To hear the service with devotion read.
Poetical Sketches in a Tour of the West of England – Marmaduke Middleton

Marmaduke never intended his work to become widespread as he published it privately in Sheffield. The intrigue is particularly in the dedication which is to:

The Misses Strutt, of Bridge-Hill, near Belper, Derbyshire, the following pages, (written to divert the solitary hours of affliction), are dedicated with great respect by their obedient servant, the author Leam, Feb. 28, 1822.

These ladies were part of the Strutt family who had Bridge-Hill House, noted above, as the family home. Jedidiah was a wheelwright, who was at the forefront of the inventions of the industrial revolution. Strutt and Arkwright would establish the heart of the spinning industry in the Derwent Valley. Jedidiah and his sons established their mill at Belper, while Arkwright had his mill, as we have seen at Cromford. The mills along this stretch of the river now form a World Heritage site and are approximately 15 miles from Leam Hall which overlooks the same river.

Our footpath will eventually lead us to a main road and we come out at Leadmill with the Plough Inn on the opposite side of the road.

Let's rest awhile at the Plough

Eyam is only a small village tucked neatly under Eyam Edge which is topped by Sir William Hill. It is surprising how many literary characters it has produced, and to this must be added the number of visitors who have penned their thoughts.

The plague in the time of Charles II has been a great source of inspiration even if there are no worthy contemporary accounts. Anna Seward through Erasmus Darwin, as her neighbour, would have been friendly with the Lunar Circle of scientists although she was ready to pounce on any interpretation of science that did not conform to the scriptures. In and around the later 1820s and early 1830s we have learned before about Earl Grey's Reform Bill, and it was at that time that Mary and William Howitt wrote about Eyam, and Thomas Denman was adding his legal skills to the formulation of the historic bill.

Currer Bell

The Plough, Leadmill to Ashopton through Hathersage

The George Hotel, Hathersage

We are outside the George Hotel, Hathersage. Try to picture the scene. In 1845, a coach draws up outside this well-known coaching inn. A young lady, 29-years-old with a pretty and delicate face, her hair parted in the middle and drawn to a bunch at the back, steps down from the coach. She is immediately greeted by a friend with whom she went to school. Standing in the background, to welcome the travellers to his inn, is Mr Morton, the manager. However, our slim, pretty traveller would not be staying at the coaching inn. Instead, she would be staying with her friend at the Vicarage. And this leads us to one of the most famous novels in English Literature. And on this walk let us add a story which has become a legend in the re-telling over the centuries. It entertains and grips us, as much now, as it did people in medieval days.

In addition, we have a picturesque village that is tucked under the dark and brooding crags of gritstone, which is where we are headed. From there we will have views over hills and valleys across which, *The Literary Way* will wend its route.

The Vicarage Visitor

At the time of her visit she had only written a few juvenile stories which were never published in her life time. She was to become one of the most famous names in English literature, and her renowned book drew insight from this village. The year following from her visit to Hathersage, she would collaborate with her sisters Acton and Ellis on their first literary adventure. They would self-publish a book entitled, *Poems*, by Currer, Ellis and Acton Bell. The book had no success at all and sold very few copies. In order to see the style of her work this is the opening lines of a poem called *Evening Solace*

But, there are hours of lonely musing,
Such as in evening silence come,
When, soft as birds their pinions closing,
The heart's best feelings gather home.
Then in our souls there seems to languish
A tender grief that is not woe;
And thoughts that once wrung groans of anguish,
Now cause but some mild tears to flow.
Evening Solace – Currer Bell

The names were pseudonyms in a similar way as when we started at Ellastone with George Eliot. Marian Evans had taken the masculine pen-name because of resistance against woman writers. The three sisters did the same. Two years later, in 1847, *Jane Eyre* by Currer Bell would be published in London. Charlotte, Emily and Anne became one of the

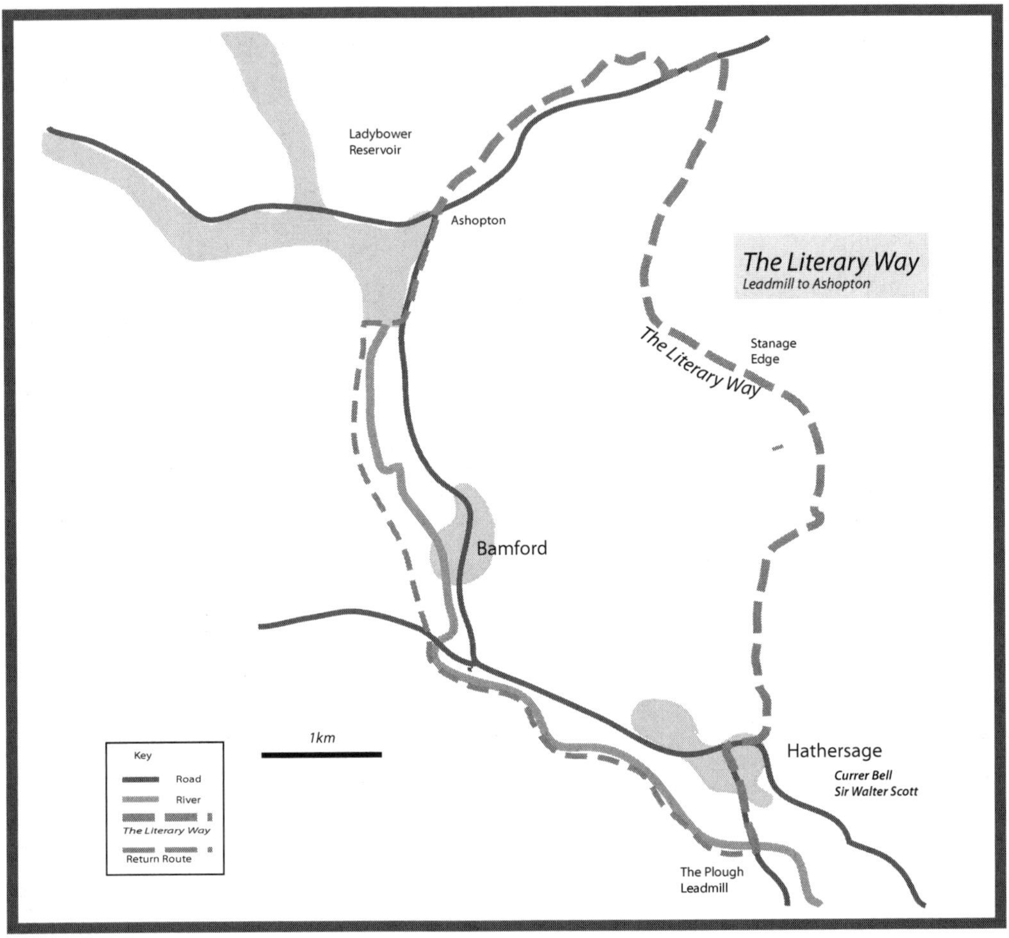

The Literary Way – Walk Seventeen – The Plough, Leadmill to Ashopton

most prominent literary families in the nineteenth century and their work endures through to the present.

Charlotte had four sisters and a brother and they lived with their widowed father in the Parsonage at Haworth in West Yorkshire, which is now the Bronte Museum. The moors around Haworth and Hathersage are very similar, as both consist of wide landscapes of heather with craggy millstone grit outcrops. A slight difference is that the edge of the crags are more noticeable in Hathersage, both behind and to the east of the village. The three girls who survived to adulthood were Charlotte, the eldest, Emily and Anne. They would all write novels that would become well-known with *Wuthering Heights,* by Emily, perhaps one of most haunting novels in English literature.

The tragedy of the family is that they would all die as young women. Anne was 29 when she died of tuberculosis. Emily, was only a year older, when she succumbed to the same disease. Charlotte would live ten years more than her sisters and would be the only one to wed. She married her father's curate. All the sisters rarely ventured far from home, although after her novels were successful, Charlotte did visit London more often and, amongst others, enjoyed the friendship of G H Lewis, who was the live-in partner of Marian Evans.

Ellen Nussey had invited her school friend to stay with her at the vicarage in Hathersage. Ellen's brother was the vicar at St Michael and All Angels church. It was during her stay, in 1845, that Charlotte conceived the sense of location for the novel. Hathersage becomes Morton in the book, after the name of the manager of the George Inn. The title, in itself, is interesting as it is one of the most prominent family names in the local area. The name is still very evident locally as it was in Charlotte Bronte's time. Charlotte used many local locations as part of the story. Before we investigate some of these, let's give the link with one of the books we have already encountered on *The Literary Way.*

Walk Directions

The Plough, Leadmill to Stanage Edge (3.0 miles)

We leave the Plough and cross the Derwent Bridge
The pavement leads us in a few hundred yards to Hathersage
We arrive at the T-junction with the George Hotel in front of us
We turn right and walk up through the village
As the road begins to rise at the end of the high street we turn left
After the school and pub there is a left turn up a hill which we take
We enter the churchyard of St Michael and All Angels
After visiting the grave of Little John we leave by the back gate
The vicarage is to our left but we turn right and then left onto a path
This crosses the fields and gradually climbs out of the valley
On our left, across the fields is Brookfield Manor
We reach the lane and cross it to go past North Lees
The path takes us up to the road, we turn left, which runs under the edge
The next footpath on our right leads us up to the edge, and we turn left

Stanage Edge to Ashopton (5.07 miles)

We follow the path along the top and take it when it descends from the edge
The path now passes along underneath the edge
This is where the abandoned millstones may be found
After a couple of miles we come to a main road
We turn left down the road which we cross and take the first turning right
Just near to the only building on the left is a path which we take
It curves round and joins another track/path
We turn left and follow it
We cross the stream at Cutthroat Bridge
We stay on the path and it brings us out next to the Ladybower Inn
The Ladybower Reservoir is directly in front of us

Ashopton to Leadmill (5.32 miles)

We turn left at the road junction and walk down the side of Ladybower
When we reach the dam we take the footpath across it.
We turn left and take the path which becomes the old railway track
Just after leaving the dam we take the path on our right and not the track
We follow this path down the valley and cross the road to continue on it
At the end of the track we turn left and after a few yards take the path on the right
It goes around the field edge and against the railway embankment
We then turn right on the path under the railway
The path leads to the edge of the garden centre and we continue on to the road
We cross the road, and the small bridge and take the footpath on the left
This is the riverside path of the River Derwent
We follow it all the way back to Leadmill

Distance: 13.4 miles Ascent: 1614ft

Samuel Johnson's book *Rasselas* was conceived while visiting Ilam Hall. In *Jane Eyre,* Jane has just gone away to school, and she is reading the inscription on the school building:

Lowood Institution.--This portion was rebuilt A.D. ---, by Naomi Brocklehurst, of Brocklehurst Hall, in this county. "Let your light so shine before men, that they may see your good works, and glorify your Father which is in heaven."--St. Matt. v. 16.

I read these words over and over again: I felt that an explanation belonged to them, and was unable fully to penetrate their import. I was still pondering the signification of "Institution," and endeavouring to make out a connection between the first words and the verse of Scripture, when the sound of a cough close behind me made me turn my head. I saw a girl sitting on a stone bench near; she was bent over a book, on the perusal of which she seemed intent: from where I stood I could see the title - it was "Rasselas;" a name that struck me as strange, and consequently attractive. In turning a leaf she happened to look up, and I said to her directly - "Is your book interesting?" I had already formed the intention of asking her to lend it to me some day.

Jane Eyre – Charlotte Bronte

The turreted North Lees Hall on the hills above the village, and which we will shortly pass on *The Literary Way* is thought to be Thornfield Hall and the home of Mr Rochester, the lead in the story. This is Jane's view of Thornfield Hall:

The Vicarage, Hathersage, where Charlotte stayed

Gathering my mantle about me, and sheltering my hands in my muff, I did not feel the cold, though it froze keenly; as was attested by a sheet of ice covering the causeway, where a little brooklet, now congealed, had overflowed after a rapid thaw some days since.
From my seat I could look down on Thornfield: the grey and battlemented hall was the principal object in the vale below me; its woods and dark rookery rose against the west. I lingered till the sun went down amongst the trees.
Jane Eyre – Charlotte Bronte

On a drive near the side of the George Hotel, a path leads to Brookfield Manor which is Vale Hall in the novel and is the industrialist's home.

Having brought my eventide musings to this point, I rose, went to my door, and looked at the sunset of the harvest-day, and at the quiet fields before my cottage, which, with the school, was distant half a mile from the village. The birds were singing their last strains. The air was mild, the dew was balm. While I looked, I thought myself happy, and was surprised to find myself ere long weeping - and why?
For the doom which had reft me from adhesion to my master: for him I was no more to see; for the desperate grief and fatal fury - consequences of my departure - which might now, perhaps, be dragging him from the path of right, too far to leave hope of ultimate restoration thither. At this thought, I turned my face aside from the lovely sky of eve and lonely vale of Morton - I say lonely, for in that bend of it visible to me there was no building apparent save the church and the parsonage, half-hid in trees, and, quite at the extremity, the roof of Vale Hall, where the rich Mr. Oliver and his daughter lived.
Jane Eyre – Charlotte Bronte

Moor House in the book is the farm, called Moorseats which is up towards the moors from Hathersage. This comes into the story when Jane sees a light and is attracted to the house. It is interesting to note that in the recent film, *Jane Eyre*, Moor House was filmed at Outseats Farm, which sits just below Stanage Edge. Moor House is where Jane was taken in:

The more I knew of the inmates of Moor House, the better I liked them. In a few days I had so far recovered my health that I could sit up all day, and walk out sometimes. I could join with Diana and Mary in all their occupations; converse with them as much as they wished, and aid them when and where they would allow me. There was a reviving pleasure in this intercourse, of a kind now tasted by me for the first time – the pleasure arising from perfect congeniality of tastes, sentiments, and principles.
Jane Eyre – Charlotte Bronte

Jane Eyre has been popular since it was published and has been made into a film at least 13 times with many of the recent productions being filmed in the local area.

North Lees Hall, the fictional home of Mr Rochester

Merry Men

You might think that because of the section title we should be in Nottingham with the famous outlaw who triumphed the plight of the poor, but we are in Hathersage with Charlotte Bronte. She is staying with lifelong friend, Ellen Nussey. They would have, on many occasions, walked through St Michael's church grounds amongst the headstones of the generations of villagers. One grave stands out from the rest. It is claimed that it is the resting place of one of Robin Hood's most loyal lieutenants, Little John.

There is speculation about the historical accuracy of many of the Robin Hood claims. It is not our intention to debate the issues here as there are many people better qualified to assess the complex historical validity of the evidence. One of the main issues is that the stories and ballads have been handed down through time and many variations and interpretations made as a result. Also the exact person is difficult to identify and hence the period he lived is also unclear. It therefore follows, whether he had merry men, which included the typically depicted giant of a man, Little John, may also be questioned.

However, it is a wonderful story, full of heroics and has been committed to literature in many forms. The recent decades of film and television media have also seen its portrayal. So let's take a romantic view of the man and legend. We'll enjoy some of the speculation as we leave the church and we begin the climb to the moors past Bronte's Thornfield Hall. As we clear the valley slope, onto the moors, we are near the rocky crags of Stanage Edge. Routes were difficult in Robin Hood's time. Forests were very prevalent in the valleys and the moors were high and their peat bogs handicapped easy travel. Careful routes were chosen either on foot or horseback that avoided both of these perilous areas. To the north-east of us about five miles away, is a village on the fringes of Sheffield called Loxley. In many versions of the historic hero, Robin Hood is taken to be Robin of Locksley. Let's add some other information to help confirm at least a plausible story of Robin Hood in this area.

Peveril Castle is about five miles to the west. This eleventh Century Norman Castle perches above the village of Castleton. We are going to visit Castleton later, for it has a close association with many writers stretching over centuries, but for now let's consider a little background to the castle, which we can see from our vantage point on Stanage Edge. Peveril Castle was at the heart of the English King's hunting forest, which was renowned for its deer. The name of a village, a few miles from Castleton, Peak Forest, is a remnant of the times. Also the nearby Chapel-en-le-Frith, was named as the church in the forest, by French prisoners of war. The castle is named after the original owner, William Peveril, who was the illegitimate son of William the Conqueror. He gained the large estate for his services in the invasion of England. There was a descendant of the original Peveril, who would also have a wide influence in the area. His principal role was as Sheriff of Nottingham.

If you know the story of Robin Hood you will immediately see the connection. Speculation again, but as well as Nottingham Castle, he also owned and occupied Peveril Castle, Haddon Hall and a small hall near Bradwell called Hazelbadge. So at least we have a tenuous link that suggest the local area could have been the heartland of Robin with the Sheriff of Nottingham also linked with the vicinity.

The popularity of the story of Robin Hood was greatly enhanced in the nineteenth century, by Sir Walter Scott, in the novel *Ivanhoe* in which Robin of Locksley appears. For Ivanhoe's inspiration, it is thought Walter Scott used the castle at Conisbrough, which is between Sheffield and Doncaster. Although as we shall see, Sir Walter wrote a book entitled *Peveril of the Peak* it was set in a time many centuries after Robin. Let's take the section in Ivanhoe when Robin meets the King for the first time.

"Thou bearest an English heart, Locksley," said the Black Knight, "and well dost judge thou art the more bound to obey my behest -- I am Richard of England!" At these words, pronounced in a tone of majesty suited to the high rank, and no less distinguished character of Coeur-de-Lion, the yeomen at once kneeled down before him, and at the same time tendered their allegiance, and implored pardon for their offences.

"Rise, my friends," said Richard, in a gracious tone, looking on them with a countenance in which his habitual good-humour had already conquered the blaze of hasty resentment, and whose features retained no mark of the late desperate conflict, excepting the flush arising from exertion,--"Arise," he said, "my friends! – Your misdemeanours, whether in forest or field, have been atoned by the loyal services you rendered my distressed subjects before the walls of Torquilstone, and the rescue you have this day afforded to your sovereign. Arise, my liegemen, and be good subjects in future.
"And thou, brave Locksley..."

"Call me no longer Locksley, my Liege, but know me under the name, which, I fear, fame hath blown too widely not to have reached even your royal ears - I am Robin Hood of Sherwood Forest."

"King of Outlaws, and Prince of good fellows!" said the King, "who hath not heard a name that has been borne as far as Palestine? But be assured, brave Outlaw, that no deed done in our absence, and in the turbulent times to which it hath given rise, shall be remembered to thy disadvantage."
Ivanhoe – Sir Walter Scott

Let's leave our mythical hero and move on so that we can reach an area with a true and well-known twentieth century hero. As we cross the moor along the Causeway we see the relics of the work that was

Stanage Edge

done here. Scattered around in the heather are partially shaped millstones. Some of them are broken, yet others have not been finished. There are many that while they appear complete have remained here where they have been hewn from the rocks. It's a fascinating reminder of the source of the key tools that brought not only the grinding of corn but also the crushing of ore. We cross the road which links Sheffield and Manchester and walk along the path, past Cutthroat Bridge, that will take us down to the Ladybower Reservoir.

Let's rest awhile at Ladybower

The legend of Robin Hood has become a very well known story over the years and has appealed to many generations, and we are happy to leave it as a myth, along with Hathersage's Little John, although it would be intriguing to know the truth behind that grave in the churchyard.

Within the church itself are the many memorials to the Eyre family, who had been a local presence for centuries with their name still very prevalent in the Hope Valley, which runs from Hathersage to Castleton. When Charlotte visited Ellen, whose brother was the vicar, the two women would have entered the church on many occasions, and it could well have been then that Charlotte conceived the name that was to be imprinted on the literary world.

From the longitudinal high street of Hathersage, with the church perched on the rising ground above the village, we went past an old hall, previously owned by the Eyre family, but designated Mr Rochester's house by Charlotte. The path took us to the millstone strewn edge with the ancient causeway running its length. Along the path, through the heather, we were met by the frequent sounds of the grouse. Before we began the descent, we had some distant views of the reservoirs, and then crossing the main road we finally reached Cutthroat Bridge. It was then a short distance down the path to come out on the edge of the very impressive Ladybower Reservoir.

Heroes

Ashopton to Hope past Derwent Dam and over Win Hill

A Helicopter Flying over Derwent Dam

Heroes come in different forms. On this walk we will deal with two very differing ones. Both men made their marks on society, one through his actions, which helped to defend this country from threatened invasion and the other by the persistent championing of the poor and working class.

Even though the latter personally made enough money for a comfortable life, he never deserted his cause. They both wrote about what they did. One was a lover of this countryside, and even as a child, had found solace in nature. He expressed his experiences through poetry. Our war hero wrote a book describing his role in the conflict.

Another person who found his poetic talents directed towards nature in this area is one of the friends of *The Literary Way* and that is Erasmus Darwin.

We have in front of us Ladybower Reservoir, which was created in the 1930s and 1940s. It involved the flooding of two villages, Ashopton and Derwent. Ashopton was at the bottom of the valley we have just come down and so the village would have been directly in front of us. The path along its east side takes us up the old river valley along which route we can clearly see what was the upper Derwent valley. The village of Derwent was halfway between Derwent Dam and the road bridge over Ladybower. The flooding of the village also included Derwent Hall, which was owned by the Duke of Norfolk. It is easy to imagine how the streams flowed down the joining valleys and created the River Derwent as it wound down the steep-sided main valley. When the reservoir is low the outline of some of the buildings from the old village are visible.

Ode to the Derwent

The Derwent River, which we have crossed several times, has its source on the peat bogs above this valley. Let's return to Erasmus Darwin for his perception of the river before it was dammed. This ode was dedicated to a patient of Dr Darwin's, who he fell in love with and would later marry. The offspring of this marriage was the intrepid traveller that lived at Sydnope Hall, Dr Francis Sacheverel

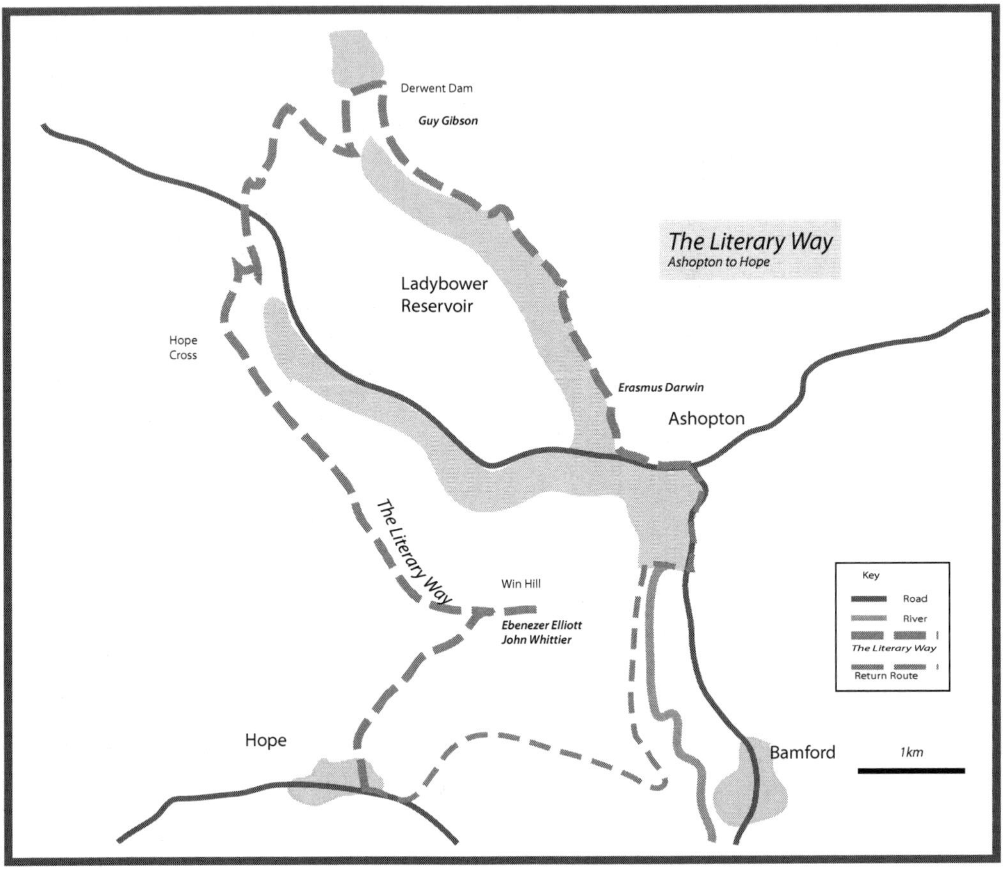

The Literary Way – Walk Eighteen – Ashopton to Hope

Darwin. Erasmus called the poem, *Ode to the River Derwent* and added that it was written in a romantic valley near its source.

Derwent, what scenes thy wandering waves behold,
As bursting from thine hundred springs they stray,
And down these vales, in founding torrents roll'd,
Seek to the shining East their mazy Way!
Ode to the River Derwent – Erasmus Darwin

Our footpath takes us past some of the old buildings of Derwent village that are above the reservoir level, and eventually brings us to the Derwent Dam. The steps near to the right tower of the dam allow us to reach the platform, which is close to the dam wall. The massive structure, topped by an edge between two turreted square towers spans the valley. If you are lucky you might arrive at the dam on one of the days on which it is overflowing. When the dam is full, the water cascades over the edge and runs down the steep slope of the front of the dam. By standing on the platform you can be a few feet away from the pouring water. The front of the dam wall is not smooth, and the protrusions create streaming white water and a superb rushing noise just in front of us.

Bouncing

It is not only for the wonderful spectacle of this dam, which has a sister of the same construction further up the valley, that we have come to see. The Derwent Dam played a significant role in the twentieth century history of the United Kingdom. There were many heroes during the Second World War, but very few captured the nation as much as Captain Guy Gibson.

Britain wanted to attack German dams at the heart of their industrial production areas. The military concluded that conventional bombing would not work and a new method of attack was needed. Scientists led by Barnes Wallis first conceived the idea, and then built a new type of bomb. It was called a bouncing bomb. It would be dropped from a very low attitude on the water behind the dam and would bounce towards the wall and slide down it. The full force of the explosion could then be applied to the dam wall and cause the breach.

There were two major problems. First, there was the altitude at which the bombers had to fly to release the bomb. It was too low for the instruments of the day to be accurate, and for obvious reasons, the raid

Walk Directions

Ashopton to Haggwater Bridge (4.93 miles)

From the main road (A57) we turn right along the east side of Ladybower
We follow the track along the edge of the reservoir
After about one and half miles we reach the few remaining buildings of Derwent village
We pass these. At low water, in a dry summer, the outline of some of the buildings can be seen
The track leads us towards Derwent Dam
We take the path to the left and reach the dam
The views from near the West Tower are excellent
From the West Tower we follow the road south to go past the entrance to Fairholmes
Just past where the exit road from the visitor centre comes out we turn right up the path
We follow the path through the trees
It joins a track and we turn left and then follow the track and then turn left to rejoin the path
We follow the path out of the woods and along the side of a field
On the track at the top we turn left past the outdoor centre (previously a farm)
At the cross paths we go ahead down the winding path
At the bottom, cross the main road, and continue on the path
At the bottom is Haggwater Bridge

Haggwater Bridge to Win Hill (3.11 miles)

Cross the bridge and follow the track
The main track winds to the right up through the woods
Follow it through the woods and emerge at the top
At the cross paths we turn left and Hope Cross is just on our left
We follow the main track (not the one by the trees)
A path bears to the left as the main path begins to descend
We take the left path and at a complex path junction we go across the cross paths
And then take the left fork (we are heading for Win Hill) the path clearly goes in that direction
Follow the path which bends round to the left, and passes behind a rise in the ground
The path then takes us to Win Hill Pike with its fine views

Win Hill to Hope (1.53 miles)

From Win Hill Pike we retrace our steps a short distance and take the downward path on our left
We follow this down the hill and then down the steep incline to go past some buildings
It now is a track which we take down and go under the railway
We take the right branch of the track and this takes us down to the road
We turn left and walk into Hope and come out by the church

Hope to Ashopton (4.16 miles)

We turn left past the church and follow the main road
After we cross the stream take the first turning on the left
We follow this lane. It bends to the right and then has a steep gradient
We pass by the buildings of Aston
Ignore the turning on the right and carry on along the lane
When we reach the road junction we turn left and follow the road around the bend
On our right is a track and footpath, we take the latter down to the old railway track
Turn left and follow until you reach the Ladybower Dam
Retrace the route across the dam and turn left to reach Ashopton

Distance: 13.7 miles Ascent: 2478ft

needed to take place at night. Second, in order for the bouncing bomb to detonate exactly in the right place, which was crucial, it had to be dropped at a very specific distance from the dam. Because of the necessary changes to normal operations, a special squadron was formed. The 617 Squadron was nick-named the Dambusters and Captain Guy Gibson, an experienced war pilot, was appointed to lead the group.

A characteristic of the dams, which were being attacked, is that they had towers. We think you can probably see where this is going. A method of manual sighting was used to determine the distance from the dam wall. When the two sights were covering the towers, the bomb was to be dropped. The correct altitude was determined by shining two angled lights to the surface of the water, when they met in a single spot of light the plane was at the correct height. The new flying and bombing methods would need practice and this is where Derwent Dam would help the squadron. The dams were used as the practice for the Wellington bombers. There have been many descriptions of his bravery and exploits, but perhaps it is better to take the words that Captain Guy Gibson wrote himself, in *Enemy Coast Ahead.*

Half an hour later we were on our way in my faithful G for George towards a reservoir called Derwent Water near Sheffield. This lake is on the Pennines, surrounded by high ground with just enough industrial haze blowing over it to make it ideal for the job; moreover the water was always calm because there was no wind in that valley.
Remembering what Geoff has said, we came screaming down at the right air speed to pull out as near 150ft as we could judge (Hoppy was sitting beside me), and released a missile. It fell short. Then we were twisting and turning our way through the valley, with high hills on either side. We climbed up again for several more tries, and in the end found it more or less fairly easy.

That night at dusk, with the fog already beginning to fill up the valley, cutting visibility down to a mile or so, we tried again. This time it wasn't so good. The water, which had been blue by day, was black – we nearly hit the black water. Even Spam said, 'Christ, this is bloody dangerous', which meant it was. Not only that. I said to Dinghy there and then, that unless we could find some way of judging our height above the level of the water, this type of attack would be impossible. 'But must we fly at this dead height? asked Hoppy.
'I'm afraid that's the snag. The scientist I met told me that in order to make this weapon work we would have to fly within a few miles an hour at the right air-speed and within a very few feet of the right height. That's our problem.
Enemy Coast Ahead – Guy Gibson

The Derwent Dam overflowing

As many will know it became a famous film in 1950, starring Richard Todd as Guy Gibson. Guy survived the Dambuster raids, but was killed in action later on in the war.

Let us cross in front of the dam and take one of the concessionary paths up through the woods. We will clear the woods and reach a track. We turn left. In between the trees we can still get fine views across the valley and down to the reservoirs. Our track leads a winding route down and then across the road. We are at Haggwater Bridge, which was a watering-place for the old packhorse trails that would have come from Edale on their way to Penistone. We take the old track up through the woods.

It is worth pausing when we reach Hope Cross, which is a square topped monolith at the junction of several important route ways. One road came from the Roman settlement at Brough, the valley in front of us, to the fort, over the moors, at Glossop. Even today it is a harsh route to walk, but it does show the determination of the Romans, who with their slaves, laid down such paths.

In summer, the hillsides here are the vibrant purple of the heather, and the path which leads to the top of Win Hill Pike cuts across a wide expanse of this luxuriantly covered countryside. This almost circular conical hill, with a small pike on its summit, can be easily recognised from miles across the peakland.

The Corn Law Rhymer

Let us introduce 'The Corn Law Rhymer', Ebenezer Elliott. He gained this title and a hero status for his campaigning against the Corn Laws of the nineteenth century. The Corn Laws were import tariffs on grain which led to the price of corn being kept high. John Bright, the industrialist, who was a friend of Joseph Whitworth, and a descendant of John Gratton, was a Member of Parliament who opposed the Corn Laws. But the approach, for the same aim, of Ebenezer and John, was very different.

Ebenezer had a life of ups and downs. He was born to a radical Calvinist family and was labelled a dunce at school. He sought solace away from his ten brothers and sisters by walking in the woods and fields. Poetry gradually came to him, when immersed in nature, through such works as Milton's.

In his teens he went to work in his father's iron foundry. It was in a poor state and, after his father's death, combined with the economic problems of the time, Ebenezer became bankrupt. Until this trauma in his life, poetry had been a recreation to do with nature. He used much of the topography around the west of Sheffield, and the Peak District, for the setting of his poems. In the extract that follows, Loxley is named, and we know that from Robin Hood. Rivelin is a nearby valley partially wooded and one of the original centres of the iron and steel making in the town. Kinderscout is the moorland past Win Hill, which we will cross later on *The Literary Way*.

Look on the clouds, the streams, the earth, the sky,
Lo! All is interchange and harmony
Where is the gorgeous pomp which yestermorn
Curtained yon orb with amber, fold on fold?
Behold it in the blue of Rivilin borne,
To feed the all-feeding seas! The molten gold
Is flowing pale in Loxley crystal cold.
To kindle into beauty tree and flower
And wake to verdant life hill, dale and plain,
Cloud trades with river, and exchange is power;
But should the clouds , the trees, the wind disdain
Harmonious intercourse, nor dew nor rain
Would forest-crown the mountains; airless day
Would blast on Kinderscout the heathy glow.
No purply green would meeken into grey
O'er Don at eve; no sound of river's flow
Disturb the sepulchre of all below.
The Ranter – Ebenezer Elliott

He would blame the Corn Laws for his bankruptcy and began his own campaign for their repeal. His biography, by his son-in-law, described this period in his life.

Ebenezer Elliott shared the fate of thousands, but thought more about it than they all, and felt it deeper. He left the tale untold because it could derive no public interest, save from its connection with such a man as himself. Thousands at the present day might tell similar tales, more instructive than entertaining to the general reader. Elliott attributed his disasters to the Corn Laws, and he was not one to suffer without seeking a remedy.
We have seen from his non-political poetry that he could sympathise with fictitious grief, nor did this make him fashionable callous to the real. Yet he dwelt not on his own grief but as an item in the general account.
Life, Poetry and Letters of Ebenezer Elliott - John Watkins

After his personal struggles, he turned his poetry to support his anti-Corn Law stance. His first poem was a long one that he called *The Ranter*. He nearly lost his money again, and joined various working class protest groups, in defence of the poor. He was never poor again, because of his merchant business, but at the same time he never forgot his roots.

He was a tireless man, with a large family and a business. His health was frequently affected by the smallpox he had as a child. He would die aged 68 in 1849, but his health had been failing for a number of years.

He believed that his poetry had developed over the years. As a young man he wrote to the Poet Laureate, Robert Southey, to ask how he could get his work published. Their correspondence lasted many years and Elliott attributed his poetic development to Southey's help. One of his topographical poems for which he was well known is *Win Hill*. This is an extract from the lengthy work. He specifically refers to the Derwent and Ashop. These two rivers previously joined each other near the village of Ashopton and just south of the village of Derwent, all of which is now under the waters of Ladybower.

To bathe with married waves their monarch's feet,
See, where the Ashop and the Derwent haste;
And how he rears him from the vale, complete
In all his time-touched majesty, embraced
By the blue, bright-blue heavens; his proud brow graced
With that stone diadem which Nature made
Ages before her practised hand had graced
With living gems the bluebell-haunted shade,
Or, high in lucid air, her wind-swift wings displayed!
Win Hill – Ebenezer Elliott

Ebenezer Elliott was always radical and passionate about the poor and the working class. One of his last works was a poem that was set to the music, *Commonwealth*. It was called the *People's Anthem*. Many years after his death it led to the suggestion that he should be named the Poet Laureate for The League of Nations.

When wilt thou save the people?
Oh, God of mercy! when?
Not kings and lords, but nations!
Not thrones and crowns, but men!
Flowers of thy heart, oh, God, are they!
Let them not pass, like weeds, away!
Their heritage a sunless day!
God! save the people!
The People's Anthem – Ebenezer Elliott

To show that Ebenezer's influence as a protest poet became widespread we can refer to John Whittier, an American poet who was passionate about the abolition of slavery. Here is John's tribute to Ebenezer.

Hands off! thou tithe-fat plunderer! play
No trick of priestcraft here!
Back, puny lordling! darest thou lay
A hand on Elliott's bier?

Hope Cross at the crossroads of ancient paths

Ladybower from Win Hill

Ebenezer Elliott – John Whittier

We leave Win Hill by retracing our steps slightly and then taking the descent into the village of Hope. This is a extremely old village with a parish that used to be one of the biggest in Derbyshire. On the edge of the village, close to the hamlet of Brough, there is evidence of Roman occupation, and there is also evidence of a settlement before the Domesday Book. The main road through the valley passes through Hope, which also has many houses along the road into Edale. In the centre is St Peter's Church. Across the road is the Old Hall pub which was built by local gentry in 1723. The market place, now with modern housing, is outside the Old Hall and opposite the church.

Let's rest awhile at Hope

Ebenezer Elliott became a much respected poet in Sheffield, which is the nearest town to Win Hill. The town was in the grip of the rapid expansion of industry and he became one of the new breed that merged industry and literature. Up to that time, in the town, many of the main literary figures came from the middle class or scholarly routes. Despite the set backs Ebenezer faced, he proved to be a shrewd business man, and despite the ups and downs of the time he succeeded in a comfortable retirement.

With the same determination and with total bravery Guy Gibson and his crews made some of the most daring raids during the Second World War. He was never content to rest and in the end his death came from always volunteering to be at the forefront of the fighting.

The lost villages are a stark reminder of the demand of the cities for water, but although man-made, they do create a wonderful countryside with the idylic mixture of hills, winding valleys and the open stretches of blue water.

Heaven and Hell

Hope to the Winnats through Castleton and past Eldon Hole

Peveril Castle above the village of Castleton

The castle and what is underneath it brings us a quite amazing literary legacy. Literary paragons have been visiting the small village of Castleton for centuries. They have left us some of the most lucid and compelling descriptions that we find anywhere on *The Literary Way.*

The Norman castle has stood proudly overlooking the village for nearly a thousand years. It was the catalyst for one of the greatest names in literature to pen a story. But it is not the only one based on the castle because a local man, from nearby Chapel-en-le-Frith, has also written a swashbuckling novel about the castle.

In this section of *The Literary Way* we will be going underground where, from ancient times to modern days, people have found intriguing experiences. One of our friends, Lord Byron, discovered he was in love when in one of the caves. Another leading poet, writer and architectural critic, reports how frightened he was when as a young boy his parents took him down one of the old mines. But a famous philosopher's mother thought even worse, and she believed that death was just around the corner. But it's not all doom and gloom in the chilling depths, as we have both a masque and a pantomime.

There is also a fascinating story of a late eighteenth century diary that came to life at the end of the twentieth century and stimulated some modern cave exploration, which eventually led to a subterranean cavern, which is taller that St Paul's Cathedral in London.

St Edmund's church stands squarely in the middle of the village and we are particularly interested in one inhabitant of the vicarage, who arrived just after King Charles I came to the throne.

We leave the village of Hope, and take the riverside path along the valley to the village of Castleton. As we approach it across the fields, we can see that the village is nestled into the broad green sweep of the hills that enclose the end of the valley. The Norman castle, which overlooks the settlement, is perched on an easily defended hill. Castleton is only a small village and so it is no time at all before we reach St Edmund's Church.

The Regretful Vicar

In 1627, a young man, 23 years old, arrived in Castleton from Brasenose College, Oxford. He had just finished his degree and had come to take up the living in the village. His name was Isaac Ambrose.

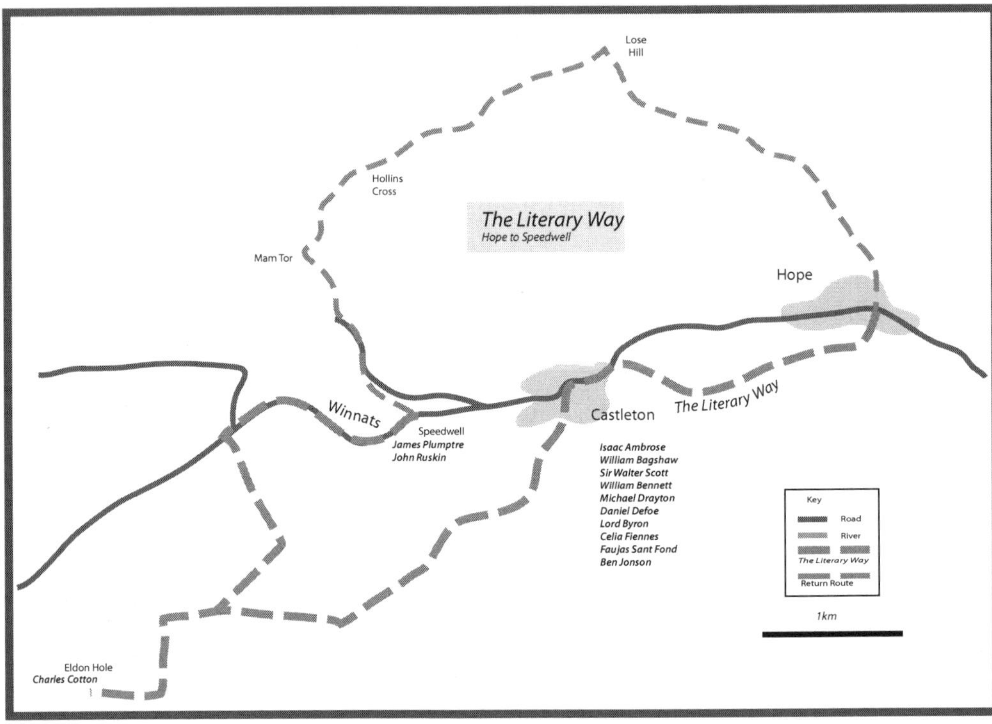

The Literary Way – Walk Nineteen – Hope to the Winnats

St Edmund's Church, Castleton

Walk Directions

Hope to Castleton (1.61 miles)

We leave Hope by taking the side road between the Church and the Woodroffe Arms
After crossing the bridge we take the path to our right
It follows a small stream to start with and then crosses fields and stiles
From early on we can see the castle over the village of Castleton
We continue to follow the path until it reaches the road where we turn left
We follow the road as it bends through the village until we turn left to reach the church.

Castleton to Eldon Hole (3.14 miles)

After visiting Peveril Castle and Peak Cavern we return to the market square with its War Memorial
Between the cottages a footpath leads into Cave Dale
We begin the walk up the dale under the castle
We have fine views of the castle from below
At the top of Cave Dale we pass through the gate and continue on the path
The path follows the wall all the way to the track
We turn right along the track
There is a track to the right which we ignore and keep going straight
We then reach a gate where six paths meet, we carry straight on
Just before the large Eldon Hill we turn left on a path
When we have passed the main height of Eldon Hill we aim for the trees in front
Turn right along the wall in front of the trees and Eldon Hole is on our right

Eldon Hole to Speedwell Cavern (2.93 miles)

We retrace our step to where the six paths meet
We take the second on our left which leads diagonally across the field
When we reach the track we turn left
At the end of the track we turn right onto the road
The road bends to the left and we take the right turn down the Winnats
The first part is on the road, but after the farm and cattle grid we can walk on the grass
We go all the way down the Winnats to the Speedwell Cavern

Speedwell Cavern to Hope (4.34 miles)

Opposite the entrance to Speedwell is a path which we take
This leads towards Treak Cliff cave and we take the path down to the road
We turn left and follow the road
After the bus turning circle continue to follow the remains of the road
At the point where the old road takes a sharp turn to the left we take the footpath to the right
We ignore any paths to the right and follow it up the side of the hill to come out at Hollins Cross
The ridge opens up before us and we turn along it to the right
There are fine views over Hope Valley and Edale
We walk to Lose Hill
The path goes down from Lose Hill
We take the left hand path (not towards the farm)
The path takes us down the convex slope of Lose Hill with Win Hill in front of us
We follow the path down to the road and turn right
We then walk along the road past the Cheshire Cheese pub and into Hope

Distance: 12.0 miles Ascent: 2344ft

Let's place him in history with reference to some other writers we have come across on *The Literary Way*. Both Thomas Hobbes at Chatsworth, and Isaac Walton in Dovedale, would have been slightly older that Isaac Ambrose, while there are a couple of writers in the chapter who would have been his contemporaries. Charles I had just come to the throne and the English Civil War would still be decades in the future.

The new vicar would only stay for about two years, and would eventually move on to Lancashire. His writings took place later in life and, while they are mainly devotional, there is one unusual book that he wrote and it was called, *The Well Ordered Family*. Let's take a small extract from a section about the governance of the household.

Of the Duties of Governors in General. In the proceedings of these family duties we are to consider the duties of: 1.The Governors 2. The Governed.
The Governors; if (as in marriage) there be more than one, as first the chief Governor, the Husband and secondly the helper, the wife, both these owe their duties to their family and to one another. The duties they owe to their families are either in general to the whole or in particular according to their several relations. That which in general they owe to the whole is either to their bodies or their souls.
The Well-Order Family – Isaac Ambrose

However, Isaac Ambrose did regret leaving Castleton. We find the source of this information in *De Spiritualibus Pecci* by William Bagshaw who had met Isaac Ambrose.

The thrice Worthy Mr Isaac Ambrose, a star of the first magnitude, for a time fixed at Castleton, by the highest hand and underneath it by the then Bishop of Chester. I had not the happiness to converse with (or see this Saint of the Lord) save once at Manchester, at that time his love of Castleton (upon the mention of it) revived. Tears shot into his eyes and from his mouth fell this ingenuous acknowledgement: It was my sin (and is my sorrow) that I left that place when the Lord was blessing my Ministry in it.
De Spiritualibus Pecci – William Bagshaw

William Bagshaw was a man of the Peak. He was born in 1628 and became a non-conformist minister. With the changing views of the monarchs in his lifetime, he varied from open preaching to secret meetings in his home. He lived for a long period at Ford Hall, which is a few miles from Castleton. *De Spiritualibus Pecci* comprises biographical fragments of his life.

Down in Yon Forest

Before we leave the religious theme that has started this chapter, we turn our attention to carol singing. Throughout the Peak District, and surrounding areas, many of the villages have their own carols. The origins of some are known, in Eyam for instance, Richard Furness wrote a carol every year, but many are shrouded in the mists of time and have undergone many changes as the new generations have taken to them.

In 1908, Ralph Vaughan Williams visited Castleton and was given some traditional local verses and their music. He included them in the *Oxford Book of Carols.* One stands out as it has grown in popularity over the years and has been recorded by many artists. Its title is *Down in Yon Forest.*

It has a fascinating history dating back to 1504 where it was noted in a London manuscript by Richard Hill. At the time it was not associated with Christmas, and it is referred to as the Corpus Christi Carol. These are the words from a more modern variant.

Down in yon forest there is a hall,
The bells of paradise I heard them ring,
Covered all over in purple pall,
I love my Lord Jesus above anything.
Traditional Carol associated with Castleton

Mineralogy

John Mawe did not live in Castleton, but he did frequently visit the village. He was born in 1764 and would build a business in mineralogy. He visited South America, collecting specimens from caves and mines. His extensive travels were possible because he had the support of the Portuguese royal family.

When he returned to England he opened a shop in The Strand, in London, which was recognised as a leading mineral establishment. He had previously worked as an apprentice in Derby making marble artefacts. In this role he knew the geologist from Bakewell, White Watson. He didn't publish many works, but did produce a ground-breaking one on conchology, or the study of shells.

He considered the area around Castleton to be the best in the country for understanding geology and mineralogy, and in 1802 published *The Mineralogy of Derbyshire.*

The ancient method of dressing and smelting lead ore is here still continued, and though new veins are frequently cut, no analysis is made of their produce; it is much to be wished sufficient encouragement was given in this science, to render it worth the attention of a person of abilities to analyze mineral substances, in order to convey mineralogical information to that part of the community that is so much interested in them.
For such a purpose Castleton seems to be the best situation, where such a variety of strata, mines, and mineral productions occur as perhaps no situation in this kingdom can boast. The various mines and veins of ore are of the first consequence, while the mountains around present a variety of strata worthy the attention of the geologist.
The Mineralogy of Derbyhire – John Mawe

John Mawe's brief introduction to the rocks of Derbyshire gives us a theme which we are going to explore in this chapter. The rocks, and the consequent caves in this vicinity, have inspired writers in many forms and so we are going under ground. We leave the church and go to the market square and turn down the short hill by the former Castleton Hall. We then cross the bridge and take the footpath between the cottages that are on the left. We are in for a surprise, for as we emerge past the last of the cottages we enter a huge rocky atrium, with an arched cave entrance at the foot of the cliffs.

The Devil's Arse

Michael Drayton is not a well-known name, but it is one that promoted a theme which many others have contributed to and commented on. In 1622, he published a quite remarkable poem that was 15,000 lines long. It was written in sections, which were called 'songs'. The poem was called, *Polyolbion.* Michael Drayton was born in 1563 and so is one of the oldest literary sources we cover on this journey.

He was born five years after Elizabeth I came to the throne. He became a page to Sir Henry Goodeere, who ensured he was well educated. In 1591, at the age of 28, he produced his first work entitled, *The Harmonie of the Church.* He would become a prolific poet, with *Polyolbion* just one of his works. Much of his poetry is either pastoral or looks back at famous events and a typical one from Michael was *The Ballad of Agincourt.* But *Polyolbion* is different. Michael describes the topography of England in his poetic songs. He must have travelled extensively and learned a great deal about the areas he visited. He often focused his attention on rivers, but also covers major features such as forests and hills.

When the Song arrives in the Peak he introduces the limestone country with the following description:

But to th' unwearied Muse the Peake appears the while,
A withered beldam long, with bleared wat'rish eyes,
With many a bleak storm dimm'd which often to the skies
She cast, and oft to the earth bowed down her aged head
Her meagre wrinkled face, being sullied with lead,
Which sitting in the works, and poring o'er the mines,
Which she out of the ore continually refines
For she a chemist was, and Nature's secret knew,
And from amongst the lead, she antimony drew
And crystals there congeal'd by her enstyled flowers
And in all med'cines knew their effectual powers,
The spirits that haunt the mines, so could command and tame,
And bind them as she list in Saturn's dreadful name.
She millstones from the quarrs, which sharpened pick could yet
And dainty whetstone make, the dull edg'd tools to whet.
Polyolbion – Michael Drayton

The path to Peak Cavern where the fictional Mary Queen of Scots had a picnic

Michael points out that the mining industry was prevalent during his tour and the extraction of minerals for medicine was also evident. The emblem of the Peak District National Park is the millstone, which was in use during his time. The caves clearly fascinated him. He described then as:

Ye dark and hollow caves, the portraitures of hell,
Where fogs and misty damps continually do dwell;
Polyolbion – Michael Drayton

The part of the Polyolbion that gripped many later writers was when Michael identified the seven wonders of the Peak. The one that interests us the most is the cavern, which lies near the castle in Castleton.

O thou my first and best, of thy black entrance nam'd
The Devil's-Arse, in me, O be thou not ashamed,
Nor think thyself disgraced or hurt thereby at all,
Polyolbion – Michael Drayton

The seven wonders were caves, wells, a hill of sand and a forest, many within the local area near Castleton. We will visit the hill of sand, Mam Tor, and Eldon Hole.

Buxton which is 15 km away had two of the wonders, namely St Anne's Fountain, which is still there, and is opposite the famous Crescent in the town. It is common today to still see people going to the fountain with water containers so they may have spring water at home.

The second of Buxton's wonder is Poole's Cavern. Tideswell, again a few miles away, was named after an ebbing and flowing well. So let us go to the Peak Cavern, which is tucked under the castle. It has been variously named the Peak Cavern and the Devil's Arse as depicted by Michael.

Let's now take the views of several visitors over the centuries as to what they thought about Peak Cavern, after that we will look at some fiction that has been inspired by the cave.

Meer Chasm

One well known figure that we have already met visited Castleton. Here is what Daniel Defoe has to say with regard to the cavern. He visited Castleton about one hundred years after Michael Drayton.

Castleton, where we come to the so famed wonder call'd, saving our good manners, 'The Devil's A ------e in the Peak',
Now not-withstanding the grossness of the name given it, and that there is nothing of similitude or coherence either in form and figure, or any other thing between the thing signified and the thing signifying; yet we must search narrowly for anything in it

to make a wonder, or even any thing so strange, or odd, or vulgar, as the name would seem to import.
The short of this story is; that on the steep side of a mountain there is a large opening very high, broad at bottom, and narrow, but rounding, on the top, almost the form of the old Gothick gates or arches, which come up, not to a half circle or half oval at the top, but to a point; though this being all wild and irregular, cannot be said to be an arch, but a meer chasme, entering horizontally; the opening being upwards of thirty foot perpendicular, and twice as much broad at the bottom at least..... But as we know they are to be found in many places in England, and that we read of them in the description of other countries, and even in the Scripture, we cannot think there is any room to call it a wonder.
A Tour thro' the Whole Island of Great Britain – Daniel Defoe

The name has changed over time from the Devil's Arse to Peak Cavern. It is a natural cavern and has only been changed slightly to avoid a section, which could only be passed, in the eighteenth and nineteenth century, by visitors lying down in a boat.

I would not Venture

The entrance to the cavern has its own fascinating history in that it was the home for a group of rope makers for many years, the practice only ceasing in the twentieth century. Any underground cave system excites the imagination of many who have gone through the caverns and caves over the centuries. Let's remember that a traveller such as Celia Fiennes visited the Peak Cavern in the late 1600s. Celia declined to take to the boat so she stopped her exploration when reaching the water:

This is what they call the Devil's Arse in the Peak, the hill on one end jutting out in two parts and joins in one at the top, this part or cleft between you enter a great Cave which is very large, and several poor little houses in it built of stone and thatch'd like little sties.....
Now none but very poor people live there which makes some small advantage by begging and by lighting the strangers into the Cave beyond this you enter so straight a passage. At the mouth you stoop very low even upon your breast and creep in, when you are about a yard or two's length you stand upright, it being lofty in manner of Poole's Hole only the rock hangs down in so many places that there is often cause of stooping very low to pass by.

The ground you tread on is all sand and lime, only the rocks do drip water in many places which makes it damp and strikes cold to you, but excepting the pillars of Rock in some places that hang down most of it is very Lofty and a great echo like a church. You pass a good way by the light of many Candles having lost sight of day from the first stooping Entrance. At last you come to a river they call it, a great water it is and very deep, they say its about 12 yards over and some do go on it with a little boat to the other side but I would not venture..
Through England on a Side Saddle in the Time of William and Mary – Celia Fiennes

Young Love

On *The Literary Way* in Matlock, we visited the Temple Hotel, where we found out that Lord Byron went there because it was a favourite visiting place for Mary Chaworth, who he was trying to court. Previously Lord Byron, Mary and others from their two families had visited Castleton and the Peak Cavern. It was when he was on the boat in the cavern that he thought about his love for her. This is how he describes it in his diary:

When I was fifteen years of age it happened that in a cavern in Derbyshire I had to cross in a boat in which two people only could lie down, a stream which flows under a rock with the rock so close upon the water as to admit the boat only to be pushed on by a ferryman, a sort of Charon, who wades at the stern stooping all the time. The companion of my transit was MC with whom I had been long in love and never told it though she had discovered it.
The Life of Lord Byron: with his Letters and Journals – Thomas Moore

Underground Graffiti

In Matlock Bath, Lord Byron was responsible for scratching on the window of the Temple Hotel, but although we have just seen him as a fifteen year old when he was in the Peak Cavern, it was not him who left his mark. A visitor scratched his name on one of the rocks in the depths of the cavern. It certainly would be frowned on today, but in the late 1700s, such an eminent visitor could get away with it. He was Sir Joseph Banks, who was President of the Royal Society at the time, a distinguished position that he held for 41 years. He was a botanist and naturalist, who came to fame after sailing with Captain Cook on his first voyage to Australia.

As well as having a great influence on the development of Kew Gardens, and the garden's specimens, he also commissioned the first geological

The cleft in the rock above Peak Cavern

map of the United Kingdom. Unfortunately, he did not record his visit to the Peak Cavern, but his name in the rock and his visit was reported by a French Professor of Geology, Barthélemy Faujas de Saint-Fond. He was on a visit to Britain to see some geological features in England and Scotland. He recorded the details in *Travels in England and Scotland.* He took the local route from Buxton.

We rode from Buxton to Castleton, a distance of twelve miles, on one of the finest days of autumn, but along a road as disagreeable and fatiguing as the worst of winter. During our stay in this little place, which is agreeably situated in the midst of some mountains, we had an opportunity of seeing the different workmen in fluorspar, and visited the magnificent cavern called the Devil's Arse, near Castleton, and likewise several mines in its vicinity. The result of my observations is a description of the cave of Castleton vulgarly known by the name of the Devil's Arse. I feel more satisfaction in telling my readers that this cave has been honoured with the visits of several respectable men of science, among the latest of whom were, Sir Joseph Banks, President of the Royal Society of London and Dr Solander, accompanied by Omai, a native of the South Seas, who was received with the most lively interest in England, where he remained a considerable time.

Travels in England and Scotland – Barthélemy Faujas de Saint-Fond

He goes further into the cave and finds the marks left by the famous men.

At the entrance of this sort of aqueduct: we saw several names engraved in the rock, among which we distinguished those of Sir Joseph Banks and Dr. Solander, and also that of Omai, who accompanied them in this subterraneous journey.

Travels in England and Scotland – Barthélemy Faujas de Saint-Fond

Our last visitor who had a different perspective visited Castleton in the early 1800's. She was visiting England from her home country of Germany.

As Miserable as Imagination could Perceive

Johanna Schopenhauer was a regular traveller in Europe in the early nineteenth century and recorded her travels in detailed diaries. Her journey around England paints a wonderful verbal description of our towns and cities and the British way of life, as perceived by someone from another country. Unfortunately her son, the eminent German philosopher, Arthur Schopenhauer, did not accompany her. To understand why we will let the British philosopher, Bertrand Russell explain:

Schopenhauer's mother was a lady of literary aspirations, who settled in Weimar two weeks before the battle of Jena. There she kept a literary salon, wrote books and enjoyed friendships with men of culture. She had little affection for her son, and a keen eye for his faults. She warned him against bombast and empty pathos; he was annoyed by her philanderings. When he came of age he inherited a modest competence; after this, he and his mother gradually found each other more and more intolerable.

History of Western Philosophy – Bertrand Russell

Let's look at Johanna's first impression of the Peak Cavern.

Once inside the cave, the black night changed to dusk as our eyes grew accustomed to the gloom. We could soon distinguish the figures of women and children, cowering like gnomes busily spinning. These creatures as miserable as imagination could perceive, live out their wretched existence in this cold damp darkness, sleeping at night in little wooden huts they have built inside the cave.

Diaries – Johanna Schopenhauer from A Lady Travels – Ruth Michaelis-Jena and Willy Merson

Johanna took a different perspective on the crossing in the small boat to our previous writers.

Never had the impression of being buried alive seem clearer to us than in this coffin-like little boat with the black roof looming over us. Our guide had to wade along, stooping; one knock against the rock above would have rendered him unconscious and we should have found ourselves alone in the most horrible situation.

Diaries – Johanna Schopenhauer from A Lady Travels – Ruth Michaelis-Jena and Willy Merson

Let's leave Johanna and move to the portrayal of Peak Cavern in fiction. After the doom and gloom of some of our writers, we will take a light-hearted view from a person who also had German origins.

The Harlequin in the Peak

Let's move from the Peak Cavern at the end of the 1700s to the famous Drury Lane Theatre in London. David Garrick, the long-term friend of Samuel Johnson, was the theatre manager there. He employed a young German artist, who would settle in England, as a scenery painter. The artist's name was Philip de Loutherbourg and he had a vision for a different way of providing scenery for plays. Up to that time backdrops were painted to set the scene. Philip introduced the technology of the time into the creation of the theatre sets. He introduced moving objects and used light and visual effects. His work helped the theatre survive during that period, as his designs were very popular. When Richard Brinsley Sheridan took over the managership of the theatre, after David Garrick died, Philip found another supportive patron.

Philip had been on his travels and painted many scenes across England. He then took the sketches he had made in Derbyshire and he built them into elaborate sets for a pantomime. The work was called *The Wonders of Derbyshire,* with an alternative title being, *The Harlequin in the Peak.* One of the scenes that came in for most praise was his representation of Peak Cavern. Chatsworth also figured in the pantomime and was also given high praise.

Cock Lorel

One prevalent story, that has been purported for years, is that an Elizabethan called Cock Lorel assembled a band of thieves who hid in the Peak Cavern. It most probably is a myth, but the name does appear in some old documents, but whether the real person was a villain is doubtful. However, the

The stream from, and the path to, Peak Cavern

legend lives on. Some versions of the myth link the people in the cave with Gypsies.

One writer drew the legend of Cock Lorel into a royal song. He was Ben Jonson, who was born in the first Elizabethan era, although he found no favour with that monarch. It would be some time later, and under King James, that Ben became successful, both as a playwright and a poet. He certainly was a character who we can warm to. He came from a poor family, but did manage to go to the nearby Westminster School, where life was hard. It was at that school that he learnt Latin and Greek, which would help him in his later life.

His first trade was the same as his stepfather's, and he became a bricklayer, but his interest lay in the theatre and so he also became a jobbing actor. In his early twenties, during a period when he struggled for work, he went to Holland where he enlisted in the army. But that life didn't appeal to him and he returned home to London the following year.

When he was 26, he became involved in a duel with another actor, who he killed in the sword fight. He was arrested and charged with murder. He pleaded benefit of clergy, which at that time, meant that he could prove to the court he could read the Bible. He was very thankful for his classical education at Westminster School in which prayers and bible readings happened several times a day. But this was not his only problem with the courts and on one occasion he had a lot to do to prove his innocence.

There were tensions in the King's realm and this was increased when the Gunpowder Plot was exposed. The immediate perpetrators were caught in the act, and there followed a hunt for other collaborators and sympathisers. Ben was suspected of being a Catholic, which he was, and had had dinner with Robert Catesby, the leader of the plot, some weeks earlier. But he convinced the court that he had nothing to do with it and only had to take some instruction to turn him away from Catholicism.

Until he came under the wing of King James, he was often in court for causing problems, mainly criticising the government, with his plays. But he gradually became a more and more successful playwright. One of his specialities came in the writing of masques. These were musicals with dancing, in which some of the audience, mainly the aristocracy, participated. The highlight of the royal year for masques was on Twelfth Night. Ben's entertainment became more and more lavish and hence expensive. In the early 1600s, his masques could cost several thousand pounds to stage even though he would normally only receive about £10 for writing each one. At the height of his popularity with the King, both as a masque writer and a poet, he was awarded a pension which adds him to the list of poet laureates.

He lived until his sixties and, despite the royal and aristocratic support, he was often in poverty and near the end of his life, he struggled and called in a few favours from his previous sponsors. He enjoyed tavern drinking with his favourite drink being the sweet white Canary wine. It seems doubtful that he ever visited Peak Cavern, although he did go to Derbyshire, especially Bolsover Castle, more than once. At one time, because of lack of money, he walked from London to Edinburgh, and after a few months, walked back again, which was quite an accomplishment as he weighed 20 stone.

Ben was a playwright contemporary of William Shakespeare, who was part owner of a successful acting group, called the Kings Men. Ben wrote many plays, which were performed by these players, and it is thought that William may have been in at least one of them, although the information about both men is very sketchy in places.

After William Shakespeare's death his work was drawn together in a first collection. Previously some of the plays had only been printed individually. Ben Jonson wrote the preface for the first folio of Shakespeare's works. At times they were rivals, but the start of the preface does imply they were friends as well.

To the memory of my beloved,
The Author
MR. W I L L I A M S H A K E S P E A R E
and what he hath left us.
To draw no envy (Shakespeare) on thy name,
Am I thus ample to thy Booke, and Fame;
While I confesse thy writings to be such,
As neither Man, nor Muse, can praise too much.
'Tis true, and all men's suffrage. But these wayes
Were not the paths I meant unto thy praise;
For seeliest Ignorance on these may light,
Which, when it sounds at best, but eccho's right;
Or blinde Affection, which doth ne're advance
The truth, but gropes, and urgeth all by chance;
Or crafty Malice, might pretend this praise,
And thine to ruine, where it seem'd to raise.
Shakespeare First Folio – Preface – Ben Jonson

Having introduced our man, let's see what he had to say about the Peak Cavern and Cock Lorel. The cavern is mentioned in two of his works, and he refers to it as the Devil's Arse. On this walk we have just met Michael Drayton, who wrote about the Devil's Arse in his *Polyolbion.* Ben and Michael were contemporaries with the latter being about ten years older. It is believed that they did not like each other. Following the publication of Michael's main topographical work Ben wrote a play called, *The Devil is an Ass.* The play was performed by Shakespeare's group, the Kings Men.

The play is based around an aspiring devil, called Pug. Satan eventually allows him to come to earth to trick a foolish old man, Fitzdottrel, who has always wanted to meet the devil. This is the first meeting.

Fitzdottrel: What's your Name?
Pug: My Name is Devil, Sir.
Fitzdottrel: Say'st thou true.
Pug: Indeed, Sir.
Fitzdottrel: Slid! there's some Omen i' this! what Countryman?
Pug: Of Derby-shire, Sir, about the Peak.
Fitzdottrel: That Hole belong'd to your Ancestors?
Pug: Yes, Devil's Arse, Sir.
The Devil is an Ass – Ben Jonson

Ben Jonson's main use of the Peak Cavern is in the *Gypsies Metamorphosed.* In this masque, the king of the gypsies invites the devil for dinner. The ingredients are different types of people. The masque was performed to celebrate the marriage, in the presence of King James, of the Duke of Buckingham. He married Katherine Manners, the daughter of the Earl of Rutland, the family that we met at Haddon Hall.

Ben Jonson could allow much more to happen in this masque as it was a private affair away from the formal court of King James. It was so popular, with the aristocratic singing and dancing that it was performed three times, which was something of a rarity. The following is from the haunt of the gypsies in the Devil's Arse.

Cock Lorel would have the Devil his guest,
and bid him home to Peak to dinner,
There fiend never had such a feast,
prepared at the charge of a sinner.
With a hey down, down adown, down,

His stomach was quesie, he came thither coached,
the joggings had caused his cruets to rise,
To help which he call'd for a Puritan poach'd,
that used to turn up the white of his eyes.
With a hey down, &c.
Cock Lorel – Gypsies Metamorphosed – Ben Jonson

For our final fictional look at the Peak Cavern we have a story set in the same Elizabethan times, but written during the Victorian Era.

The Peak Cavern, Madam!

On *The Literary Way,* at Dethick, we introduced Charlotte Yonge and the novel she wrote, *Unknown to History,* about Mary, Queen of Scots. It is unlikely she ever visited Castleton as she stayed virtually her entire life in the quietness of rural Hampshire, where she wrote many novels and other works, principally for young Christian women. However, her description in *Unknown to History* is realistic, especially the scenes set in Sheffield where Mary is held on house arrest.

At Elizabeth's request Mary spent a long time under the guardianship of the Earl of Shrewsbury. In the story Mary asks to go to Castleton and down the Peak Cavern. The Earl of Shrewsbury is not pleased with Mary's idea of visiting the cave.

So on the ensuing morning, when the Earl came to pay his respects, Mary assailed him with, 'There is a marvellous cavern in these parts,my Lord, of which I hear great wonders.
'Does your grace mean Pool's Hole?'

Peveril Castle Keep and Mam Tor from the top of the slope in Cave Dale

'Nay, nay, my Lord. Have I not been conducted through it by Dr. Jones, and there writ my name for his delectation? This is, I hear, as a palace compared therewith.'
'The Peak Cavern, Madam!' said Lord Shrewsbury, with the distaste of middle age for underground expeditions, 'is four leagues hence, and a dark, damp, doleful den, most noxious for your Grace's rheumatism.'
'Have you ever seen it, my Lord?'
'No, verily,' returned his lordship with a shudder.
'Then you will be edified yourself, my Lord, if you will do me the grace to escort me thither,' said Mary, with the imperious suavity she well knew how to adopt.
Unknown to History – Charlotte Yonge

Of course, Mary gets her way and they set off for Castleton.

Deep beds of rich ferns clothed the lower slopes, and sheets of that delicate flower, the enchanter's nightshade, reared its white blossoms down to the bank of a little clear stream that came flowing from out of the mighty yawning arch of the cavern, while above the precipice rose sheer the keep of Peak Castle. The banquet was gracefully arranged to suit the scene, and comprised, besides more solid viands, large bowls of milk, with strawberries or cranberries floating in them. Mr. Eyre, the keeper of the castle, and his daughter did the honours, while his son superintended the lighting and fumigation of the cavern, assisted, if not directed by Dr. Jones, whose short black cloak and gold-headed cane were to be seen almost everywhere at once. Presently clouds of smoke began to issue from the vast archway that closed the ravine. 'Beware, my maidens,' said the Queen, merrily, 'we have roused the dragon in his den, and we shall see him come forth anon, curling his tail and belching flame.'
Unknown to History – Charlotte Yonge

Let's leave the Devil's Arse and head upwards, as we are going to the castle. If we retrace our steps to Castleton Hall, the entrance to Peveril Castle is opposite. The keep was built by Henry II in 1176. Let's wander round and take in the fine views across the valley.

Waverley

Our journey, *The Literary Way,* started near Ashbourne and we soon met Samuel Johnson whose name stands out in the history of English literature. In Castleton, we meet another prominent doyen of literature, Sir Walter Scott. He was given his baronetcy in 1822 as a result of his writings. His novels and poems became very famous in his lifetime, and with the increased travel across the world at the time, he became one of the first writers to be known in many countries during his own lifetime. His works are still read today and many of his writings are classics of both English and Scottish literature.

His most well-known works include *Ivanhoe, Rob Roy* and *The Lady of the Lake.* These and others form the Waverley Novels, for which he is best remembered. He had a quite amazing output of writing and completed sixteen novels in fifteen years. Many of these novels involved detailed research. Simultaneously, he also published poetry. Scott qualified as a lawyer but, at the age of 25, he began to write and publish poetry. By the age of 43, he had begun a printing press and had become acclaimed for his poetry. However, the printing press started to get

Cave Dale overlooked by Peveril Castle

into financial problems and he chose to write a novel to bring in some much needed income.

Then started one of the more intriguing stories of publishing in the nineteenth century. *Waverley*, the first of the novels, was published anonymously in 1814. But it would be some 13 years later before he would actually admit to being the author of *Waverley,* the novel, and all the other novels classified under the same heading. It is thought that he only admitted authorship because, despite the success of the books, his business was again in financial difficulties. The initial novels were all based in Scotland, but the fifth book, *Ivanhoe,* was based in England, and we introduced a section from it when we told of the Robin Hood connections with the local area.

This English theme he carried further forward with the ninth book, *Peveril of the Peak*. The story is not based at the origins of the Castle, but during the English Civil War. This is the introduction.

William, the Conqueror of England, was or supposed himself to be, the father of a certain William Peveril, who attended him to the battle of Hastings, and there distinguished himself. The liberal minded monarch, who assumed in his charters the veritable title of Gulielmus Bastardus, was not likely to let his son's illegitimacy be any bar to the course of his royal favour, when the laws of England were issued from the mouth of the Norman victor, and the lands of the Saxons were at his unlimited disposal. William Peveril obtained a liberal grant of property and lordships in Derbyshire, and became the erector of that Gothic fortress, which, hanging over the mouth of the Devil's Cavern, so well known to tourists, give the name of Castleton to the adjacent village.

Peveril Castle by Sir Walter Scott

The novel then introduces the characters of this post-English Civil War conflict. Sir Walter published this novel in the 1830.

Banner Cross

William Bennett was a writer of a novel, also based on Peveril Castle, but his was set some thirty years earlier than Sir Walter's at the beginning of the Civil War. William was a solicitor, who had his family home in Chapel-en-le-Frith, which is about six miles from Castleton. In the Preface, he gives a lengthy description of finding an old manuscript, from which he claims he wrote the story, and notes that Banner Cross is now known as Castleton. We have come across William before, but we knew him as Lee Gibbons, when he wrote the three-volume *King of the Peak* about the Haddon Hall elopement.

The book based at Banner Cross, called *The Cavalier*, was also written under the same pseudonym, Lee Gibbons. The most obvious reason for this was to protect his professional reputation. He was an active solicitor in Chapel-en-le-Frith and Manchester, and so it might appear frivolous to his clients to see him as a novel writer.

His family went on to have a large influence in the development of Buxton with one of his sons responsible for the hospital.

Eldon Hole is fenced in the background

The Cavalier is set in and around Banner Cross and he retains several local names such as Hope Dale and Mam Tor. It is a tale about the growth of Puritanism and the ensuing fighting that the civil war brought. In the first chapter, William introduces the principal family and at the beginning of the second chapter is the description of Banner Cross.

To those of our readers, who have visited the grand cavern of the Peak, will not need to be reminded of the strength and beauty of the site, whereon stood the castle of Banner Cross; its ruins are now seen, hanging over the yawning ravine which leads immediately into the Devil's Cave: but, for the benefit of those who are strangers to the romantic scenery of the High Peak, we will endeavour to sketch an outline of the picture.
The Cavalier – William Bennett

We leave the castle and, returning to the Market Square, take the path between the cottages that leads us into Cave Dale, which is a collapsed limestone valley. Peveril Castle perches on the cliff top above our heads. The next part of our journey is across some fascinating limestone country features, which are part of an area of Special Scientific Interest, due to the geology of the area. Cave Dale takes us up on to the limestone moors and out onto Dirtlow Rake which shows the remnants of lead mining and mineral extraction.

Eldon Hole

It is now time to visit the gaping hole in the ground called Eldon Hole. It is a natural deep cavern about which there have been plenty of myths and stories. This is how Charles Cotton describes Eldon Hole, which is one of the wonders of the Peak. His poem was written in 1683.

Hence two miles east, a fourth wonder lye,
Worthy the greatest curiosity,
Call'd Eldon Hole, but such a dreadful place,
As will procure a tender muse her grace,
In the description if the chance to fail,
When my hand trembles and my cheeks turn pale.
Betwixt a verdant mountain's falling flanks,
And within bounds of easy swelling banks,
That hem the Wonder in on either side,
A formidable scissure gapes so wide,
Steep, black, and full of horror, that who dare
Looks down into the chasm, and keeps his hair
From lifting off his hat, either has none,
Or for more modish casheers his own.
It were injurious I must confess,
By mine to measure braver courages:
But when I peep into't, I must declare,
My heart still beats, and eyes with horror flare.
And he that standing on the brink of hell,
Can carry it so unconcern'd, and well,
As to betray no fear, is, certainly,
A better Christian; or a worse than I.
The Wonders of the Peak – Charles Cotton

It really is quite astonishing the number of people over the centuries that have come to visit this limestone feature. Compared to Peak Cavern and Mam Tor it is somewhat of a disappointment, as it is only a hole in the ground. Even today it is a fairly difficult place to access whether you come from Castleton or from Peak Forest, which is the village we can see in the distance, when we are at Eldon Hole.

If we return along the path and take the track that takes us near to the top of the Winnats which we descend through the steep limestone pass.

At the bottom of the Winnats Pass is the Speedwell Cavern, which is an old lead mine but is now a show cave and it is open to the public. The great interest for many tourists is the trip through the old mine taken on a flat-bottomed boat.

A Vicar, Leviathan and Titan

In 1771, a son was born into the very respectable home of Robert Plumptre, who was President of Queen's College, Cambridge. The baby's name was James, and as we would expect from his background, he was raised in an atmosphere of knowledge and learning. His family were also strongly connected with the church, with his father having taken holy orders. James, as the third son, took the same preferment at University and went into the church. This was a familiar situation for many such families, however, James did have a little bit of rebellion in him. At Cambridge, he left his father's college and transferred to Clare College, and this was an unusual occurrence.

His other slightly unusual leaning for a man about to enter the church was his love of the stage. With the often ribald nature of the acting and theatre life, there seemed little hope of easy reconciliation, but James was not deterred. He was determined to make the stage and theatre morally acceptable. He wrote a number of plays and even a comic opera. He wanted some of the major works to be available in an acceptable form, both morally and family related and so re-edited many plays and stories. Whilst much of this was done in his youth, even after taking the cloth, he still mixed literary related activities with more religious writings.

But it wasn't his religious writings or his theatrical talents that have brought him to our attention here at the Speedwell Mine. As a young man at University, he did what so many do today and set off travelling. He made a number of excursions and kept a rather spasmodic account of some of the places he visited and the people he met. He often travelled with his tutor, from Clare College, and on one trip to Derbyshire he had an interest to go underground.

Speedwell, at the time, was a working mine. Apart from Peak Cavern, which regularly had visitors, the other way people went underground was to pay miners to take them down. This is what James did, and he recorded the details in the journal of his travels. They went underground with two miners at the Speedwell Mine in 1793. So let's go down Speedwell and relive the first part of James' route, although we will do so with the benefit of electricity.

We entered a hut at the side of the hill, where our guides provided themselves with lights, which they carried in their hands by sticking several in a lump of clay, and then proceeded down the steps for near fifty yards, till we came to a canal.
James Plumptre's Britain – Ian Ousby.

They travelled in a boat in the same way as visitors do today. But at the end of the canal the miners led them onwards.

.. we chained our boat to the rail; and with each of us a light proceeded upon planks, laid upon rafters over the stream... At the end of this board walk we reached a small cavern and stood upright to rest ourselves. The miners told us, if we went farther, we must climb up the rock by rails fixed into the side: that many went no further than this place; but if we weren't afraid, we might proceed. We told them to lead on.
James Plumptre's Britain – Ian Ousby

After James Plumptre's death his papers went to his University. In the late twentieth century his diary was found to contain some interesting travel details, but it was the details of his trip down Speedwell Cavern that attracted attention. It wasn't a route that was currently used by cavers.

We climbed ten yards up a rock, by rails sometimes a yard asunder and at length into a large cavern dimly lit to be seen by our candlelight; the dashing noise of a waterfall, to be heard and not seen added to the terror of the place... with much labour and difficulty got to the end of it scrambling, which was sometimes through holes in the rocks just big enough to admit the body... From this place we went on slanting up the rocks to the place they worked at. We stopped to rest and take some of our brandy, which we found refreshing, and the miners explained the whole process of their work... At the top of the cavern, the place where we left off climbing, one of the men left a piece of candle alight, which he had brought for that purpose... We soon got to the bottom of the cavern and our guides told us to look up. The sight was dreadful: the candle forty yards above us, appeared like a star and afforded a dim light just sufficient to give an idea of the danger we had braved...
James Plumptre's Britain – Ian Ousby

At the top of their climb James and his companion had been offered a further climb but as that was through another miner's working they declined and retraced their steps.

At the large cavern I first mentioned, we left another light, which when we got to the end (600 yards) had a most beautiful effect, appearing like a star with beams playing on the water. We, at length, after two hours absence from it, got to daylight again, highly satisfied and pleased with our excursion, and returned to Castleton with mixed emotions of terror and admiration.
James Plumptre's Britain – Ian Ousby

James Plumptre's account led cavers to the cavern he climbed and this is now called Leviathan. From there, after much hard work in the clearing of routes, the cavers then found the large cavern which has the deepest shaft in the UK, which is 464ft. For comparison St Paul's Cathedral in London is 365ft.

A Frightened Boy

John Ruskin, the art and architecture critic and social writer, visited Speedwell Cavern as a young boy of about eleven years old. The visit was part of his interest, encouraged by his parents, in collecting minerals.

I pursued my mineralogical studies on fluor, calcite, and the ores of lead, with indescribable rapture when I was allowed to go into a cave. My father and mother showed far more kindness than I knew, in yielding to my subterranean passion; for my mother could not bear dirty places, and my father had a nervous feeling that the ladders would break, or the roof fall, before we got out again. They went with me, nevertheless, wherever I wanted to go, — my father even into the terrible Speedwell mine at Castleton, where, for once, I was a little frightened myself.
Praeterita – John Ruskin

We came across John Ruskin in Monsal Dale where he complained about the railways spoiling the valley. His comments and opposition to the emergence of the steam train did not stop there. Among others he was instrumental in stopping the railway coming to Castleton. Instead it passed along the next valley, Edale.

Let's rest awhile at Speedwell

Castleton has for centuries been a place to visit. The castle and particularly Peak Cavern, have attracted many visitors,who started coming in the seventeenth century. In many cases, the picturesque setting of Castleton, tucked into the end of the sweeping Hope Valley, with its dominant castle,

Speedwell Cavern at the foot of the Winnats

subterranean explorations and the steep Winnats Pass, has inspired many writers.

One of the doyens of literature, Sir Walter Scott, chose the setting of Peveril Castle for a tale named after the Norman fortification. Of the other Victorian writers, one chose the castle, but he was a local man and would know it well, while the other picked the impressive story of Mary Stuart and gave one setting as Peak Cavern. It is also the last time that we encounter Lord Byron with the touching scene, on a cold, damp flat-bottomed skiff with rocks near their heads, where he found one of his first loves.

Our favourite period though, is long before the Victorians, it is near the beginning of the seventeenth century, when we can see the links between this small village and the centres of society in London and Oxford. From the latter, the young man, Isaac Ambrose, newly ordained, chose this sleepy village for his first parish and then regretted leaving it so soon. Attached to the royal and aristocratic ensembles were two writers, who, although not friends, took to the wonders of the Peak Cavern, firstly in *Polyolbion* and then in *Gypsies Metamorphosed.* We can therefore say that Isaac Ambrose and Ben Jonson gave us a real feel for sixteenth century heaven and hell.

The rolling limestone landscape with the deep valleys and underground caves, caverns and mine workings gave us the fascinating story of the modern find of Titan Cavern. From near the Speedwell Cavern, we can see the broad sweep of the Hope valley and can easily pick out Ebenezer Elliott's Win Hill and Lose Hill. The top of the latter was presented to one of the authors from a previous chapter, G H B Ward.

Mystery under the Shivering Mountain

The Winnats to Edale Cross via Mam Tor and Rushup Edge

Mam Tor

The Shivering Mountain is one of the wonders of the Peak, and on this walk we look forward to the comments of two of our intrepid travellers. To this we add one of the most celebrated mystery writers, who as a doctor, spent a few weeks in nearby Sheffield, but found time to write a short story. For the substance and background to the story, we again need to go underground, and again it is an old mine, that is now a show cave.

Not far away is a natural cave, where late Victorian geologists and archaeologists made some interesting discoveries. It's then up on to a long ridge with superb views across the landscape. We can see the bleakness of the moors to which we are heading, but before that there is a secluded valley. It has stimulated the eloquence of a Victorian working-class poet from Manchester.

We leave Speedwell Cavern and take the former A road towards Mam Tor, and we go past the old Odin's lead mine with the crushing circle still preserved opposite to the mine entrance.

After a series of landslips, in the 1970s, the 'shivering mountain', Mam Tor, won the battle over the road and it was deemed too unstable to re-build. Let's follow the road up and over the heavily ruptured remains.

Elementary, My Dear Watson

The Terror of Blue John Gap is a typical Conan Doyle title. Sir Arthur is known for the creation of the famous sleuth Sherlock Holmes, who incidentally, was modelled on a top doctor at Edinburgh, where Arthur completed his medical training.

The Sherlock Holmes books became famous in his day, and he also wrote a large number, over forty, of other novels as well as about ten non-fiction works. Arthur was an interesting character who turned his clever mind to many topics. He moved around the country during his medical training. In his first years as a qualified doctor, before settling down, he went abroad, as he was particularly taken with the sea, and served as medical officer on trips to the Arctic and Africa. He wasn't successful in setting up a doctor's practice in Plymouth and finally moved to Portsmouth. He lived the latter part of his life in Sussex, which is where he died in 1930.

On his travels, while he was in South Africa during the Boer War, he wrote a keenly observed description of the circumstances of the soldiers. On his return to England he took up the cases of, what is now known in the press as, 'miscarriages of justice', in which he was successful.

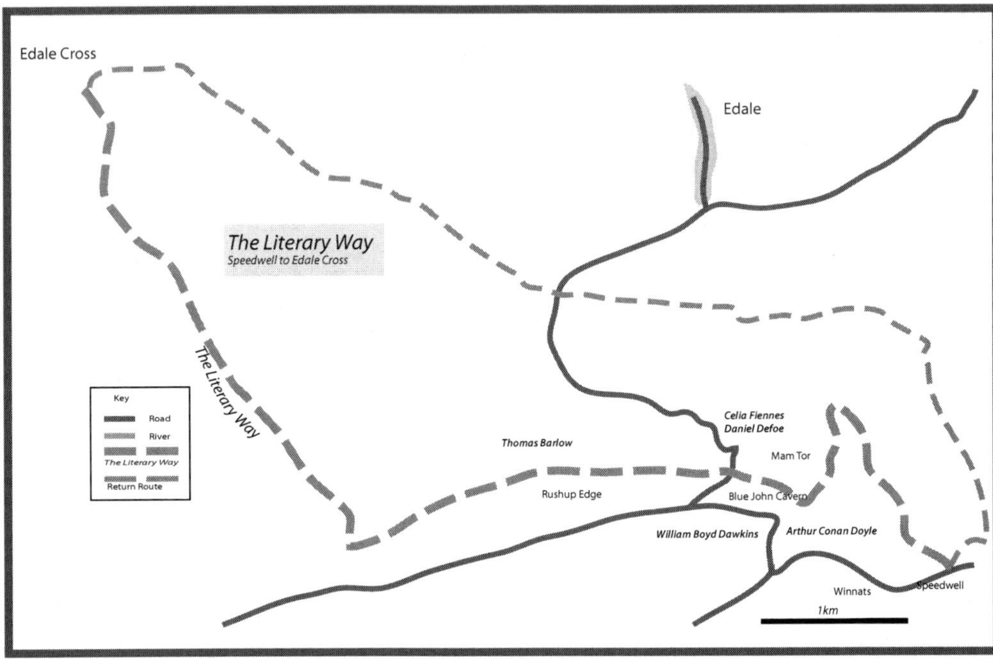

The Literary Way – Walk Twenty – The Winnats to Edale Cross

A medical career filled his ambitions as a young man but during the early part of his life he was also an active sportsman, and made several appearances, principally as a batsman, in first class cricket.

The development of Sherlock Holmes and other thriller writing came to the fore during one part of his life, but it is believed he became bored with Holmes and killed him off at the Reichenbach Falls. However, due to popular demand he had to resurrect his detective. In his latter life, mysticism gripped him and he devoted his writing to books and articles on the subject. He was a firm believer, and could not even be dissuaded from it by his friend, Houdini, who tried to demonstrate it was illusions.

As we round the top of the disintegrated road there is a sign to the Blue John Mine and this is why we have introduced the Conan Doyle story, *The Terror of Blue John Gap*. So how did Conan Doyle come to write his story about this location? It was due to his travelling for his medical training. Conan Doyle spent a short time, in 1878, in nearby Sheffield, so it is reasonable to assume he was familiar with the area. The short story might have been in his thoughts for a while, as it would be 1912 before he would publish this work.

Blue John is a derivation of Bleu-Jeune. It is a banded variety of fluorite. It is mainly worked into jewellery but some larger pieces have been made into vases and dishes. One of the prime designers and makers of Blue John ornaments was Matthew Boulton, who lived in Birmingham in the late eighteenth century and was a member of the Lunar Circle along with Erasmus Darwin and Josiah Wedgwood.

For Conan Doyle's story, the context of the piece we have selected is from a diary entry of Dr John Hardcastle and it comes from near the beginning of the story when he described staying on a farm:

Already I feel the benefit of this wonderful upland air. The farm of the Allertons lies fourteen hundred and twenty feet above sea-level, so it may well be a bracing climate...... It is a most lonely spot, and the walks are picturesque in the extreme. The farm consists of grazing land lying at the bottom of an irregular valley. On each side are the fantastic limestone hills, formed of rock so soft that you can break it away with your hands. All this country is hollow. If you could strike it with some gigantic hammer it would boom like a drum, or possibly cave in altogether and expose some huge subterranean sea...

But there is one of these strange openings in the earth which has a special interest, for it is the handiwork, not of nature, but of man. I had never heard of Blue John when I came to these parts. It is the name given to a peculiar mineral of a beautiful purple shade, which is only found at one or two places in the world. It is so rare that an ordinary vase of Blue John would be valued at a great price. The Romans, with that extraordinary instinct of theirs, discovered that it was to be found in this valley, and sank a horizontal shaft deep into the mountain side. The opening of their mine has been called Blue John Gap, a clean-cut arch in the rock, the mouth all overgrown with bushes. It is a goodly passage which the Roman miners have cut, and it intersects some of the great water-worn caves, so that if you enter Blue John Gap you would do well to mark your steps and to have a good store of candles, or you may never make your way back to the daylight again.

I have not yet gone deeply into it, but this very day I stood at the mouth of the arched tunnel, and peering down into the black

Walk Directions

Speedwell to Mam Tor (2.07 miles)

Take the path opposite to the entrance of Speedwell Cavern
Go towards Treak Cliff Cave and take the path down to the road and turn left
Follow the road past the coach turning point
The remains of the road turn sharp left
Follow the road over the old broken pieces of tarmac that are still left
Pass through the gate at the top
On your left is the Blue John Mine
Continue past Blue John Mine until you reach the road
Turn right and then cross the road
A little way up on the left is a gate
Go through the gate and Windy Knoll cave is on the left amongst the mounds
Retrace your steps to the gate and take the path up to Mam Tor
Enjoy the view from the top

Mam Tor to Edale Cross (4.54 miles)

Come back down Mam Tor and when you reach the road go down a little
Then cross over and join the path along Rushup Edge away from Mam Tor
Follow this path along the edge with views in all directions
After about one and half miles the path begins to dip to the road
On our right is a track which we take
In a short distance there is an old signpost on the left that points to a path across the moors
We take that path across the moors
It is regularly walked so it can normally be quite easily followed
It goes straight ahead
When you reach the highest point the path can be seen to descend to a wall
Follow the path and cross the stile in the wall
The path then stays close to the wall down to Edale Cross

Edale Cross to Speedwell Cavern (5.58 miles)

Turn right along the track at Edale Cross
Go down Jacob's Ladder (a steep path) into Edale
Follow this path. It passes an Information Barn
Just before the houses it joins a road
Follow the road which takes us towards Barber Booth
We go under the railway and come out at Barber Booth
There is road junction and we take the path directly opposite
This crosses several fields and then comes out on a lane/track
Turn to the right and follow around the right bend
Then take the path on the left that leads us to Hollins Cross
Enjoy the views back across Edale
On Hollins Cross there is a main path along the ridge
Looking into Hope Valley there are two paths
Take the one down to the left
After a short distance take the path to the right (not the main one)
At the path cross, go straight ahead
The path crosses the fields towards the trees
It then goes round Dunscar Farm and goes to the road
At the road cross into the car park and return to Speedwell

Distance: 12.2 miles Ascent: 2301ft

The Winnats from Mam Tor

recesses beyond, I vowed that when my health returned I would devote some holiday to exploring those mysterious depths and finding out for myself how far the Roman had penetrated into the Derbyshire hills.
The Terror of Blue John Gap – Sir Arthur Conan Doyle

Bison and Reindeer

Having visited the Blue John mine, if we follow the road to the junction, we need to cross into the rough pasture area in front of us, where we will find Windy Knoll Cave, which has railings in front of it. This was the subject of a significant investigation, in Victorian times, when William Boyd Dawkins, along with his exploring colleague Rooke Pennington, extracted the remains of several thousand animals from Windy Knoll Cave. William was Professor of Geology in Manchester, and Rooke was a solicitor from Bolton, who had an amateur enthusiasm for geology. The latter opened his own geological museum in Castleton with a range of rocks and minerals.

From the last (Windy Knoll) Mr. Rooke Pennington and myself obtained no less than 6800 specimens, irrespective of fragments thrown aside, belonging principally to the bison and

The top of Mam Tor during winter

reindeer, together with bears, wolves, foxes, and hares. This vast accumulation of bones, in an area not more than 25 by 18 feet, had been formed in the bottom of a swallow hole used as a drinking place by migratory bodies of animals. It is about 1600 ft above the seas, at a point in the Pennine Chain where the magnificent ravine of the Wynnetts and the pass by Mam Tor lead from the Vale of Hope and Castleton into the plains of Cheshire and Lancashire, and it evidently marks the route by which the animals passed to and fro from one set of pastures to another, after manner of the bison in North America and the reindeer in Siberia.

Early Man in Britain – William Boyd Dawkins

Shivering Mountain

As we leave Windy Knoll, the massive hill of Mam Tor is in front of us, as is the path that will take us to the top. Once at the peak we can see the mast above Eyam that we passed some time ago. We can also see Peveril Castle. In the distance to the east, there are the gritstone edges, with Stanage Edge being prominent. If we walk to the other side of Mam Tor, we look out over Edale, and the high peat moors of Kinderscout stretch out in the distance. Let's return to our discussion of rocks. The gritstone forms a huge horseshoe around the limestone and these two rocks type comprise the Peak District. Mam Tor is sandwiched between the gritstone and the limestone. It is made of a series of thin layers of shale and sandstone. These rocks are friable and when water enters between layers, failures in the rock structure can occur. As can be seen Mam Tor is a circular hill, with a ridge extending either side. One is the edge we will walk along, Rushup, and the opposite is called the Great Ridge. It separates Edale from Hope Valley and ends at Lose Hill. Win Hill, so well described by Ebenezer Elliot, is beyond Lose Hill.

Mam Tor is a very distinctive landmark, because the southern face of the hill has slumped down leaving the layers of rocks exposed. The slumped rocks can be seen as irregular mounds at the base of the hill. The collapse of the rocks from the face has been a process that has taken place over a long period of time. Let's take the briefest of interludes to look at the history embedded on the landscape that surrounds us. Right under our feet we have the oldest of man's habitation. On the top of Mam Tor is an Iron Age fort, the remains of the embankment can still be seen. Why live up here? The principal reason was that the valleys would have been heavily wooded. Let's try and get the times in perspective. There are suggestions that the hill fort at Mam Tor would probably have been abandoned several centuries BC. To put it in historical context, this hill fort would have been abandoned about the same time as Socrates and Plato were flourishing in Ancient Greece.

Let's move on in history. Just behind Hope, the village under Lose Hill, is the former fort of Navio. We crossed a Roman road that had come around Win Hill, the road originated from Navio, which is believed to have been established 80AD, that is, several centuries after the Mam Tor hill fort was abandoned. We move on a thousand years and there are two places to look at now from Mam Tor. The first is Peveril Castle. It was given, along with the surrounding hunting forest, to William the Conqueror's illegitimate son. On the other side of Mam Tor we look down into Edale. The village with that name is easy to pick out. Edale was mentioned along with many other local settlements in the Domesday Book of 1086 just under a thousand years ago.

Before we move on we want pick up the idea introduced by Michael Drayton, the Seven Wonders of the Peak. It origins are a little cloudy, but Michael was one of the first to suggest them, however there have been slightly different interpretations over time. But one of those wonders has always been Mam Tor. Let's see what a couple of our travellers thought of this 'wonder'.

Celia Fiennes, we first met in Bakewell. She was the early eighteenth century woman who toured England just accompanied by her servant.

The fifth Wonder Mam Tour which is a high hill... It looks just in resemblance as a great Hay-Ricke that's cut down one half, on one side that describes it most natural, this is all sand, and on that broken side the sand keeps trickling down allwayes especially when there is the least wind, of which I believe this Country is scarce ever without it, many places on the hill looks hollow and loose which makes it very dangerous to ascend and none does attempt it, the sand being loose slips the foot back again.
Through England on a Side Saddle in the Time of William and Mary – Celia Fiennes

Another view was added by Daniel Defoe some thirty years later.

Mam Tor, as the word in the mountain signifies, the Mother Roc, upon a suggestion that the soft crumbling earth, which falls from the summit of the one, breeds or begets several young mountains below. The sum of all the wonder is this, that there is a very high hill, nay I will add (that I may make most of the story, and that it may appear as much like a wonder as I can) an exceeding high hill. But this in a country which is all over hills, cannot be much of a wonder, because there are several higher hills in the Peak than that, but not just there. The south side of this hill is a precipice, and very steep from top to bottom; and as the substance of this hill is not solid stone, or rocky, as in the case of all the other hills thereabouts, but a crumbling loose earth mingled with small stones, it is continually falling down in small quantities, as the force of hasty showers or solid heavy rains loosens and washes it off, or as frost and thaws operate upon it in common with other parts of the earth.
A Tour thro' the Whole Island of Great Britain – Daniel Defoe

Daniel's words show that he was not impressed. However, it is also clear that he had a rudimentary understanding of geomorphology.

The Calico Printer

Let's leave Mam Tor and stride out along Rushup Edge, from which the views are magnificent. On one side we look over a shallow valley and undulating landscape and we can see the, now disused, quarry workings of Eldon Hill, which shields from our sight Eldon Hole. On our right we look down into Edale, which is a wide sweeping valley faced with the steep sides and crags of Kinderscout. The small village of Edale nestles on the far side and the booths of the old packhorse trail follow the line of the far declivity.

In Ebenezer Elliott we met a working man who used poetry, first as a means of solace, and then as a method of communication to reveal the visions of the working-class. Thomas Barlow was born in 1826 in Lancashire and took up the trade of calico printing at Hyde near Manchester. He became one of the first working class magistrates in the town of Glossop, which is about 15 miles north of where we are now. At the age of 41 he published a collection of his works, entitled *A Picnic at Woodhead,* which includes a lengthy poem, *Scenes Around Castleton.*

Thomas describes both the landscape and the specific features such as the castle. He also praises Richard Furness, who we met at Eyam, as the poet of the Peak. We are now overlooking the delightful valley of Edale and so we have selected Thomas's description of this sheltered landscape, which forms the end of the poem. Edale from Rushup Edge looks particularly splendid in the late summer months when the hills behind the booths and Edale village are purple with the flowering heather.

Then, Edale sunny-sided Edale!! Thoughtful
Wilt seem as bright, as beautiful as now!
Thy sister valley, too, will seem as fair;
For ye, together, are a lovely pair:
Edale and Castleton, Mam Tor between,
How wondrous one! The other how serene!
Not till the tide of memory cease to flow,
Shall I the grandeur of your scenes forgo;
Nor till life's sun shall set and pass away,
Shall I forget this bright and happy day!
Green hills and dales, and purple moors adieu,
I leave one last fond loving look with you
Resolved, if spared till next year's summer reign,
And health permit, to visit you again.
Picnic at Woodhead – Thomas Barlow

Rushup Edge gives us wonderful views in summer but, at other times of the year, bleakness soon appears over the rough grassy knolls. This is a windswept area and we begin to get the first taste of the moors. Near to the gate that leads to the track down to the road we turn right to cross the moor. If there has been no rain for several weeks you will find it dry but after even a small amount of precipitation

Low cloud gradually clearing over Edale

the black peat will cling to your boots. The route is straight across the moor and finally reaches a stile after which we descend down a track which crosses our path. Just to our left is the old Saxon Edale Cross.

Let's rest awhile at Edale Cross

On this walk it has been the rocks and the scenery that have been so much to the fore. The Blue John mineral has given us ornaments and jewellery since the late eighteenth century. The tradition continues today with minor extraction, cutting and polishing still taking place.

The area and the mineral inspired one of the most well-known detective writers to a story. Arthur Conan Doyle not only gives us a mystery but also includes a splendid description of the landscape, rocks and the minerals. Since we left the village of Hope, we have been able to see how Mam Tor dominates the western end of the Hope Valley. It has been in the list of the wonders of the Peak since the seventeenth century and so it has been interesting to see how it has been described by two contemporaneous writers, Daniel Defoe and Celia Fiennes. Our final contribution in this chapter was from one of our working-class Victorian poets, who gave us his personal description of Edale.

Howling Wilderness

Edale Cross to Hayfield across Kinderscout

Edale Rocks and the Pennine Way

We are now on the last leg of our journey, and the final point on *The Literary Way* beckons us, but it will be a hearty walk. To complete our route we will cross some bleak countryside, but it is an area with spectacular views. It was described by Daniel Defoe as a 'howling wilderness.' It is a remote, harsh landscape, but a wonderful contrast to some of the verdant valleys and historic villages through which we have passed. As we walked along Rushup Edge and then turned across the moors, the bleakness of this area began to hit us. So apart from the graphic descriptions of these moors why else are we up here? There are four reasons and what a mixture they make!

There is a person who came about 100 years after Ebenezer Elliott, but we are sure that, if they had been of the same time, they would have been good friends and the ringleaders of the movement that campaigned for the working class. Our twentieth century man would start a campaign that gained public momentum and eventually has given us what we have today, that is, open access land on some of the most beautiful moors in the country. Indirectly, it gave rise to National Parks, where the emphasis is placed on the countryside and people's access to it, rather than the relentless spread of towns and restrictive landowners.

Let's add to this a vastly different inspirational man, who, in the early part of the twentieth century, was flying kites over these moors. There is much supposition about this man's writings, but not long after he was on Kinderscout he decided to change the direction of his life. That decision, which has a backdrop of some of the most famous events of the time, gives us a brief view of the complex mind of this individual. He would go on a few years later to write a short book that would become a definitive literary work in the twentieth century.

One of the undoubted challenges of devising a walk of such well known literary characters is how do we give it a good finish! Throughout most of this part of the walk there is a house that will be in our view. It is tucked under the craggy rocks of the west facing edge of Kinderscout. In summer, it looks a wonderful setting, and we could say almost the perfect composition for a painting, but in winter it is cold, with gale force winds, and is very remote. In this part of the countryside winter is the time for hardy souls.

This single house stands a good distance from other buildings and farms and brings us two writers. The first wrote a book, the first part of which is set in this house and gives us an impressive description of the moors and areas around Kinderscout. It be-

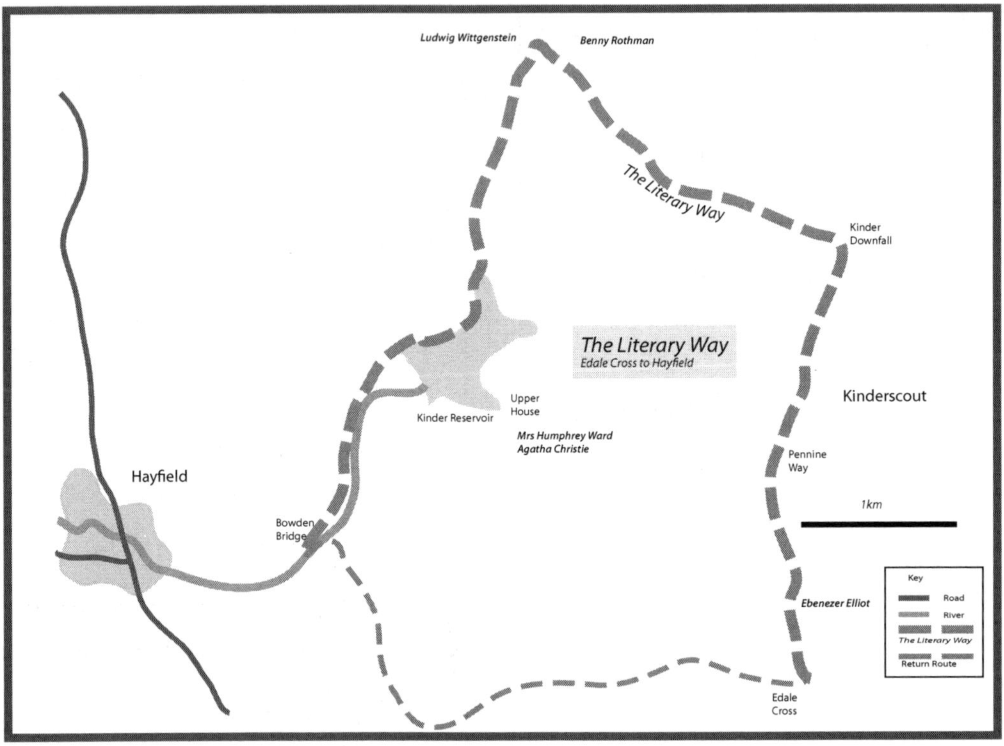

The Literary Way – Walk Twenty-One – Edale Cross to Hayfield

came a million copy best seller in Edwardian times, which is probably a greater achievement during that era, than it is today. She is unusual in that she wrote under her husband's name, which was an accepted form of address during that period.

Our second writer associated with this house has a more indirect link. She wrote a story based on a remote shooting lodge, and her brother in-law, who she frequently visited, owned the house. She is reputed to have sold approximately 4 billion novels.

Whilst this is the howling wilderness of Daniel Defoe, it is also some of the most dramatic countryside there is. William Bennett, the author of *The Cavalier,* set in Castleton, lived at Chapel-en-le-Frith, which we saw tucked down in the western valley as we began our trek across the moors. The preface to the book is a letter to a friend and in it he describes Kinderscout.

Winter is the season for beholding the Derby Hills in their sublimity; the warm aspect of summer softens down their rugged features, and covers them in purple bloom, whilst the snows of winter, falling on their unsconced heads, make then show as desolate and cheerless, as they are wide and extravagant.
Preface – The Cavalier – William Bennett

On Desolation – This is Liberty

We are now on the Pennine Way. It started a few miles away, at the Nag's Head, in that small village named after the dale, Edale, which was clearly visible from Rushup edge. This long distance route then follows the spine of England and, 429km (267miles) later, arrives at Kirk Yetholm in Scotland. The Pennine Way was the first of the long distance paths and is now even more popular than ever. Since the 1960s long paths have developed all over the country. Each has its uniqueness and some wonderful landscapes. The Pennine Way came in from our right while we were at Edale Cross. The track that we crossed was the old packhorse trail from Hayfield to Penistone. To our right the trail descends steeply down Jacob's Ladder and takes the route along the edge of the valley into the village of Edale.

We climb the steep path to Edale Rocks and now we are fully on Kinderscout. This is a stunning area and such a contrast to some of the beautiful spots we have passed through. It is without doubt dramatic country. On these moors it is very easy to get lost going across the peak bogs. In many places there are no landmarks on view, just black peat grykes and mounds of heather. Every direction can look the same. When you combine these difficulties of navigation, with the potential sudden change in the weather, it is a dangerous area. This is an area where the mountains rescue teams are frequently called out to find those injured, lost and in distress.

Walk Directions

This final section is slightly different to the other walks. We finished the last part of The Literary Way at Edale Cross. Given that this is not the easiest place to access and there is no parking anywhere nearby we will start at the end of the walk and go to Edale Cross and then follow The Literary Way to the end

Bowden Bridge, Hayfield to Edale Cross (2.35 miles)

Bowden Bridge car park is reached through Hayfield when we then turn up Kinder Lane
Leave the car park and cross the road and the bridge and turn immediately left
Follow the track as it curves round to the right
Continue on the track (do not take the Pennine Bridle way)
The track turns to the left at Coldwell Clough (by the farm)
Continue on the track as it begins to climb
Follow the track past the fields and then to the Open Access land
Continue on the track until you reach Edale Cross

Edale Cross to Kinder Downfall (2.07 miles)

Go past the cross, through the next gate, and turn left up towards Edale Rocks
The path dips at first and then rises past the rocks
We are now on Kinderscout
Carry on forward and you will see a path ahead along the edge of the moor
On the right is a trig point and a fine example of 'moonscape'
To the left we have a view towards Manchester and below we can see Kinder Reservoir
Continue to follow the path along the edge.
As you reach some of the large rocks the path gradually turns to the right
From in between the rocks you will get the first glances of Kinder Downfall
Carry on along the path to cross the Kinder Stream just above the Downfall

Kinder Downfall to Bowden Bridge (4.01 miles)

Cross the Downfall and stay on the same path along the edge
It gradually drifts away from the steep edge
When the path descends across some steep rocks in front there is a cross of paths
Straight on would lead to The Grouse Inn and right would take us to Ashop Head
We turn left
(Do not take the first path left down the valley)
Go on a little further and take the second path at the cross of paths (it is much easier)
Near the bottom as you near the reservoir take the left path to go along the edge of the water
The path goes along the wall overlooking the water
As you clear the inlet you will be able to see Upper House set next to the trees on the opposite side
Continue along the waterside path until it turns inland for a little while
This will join a track and comes out past the dam onto the lane
Turn right along the lane
Follow it back to Bowden Bridge.

Distance: 8.43 miles Ascent: 1980ft

Ebenezer Elliott wrote a sonnet about Kinderscout.

We are not lonely, Kinderscout! I stand
Here, with thy sire, and gaze, with him and thee,
On desolation. This is liberty!
I want no wing, to lift me from the land,
But look, soul-fetter'd, on the wild and grand.
Oh! that the dungeon'd of the earth were free
As these fix'd rocks, whose summits bare command
Yon cloud to stay, and weep for Man, with me!
Is this, then, solitude? To feel our hearts
Lifted above the world, yet not above
The sympathies of brotherhood and love?
To grieve for him who from the right departs?
And strive, in spirit, with the martyr'd good?
"Is this to be alone?" Then, welcome solitude.
Sonnet 28 by Ebenezer Elliott

Daniel Defoe also had his views on this landscape.

There is indeed an extended angle of this county, which runs a great way north west by Chappel-en-le-Frith and which they call the High Peak. This, perhaps, is the most desolate, wild, and abandoned country in all England. The mountains of the Peak, of which I have been speaking, seem to be but the beginning of wonders to this part of the country, and but the beginning of mountains, or, if you will, as the lower rounds of a ladder. The tops of these hills seem to be as much above the clouds, as the clouds are above the ordinary range of hills.
A Tour thro' the Whole Island of Great Britain – Daniel Defoe

We are going along the edge of the moor so navigation is not difficult. See if you can pick out the 47-storey Beetham Tower in the centre of Manchester. You might well need binoculars to be able to select the Old Trafford football ground, which is twenty miles away, but the power station with its cooling towers, near Warrington, is easy to find, although it is 45 miles. By now you might have noticed planes overhead. On a clear day, sit, enjoy the view, and watch the plane now flying over your head curve round and land at Manchester Airport.

We pass over the peat moor's 'moonscape'. The white feldspar crystals, which have been weathered from the millstone grit rock, cover parts of the moor and make it more akin to a beach. It has often been suggested that it looks more like the moon's surface. It is these crystals that have created the wonderful aeolian shaped rocks that edge the moors. As we pass along the edge of Kinderscout we can begin to pick out our literary house. It is practically obscured by the trees on the crag side of Kinder Reservoir. Views of it will remain for a good while.

As the edge takes us slightly in towards the moors so the jumble of rocks which shields Kinder Downfall becomes evident. This 30 metre fall from a small stream flows over the edge of the moors and tumbles down to the early twentieth century Kinder Reservoir. The catchment area for the stream is

The path across the moors

the peat bogs behind it and so it is no more than a stream, but when the wind blows hard from the west, then it shows the power of the air as it is forced into the V-shaped crags. The wind picks up the stream as it falls and blows it back as spray!

Let us continue to follow our path and, after a steep but short descent, we come to a cross of pathways. To our right the path leads across the moor to the Snake Inn. This was opened in late Victorian times and was the only path in the area, although it was frequently closed by gamekeepers in the shooting season.

The Duke's Apology

The moors were for many years the shooting havens of the landed gentry. They were guarded by the gamekeepers who kept all away from the area, which is the natural habitat of the grouse. The number of birds, although wild, would be managed by the gamekeepers so that their landowners could enjoy the shooting season. Effectively the moors were closed and private areas, and there are rarely any rights of ways across them. The main reasons for this is that rights of ways were determined by regular travelled routes and very few people would need to cross these inhospitable moors, hence accessible paths were often found in valleys. As we saw with the *Clarion* call of Bert Ward on the Eastern Moors, the early twentieth century saw the rise of the people in the towns who wanted to walk in the countryside. Ashop Head is just along the path to our right.

In 1932 there would be a major challenge to the landowners and the gamekeepers. This is an extract from the *Guardian* newspaper, 25 April 1932.

Four or five hundred ramblers, mostly from Manchester, trespassed in mass on Kinder Scout to-day. They fought a brief but vigorous hand-to-hand struggle with a number of keepers specially enrolled for the occasion. This they won with ease, and then marched to Ashop Head, where they held a meeting before returning in triumph to Hayfield. Their triumph was short-lived, for there the police met them, halted them, combed their ranks for suspects, and detained five men. Another man had been detained earlier in the day.

On Ashop Head itself a victory meeting was held, and the leader who at an earlier stage had asked us to trespass in spite of all danger now congratulated us on having trespassed so successfully. We were warned that some ramblers might be unfortunate enough to be fined, and for their future benefit the hat was passed around.

Guardian Newspaper, 25 April 1932

The leader behind the idea was a trade unionist called Benny Rothwell. As well as being active in local socialism in the south of Manchester, he also enjoyed access to the countryside. One of the nearest stations to the Peak District from Manchester was Hayfield. The direct train would end its journey in the valley below the towering crags of Kinder and the Downfall.

The day after the trespass five men were arrested for unlawful assembly and the breach of the peace, including Benny Rothwell. They were later jailed at Derby Crown court for between two and six months. There has been much symbolism attached to the trespass and the leading of Benny Rothwell. It has been captured in songs celebrating protest, as well as cited as being a key step in the formation of National Parks. The landowner for the moors when the trespass took place was the Duke of Devonshire. In 2002 there was the 70th year celebration of the events. The Duke of Devonshire, at the time, was Andrew Cavendish, who came to meet the walkers on their symbolic celebration to apologise for the actions of his grandfather.

Let's Fly a Kite

We are where the four paths meet. In was in this vicinity where our man was flying kites. The path leads in about a mile or so to the road, and joins it near the Grouse Inn. The pub was used as a base to fly the kites, which took place all over this part of the moor. The complexity of the origins of a book from our intrepid kite flier is tricky, but do bear with us as it is a fascinating story.

We are indebted to the acute observations of Susan Stebbett in defining this story. It begins a long way from the Peak District, in Vienna, Austria, in 1899. A family, who had become very rich from the steel industry of that country, had another son. He was called Ludwig and he joined four brothers and three sisters. In his childhood he led a life of luxury. The family home was a centre of intellectual and musical development. As part of the high society of the time, the family attracted many of the leading musicians of the day including, Brahms, Strauss and Mahler.

But Ludwig's learning was not focused on music but on his father's technical empire. Engineering attracted him. So it was it was no surprise that in

Moonscape on Kinderscout

Kinder Reservoir with a hazy Manchester

1906, at the age of 17, he went to Berlin to study mechanical engineering. After a short period there he moved to Manchester University to further the same studies.

Manchester had become a centre for engineering excellence. It was enjoying both the practical and philanthropic benefits of our Darley Dale man, Sir Joseph Whitworth. His principal works were in the city and as we know he lived there for many years. He left a substantial sum for the education of future engineers and it was these bequests that brought together engineering excellence from which our writer, Ludwig, intended to benefit. It was at the time when a certain aspects of mechanical engineering was about to take a major leap forward.

The Wright brothers in the USA were laying patents for controlled man-made flight. There was huge scepticism in Europe, but there was also lively debate in papers and magazines about competing methods for achieving flight, and whether the Wrights had actually truly achieved it.

So what is the link with kites? At the time meteorological understanding was being enhanced by lifting instruments into the atmosphere by the use of kites. This could be controlled, under certain weather conditions, and could return the instruments safely to the ground. By the early 1900s the kites had sufficient lift to rise several thousand metres with instruments. Generally Ludwig was a mechanical engineer interested in aeronautics. Kite flying on the Kinderscout moors was to help the University of Manchester make progress in meteorology. But mechanical engineers were very interested in kites, because of the lift they generated and whether it could be harnessed for man-made flights. The designs being used by Ludwig were box kites with wings attached.

We know with hindsight that the Wright brothers' invention went on to be the basis of manned flight as it is today, but at the time there were sufficient challenges of the alternative methods, all of which were to disappear, as the Wrights established their superiority. But we are talking of a time in 1908 when it was still thought other methods could be better.

Enter Samuel Franklin Cowdrey, who had a hero called William Cody, or as he was frequently known, Buffalo Bill. Cowdrey not only changed his name to Cody, but also set up Wild West shows with the associated riding and shooting skills, to emulate his hero. In 1890, Samuel Cody arrived in England and acquired British nationality. In addition to touring with his shows he also experimented with man-lifting kites. These were immediately taken up by the military at Farnborough as a method of artillery spotting that was much more controlled than balloon flight. The kites certainly had the lift to raise a man on the end of the tether, but it was at the mercy of the wind as to the direction that could be realised. In order to overcome this Samuel added a small engine so that he could fly the kite. The control of direction was haphazard but the device worked and flew for 27 minutes.

So Ludwig had an interest in aeronautics and was using powerful kites to get the lift for experiments at the same time as the Wright brothers and Cody were developing their respective ideas for manned flight. In 1910 Ludwig would register a patent in the UK, *Improvements in Propellers applicable for Aerial Machines.*

Date of Application, 22nd Nov., 1910
Complete Specification Left, 21st. June, 1911 – Accepted, 17th Aug., 1911

PROVISIONAL SPECIFICATION

I, LUDWIG WITTGENSTEIN, of Wilmslow Road, Fallowfield, City of Manchester, Researching Student, do hereby declare the nature of this invention to be as follows:

This invention relates to propellers for aeroplanes, helicopters, dirigible balloons, or other forms of aerial machines. It consists essentially of a radially armed motor each arm carrying a combustion chamber, and exhaust nozzle at its extremity and each arm formed as, or fitted with, a propeller blade.
Patent Application – Ludwig Wittgenstein

The idea of reciprocal mechanics, that is the up and down movement of birds, held virtually no adherents in the aeronautical debate. The ideas seemed to centre on thrust and lift. The latter came from the various types of wings and structure that were being constructed and how the lift could be varied and the direction controlled. Humans could not produce the thrust necessary to get the lift and therefore inventors looked at the use of engines to achieve the necessary dynamics. Ludwig was particularly interested in the gain of thrust from the design of propellers and the engines to drive them. As he studied the area he moved the focus of his attention away from the mechanics of operation to the mathematics behind the engineering. In doing so he came across another work of the very early years in the twentieth century.

Bertrand Russell, in 1903, by then a fellow at Trinity College Cambridge, published a work called, *The Principles of Mathematics*. Bertrand would become one of the great intellectuals of the twentieth century in both mathematics and philosophy. Ludwig wrote to Russell and then visited him at Cambridge. It was the start of a lifelong relationship, that wasn't always smooth, and had long periods of abstinence, however, it did draw together two minds that stimulated much thought and discussion in twentieth century intellectual circles. From the build up we have given, you could think that Ludwig would produce a book that united the different areas of his expertise, particularly in the linking of mathematics to aeronautics. However, another twist came when Ludwig abandoned aeronautics.

After moving to Cambridge he spent a few years in debate with others, but decided he must isolate himself to concentrate on his work. With this in mind he moved to a remote part of Norway. It was here, in 1909, that he would lay the foundations for one of the major works of philosophy. It would not be published for another twelve years, partly due to Ludwig not being able to decide on the exact structure, but also because of the First World War, where he served with distinction in the Austrian army. Ludwig Wittgenstein, with the help of his Cambridge friends, Bertrand Russell and the future Chancellor of the Exchequer, the economist Maynard Keynes, published, *Tractatus Logico-Philosophicus* in 1921. The book is about the theory of knowledge and the attempt to define the relationship between language and reality. We will let Bertrand Russell, in his Introduction to the book, explain the deeper meaning and significance of the book.

MR WITTGENSTEIN'S Tractatus Logico-Philosophicus, whether or not it proves to give the ultimate truth on the matters with which it deals, certainly deserves, by its breadth and scope and profundity, to be considered an important event in the philosophical world. Starting from the principles of Symbolism and the relations which are necessary between words and things in any language, it applies the result of this inquiry to various departments of traditional philosophy, showing in each case how traditional philosophy and traditional solutions arise out of ignorance of the principles of Symbolism and out of misuse of language.

Tractatus Logico-Philosophicus – Ludwig Wittgenstein

There is no doubt that not only is it a highly com-

Crossing the Kinder stream with the black peat moors in the background

plex book, but it is also very difficult to read. Just to give you a flavour of the book here are the first few lines.

TRACTATUS LOGICO-PHILOSOPHICUS

1 The world is all that is the case.
1.1 The world is the totality of facts, not of things.
1.11 The world is determined by the facts, and by their being all the facts.
1.12 For the totality of facts determines what is the case, and also whatever is not the case.
1.13 The facts in logical space are the world.
1.2 The world divides into facts.
1.21 Each item can be the case or not the case while everything else remains the same.
2 What is the case a fact is the existence of states of affairs.
2.01 A state of affairs (a state of things) is a combination of objects (things).
2.011 It is essential to things that they should be possible constituents of states of affairs.
2.012 In logic nothing is accidental: if a thing can occur in a state of affairs, the possibility of the state of affairs must be written into the thing itself.
2.0121 It would seem to be a sort of accident, if it turned out that a situation would fit a thing that could already exist entirely on its own.
Tractatus Logico-Philosophicus – Ludwig Wittgenstein

You might wonder if there was a link between the kites and his later philosophical thinking. There is, in fact, a very distinct link. Aeronautics began many of its ideas with the development of models, which would then be attempted to be scaled up to full- sized versions. The development of flight was an area where many models worked, but they could not be scaled up. Getting the thrust and lift correct across different scales was a complex task. So Ludwig would have been very familiar with the models, kite and mechanics, which many were trying to turn into large human-scale working systems. He carried forward his views on models and their relationship to reality in the *Tractatus* which attempts to explain the relationship between language, thought and existence.

The Edwardian Anti-Suffrage Campaigner

We are going to leave the moors by taking the path down to Hayfield. We shall leave it to J B Firth in *Highways and Byways of Derbyshire,* written in 1905, to describe the scene, and to introduce the novel that is set there.

With our backs to the moor we gaze down upon a deep broad valley of cultivated land whose exit lies to the right along the course of the river Kinder, while it runs up on the left towards a big amphitheatre of hills the western side of lofty Kinderscout. Out of the valley itself there rises a great mound if we were below we should think it a hill so rounded that were it not for the stone walls, which trace their zig-zag patterns on its sides, one might think it had been patted smooth by some giant in play.

This valley has its place in literature; it is the Derbyshire home of David and Louie Grieve. Their thin-lipped, shrewish, grasping Aunt Hannah and her shambling husband, Reuben, lived in one of the little farms which we see below us. Needham's Farm is its name in the novel, and the novelist herself, Mrs. Humphry Ward, stayed, while she wrote the book, at Marriott's Farm or Upper House, which, as its name suggests, is the highest inhabited house on this side of Kinderscout.

The indefinable atmosphere of the moors is transferred to the pages of her book. In this respect, Mrs. Ward has done for Kinderscout what the Brontes did for the Hayworth and Keighley moors, and those who have time to spare will find reward in exploring for themselves the course of the Kinder.
Highways and Byways of Derbyshire – J B Firth

Mary Augusta Arnold was born in Australia into a literary family with the most famous members being Matthew Arnold and Thomas Arnold. Her sister married into the Huxley family and thereby extended the contacts she gained with the world of writing. In 1872, just as she was reaching 21 years old, she married Humphrey Ward who was a Fellow of Brasenose College, Oxford, which is where she first settled in her married life. As a young wife she spent the initial years of her marriage developing her own education especially in the learning of languages.

She began to write articles and then produced her first book, which was for children. It would be sixteen years after her marriage that she produced her second novel, *Robert Elsmere,* which was to make her famous. It very much reflected her own beliefs and that of the Victorian times that she lived in, with the novel's theme being centred around religious faith and doubt. Her theme for her following work, *The History of David Grieve,* was based on a poor boy making his way in the world. In total, she would write 25 novel-length works, but it would be *Robert Elsmere* and *The History of David Grieve,* that would make her famous through Britain and the United States of America. It is reputed that *The History of David Grieve* sold more than one million copies.

Aside from her writing she became notable for two reasons. She was the leading woman in the anti-suffrage movement of the early twentieth century; she actively campaigned for women not to be given the vote. However, she did believe in helping the working classes and had a great deal of respect for them. She established educational centres for those that could not afford to pay and put great energy into ensuring their success. The Mary Ward Centre for adult education still exists in Bloomsbury, London.

In order to see the description of the area it is perhaps best to take the opening to *The Life of David Grieve.* You will notice how she writes with the local dialect in the speech. Mary also gives a description of the house, which was much smaller when she stayed there and wrote her book. It was extended in the early twentieth century.

'Tak your hat, Louie! Yo're allus leavin summat behind yer.'
'David, yo go for 't,' said the child addressed to a boy by her side, nodding her head insolently towards the speaker, a tall and bony woman, who stood on the steps the children had just descended,

People at the top of Kinder Downfall

holding out a battered hat.
'Yo're a careless thing, Louie,' said the boy, but he went back and took the hat.
'Mak her tie it,' said the woman, showing an antiquated pair of strings. 'If she loses it she needna coom cryin for anudder. She'd lose her yead if it wor loose.'

The top gate was fast, but David climbed the wall and stood there a while, hands in his pockets, legs apart, whistling and looking. 'They can't see t' Downfall from Stockport to-day,' he was saying to himself; 'it's coomin ower like mad.'

Some distance away in front of him, beyond the undulating heather ground at his feet, rose a magnificent curving front of moor, the steep sides of it crowned with black edges and cliffs of grit, the outline of the south-western end sweeping finely up on the right to a purple peak, the king of all the moorland round. No such colour as clothed that bronzed and reddish wall of rock, heather, and bilberry is known to Westmoreland, hardly to Scotland; it seems to be the peculiar property of that lonely and inaccessible district which marks the mountainous centre of mid-England the district of Kinder Scout and the High Peak.
The History of David Grieve – Mrs Humphry Ward

Let's take the path down the clough to get a better view of Upper House which is tucked away on the far side of the reservoir. When Mary stayed at the remote house in the late 1800s the reservoir had not then been built.

Agatha Mallowan

Agatha Mallowan preferred to use this name in her private life, but the publishers insisted on her sticking with the name she wrote her first novels by, Agatha Christie. She was born in 1890 into the Miller family. Agatha had an older brother and sister. In 1914, she married Archibald Christie but the marriage did not last and in 1930, Agatha married archaeologist Max Mallowan. As many will know, she is one of the most prolific authors of the twentieth century. While she did not define the detective genre, she went a long way to making it her own.

She is very coy about the settings of many of her books and stories, but we want to take you through why the house in which Mary Ward stayed is the likely setting for one of her tales and where there is a very definite connection between the former shooting lodge and Agatha. But in order to do so we need to look a little at part of Agatha's life, and the surrounding area.

As we have seen from Kinderscout the views look out over the Cheshire Plain and Manchester. The quote from *The Life of David Grieve* is interesting because it says that from Stockport, it is possible to see

Upper House

the Kinder Downfall.

Just outside Stockport is the small area of Cheadle, which has a grand building called Abney Hall, which originally had 200 acres of grounds. Agatha's sister Madge married Jimmy Watts, who was the heir to the hall. Jimmy worked in the family business and would eventually take charge of it. His grandfather who had founded the firm had also been the Mayor of Manchester. It was he who had bought the hall from Mrs Orrell, Joseph Whitworth's wife's name by her first marriage, and changed the name to Abney Hall. Agatha's mother had been to boarding school in Cheshire and already knew the Watts family, and Agatha had even visited the hall as a child. But it would be years later after her sister, Madge, had married Jimmy Watts that the visits became frequent.

She particularly enjoyed the Watts' family atmosphere, especially at Christmas, and it provided a stimulus to use the hall as the setting in several of her stories. The feast in *The Affair of the Christmas Pudding* was based on her visits there. Here is how she described the festive food in her autobiography;

Christmas was the supreme festival, something never to be forgotten. Christmas stockings in bed. Breakfast, when everyone has a separate chair heaped with presents. Then a rush to church and back to continue the present opening. At two o'clock Christmas Dinner, the blinds drawn down and glittering ornaments and lights. First oyster soup (not relished by me), turbot, the boiled turkey, roast turkey and a large roast sirloin of beef. This was followed by plum pudding, mince pies, and a trifle.....In a story I once wrote, the Affair of the Christmas Pudding, I have described just such a feast.
Autobiography – Agatha Christie

Agatha also used the hall in other stories including *After the Funeral* and it was Stoneygate in *They Do It With Mirrors*. The Watts family moved in the exalted circles in Manchester and two Prime Ministers, William Gladstone and Benjamin Disraeli, stayed there. Her good relationship with Jimmy could also be seen with reference to one of her most successful books, *The Murder of Roger Ackroyd*.

The Murder of Roger Ackroyd was far and away my most successful to date; in fact it is still remembered and quoted. I got hold of a good formula there – and I owe it in part to my brother-in-law, James, who some years previously had said somewhat fretfully as he put down a detective story: 'Almost everyone turns out to be a criminal nowadays in detective stories – even the detective. What I want to see is a Watson who turned out to be the criminal.'

It was a remarkably good thought and I mulled it over lengthily. Then, as it happened, very much the same idea was also suggested to me by Lord Louis Mountbatten, as he then was, who wrote to suggest a story should be narrated in the first person by someone who later turned out to be the murderer. I thought it a good idea, and considered it for a long time. It had enormous difficulties of course. My mind boggled at the thought of Hastings murdering anyone.
Autobiography – Agatha Christie

Six or seven miles from Upper House at Kinder is the village of Marple. Agatha didn't indicate how she came up with the name Marple, but there is plenty of supposition that, as she passed through Marple on the train, it gave her the idea for the name. She was known to frequently travel by train and her trips with her husband, Max, to the middle east would frequently be completed on the Orient Express, which, as we know, became one of her most famous novels.

As for trains – what can beat a train? Especially before diesels and their smell arrived. A great puffing monster carrying you through gorges and valleys and past snow mountains, alongside country roads with strange peasants in carts. Trains are wonderful and I still adore them.
Autobiography – Agatha Christie

To add to the supposition that the small town of Marple gives its name to the famous detective, it was at one time on a main route from London. As we have transversed the Peak District we have commented on several occasions on what is now the Monsal Trail, but before its closure it was a steam route from Derby and then Matlock to Manchester. This is how William Bradbury described the end of an express train journey from St Pancras, in *All About Derbyshire*. He wrote the book close to the time Agatha was born. He refers to New Mills which is a couple of miles from Hayfield.

Viaducts carry us over Chapel-en-le-Frith, and give us Amadeus-like privileges with regard to peeping down cottage chimneys and into bed-room windows. Down the hill-side now as if the Iron Horse were a frightened Pegasus and were running away altogether. The steam is shut off; ever and anon the sibilant sound of the air brake is heard. That station I think was New Mills but the pace is so rapid that the letters on the platform name-board were running into each other. The rivulet running by the line is the Kinderbrook. To the right,Kinderscout—the king of the Peak mountains—sets his shoulders against the sky.
At Marple the charm of the scenery diminishes. We have passed through the Peak. The Rubicon is crossed, and the poetry of Derbyshire gives way to Cheshire and Lancashire prose. God's country is forsaken for man's town, and presently the engine, breathless and palpitating, pants into the Cottonopolis terminus.
All About Derbyshire – William Bradbury

Having described how Agatha was so involved with the region let us return to our house, cum shooting lodge, under Kinderscout. What is the connection with Agatha? The building has variously been called Upper House or Marriott's Farm. It was owned for many years by the Watts family. Jimmy became very much involved in the discussion to open up the moors for visitors because they had to cross his land.

Before the time of Benny Rothman, a local footpath society tried to negotiate access and Jimmy did make limited concessions on his land. There is no direct evidence that Agatha visited Upper House, but it would seem highly likely that at some time she visited with some of the large Watts family. The route of 14 miles to Upper House from Abney Hall would have either been by train or road.

Hayfield Church and Memorial Gardens

Hayfield lost its station during the Beeching cuts of the 1960s but it was the main point for people travelling from Manchester and Stockport to approach the Derbyshire moors and hills which are visible from those towns. A short distance from Hayfield is the main A6 which goes across the Peak District to Matlock and then on to London.

Let us look at Agatha's short story, *The Mystery of the Hunting Lodge*. It opens with an arrival of a man at Poirot's flat in London who requests help in solving the mystery of a man shot in a Hunting Lodge on the Derbyshire Moors. Captain Hastings, Poirot's associate, travels with the man to Derbyshire.

'To begin with, Captain Hastings, you must understand that Hunter's Lodge, where we are going, is only a small shooting box in the heart of the Derbyshire Moors.'
The Mystery of the Hunting Lodge – Agatha Christie

They arrive in Derbyshire.

It was about three o'clock when we arrived at the little station of Elmer's Dale. From there a five mile drive brought us to a small grey stone building in the midst of the rugged moors.
The Mystery of the Hunting Lodge – Agatha Christie

Captain Hasting visits the Lodge and then sets off to find Inspector Japp.

I had seen all that Hunter's Lodge has to show me. I must go back to Elmer's Dale and get in touch with Japp. Accordingly I took leave of the Haverings, and was driven off in the car that had brought us from the station. I found Japp at the Matlock Arms and he took me forthwith to see the body.
The Mystery of the Hunting Lodge – Agatha Christie

So we have the lodge and its setting coupled with a nearby express to London and the main road that leads to Matlock.

Let's rest awhile at Bowden Bridge

We take the path along the edge of Kinder Reservoir and then along the lane to Bowden Bridge. On our right is a small quarry now used as a car park. It is appropriate to finish our walk along *The Literary Way* here, as it was where those involved in the mass trespass assembled prior to walking up onto the moors. Since that time, rights of way have been established and it is along these, and across the open access land, that we have travelled the entire distance from Ellastone. A plaque on the wall of the quarry commemorates the event. It was especially pleasing to us to be able to finish the walk with giants in the world of twentieth century literature. Agatha Christie's style and intrigue has captured so many all over the world and she had a claim to be the best selling novelist in the history of books. Ludwig Wittgenstein is perhaps far less known, but in the august world of philosophy he stands out as a paragon of the last century. Mary Ward's dedication to the working classes lives on in London, but she came on holiday here, at Upper House, to write one of best-selling books which has as its initial setting the same farm.

After walking through some quite magnificent countryside it is fitting that some of the most spectacular and impressive landscape forms the basis for our last walk. The wild and desolate moorlands have their own majestic character and as we have strolled along the fringes of the vast peat plateau we have had the most magnificent views westwards across Cheshire and Lancashire.

Final Words

We set out in hearty spirit to explore the countryside of the Peak District and the writings of the people who were inspired by it. Our authors have ranged from those who have been famous for centuries, such Daniel Defoe, to some like Frances Jacson that are little known. In between, there are an intriguing group, which is those authors that were famous in their day, but now are little known names. These included the prolific writer of horse racing novels, Nat Gould, who was a true predecessor of Dick Francis, and Charlotte Yonge who wrote about Mary Queen of Scots.

One of our most pleasing discoveries was the visit to Ashbourne by Alexandre Dumas. It is not a name that we would have expected to find on our route, but we were delighted when we found that he had written a novel based on the town. Another surprise came when we investigated the antiquarians. We expected to find rather dry and uninteresting works, but the scope and passion that both Llewellyn Jewitt and Thomas Bateman had for their studies shone through in their work and writings. And to these two we add Eliza Meteyard who knew both of these men. The two stories of hers that occurred on our route, *Lillian's Golden Hours* and *Dora and her Papa* are first-rate books even though they were meant for children.

The compassion and sorrow associated with the children struck us as very touching given the harsh and untimely deaths of the period. The sculpture of Penelope, daughter of Brooke Boothby, and her father's words, show what she meant to him. The death of Thomas Moore's young daughter would have not only brought sorrow to him but also to his friend, Lord Byron, whose name she took. Perhaps it is one of the simplest of poems in this book, but Michael Sadler's *The Factory Girl's Last Day* was a touching reminder of the harshness of nineteenth century mills.

The quiet and peaceful Cordwell Valley provided us with an outstanding collection of writers who gathered around Edward Carpenter. He must have been an interesting man to meet as so many came to visit him. The foursome of Edward, Henry and Kate Salt along with George Bernard Shaw would have provided a raft of entertaining evenings. And to those we can add classic writers such as E M Forster and Olive Schreiner.

It was not only the hills and vales that spawned literary merit. The show caves of Castleton created rich and intense writing both factual and fictional. James Plumptre writing from two hundred years ago stimulated modern cave exploration in the area, and Conan Doyle used the setting for one of his typical mysteries. One of our favourite stories from *The Literary Way* is *Unknown to History* by Charlotte Yonge. It is a good fictional take on the story of Mary, Queen of Scots, laced with many of the historical facts.

One of the most intriguing connections focused on Peak Cavern. It remains somewhat of a mystery why the Jacobean writers, Michael Drayton and Ben Jonson both picked the Castleton cave to include in their works. The cave also appeared as the unlikely set in the de Loutherbourg pantomime over 200 years ago.

The two great stately homes of the area, Haddon and Chatsworth, have provided us with a large variety of novels and poems. The philosopher of Chatsworth, Thomas Hobbes, appeared in an intriguing story written by Joseph Shorthouse. The name of the novel is the lead person John Inglesant who deals with the machinations of the English Civil War. It is a well-researched and intricate story. Haddon and Chatsworth produced a great deal of poetry but surprising little by the leading poets of the ages, although Dorothy Vernon has stimulated all forms of media.

These magnificent old houses have families that go back many generations and we found it most interesting to be able to link literature and writing through the family links at Chatsworth. Caroline Lamb had a frenetic lifestyle with outrages more typical of those today that in the early 1800's. The family links between her famous aunt, Georgiana and the modern day Princess Diana and the Duchess of York were an interesting find. Although we only included a snippet of Nancy Mitford's work, her family and its links with the leaders of the twentieth century was compelling reading.

One of the most captivating villages to visit is Eyam. The famous plague of 1666 provided many later writers with the basis for novels and poetry, although some local writers such as Murray Gilchrist and Richard Furness preferred other topics. Joseph Hutton's *The Dagger and the Cross* stands out as a good read with a clever ending for its time.

We have covered a good number of main writers and what is quite outstanding is the amount of books that they wrote between them, with one of the most prolific authors of novels being Nat Gould with over 125. There are many writers that we encountered that have published over fifty books. *The Compleat Angler* stands out as one of the most printed books, with the exception of the Bible. Whether that is true, or some form of myth, it has certainly been around for a very long time and has been produced in millions.

One of the greatest revelations in the books we have read have been the different styles of writing. It is easily accepted that styles change, and no more so than in the way authors address their readers. If we combine this with the language and descriptors that are used then we have sought out many different approaches from the very formal to the anecdotal. Perhaps this is no more evident than in William Adam's *Gem of the Peak.* It is a wonderful combination of enthusiasm, real stories and delightful flowery language.

It has also been fascinating to bring together at one end of a range, work for children including the thoughtful *The Time Traveller,* Alison Uttley, and the hero of all young boys, *Just William,* Richmal Crompton. At the other end we have the deep and profound work of Jean-Jacques Rousseau's *Confessions.* Correspondingly we have serious and studied works, such as Samuel Johnson's English Dictionary and this contrasts to the humour of Richard Graves with the wonderful satire on Methodist evangelism, *The Spiritual Quixote.* When we put together a book, such as this one, there is a lot of research, many blind alleys and some first-rate surprises. Two of the latter occurred virtually in the same area, on Kinderscout near Hayfield. To find that the very important, but enigmatic philosopher, flew kites there before he switched his intellectual prowess from engineering to epistemology was an unexpected find. Then to discover just down the hill at Upper House there were two literary connections led to a lot of further investigation of both Mary Ward and Agatha Christie. It was this unique combination that, to us, makes a fitting finale for the whole of *The Literary Way.*

Principal Books

Chapter One – Rural Bliss

Adam Bede – George Eliot, William Blackwood, 1859
Autobiography and Correspondence of Mary Delany – Mary Delany, R Bentley, 1861
The Vales of Weaver – John Gisborne, J Stockdale, 1797
The Social Contract – Jean-Jacques Rousseau, M Rey, 1762
Confessions – Jean-Jacques Rousseau, 1782
Childe Harold's Pilgrimage – Lord Byron, J Murray, 1812
The Life and Times of Gilbert Sheldon – Vernon Staley, W Gardner, 1913
The Banks of the Dove – Michael Sadler, Saturday Magazine, 1832
The Factory Girl's Last Day – Michael Sadler, Published by Michael Sadler, 1830
Juvenilia – Charlotte Bronte, Penguin, 1996
The Life of Charlotte Bronte – Elizabeth Gaskell, Smith Elder, 1906
Botanic Garden – Erasmus Darwin, Johnson, 1791
Flagellum, or the Life and Death, Birth and Burial of Oliver Cromwell – James Heath, S Gent, 1663
Burlesque upon the Great Frost – Charles Cotton: The Lives of the English Poets, Samuel Johnson, 1779–1781
The Bells of St Petersburg, Melodies, Songs, Sacred Songs and National Airs – Thomas Moore, Williams, 1836
The Life of Lord Byron: with his Letters and Journals – Thomas Moore, Six Volumes, John Murray, 1854
Elphinstone – Alfred Butler, Richard Bentley, 1841

Chapter Two – Great Poor Writers

A Treatise on Hunting – Sir Thomas Cockaine, 1591
The Tragedy of Ovid – Aston Cokain, 1669
Le Pasteur d'Ashbourn – Alexandre Dumas, Oeuvres Complete, Michel Levy Feres, 1860
Dictionary of the English Language – Samuel Johnson, Straban, 1755
The Life of Samuel Johnson – James Boswell, 1791
A Short Account of the Extraordinary Life and Travels of HLL – Parkes, 1804
Female Ministry: Or Woman's Right to Preach the Gospel – Catherine Booth, Morgan & Chase, 1859
Sorrows, Sacred to the Memory of Penelope – Brooke Boothby, 1796
De Vere: Man of Independence – Robert Plumer Ward, Henry Colburn, 1827
The Tour of the Dove – John Edwards, Longman, Hurst, Rees, Orme and Brown, 1821

Chapter Three – A Limestone Desk in Happy Valley

The Old Batchelor – William Congreve, London, 1693
The Mourning Bride – William Congreve, 1697
The Life of Samuel Johnson – James Boswell, 1791
Rasselas – Samuel Johnson, 1759
The Tour of the Dove – John Edwards, Longman, Hurst, Rees, Orme and Brown, 1821
The Lives of the English Poets – Samuel Johnson, 1779-1781

Chapter Four – A Contemplative Man's Recreation

Gem of the Peak – William Adam, Fifth Edition, John & Charles Mozley, 1851
The Poetical Works of Eliza Cook – Eliza Cook, Frederick Warne, 1872
The Compleat Angler – Isaac Walton, London, 1653
The Compleat Gamester – Charles Cotton, London, 1674
In Dovedale – Henry Glassford Bell, H W Longfellow, Poems of Places, 1876–1879
The Jewel of Joy, Writings of Thomas Becon – Thomas Becon, 1560?
Maxims and Reflections – Sir William Fitzherbert, 1784
Rhoda – Frances Jacson, Henry Colburn, 1816
The Florists' Manual – Maria Jacson, Joseph Johnson, 1816
Life of the Author, The Spiritual Quixote – Richard Graves, J Dodsley, 1774
The Spiritual Quixote – Richard Graves, J Dodsley, 1774

Chapter Five – Horse Tales

The Magic of Sport – Nat Gould, John Long, 1909
Horse or Blacksmith – Nat Gould, Routledge, 1897
Rider in Khaki – Nat Gould, J Long, 1918

Chapter Six – Caves and Down Under
A Tour Through the Whole Island of Great Britain – Daniel Defoe, London, 1724
The Wintry Peacock, England My England – D H Lawrence, Selzer, 1922
Kangaroo – D H Lawrence, Martin Secker, 1923
Passages from English Notebooks – Nathaniel Hawthorne, James Osgood, 1870
Frankenstein – Mary Shelley, Lackington, Hughes, Harding, Mavor & Jones, 1818
The Isle of Man; its history, physical, ecclesiastical – Joseph Cumming, J van Voorst, 1848
The Life of Lord Byron: with his Letters and Journals – Thomas Moore, Six Volumes, John Murray, 1854
Childe Harold's Pilgrimage – Lord Byron, J Murray, 1812
Chatsworth – P G Patmore, H Colburn, 1844
The Half-Sister – Geraldine Jewsbury, Chapman & Hall, 1848
Charlotte Cushman : Her Letters and Memories of her Life – Emma Stubbins, Boston, Houghton & Osgood, 1878
Botanic Garden – Erasmus Darwin, Johnson, 1791

Chapter Seven – A Dark Wood, Dark Deeds and a Lamp
Puck – Ouida, J B Lippincott, 1900
View and Opinions – Ouida, Methuen, 1896
The Country Child – Alison Uttley, Faber & Faber, 1931
Florence Nightingale, Eminent Victorians – Lytton Strachey, Chatto & Windus, 1918
Notes on Nursing, What it is and What it is not – Florence Nightingale, Appleton & Company, 1883
The Time Traveller – Alison Uttley, Faber & Faber, 1939
Unknown to History – Charlotte Yonge, Macmillan, 1882
Mary Stuart - Friedrich Schiller, David McKay, 1898

Chapter Eight – Boys, Trees and Water
Monady written at Matlock, The Poetical Works – William Lisle Bowles, J Nichol, 1855
Practical Hydropathy – John Smedley, J Caudwell, 1864
Kidnapped – Robert Louis Stevenso, Cassell, 1891
Just William – Richmal Crompton, George Newnes, 1922
Travels in Spain and the East, 1808–1810 – Francis Sacheverell Darwin, Cambridge University Press, 1927
Broken River – Crichton Porteous, Robert Hale, 1956
Miscellaneous Papers on Mechanical Subjects – Joseph Whitworth, Longmans, 1858
Reflections – John Gisborne, Blackwood, 1833
A Tradition of Darley Dale – William Wordsworth, H W Longfellow, Poems of Places, 1876–1879

Chapter Nine – Seventeenth Child
The Ceramic Art of Great Britain – Llewellyn Jewitt, Virtue & Company, 1878
The Wedgwoods – Llewellyn Jewitt, Virtue, 1865
Half Hours Among Some English Antiquities – Llewellyn Jewitt, Hardwicke & Bogue, 1877
The Ballads and Songs of Derbyshire – Llewellyn Jewitt, Bemrose, 1867
Florence Nightingale, Antennae – Llewellyn Jewitt, Longman & Brown, 1858
The Life and Death of Llewllyn Jewitt – William Goss, Henry Gray, 1889
Mary Howitt – An Autobiography, W Isbister, 1889
Lillian's Golden Hours – Eliza Meteyard, Routledge, 1858

Chapter Ten – The Barrow Knight
Ten years Diggings in Celtic and Saxon Grave Hills – Thomas Bateman, J R Smith, 1861
Dora and Her Papa – Eliza Meteyard, Routledge, 1869

Chapter Eleven – A Gothic Elopement
Journal of the Life of John Gratton – John Gratton, James Phillips, 1795
The Life of John Bright – George Macaulay Trevelyan, Boston, Houghton, Miflin, 1913
The Works of George Herbert – Robert Willmott, Routledge, 1856
Gem of the Peak – William Adam, 5th Edition, John & Charles Mozley, 1851
The Mysteries of Udolpho – Ann Radcliffe, G G & J Robinson, 1794
Pen & Pencil – Mary Balmanno, D Appleton & Company, 1858
Evenings at Haddon Hall – Baroness Calabrella, Henry G Bohn, 1853
Poems – Benjamin Fenton, Saunders & Otley, 1843
Holiday Excursion of Three College Girls through the Mother Country – Elizabeth Champney, Estes & Lauriat, 1883

Peak Scenery – Ebenezer Rhodes, Longman, 1824
The King of the Peak – Lee Gibbons. Longman, 1823
Dorothy Vernon of Haddon Hall – Charles Major, Grosset & Dunlap, 1902

Chapter Twelve – Satanic Mills in Arcadia

Haddon Hall, Flowers from Sheffield Park – John Holland, London, 1827
Through England on a Side Saddle in the Time of William and Mary – Celia Fiennes, Scribner & Welford, 1888
A Delineation of the Strata of Derbyshire – White Watson, W Todd, 1811
Pride and Prejudice – Jane Austen, T Egerton, 1813
Friends – Francis Hodgson, John Murray, 1818
New Zealand, Rulers and Statesman, 1840–1885 – William Gisborne, S Low & Marston, 1886
Botanic Garden – Erasmus Darwin, Johnson, 1791
The Poetical Works of Eliza Cook – Eliza Cook, Frederick Warne, 1872
Fors Clavigera – John Ruskin, Greenwood Press, 1871
Peak Scenery – Ebenezer Rhodes, Longman, 1824
The Old Armchair – John Holland, Henry Fisher, 1824
Vignettes of Derbyshire – Mary Sterndale, G & W B Whittaker, 1824
The Life and Adventures of Michael Armstrong – Francis Trollope, Henry Colburn, 1840
The Miner's Daughter – William Howitt, Household Words, Volume 1, 1850

Chapter Thirteen – Sylph, Leviathan and Families

The Horticultural Register – Jospeph Paxton & Joseph Harrison, 1832
Prelude to Leadership – John F Kennedy, Regnery Publishing, 1995
John Inglesant – Joseph Shorthouse, Macmillan, 1881
De Mirabilibus Pecci – Thomas Hobbes, 1683
The Leviathan – Thomas Hobbes, Andrew Crook, 1651
Through England on a Side Saddle in the Time of William and Mary – Celia Fiennes, Scribner & Welford, 1888
The Sylph – Georgiana Cavendish, T Lowndes, 1779
Glenarvon – Caroline Lamb, Henry Colburn, 1816
The Complete Poetical Works of William Wordsworth – E Moxon, 1870
The Pursuit of Love – Nancy Mitford, Hamish Hamilton, 1945

Chapter Fourteen – Victorians

Thoughts and Sketches – John Hall, Pawson & Brailsford, 1877
The Life and Letters of Sebastian Ziani Ferranti – G Ferranti & R Ince, Willams & Norgate, 1934
The Poems of William Watson – William Watson, Macmillan, 1893

Chapter Fifteen – The Sage

Towards Democracy – Edward Carpenter , Labour Press, 1896
Civilisation, its Cause and Cure – Edward Carpenter, Allen & Unwin, 1921
Edward Carpenter, The Man and His Message – Tom Swan, Arthur C Fifield, 1905
On the Threshold – Isabella Ford, E Arnold, 1895
Maurice – E M Forster, Edward Arnold, 1971
The Logic of Vegetarianism: Essays and Dialogues – Henry Salt, G Bell, 1906
Candida A Pleasant Play – George Bernard Shaw, 1898
Clarion Ramblers Handbooks – G H B Ward
The Truth about Spain – G H B Ward, Cassell & Company, 1911

Chapter Sixteen – The Plague

Life of Thomas, First Lord Denman – Sir Joseph Arnould, Longmans, Green & Company, 1873
The History and Antiquities of Eyam – William Wood, Miller, 1842
The Desolation of Eyam – William and Mary Howitt, Wightman & Cramp, 1828
The Dagger and the Cross – Joseph Hatton, R F Fenno, 1897
The Poetical Works of Anna Seward with Extracts from her Letters and Literary Correspondence – Sir Walter Scott, J Ballantyne, 1810
Memoirs of Dr Darwin – Anna Seward, W Poyntell & Company, 1804
The Poetical Works of the Late Richard Furness – G Calvert Holland
The Last Posset, Peakland Faggot – R Murray Gilchrist, G Richards, 1897
The Basilisk – R Murray Gilchrist, (The Basilisk & Other Tales of Dread, Pelan & Roden, Ash-Tress Press,

2003)
Poetical Sketches in a Tour of the West of England – Marmaduke Middleton, Hartshead: Montgomery, 1822

Chapter Seventeen – Currer Bell

Poems – Currer, Ellis and Acton Bell, Smith Elder, 1846
Jane Eyre – Charlotte Bronte, Smith Elder, 1847
Ivanhoe –Sir Walter Scott, J Ballantyne, 1820

Chapter Eighteen – Heroes

Memoirs of Dr Darwin – Anna Seward, W Poyntell & Company, 1804
Enemy Coast Ahead – Guy Gibson, Pan, 1946
The Poetical Works of Ebenezer Elliott – Ebenezer Elliott, Steill, 1840
Life, Poetry and Letters of Ebenezer Elliott – John Watkins, J Mortimer, 1850

Chapter Nineteen – Heaven and Hell

The Well-Ordered Family – Isaac Ambrose, Boston, 1762
De Spiritualibus Pecci -- William Bagshaw, Neville Simmons, 1702
The Mineralogy of Dersbyhire – John Mawe, William Phillips, 1802
Polyolbion – Michael Drayton, M Lownes, J Browne, J Helme, and J Busbie, London, 1612
A Tour Through the Whole Island of Great Britain – Daniel Defoe, London, 1724
Through England on a Side Saddle in the Time of William and Mary – Celia Fiennes, Scribner & Welford, 1888
The Life of Lord Byron: with his Letters and Journals – Thomas Moore, Six Volumes, John Murray, 1854
Travels in England and Scotland – Barthélemy Faujas de Saint-Fond, J Ridgeway, 1799
History of Western Philosophy – Bertrand Russell, Allen & Unwin, 1945
Diaries – Johanna Schopenhauer from A Lady Travels – Ruth Michaelis-Jena and Willy Merson, Routledge, 1988
Shakespeare First Folio, Preface – Ben Jonson, London, 1623
The Devil is an Ass – Ben Jonson, London, 1631
Cock Lorel, Gypsies Metamorphosed – Ben Jonson, London, 1641
Unknown to History – Charlotte Yonge, Macmillan, 1882
Peveril of the Peak – Sir Walter Scott, J Ballantyne, 1822
The Cavalier – William Bennett, Longmans, Hurst, Rees, Orme & Brown, 1821
The Wonders of the Peak – Charles Cotton, London, 1681
James Plumptre's Britain – Ian Ousby. Hutchinson, 1991
Praeterita – John Ruskin, Wiley, 1885

Chapter Twenty – Mystery under Shivering Mountain

The Terror of Blue John Gap – Sir Arthur Conan Doyle, Strand Magazine, 1910
Early Man in Britain and his Place in the Tertiary Period – William Boyd Dawkin, Macmillan, 1880
Through England on a Side Saddle in the Time of William and Mary – Celia Fiennes, Scribner & Welford, 1888
A Tour Through the Whole Island of Great Britain – Daniel Defoe, London, 1724
Picnic at Woodhead – Thomas Barlow, John Heywood, 1867

Chapter Twenty-One – Howling Wilderness

The Cavalier – William Bennett, Longmans, Hurst, Rees, Orme & Brown, 1821
The Poetical Works of Ebenezer Elliott – Ebenezer Elliott, Steill, 1840
A Tour Through the Whole Island of Great Britain – Daniel Defoe, London, 1724
Guardian Newspaper, 25 April 1932
Patent Application – Ludwig Wittgenstein, 1911
Tractatus Logico-Philosophicus – Ludwig Wittgenstein, Harcourt, Brace & Company, 1922
Highways and Byways of Derbyshire – J B Firth, Macmillan, 1905
The History of David Grieve – Mrs Humphry Ward, Smith Elder, 1892
Autobiography – Agatha Christie, Collins, 1977
All About Derbyshire – William Bradbury
The Mystery of the Hunting Lodge from Poirot Investigates – Agatha Christie, 1924

Acknowledgements

In the course of researching materials for this book there are a numbers of thanks that must be given.

Our thanks to

Haddon Hall for permission to use the photographs from within the Hall and Grounds

The Vicar of St Oswald's for the use of photographs taken within the church

The photographs of Chatsworth Gardens, reproduced by permission of Chatsworth Settlement Trustees.

We would also like to thank the landowners over whose land the paths and rights-of-way have crossed. There are too many individuals to name but grateful acknowledgments go to the National Trust and English heritage and the churches along the route.

It might seem a little unusual when discussing acknowledgements for a book that deals with historical literature but two major corporations have made the on-line access to old books very easy, and so our thanks go to Google and the Microsoft Corporation.

One of our biggest appreciations go to the *Internet Archive (www.archive.org)* who have made possible the accessing of masses of old literature. Thank you Internet Archive, you are a real gem.

We also are grateful for the advice from Laura Walker and Shaun Puckering.

While we have endeavoured to be accurate throughout we wholeheartedly acknowledge that any mistakes in this book are entirely our responsibility

Index

Names are classified by first name

Works are in italics

A

B

C

D

E

K

L

M

N

O

P

Books from The Creative Peak - Fiction

Weaving a Tangled Web
Terry Melvin

(Paperback and e-book)

ISBN 978-1-910236-01-7 (Paperback)

Will He Come Back?
T A Cherry

(Paperback and e-book)

ISBN 978-1-910236-02-4 (Paperback)

Model for Murder
Mel Cope

(Paperback and e-book)

ISBN 978-1-910236-00-0 (Paperback)

Cocktail of Secrets
C T Luxon

(Paperback and e-book)

ISBN 978-1-910236-03-1 (Paperback)

The Elusive Quest
T M Elvey

(Paperback and e-book)

ISBN 978-1-910236-04-8 (Paperback)

All of the novels above have locations within the stories in either the Peak District or Sheffield

For all books please visit the website www. thecreativepeak.com

Books from The Creative Peak - Non-Fiction

Food for Countryside Moods -
Terry Goble

(Paperback and e-book)

ISBN - 978-1-910236-06-2

"Recipes inspired by the weather, season and the countryside"

The Countryside Awakes

Lazy Hazy Days

The Fires of Autumn

Grey Days

Crisp and Even

The fresh air and ambience of the delightful countryside of the Peak District builds our appetites as we cross the hills, valleys and moors of one of England's premier areas of natural beauty. The different moods of the landscape, whether it is the dark grey days of heavy mist, or the scintillating brightness of a fresh spring, engender the desire for food that responds to those moods.

The recipes drawn their originality from the countryside moods combined with the international flavours and tastes that are so much part of our modern cuisine. We present of fusion of cookery created from readily available fresh ingredients. The healthiness of walking the countryside is complemented by the carefully considered cooking methods which use tasty ingredients cooked in a light and nutritious way.

www.foodforcountrysidemoods.com

For all books please visit the website www. thecreativepeak.com